FIRST LADIES OF MISSOURI

Best wishes

Jerena East Giffen

FIRST LADIES

OF MISSOURI

Their Homes
and Their Families

by Jerena East Giffen

Library of Congress Catalog
Card Number: 96-77024

Manufactured in the United States of America by
Walsworth Publishing Company

Published by Giffen Enterprises
1606 Hayselton Drive
Jefferson City, MO 65109

Photography by Wright Studio

Jacket Illustration by Pat Jones

to my First Ladies
Jerena Giffen Dik and Sarah Jerena Dik

Acknowledgements

Hundreds of hands have a role in the production of a volume concerned with nonfiction. The author is merely the chronicler of the facts. This volume, in particular, is an accounting of the activities of a multitude of persons who lived and created the story throughout the history of Missouri. As indicated by the title, the pages that follow record the actions and lives of certain select persons -- those who occupied the position of executive family of Missouri and, more precisely, the position of First Lady. Occasionally, it was merely a political quirk that thrust a family into executive office. A First Lady gained her title by the circumstance of having chosen a particular husband. But, without exception, each First Lady helped create this story.

A great debt is owed by the author to the former First Lady, Eleanora Gabbert Park. In 1936, Mrs. Park published an earlier accounting of women who lived in Missouri's executive mansion. Without her gracious cooperation, many of the anecdotes and, particularly, many of the photographs in this book would not have been available. Also deeply appreciated was the assistance of other First Ladies and descendants of first families who contributed their time and personal records to this effort.

Production of a book entails a unique set of occupational hazards and fortunate is the author who can benefit from the advice and experience of professionals in the field. The author so benefited from the innumerable and invaluable suggestions for the first edition by the late Dr. Richard S. Brownlee, director of the State Historical Society in Columbia. Many comments for historical accuracy were contributed to the first edition by Dr. William E. Parrish, formerly of Westminster College, Fulton and Dr. David D. March, history professor emeritus at Northeast Missouri State University in Kirksville.

A great debt is owed to two friends, Lucile Geary and Genevieve O'Halloran of Jefferson City, who contributed suggestions for clarity and style and assisted with proofreading the finished manuscript for the second edition. Special thanks are extended to my special friend, my husband, Larry.

Jere Giffen
Jefferson City, Missouri
June, 1996

Foreword

An earlier First Lady describes well the experience of living in Missouri's Mansion. Jerry Dalton noted that walking into this magnificent building is a "handclasp with history." I have enjoyed such a handclasp in the three years I have been privileged to call the Mansion my home. Over the last 125 years, the stately old building has survived the neglect of legislators and the good intentions of decorators to become one of the finest examples of Victorian restorations in the nation.

Historically, the Mansion has been a lively part of the capital community -- its doors open to officials, citizens and distinguished visitors from around the world. That dedication to hospitality is no less true now. In 1995, Missouri's Mansion extended its traditional, warm openness to more than 58,000 guests.

Living in the Mansion, I share a common bond with the other First Ladies who have served the state since 1821. None sought the position that cast her into the spotlight, and yet each, in her own way, made a unique contribution to her own time.

In this volume, First Ladies of Missouri: Their Homes and Their Families, Jerena Giffen takes the reader behind the doors of the state's executive residence for an intriguing, close-up view of the wives of the state's governors. The author brings an appreciation for the women who have served the needs of their families, their communities and their state.

Jean Carpenter Carnahan
June, 1996

Contents

Illustrations

FIRST LADIES OF MISSOURI

Chapter I

An Indian princess, daughter of the great chief of the Missouris, danced for the court of Louis XV in France in 1725. Her hair was long and dark and her eyes black, contrasting with the fair skin and powdered hair of the ladies of the court. Her dress for the occasion was a damask gown of bright red and gold. One of her ornaments was a repeating watch set with diamonds. The dress and the watch were gifts from her royal French audience. Her dancing finished, the princess returned to her faraway village on the bank of the Missouri River and started her reign as the first, first lady of a New World area later to bear the name of her Indian tribe.

This daughter of the grand chief of the Missouris was a member of a vanishing tribe of Indians eventually pushed aside by the inroads of European explorers and adventurers into the New World. The land later to become the state of Missouri was owned and governed by French and Spanish monarchs for more than one hundred and twenty years before it was purchased by the United States in 1803. Even under United States control, the area experienced seventeen years as a territory with governors appointed by presidents. Thus, an accounting of Missouri's first families begins with the earliest executives assigned to the area and follows the transfer of power from the French, to the Spanish, to the United States and, finally, to the state of Missouri.

Records uncovered by historians contain but brief glimpses of the princess of the Missouri tribe. However, a French fort near her village represented the first recorded establishment of European authority in the lower Missouri River Valley. Actual site of the fortification, known as Fort Orleans, remains a matter of conjecture but it was completed by 1724 somewhere on the north bank of the Missouri River in what is now Carroll County. When the seat of state government was permanently established one hundred years later, the capital was located one hundred miles downstream from the French fort. The title of the Indian princess was passed to American first ladies but only after a century of adventure which included the kidnapping by river pirates of one governor's wife and the necessary involvement of another first lady with a secret agent later branded one of the blackest traitors in American history. All this was yet to come when the daughter of the Missouri chief danced her way into the history of Missouri.

The princess of the Missouri tribe was the protege, some called her the mistress, of a French officer, Etienne Veniard de Bourgmond, who found as much or more time for romantic interludes as he did for soldierly duties. Sieur de Bourgmond enters the story of the Missouri Valley only after deserting his military post in Detroit and living for a while with a runaway French woman and other fugitives on an island in Lake Erie. De Bourgmond's charm must have worked equally well on his military superiors as on the irate husband because soon after he was captured he was acquitted.

A prolonged imprisonment at this point might have ended his adventures and cheated history of later events. However, De Bourgmond was freed and in 1712 deserted again to follow a group of Missouri Indians back to their homes on the Missouri River near the mouth of the North Grand River. Here, for six years, he lived among the Indians, married into the tribe and fathered a son. This son, born about 1714 or 1715, traveled with his father to France where De Bourgmond apparently again was in good standing with authorities for he was commissioned to build a fortification on the Missouri River to deter encroachment of the Spanish from the southwest sections of the New World.

De Bourgmond was given the title of "Commandant of the Missouri." He returned to America and built Fort Orleans across the river from the Missouri Indian village. The next months were spent by De Bourgmond exploring the river and pursuing peacemaking missions among the various Indian tribes. The amazing affection and respect of the Indians for this Frenchman were evidenced repeatedly. On one of his peace missions he was offered an Indian maiden as his wife but he declined, saying a Frenchman was allowed only one wife. The Indian girl was offered to his son, but the second suggestion was rejected since the lad was not yet ten years old.

At the height of his success among the Indians, De Bourgmond made plans to display his accomplishments to his superiors in France. He persuaded a representative group of Indians to travel with him to Paris. This was a popular practice of the times, occasioned partly by the curiosity of the French and English concerning the aborigines of the American colonies and partly to cultivate the good will of the Indians. Whatever his personal motives, De Bourgmond arrived in Paris in the fall of 1725 with the Missouri Indian princess and others from the Oto, Osage and Missouri tribes.

Court society lavished presents on the visitors and dressed the princess in damask and silk stockings. She was given a costly and intricate jeweled watch which would strike the time. She even was converted to Christianity and baptized at Notre Dame de Paris. But here the quixotic De Bourgmond deserted his princess and his life of adventure in the colonies. He accepted from the king a patent of nobility and a coat of arms which featured a naked savage reclining on a pile of silver. De Bourgmond retired into historical obscurity and a secure life with a rich widow in Paris. The princess, not one to pine, married one of De Bourgmond's officers, a Sergeant Dubois who had accompanied the Indians on the trip from the Missouri River to France. Dubois was granted an officer's commission and named the new commander of Fort Orleans. Sieur and Madame

Gerald Massie

Missouri Princess returns to her Indian village with French husband. Lunette, painted by Ernest L. Blumenschein, on second floor of Missouri capitol

Dubois returned to America and set up housekeeping in the officer's house built by De Bourgmond.

Thus, the wife of the commander of Fort Orleans – the only white settlement of its time within the lower Missouri Valley – reigned in a "mansion" with a thatched roof. Records in Paris contain a description of this house written by De Bourgmond himself. It was "a house of round posts in the ground and not framed . . . without ceiling, floor or chimney . . . the fire being made in the middle of the floor, Indian fashion, and a roof of grass supported on rafters just as God grew them in the woods, being neither squared nor finished." Here, the Missouri princess lived as Madame Dubois – First Lady of the Missouri Valley. Her husband apparently died soon after their return from France and Fort

Orleans was abandoned sometime in late 1728 or early 1729. Madame Dubois was reported a few years later living on the banks of the Mississippi River and married to another French officer by whom she had a daughter. This girl, in all probability, became heiress to the repeating watch given her mother in a faraway French court. The child, no doubt, provided a rapt audience as her mother described her appearance before Paris society dressed in silk stockings and a gown of flame damask.

With the closing of Fort Orleans, the thread of established authority within the area of the lower Missouri Valley was broken. The territory had been under French control since 1682 but no commander in residence appeared to replace De Bourgmond and protect the new possession which was part of the larger area known as the Louisiana Country. A few permanent settlements were established along the Mississippi River including Ste. Genevieve about 1735, but local civil and military authority, what little existed, was limited to the confines of the settlements. It took a change of ownership before any executive with extensive authority arrived again in the area to be known as the state of Missouri.

During French control there was no division of the land along the Mississippi River and areas on both sides in the region around St. Louis were referred to as the Illinois Country. This designation often was used even after treaties following the French and Indian War split the area and England took over all the land east of the Mississippi and Spain controlled the west side. Although the Spanish gained possession in 1763, several years passed before they officially assumed control of their newest possession. The first person to appear with authority delegated by the ruling Spanish arrived in 1770 with the title of lieutenant-governor. This was a powerful position with control over all of the area known as Upper Louisiana and with a residence in St. Louis.

When the first Spanish lieutenant-governor came to St. Louis, he found the community governed, perhaps unofficially, by a French officer, Louis St. Ange de Bellerive. This officer had been commanding French forts on the east side of the Mississippi until that area was surrendered and St. Ange moved across the river to St. Louis. At this point, the thread of the Missouri Valley story again connects with the French Fort Orleans for St. Ange was one of the men who accompanied De Bourgmond on his peacemaking missions among the Indians in the 1720s.

St. Ange was a bachelor. But even if he had had a wife, her title of first lady would have been questionable for St. Ange was in the anomalous position of a French official reigning over an area owned by the Spanish. The only woman of importance, as far as influence in the lives of the men of authority prior to the arrival of the Spanish in St. Louis, was Madame Marie Therese Chouteau. This courageous French lady traveled up the Mississippi River with

Missouri Historical Society

Madame Marie Therese Chouteau

Laclede to be on hand for his selection of the site of St. Louis. It was Madame Chouteau's son, Auguste, who, although barely fourteen years old, was assigned by Laclede to supervise construction of the new community in 1764. In a personal diary, Chouteau recorded how the largest house built in the new village was constructed of stone for the use of Laclede. The cellar of the house was dug by the women and children of curious Missouri Indians who were attracted by the activity in the new settlement. The Indians carried the earth away from the excavation in baskets on their heads and were rewarded with beads and trinkets.

Besides being used by Laclede as headquarters for his fur-trading company, this stone house was occupied by Madame Chouteau as a residence and was selected by St. Ange as the seat of his government. When Madame Chouteau moved her family into another large stone house a block away, St. Ange boarded in her new home but the seat of government remained at Laclede's house. It was in Madame Chouteau's second home that Pontiac, the great chief of the Ottawa

Indians, stayed during a visit with St. Ange in 1769. The chief was welcomed warmly by the leading citizens of the new settlement. When the Indian leader was killed soon after the visit, St. Ange buried his friend along the St. Louis riverfront. St. Ange still was boarding with Madame Chouteau when he died in 1774 and among his debts was a fifteen-month board bill owed his landlady. The original stone Laclede house continued as the seat of the Spanish government and as the "mansion" of the lady of the first Spanish commander of Upper Louisiana.

With the arrival of Spanish officials in St. Louis, a recognized chief executive was to serve and live continuously, except for a few months, during the next two hundred years within the still unmarked confines of the state of Missouri. As the years changed the status of the land from a colony to a territory and finally to a state, the titles of the chief executives changed from lieutenant-governor to territorial governor and to governor of Missouri. But the titles and duties of their wives were not defined. Historical records fortunately preserved brief accounts of the Missouri Indian princess, but other executive wives took their places with a minimum of public recognition.

During the first one hundred years of Spanish and then United States government in the area of Missouri, the official hostesses received recognition only when incidents forced them before the public. Generally, the early first ladies played their roles backstage or from the wings as observers of the unfolding historical drama. Political and governmental leaders and executive husbands considered the wives successful first ladies if they merely smiled charmingly, entertained graciously and spoke rarely. It was only in the late 1800s that public recognition was given to the part played in an administration by governors' wives. And finally in the twentieth century the first ladies emerged with an important identity of their own. Some even suggested – perhaps partly seriously – that a governor's wife might be considered as a successor to her husband. These suggestions were stilled for awhile when such a change-about became a reality in another state. A governor's wife was viewed in the last half of the twentieth century as a person who could have a major individual impact not only on the image of her husband's administration but on the image of the entire state.

It took two hundred years for the first ladies of the Missouri region to acquire identities before the public, but an important personal role was performed by them throughout the years. And herein lies a story as vital to history as any more tangible record of accomplishments.

One young first lady dies and less than a year later her husband is accused of misconduct during the defense of his village. An unrequited love adds to the melancholy of a successful explorer and he dies – perhaps by suicide – while serving his first term as a young territorial governor. At least two governors choose to curtail their careers at their wives' requests. Many more incidents discussed only in the intimacy of family circles have moulded the lives of the executives of Missouri. The public accomplishments of the governors' wives can be readily reviewed. The more personal contributions can only be glimpsed and guessed. The recounting of these incidents is the story of the first ladies of Missouri. And, other than the Indian princess, the service of first ladies started with the establishment of Spanish authority in St. Louis in 1770.

Chapter II

When the earliest settlers of America attempted to establish European authority in the New World, they encountered hostility from the Indians. When Don Pedro Joseph Piernas arrived to establish Spanish authority at St. Louis, he also encountered hostile residents, but this time they were French. However, Captain Piernas brought with him a French wife as a most charming means of quick entree. When Captain Piernas and his wife, Felicite Robineau de Portneuf, arrived at the St. Louis riverfront in 1770, the French colonists were not in a receptive mood. They felt forsaken by their king. They had watched sadly as the flag of France was replaced by the banner of Spain. But their despair was eased when twenty-four-year-old Dona Felicite stepped ashore and responded quickly to their French greetings.

The first, First Lady under Spanish rule in Upper Louisiana found her new home a little more civilized than many of the pioneer communities of other areas. St. Louis by 1770 had about five hundred residents. There were fifteen larger homes of stone and one hundred houses of wood. Many settlers had brought with them the fine furniture used in older communities on the eastern side of the Mississippi River. They also had clothes of silk and satin and lace which they donned for holidays and other occasions such as welcoming a new French First Lady.

Dona Piernas took up residence in the largest house of the settlement – the stone home of Laclede, the community's founder. She quickly assumed her place in the fun-loving community where the colonists had preserved many customs of the Old Country, particularly those affairs which called for singing, dancing and feasting. The height of celebration was reserved, of course, for *Noel* and *le Jour de l'An.* However, every Sunday was a feast day. Families returning from church at noon gathered around a table laden with the fineries of French cooking such as gumbos and stews flavored with cherished garlic and pepper and accompanied by wines and liqueurs. Occasional added treats were pralines, a type of candy made from brown sugar and nutmeats, and *crocquecignoles,* pastries made from strips of dough fried in lard. When the meal was over, young and old turned to dancing to the fiddle or a card game called "loo" or the men adjourned to the billiard hall.

Howe, Historical Collections of Great West

Early French settlers in Illinois, dancing and celebrating

Even household chores took on festive airs as laundry day by the river served as a gathering for gossip. Although it is not known whether the wife of the Spanish commanding officer did her own laundry, it is safe to presume she was a favorite among the gossipers. She had news from faraway French New Orleans; she had the latest word on fashions in that larger community where ships brought gowns from Paris. And the description of French fashions was eagerly received by the St. Louis creoles who on weekdays replaced the satins and laces with dresses of cotton. Men and women alike tied blue kerchiefs tightly over their hair and frequently adopted the footwear of Indians.

Despite the facade of a light-hearted life, St. Louis still was too close to the frontier of American civilization not to experience some limitations. The homes which might contain a fine piece of French furniture were freqently built of logs. These logs were placed in the ground vertically, stockade style, contrasting to the horizontal style more common in the American colonies. Water for household and table use was brought daily from the Mississippi River and poured into earthen jars where the mud settled to the bottom. The cherished spices had to be transported from New Orleans along with many other household needs and a housewife's grocery order would have had to cover requirements for about one year.

Although the trip down the Mississippi River from St. Louis to New Orleans required only a few weeks, the arduous return took several months of pulling, poling and sailing against the current. The key to the storeroom of a home never left the hand of the housewife and each day she doled out the basic requirements. The duties of the early French housewife, of necessity, extended to the refinement of supplies native to the area such as the preparation of cordials from gooseberries, currants and grapes. She clarified bear's oil for salads. She dissolved brown or maple sugar and dripped it through clean straw and a blanket to make white sugar. In the spring, she supervised the planting of a small garden near each house to produce okra and beans for the favorite gumbo.

But the role of the early creole housewife in St. Louis extended with equal importance beyond the kitchen, garden and storeroom into other areas of the home. Her counsel was sought by *le pere* and her advice weighed heavily in important decisions. She was teacher to the children and medical adviser to the entire household. Although St. Louis had a physician very early in its history, his limited skills could add but little to the bedside vigil of the wife and mother. As a result of the grossly inadequate medical treatment, many of the frequently arriving babies did not survive infancy. This greatest of sorrows – the loss of young children – also occurred in the home of the Spanish commander. Among the events recorded in the little church of St. Louis were the burials by the Governor and Dona Piernas of a son and a daughter. Outside the church, a new bell hung on a temporary scaffold and tolled for the burials. The bell was a gift of the commander and his wife and was named Pierre Joseph Felicite in their honor.

Captain Piernas and his five successors in St. Louis during the thirty-four years of Spanish rule held the title of lieutenant-governor. For administrative purposes, the Spanish divided the territory of Louisiana in half with the upper or northern half generally referred to as Upper Louisiana or, particularly around St. Louis, as the Illinois Country. This upper half contained all the area later to become the state of Missouri as well as land reaching north to Canada and west to the Pacific Ocean. The lieutenant-governor, with headquarters in St. Louis, was accountable to a governor-general in New Orleans and a captain-general in Havana, Cuba. However, owing to the difficulties and delays in communication, the lieutenant-governor's position was much more powerful than might first appear. He was commander of the militia and had general superintendence of public works and property. He acted as judge of crimes. All papers, including wills, were executed in the presence of the lieutenant-governor to give them validity. The various lieutenant-governors apparently were at liberty to choose the language of their administrations and they frequently chose French for everything except some of the official documents exchanged with New Orleans.

The only area in which the Spanish higher command seems to have extended a heavy hand was in the office expenditures of the lieutenant-governors. A heated exchange of letters with New Orleans was occasioned when one lieutenant-governor bought four pounds of nails to repair the soldiers' quarters in St. Louis. Apparently most of the money spent in the households of the lieutenant-governors was charged against their salaries. The salary of Captain Piernas was 375 pesos a year, so the household of the first executive assigned to St. Louis probably was operated by his French wife on much the same scale as most of their neighbors.

However, the home of the first lieutenant-governor was a "mansion" of its time. The Laclede house, as it was called, was built on the St. Louis riverfront at the central point of the town. The building was described as sixty feet wide in the front, facing the river, and about twenty-four feet deep. The main floor was divided into five rooms – a large square central area and four smaller rooms at the sides. The center hall was used by the Governor as his executive office and since it completely separated the two family rooms on each side, Dona Felicite must have experienced difficulties conducting her family affairs during business hours. She may have had greater access to the family rooms by using the attic since there were narrow stairs to the garret under the steep roof at two of the inside corners of the building. Below the main floor was a basement about ten feet above ground level used to house the Spanish troops which arrived with Piernas. The Laclede house was occupied by the Spanish governors as their executive mansion and capitol until 1783 when another building was purchased across the street.

Spain's first executive family assigned to Upper Louisiana remained in St. Louis five years. The take-over of Spanish rule did not prove as traumatic as was feared, for Piernas set a pattern of a soft command. He and his French wife were quickly accepted and the only major ruffling of feathers occurred among the Indians. It seems the Spanish Governor Piernas had a manner more haughty than the French and this was resented by the Indians. An assassination plot was stopped only when the tongue of one of the plotters was loosened by overindulgence and the would-be assassin was stabbed by an Indian from another tribe.

Dona Piernas reigned with ease. In fact, her service in St. Louis was the occasion for her return to the region of her infancy since records indicate she was born on September 24, 1745 at Fort Chartres located across the Mississippi River near St. Louis. She apparently was a lady of substance – she was heiress to two estates in New Orleans and her income was augmented several years after her husband's service as commandant by a pension from the Spanish authorities. When the Governor and his lady arrived in St. Louis, the Piernas family included an infant daughter. Church records note the baptism of Marie Raphael Firmin, daughter of Pedro de Piernas and Felicite on September 25, 1770 – one day after her mother's twenty-fifth birthday. During their assignment to St. Louis, the Piernases baptized three children and buried two other babies.

In the spring of 1775, the Piernas' term in St. Louis ended. Spanish lieutenant-governors did not serve a specific number of years in office but were subject to reassignment at the pleasure of their superiors in New Orleans. When authorities reassigned Don Piernas, a written testimonial of praise for his service was signed by the leading men of St. Louis.

Francisco Cruzat was the second executive sent to St. Louis. This Spanish officer and his wife – who also was Spanish – were to serve two separate terms for a total of ten years. The Cruzat regime was to be the longest of a Spanish commander in St. Louis and was to be marked with events which left deep imprints on the early history of the area later to be the state of Missouri. The first term of Governor Cruzat and his wife, Nicanora Ramos y Tibaldo, started in the summer of 1775. St. Louis by then had a population of some eight hundred persons. The executive and his family continued to rent the Laclede house as a combination capitol-mansion and officers' quarters. Dona Cruzat evidently reigned with the same congeniality as her French predecessor. There was no outstanding event recorded concerning the family of the Spanish executive during his first three years of residence. In the summer of 1778, the Cruzats' first term in St. Louis ended. They were reassigned and officials in New Orleans announced the appointment of Don Fernando de Leyba who was to prove to be an unfortunate choice for the post.

Citizens of the Illinois Country had enjoyed eight years of a pleasant paternalistic government under the Spanish. No taxes other than minimal duties on imports and exports were imposed. The St. Louis citizens and the friendly Indians of the area came forth with gifts and money when the Spanish administration was short of funds. Grants of land were made without charge by the lieutenant-governors and the unofficial grants made by St. Ange and by Laclede at the time of the founding of St. Louis were recognized by the first Spanish lieutenant-governor. The administration of the second executive, Governor Cruzat and his wife, left no record of disruption of the relationship between the Spanish first families and the French creoles. Thus, the conduct of the third Spanish official, Don De Leyba, was at first puzzling and then infuriating to the citizens of St. Louis. De Leyba's actions as an extremely strict administrator led to formal charges of misconduct filed by citizens following an Indian attack on the village. But there was a prefacing event – the death of his wife – that cannot be appraised as to its effect on De Leyba's behavior.

De Leyba, a native of Spain, arrived in St. Louis with his family in the summer of 1778. Fourteen months after their arrival, the young wife, Marie of the Conception y Zezar, died leaving two young daughters alone with their father in the Spanish executive residence. On May 26, 1780, less than a year after the First Lady's death, a band of Indians backed by the British staged a one-day attack on the Spanish outpost. Reports of the Governor's behavior

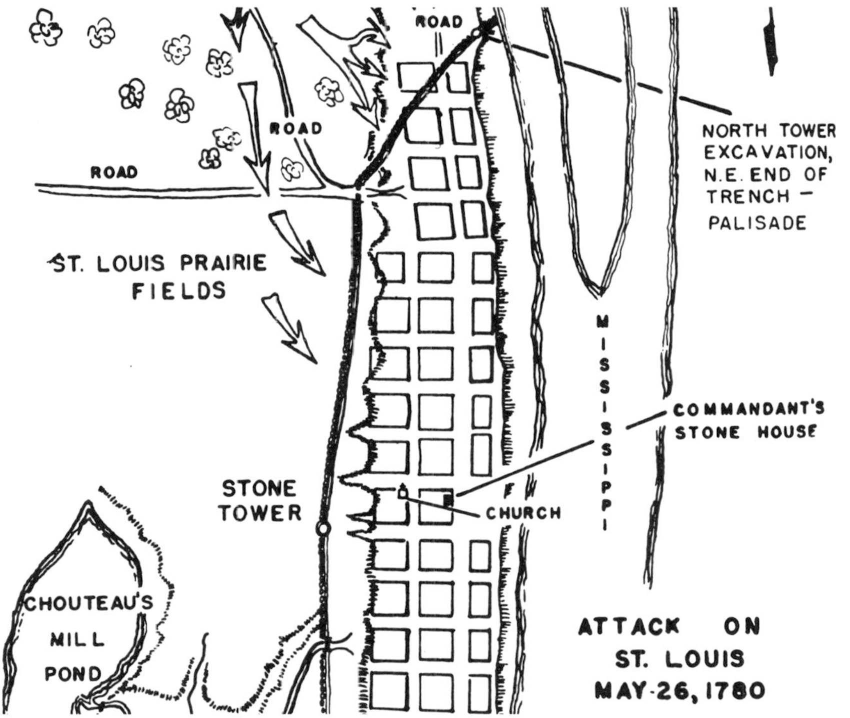

State Historical Society of Missouri

Map showing location of commandant's house. Published in *Missouri Historical Review,* Oct., 1960, "The British-Indian Attack on St. Louis," by Don Rickey Jr.

during the battle vary with the reporter. He was accused of ordering the town gates closed, leaving several townspeople working in the fields west of the village to the mercy of the Indians. One writer stated the Governor was drunk during the attack. Less emotional accounts in later years contend the bitterness of the St. Louis residents resulted entirely from De Leyba's parsimonious handling of government funds.

After the Indian attack had been repulsed, ending the only involvement of Spanish Missouri in the American Revolution, the angry citizens dispatched a protest letter to New Orleans demanding the recall of De Leyba. They accused De Leyba of gross misconduct before and during the attack. The Governor died – some said by suicide – before a replacement arrived. Church records show that on June 28, 1780 – one month after the battle – De Leyba was buried beside his wife under the floor of the little St. Louis church. Burial within the church building was an honor reserved for the governors and their families, the clergy, the sextons and those who donated one hundred pesos for the construction of the church. Others of lesser position or wealth were buried in the cemetery beside the church.

Governor De Leyba, in a will written less than three weeks before his death, left part of his estate to his mother and the rest to the benefit of his two orphaned daughters, Pepita and Rita. His will gave further insight into the life of the Spanish first families for it mentioned that all the furniture in the executive residence was De Leyba's personal property. Thus, De Leyba's replacement would have had to transport furniture up the Mississippi or perhaps buy the furnishings of his ill-fated predecessor. The successor selected by Spanish authorities was the previous lieutenant-governor, Francisco Cruzat.

It undoubtedly was a wise move which resulted in the return of the Cruzats to St. Louis. The disrupted and disturbed conditions following De Leyba's reign could best be settled by an experienced executive already accepted by the citizens. No portrait of either the Governor or Dona Cruzat is available but a mental picture of the courageous lady emerges from her own description of her capture by river pirates.

Dona Cruzat's river adventure took place in the summer of 1782. Records indicate that some months earlier she had traveled down the Mississippi to New Orleans for a visit. In the spring, she started the laborious return voyage up the river. She was a passenger on a large barge owned by Silvester Labbadie, a wealthy merchant and trader. Also on board were her children and, more important to pirates, a cargo of goods for Indians, clothing for the Spanish soldiers and 4,500 pesos for maintenance of the garrison. On May 2, 1782, the barge was hailed and stopped under the pretext that the stranger had letters from Governor Cruzat for his wife. Immediately, the passengers were overwhelmed by forty armed men, described as Englishmen, who had hidden in the woods. The captain of the pirates, James Colbert, reassured Dona Cruzat that she would not be harmed.

While others from the barge were tied, Dona Cruzat and her children were taken by boat up a smaller river and placed in a rough prison. They remained in captivity nineteen days before the Spanish lady, by some intrigue or display of temper, or both, persuaded Colbert to release her for a ransom of four hundred pesos. She signed a promisory note and was granted the original barge and its owner, Labbadie, as a guide, with the understanding that she would return to New Orleans rather than continue to St. Louis. She and her family and the riverman, left only with his leather breeches, arrived back in New Orleans on May 29, 1782. Within a few hours she had made a detailed statement before the Spanish commander.

She recalled that her prison was made of trees placed one upon the other after the limbs were removed. The only opening was a wicket closed with a board and a log. Light and air were admitted through a hole in the top. Her testimony mentioned that four of her children were with her in the prison. Records indicate that the children probably included two of her sons, one of them about six years old. There was no indication that the ransom was paid. However, Dona Cruzat apparently soon set out again for St. Louis and this time arrived without incident. It must have been a wildly concerned husband and father who awaited the return of his family for he could have received only sketchy reports of her kidnapping.

With his family safely restored to their home, the Governor, probably prodded by his wife, took a long look at their quarters. Laclede had been dead for more than four years and the executive residence was poorly tended by the surviving partner in Laclede's company. It was described a few years later as a "stone house falling to ruin with a rotten roof." This original Spanish government mansion in St. Louis later was purchased at auction by Auguste Chouteau and remodeled into an impressive showplace on the St. Louis riverfront. However, it was only rental property to the Spanish government and the solution for the Governor was a different house. This was accomplished in the summer of 1783 – one year after his wife's kidnapping. Cruzat bought a home diagonally across the street, again facing on Rue Royal or Main Street.

Original Laclede house after it was remodeled by Auguste Chouteau *Missouri Historical Society*

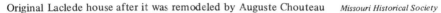

The new government house and executive residence was built by a French-Canadian merchant, Jean Baptiste Martigny, who was one of the original settlers of St. Louis. The Martigny house was constructed of stone and, like the Laclede house, was situated in the center of the community. It was extremely commodious for the times although not as large as the first Spanish governors' residence in St. Louis. The Martigny house was to continue as an executive mansion for all the succeeding lieutenant-governors assigned to St. Louis by the Spanish.

A change of homes by the Cruzats was not destined to remove them from the shadow of sadness which seemed to frequent the families of the Spanish executives. Two children of the first governor had died in the Laclede house. The third governor, De Leyba, and his wife died and were buried in the little St. Louis church. The Cruzats, during their first term in St. Louis, baptized one son, Antoine, and a daughter, but also buried another son. During their second term, the Cruzats' daughter, Josette, died in October, 1784 and another daughter, listed only as very young, died in February, 1786. In the spring of 1786, the Spanish First Lady died. The heroine of the river adventure who had proven a match for the English pirates succumbed to the inadequacies of primitive frontier medicine. She, too, was buried beneath the floor of the St. Louis church.

Available records list only two surviving children of this remarkable woman – an older son, Jose Ignacio, who evidently was born before the Cruzats' first assignment to St. Louis, and the second son, Antoine. One year after his wife's death, the Governor left St. Louis on reassignment but the Cruzat name was destined to reappear on the pages of American history. Antoine married a daughter of the Chalmette family of New Orleans and their son fought British invaders on the grounds of the Chalmette plantation during the Battle of New Orleans. Young Cruzat watched or even helped carry out orders to destroy the plantation home of his family so the building might not protect the enemy. But this battle was in 1815, many years after Antoine Cruzat had attended his mother's funeral in St. Louis.

Manuel Perez, a veteran soldier in the Spanish service, succeeded the widower Cruzat in November, 1787. Perez was described as amiable and apparently his reign continued the congenial relationship between the Spanish executive families and the French creoles of St. Louis. Although the new Governor was past fifty when he came to St. Louis, his wife undoubtedly was several years younger. The first lady, Jeanne Catherine Dubois, did her part to endear the new executives to the Catholic community when she increased their sizeable family soon after their arrival. St. Louis church records contain the notice of two children, Etienne Michael and Michele Eugene, born to Manuel and Dona Perez on September 27, 1789. Whether the first family of St. Louis was blessed with twins or the notations were a mistaken double listing is a matter lost to history. But the event or events, added to the four or five other children of the family, cast the First Lady in the same role of a busy mother so familiar to other wives of the community.

Governor Perez was the last Spanish-born official to serve as commander of the Spanish post of San Luis des Illinois. The residence of the Perez family ended in the summer of 1792. The Governor evidently was sick at the time because a year later he applied for retirement noting that the five years in St.

Seebold, Louisiana Plantation Homes and Family Trees

Jeanne Catherine Duboise, wife of Don Manuel Perez

Louis had affected his health. When he left, the Governor sold at auction his furniture used in the executive residence, the building most frequently referred to as the Government House.

Zenon Trudeau was the fifth executive to serve in Upper Louisiana under the Spanish regime. Although an officer in the Spanish service, Trudeau was born in Canada of French parents. The First Lady might well have shared his national origin although records reveal only that her name was Eulalie de Lassize and that her father, like her husband, was a high-ranking officer in the Spanish service. For the last time, the Spanish executive residence in St. Louis was to shelter new babies of the official family – Emile Auguste Trudeau, born March 19, 1796, and Jn. Valery Trudeau, born May 6, 1798.

Although the Trudeaus shared the joys of birth, the pattern of bereavements seems to have ended with the Cruzats. There are no records of family deaths during the terms of the last three governors under the Spanish flag. Since the time was far distant when first ladies would be considered individuals worthy of public recognition, the service of Eulalie Trudeau may only be imagined as conforming to the feminine pattern of the times. Her hours must have been divided among her duties as mistress of the storeroom and nurse to her family of seven or eight children. The Trudeau children had one unique advantage for they attended a schoolroom outside their home. They were students in a nearby building which housed the first school in St. Louis tended by the Governor's relative, Jean Baptiste Trudeau.

Don and Dona Trudeau and their several children were to be the last large family to occupy the Spanish executive residence in St. Louis. The final lieutenant-governor to serve the rulers of Spain at the Spanish post of the Illinois Country was Colonel Carlos de Hault de Lassus. Governor Trudeau had been stationed in St. Louis for seven years when his transfer was effected in the late summer of 1799. His replacement, De Lassus, did not have far to travel from his previous assignment at New Madrid. Like St. Ange, the first executive to reign unofficially in St. Louis, the last provincial governor was without a wife or a family to assist in his service to the people of St. Louis. De Lassus' marriage occurred after his term in St. Louis ended. In 1811, the last Spanish Governor married the daughter of a Spanish official in New Orleans. The young Madame De Lassus, Adelaide Feliciana Mariana di Leonardo, had three children but only one son, Auguste, survived. This son and his father returned to St. Louis shortly after the death of Madame De Lassus in 1816 and the child of the provincial governor remained to add his father's name to the generation which was to see the former Spanish possession grow and flourish as the state of Missouri.

Although he lacked a hostess while he occupied the Spanish executive residence in St. Louis, De Lassus had one advantage which endeared him to the people of his charge. The Governor was a native of France where his father was one of the many men of noble birth who fled the Revolution. It was De Lassus' final duties in St. Louis which made him an important figure in Missouri history. He took part in a three-way exchange which permitted the beloved flag of France to fly again over the community of St. Louis – although only briefly.

Chapter III

On March 9, 1804, the flag of France was raised for the last time over the village of St. Louis. It was a twenty-four-hour grace period for the loyal French creoles – a time for a last celebration and a final adieu to their national emblem. Records fail to note who was responsible for the bit of benevolence which permitted the flag ceremony to extend into a second day, thus leaving the flag of France aloft overnight. But it was a gentle gesture found seldom in the annals of military and political history. Prefacing events had included a secret treaty in 1800 under which the Louisiana Territory was sold by Spain to France and a second negotiation in 1803 which occasioned the final transfer of the vast territory from France to the United States.

It was the soft-spoken, displaced Frenchman, Don Carlos de Hault de Lassus, who handled the first exchange of flags in the name of Spain. Paradoxically, this native-born Frenchman who served as the last ruler for Spain stood by and watched as a very correct and polite native-born American, Captain Amos Stoddard, raised the flag of France. Since the French never had formally claimed Upper Louisiana before the area was resold to the United States, Stoddard acted both in the name of France and the United States in the three-way transfer. And it was the third flag ceremony – the lowering of the French emblem and its replacement by the Stars and Stripes – that was witnessed with the greatest pathos by the St. Louis residents who still remained predominantly French in speech, manners and loyalties.

The St. Louis creoles had found life under the Spanish flag very much to their liking. Their days were filled with feasting and frivolity. But the Americans were something else. The pioneers who had begun to move into Upper Louisiana in ever-greater numbers were a different breed. Theirs was a life dedicated to long hours of work and industry. The American men were just as eager to plow the ground as to row the rivers in search of furs. The American women were observed making butter in churns instead of shaking the cream in a jar or beating it in a bowl. They also were adept at the spinning wheel. Thus, in St. Louis, two contrasting cultures met and the American flag seemed a harbinger of the way of life which would survive.

But the St. Louis French were not going to forget their good manners. Barely had the new temporary executive arrived when Governor De Lassus held a public dinner in Captain Stoddard's honor. This was followed by a dinner and ball given by the citizens of St. Louis. The new executive was aware of the requirements of his position and he reciprocated with a dinner and ball open to the public. Captain Stoddard noted in personal correspondence that his entertainment – which might be classed as the first inaugural ball of an American governor in the area of Missouri – cost a total of $622.75. Stoddard stated that he had hopes the government would reimburse him for this expense. Perhaps Captain Stoddard's entertainment costs would have been more conservative if he had had a hostess to oversee the entertainment. But he was a bachelor and his official residence was without a family just as it had been with the last Spanish governor.

Captain Stoddard continued to rent the Government House as his home and office. It was in front of this house on the St. Louis riverfront that the ceremony of the Three Flags had taken place. Stoddard served as temporary governor in St. Louis from March until September, 1804 when he was relieved of his civil duties and reassigned by the United States Army. As Stoddard moved out, the Government House, the second executive residence under the Spanish regime, was turned into a hotel and was occupied only briefly a few years later by a man destined to serve as a territorial governor. There never again was to be a single building which could be designated as an official executive residence of more than one reigning family until the state of Missouri emerged from the Territory of Louisiana and the seat of government was removed from St. Louis.

But before it was to receive the badge of statehood, the area had to fulfill a probationary period. Four permanent governors were to serve during territorial days including two who had greatly enhanced their country as explorers and one who betrayed his country as a traitor. After Stoddard's brief service as a temporary executive, only one other governor was to serve without a wife as his companion and hostess. For several months, the area of Upper Louisiana did not have an executive in residence. Congress had attached the area to the Indiana Territory and only a deputy was assigned to St. Louis. This deputy governor, Colonel Samuel Hammond of Virginia, remained long enough to completely Americanize the executive office. One historian noted that he built a house in the American style and entertained lavishly. This evidently signified that his home was an architectural break with the quaint French style of steep roofs and wide verandas. Serving with Colonel Hammond was a wife with an utterly Anglo-Saxon name – Eliza Amelia O'Keefe Hammond. In 1805, after repeated protests from the citizens calling for a greater voice in their government, the area of Upper Louisiana was renamed the Louisiana Territory. The same act of Congress provided that the territory would again have its own governor

Jacobs, Tarnished Warrior

Ann Wilkinson

appointed by the president to serve, for the first time, a set term of three years.

In the spring of 1805, President Jefferson appointed James Wilkinson, a brigadier general in the United States Army, as the first permanent governor to serve in the Territory of Louisiana. This presidential decision meant the executive office in St. Louis was to be filled by a man whom history would brand as a traitor to his post and his country. Many volumes have detailed Wilkinson's service as Secret Agent Number 13 on the payroll of the Spanish government and his part in the Burr conspiracy. But undenied in the blackened record of the Governor was the role of undaunted loyalty to her husband played by Ann Biddle Wilkinson. The dark-haired Ann had broken with her Quaker faith to marry Wilkinson in 1778 and for this act she was read out of the Friends Society. This was but the first of many incidents which illustrated Mrs. Wilkinson's complete devotion to her husband. She was born in Philadelphia into a family of wealth and social standing. This did not deter her from accompanying her husband to whatever frontier post he was assigned, occasioning long journeys by riverboat and across mountain areas. A traveler who visited one of these frontier posts described Mrs. Wilkinson as slender and attractive with affable deportment and elegant manners. Her childhood years among people of ability and means had inbred the qualities of a good hostess. It was mentioned repeatedly how easily she gained friends and how her popularity exceeded that of her husband.

When the Wilkinsons arrived in St. Louis in mid-summer of 1805, one of their first social engagements was a dinner given by Auguste Chouteau and held in the original Laclede house and former Spanish executive residence which by then had been turned into the leading mansion of the town. For their own residence, the Governor and his family moved into a home on Main Street close to the mansion of Pierre Chouteau, younger brother of Auguste. Accompanying the Wilkinsons was their second son, Lieutenant James Biddle Wilkinson. An older son, John, had died in Philadelphia in 1796 and a younger son, Joseph, was a recent graduate of Princeton College, later Princeton University.

Auguste Chouteau's entertainment was one of the few invitations extended by the St. Louis residents to the new first family. An officer of the post observed that the Governor seemed determined to dissatisfy the French and alienate the Americans. However, the fun-loving creoles were temporarily placated when the news arrived, in January, 1806, of Wilkinson's confirmation by Congress and the Governor ordered a celebration. Barrels of tar were set afire, church bells sounded and cannon were fired. Wilkinson was toasted with wine and whiskey in a celebration that extended into the early morning. The role of Ann Biddle Wilkinson in this riotous inaugural ball is not recorded. Ill health apparently prevented her from playing the role of a charming wife which had gained her notice and acclaim in her husband's previous assignments. Her days in St. Louis were clouded by sickness and she seldom appeared in public except to take daily rides in a carriage. Had her strength not failed perhaps she could have countered her husband's unpopularity. However, it is doubtful she could have redirected her husband's destiny. Wilkinson continued on his devious path while serving as governor, even entertaining Aaron Burr in St. Louis where, it is believed, the two plotted the infamous conspiracy generally attributed to Burr.

After serving less than a year, Wilkinson was removed from St. Louis. The president ordered Wilkinson to New Orleans for additional military duties, but the Governor's departure was delayed for three months because of his wife's failing health. Finally, the Wilkinsons started their trip down the Mississippi River – a departure route used by so many of the Spanish first families. Ann's health worsened and she died on February 23, 1807 of tuberculosis – an illness undoubtedly contracted during her years of frontier hardships. She was buried in New Orleans six months after she left her home in St. Louis and her position of first lady of the Territory of Louisiana. Three years after Ann's death, Wilkinson, then in his early fifties, married a young French girl, Celestine Laveau

Trudeau. They had three children – twin girls, Stephanie and Theofannie, born in 1816, and a son, Theodore, born about 1818.

Again, for nearly a year, the Territory of Louisiana was without an executive family in residence. But the vacancy created no real problems such as it might a century or so later. Residents of St. Louis and the surrounding area were too busy with the details of daily existence to be very concerned with the absence of an official host and hostess. The only heads of state who might need to be welcomed in the Midwest were a few visiting Indian chiefs and they were the province of the Indian agent. Fortunately for the president, a new director of Indian affairs and a new territorial governor became available at the same time – both already companions in high adventure.

When President Jefferson formally removed Wilkinson as governor in March, 1807, he named Meriwether Lewis the new executive for the territory. Lewis' companion in the famous exploration, William Clark, was named Indian agent. And a month later, in April, 1807, another historic name was to appear on official papers when Frederick Bates was appointed secretary to the territory. Bates succeeded Joseph Browne and the two were to bridge the gaps, as acting executive, between the departure of the beclouded Wilkinson and the arrival of a melancholy Lewis.

Although he had achieved high success as an explorer, Lewis at thirty-two still was a bachelor. His letters mentioned various lady friends but there was no bride. During the twelve months that he delayed his trip to take over his executive post in St. Louis, his biographers tell of Lewis dining in Richmond, Virginia, with a former love. The story is told of her promise of later meetings but the young lady already was married and Lewis was more saddened than cheered by their evening together. The dejection was noted by his friends, the Clarks, when he arrived in St. Louis in March, 1808, and his mood apparently was not much changed more than a year later when he left again for a trip to Washington. It was during this trip that Lewis died of gunshot wounds while lodging at a tavern in eastern Tennessee. The tavern keeper was brought before a grand jury but a murder charge was dismissed. Even Lewis' greatest admirer – President Jefferson – believed Lewis had taken his own life. How can the various pressures of life be measured as the major or minor contributing factors to melancholy? How could even his close friends determine the true effect of his unrequited love on the pattern of Lewis' life which ended so abruptly along the Natchez Trace?

Louisiana Territory again was without a governor and a first lady. In fact, as for a hostess to tend to official entertainment and an official residence to house the reigning executive family, the area of Louisiana under the United States fell far short of the pattern set by the Spanish officials. It was not until late in the territorial period that the American governor spent much time tending to his duties. It was not until the appointment of General Clark with his young Southern wife that a single dwelling became known as the center of official territorial hospitality. The bachelor Stoddard had lived in the old Spanish Government House during his brief tenure. The Wilkinsons had lived in the center of town in a private dwelling. Lewis had been asked to live with his friends, the Clarks, but he chose to room with Auguste Chouteau in the latter's riverfront mansion.

In the spring of 1810, following Lewis' death in October, 1809, a presidential directive designated a new governor for Louisiana. The next appointee, again a bachelor, was Benjamin Howard of Lexington who resigned as a member of the Kentucky congressional delegation to accept his new position. Accept he evidently did – but arrive he did not until several months later. Finally, in the fall the new Governor made his appearance and the St. Louis citizens took time to entertain the new executive. A St. Louis newspaper reported that on Monday, September 24, 1810, a "public dinner was tendered by the citizens" of St. Louis to Governor Howard. "In the evening," the story continued, "the Assembly Room was thrown open to a crowded assemblage of beauty and fashion, when the lovers of the mazy dance enjoyed themselves until morning."

A month after the public dinner, Governor Howard again took leave of his post for another of his many absences which resulted in his being away from St. Louis as many months as he was present in the village. Secretary Bates dutifully recorded the arrivals and departures of Governor Howard, but he made no mention of the cause of his many trips – whether official or personal. However, an event occurred in Virginia less than a year after Howard's appointment as governor which accounted in part for his frequent trips. On February 14, 1811, Governor Benjamin Howard was married in Loudon County, Virginia, to Miss Mary Armistead Mason. Sometime after the wedding, the Governor and his new bride arrived in St. Louis where the First Lady may have entertained at a log house owned by Howard. This house was on a tract of land later bordered by Howard Street in an area quite far north of the main settlement of St. Louis.

In June of 1812, shortly after Governor Howard introduced his bride to their new home, the name of his jurisdictional area was changed. Congress raised the Territory of Louisiana to a second-class territory and renamed it the Territory of Missouri. Thus, the title of Missouri was for the first time officially attached to the land bisected by the great river of the same name. The change may have been ordered to avoid confusion with the state of Louisiana which was admitted into the Union in the spring of 1812. Governor Howard, in his executive capacity, divided the newly named Missouri Territory into five counties – St. Charles, St. Louis, Ste. Genevieve, Cape Girardeau and New Madrid.

Soon after these changes went into effect in December, 1812, the reign of the new First Lady must have ended with her departure from St. Louis. On March 21, 1813, Mrs. Howard died at the home of a relative in Lexington, Kentucky. Her childless marriage had lasted two years. A newspaper account of her death mentioned that Governor Howard "obeying the call of duty, had shortly before set out for his territory, under the fullest expectation of her recovery." About the time of his wife's death, Governor Howard resigned as territorial governor to accept an appointment as a brigadier general in the army and left for duty in the War of 1812. He died in St. Louis in September, 1814.

In the summer of 1813, General William Clark was named to the vacant executive office. Clark had been living in St. Louis during his tenure as superintendent of Indian affairs. He had assumed the Indian post in 1807 and in the same year became engaged to a childhood sweetheart, Julia Hancock of Fincastle, Virginia. This was the "young lady fair" for whom a major tributary of the Missouri River in Montana was named Judith's River during Clark's expedition with his friend, Lewis. The explorer evidently was mistaken in this gesture concerning the origin of "Judy," his fiancee's nickname.

In writing to Lewis about the betrothal Clark described his fiancee as "a most lovely girl, beautiful, rich, possessing these accomplishments which are calculated to make a man happy." Clark was thirty-seven years old when he married his sixteen-year-old Judy on January 5, 1808. The two spent their honeymoon on a boat trip on the Ohio River and in a few weeks returned to Clark's duties in St. Louis. As their honeymoon "cottage," General Clark took his bride to the stone house on Main Street in St. Louis which for years had served as the government mansion of the Spanish executive families and where the transfer of the area to the United States had taken place. It apparently was this home that the Clarks offered to share with the bachelor Lewis who had been named territorial governor. Lewis declined and the Clarks later moved to other quarters. Records show that in October or November, 1808, the old Spanish Government House became the Eagle Tavern.

By the time Clark was elevated to territorial governor the family had moved into a French-style house of posts at Main and Pine Streets, again in the heart of the community. Julia Clark's added duties as first lady of the territory had to be interwoven with her growing family responsibilities. The Clarks' first child was born in January, 1809 and was named Meriwether Lewis Clark to honor their friend. It was hoped in vain that Lewis' visits to his namesake might help break the pattern of his melancholy. A second son, William Preston, was born in their second home. It was in this home that Mrs. Clark gained fame for an accomplishment other than her duties as first lady and mother. A magazine article of the time noted that Governor Clark bought a piano for his wife and its arrival from New York was a great event. The magazine stated that "Mrs. Clark was the only lady in St. Louis or the surrounding settlement who could play it and Mrs. Clark's piano and her wonderful musical ability soon became the pride and admiration of the good people of St. Louis." This musical success apparently was a social and economic coup for St. Louis in a competitive struggle with neighboring communities on both sides of the Mississippi River.

Two more children were born in this home with the piano – the Clarks' only daughter, Mary Margaret, on January 1, 1814 and a third son, George Rogers Hancock, in May, 1816. About the time the son was born and named in honor of the Governor's famous older brother, the Clarks started plans for their

Turner, The Chouteau Family

Julia Clark

most famous home – also to be located on Main Street. This was a two-story brick house. The part of the new construction which attracted the most attention was a large chamber built to the east of the residence toward the river. This room, measuring about one hundred feet long and thirty or thirty-five feet wide, was known as the Council Chamber where the Governor received visiting Indian chiefs. In this chamber, the Governor displayed a collection of Indian and archeological trophies gathered during his exploration and from his many Indian friends. Birch-bark canoes hung from the ceiling and minerals and fossils were displayed around the walls, including the bones of an animal identified as a mammoth or mastodon. Also on display were the remains of a rattlesnake nine feet long and the skin of a crocodile twelve feet in length. This primarily was the province of the Governor but one could imagine that Julia on occasion might take her visitors for a peek at the awesome sights in the Council Chamber.

Little has been preserved concerning the social life of the last territorial Governor and his First Lady. The frivolity of the French society had been considerably tempered by the sober devotion to economic improvement of the reigning Americans. By 1819, steamboats were making more frequent trips on the Mississippi and had ventured into the Missouri River. The increased bustle on the wharf continued to improve the business life of the St. Louis community. The Clarks' home was the center of hospitality for river passengers and neighbors – both red men and white – and Julia, with her southern upbringing, undoubtedly played the busy and gracious hostess. The Clarks, for the first time since the United States had taken possession, provided the territory an ideal first family by all standards – a respected executive, a charming chatelaine and a houseful of young children. The Clark family was increased again in 1818 with the birth of a fifth child – John Julius.

It was shortly after the birth of the son John that friends noticed the failing of Mrs. Clark's health. As was the vogue of the time, the Governor decided to take his wife on an ocean voyage. The family traveled by steamboat to Louisville and New Orleans and then on an ocean vessel to Washington, D.C. Julia rested in a Washington hotel where she was visited by the ladies of the White House including Mrs. Dolly Madison. A further trip to an Eastern spa also failed to improve the health of the young First Lady from the Missouri Territory and Julia had to be carried on a bed to Fotheringay – the home of her parents. She seemed to improve during a winter of rest in the Roanoke Valley and the Governor left his family to attend to duties in St. Louis.

The nature of Mrs. Clark's illness never was stated in records of her life. This apparently resulted not so much from the inability of physicians to diagnose disease as from a reluctance to make public statements concerning the types of disorders common to women. This same hesitancy omitted from public records the types of illness suffered by previous first ladies – Dona De Leyba and Dona Cruzat of the Spanish period and Mrs. Howard, wife of the early territorial governor.

Governor Clark's return to his duties in St. Louis was cut short when a message arrived that his wife had died on June 27, 1820. The twenty-eight-year-old First Lady of Missouri was buried near her childhood home in Virginia. Governor Clark evidently stayed with his children in Virginia for several months before they started the long trip back to St. Louis. However, the shadow of bereavements which seemed to follow both the Spanish and now the early American executive families was destined once again to fall upon the last territorial governor. When Clark had traveled with his family as far as Louisville, his only daughter, seven-year-old Mary Margaret, became ill. She died in Kentucky in October, 1821.

Affairs at home had undergone historic changes during Governor Clark's absence of nearly two years. A state constitution was enacted and put into effect in July, 1820. It evidently was during Clark's brief return from Virginia earlier that summer that he consented to have his name entered as a candidate for the first governor of the prospective state. But it was only his friends who were on hand to carry Clark's campaign. The widowed Governor was in Virginia to close the affairs of his young Judy and provide fatherly solace to his children. Records of the period fail to evaluate the effect of Clark's absence on his appeal to voters but it is difficult to imagine how an absentee candidate, even the highly popular explorer and territorial executive, could expect victory. He was defeated by a large margin and by the time of his return to St. Louis with his children, a new governor had assumed office.

In November, 1821, the fifty-one-year-old Clark married Mrs. Harriet Kennerly Radford, a widow and a cousin of his first wife. Although the second Mrs. Clark did not serve as first lady, she stepped into a busy life, assisting General Clark in his continued duties as Superintendent of Indian Affairs and tending their combined families. She assumed the care of her cousin's four boys, along with her own three children and, later, the two boys by her marriage to General Clark. The last of Clark's six sons and his final child, Edmund, was born in 1826, but died before he was one year old. The Clarks lived out their years in St. Louis, receiving relatives and friends and, more particularly, welcoming visitors to the world-famous Indian Council Chamber.

Chapter IV

Good fortune was the lot of Missouri in 1820. The territory was on the threshhold of statehood. The first state governor was elected and a new and accomplished first lady assumed the position of official hostess. Although a popular explorer had been defeated in that first race for governor of the state, the victor, Alexander McNair, was an equally well-known, native-born American whose journey to St. Louis, the unofficial capital of the territory, had taken place in time for him to witness the ceremony of the Three Flags. McNair had served in various offices while the new territory was building toward acceptance into the Union. And his own personal union in 1805 with Marguerite Susanne de Reilhe provided the state with a hostess steeped in the ways and manners of the original and proud French society of St. Louis. The first, First Lady of the state of Missouri also was the first governor's wife to be born in the state.

Alexander and Marguerite de Reilhe McNair represented a combination of cultures which mirrored the history of the state and the nation. The Governor, born in Pennsylvania of Scotch ancestry, brought to his office the heritage of thrift and industry typical of early colonists on the eastern seacoast. State documents reveal that McNair opposed, as too high, a minimum salary for the governor of Missouri set at the same $2,000.00 a year paid the territorial governors. His wife was the granddaughter of a pioneer Episcopal minister who settled along the Mississippi River in the St. Louis area before the American occupation of that region. After the death of the Reverend Dr. Ichabod Camp, Mrs. McNair's grandmother moved her family of daughters to St. Louis. One of the daughters, Stella Camp, married Antoine de Reilhe, a pioneer St. Louis merchant who had been born in France of noble ancestry.

Madame De Reilhe died in 1793 when Marguerite was six years old and the father of the family devoted his time to educating his three motherless children. Marguerite, reared with the ability to speak French and Spanish as well as English, attained an educational level rare for women of the time. She was fifteen when her father died and three years later, in March, 1805, she married Alexander McNair. Her bridal trip, according to family records, was a journey by horseback to visit her new in-laws in Pennsylvania. Several months later the

Park-Morrow, Women of the Mansion

Marguerite McNair

couple returned to St. Louis, riding this time in government boats. Mrs. McNair set up housekeeping in a building on the principal street of the community where her husband also conducted a fur business. This home was sold in 1811 to General Clark, the territorial official whom McNair was to defeat in the first state gubernatorial campaign. The McNairs moved into a log house at Main and Spruce, which records describe as a double house, two rooms deep, built of logs set upright in the ground in the old French style. A wide veranda supported by cedar posts surrounded the house on three sides. Pictures of this house, in a later dilapidated condition, have been published frequently as Governor McNair's "Mansion." However, the McNairs by the time of his campaign and election as governor had moved into a large brick home on Third Street, later Broadway. Near this brick home was one of the Indian mounds in the original St. Louis area which caused the community to be known at times as the Mound City.

Mrs. McNair's early married life apparently was extremely tranquil but the Governor's election marked the start of personal tragedies. During the three weeks between his election and his inaugural address, two of the McNair's children died of typhoid fever. Stella Ann, born the first year of their marriage, returned from school in Kentucky to help celebrate her father's success and died at the age of 14; the youngest son, Benjamin Howard, died at the age of six. A biographer noted: "The weight of this double blow that fell . . . could be best appreciated by those who knew the deep affection he (McNair) had always shown for his children." Within another six years, Governor McNair was to die of influenza and the widowed former First Lady was faced with the upbringing of eight children – the oldest eighteen and the youngest two weeks. Her husband's sudden death also left the family deeply in debt and even Mrs. McNair's small newspaper advertisement opening her home to "a few gentlemen boarders" did not result in sufficient income to save the family's numerous properties. When Mrs. McNair died in 1863 she had outlived six of her ten children. Four of the McNair sons served in the various wars of the nation, two dying in the service. Only one of the six sons, Antoine de Reilhe McNair, married and continued the name of both his American father and his French grandfather and he had been badly crippled in the Black Hawk War.

Overcoming the family tragedies which marred her husband's inaugural and still not confronted with later bereavements, Mrs. McNair took her place as first lady and set high standards for the first ladies who were to follow. An early St. Louis school teacher, E. H. Shepard, preserved for history the greatest detail of the family side of the McNairs' years as governor and first lady. Shepard recorded how his wife was visited by Governor and Mrs. McNair and invited "to come to their home and stay as one of their children while I taught their sons." Although the Shepards refused, they did take rooms in part of the McNairs' property and former home, the old French house of logs. Mr. Shepard opened a school at another site and his pupils included three of the McNair sons. Mr. Shepard also wrote about the McNairs' new brick home which he described as "the high school of refinement in St. Louis and Missouri." Shepard said people from all parts of the state visited Governor McNair's residence "and were

One of early McNair houses

Missouri Historical Society

received by his accomplished wife with the affection of a sister or a mother and made welcome to all it afforded." The McNair home also served as the focal point of political activity in the young state with "information sought and given by politicians of all parties with the utmost freedom and kind feelings." Another account states that the McNair home was the scene of frequent parties for the children of the household along with other young people of the community and officers from a nearby military post. It described how the servant girls would line up near the entrance to the ballroom and hand to each of their mistresses a freshly ironed handkerchief for her to carry into the party.

Perhaps the greatest tribute to Mrs. McNair was paid a century later at the dedication in St. Louis of a memorial to the first state Governor and his wife. Archbishop John Joseph Glennon spoke on the qualities of Mrs. McNair and attributed much of the Governor's success to her helping hand. "I would to God that the women of her day were reproduced in the women of today," the Catholic official concluded. Mrs. McNair's areas of concern also extended beyond the family threshold. Although a Catholic, she is credited with joining women of all creeds to start the first organized charitable service in St. Louis which met in the executive residence.

During most of Governor McNair's term, the temporary seat of state government was established upstream on the Missouri River at St. Charles which like St. Louis was a village founded as a headquarters for hunters and Indian traders. By the time the first legislative session was held in St. Charles, the community had some one hundred houses, many substantial brick buildings, and had evolved as the center of an agricultural population. It is doubtful that Mrs. McNair's presence was required at state functions in St. Charles but she very likely visited the village, staying in the home of a McNair relative. Although the Governor, wearing a "pigeon-tail" coat, traveled by horseback to St. Charles, his wife and family undoubtedly used the McNair carriage which was one of the few conveyances of its type in the area. Tradition records that Governor McNair on occasion rented rooms in a rock house near the buildings used as the state capital in St. Charles. It also is recorded in old newspapers that the Governor had a standing reservation for a table by the window in the old Chambers Tavern where forty cents provided a meal, with such offerings as prairie chickens, bear steaks, guinea eggs, wild honey or "almost anything else obtainable and edible." Another St. Charles tavern advertised lodgings for legislators at "two bits" a night. Also available were meals of "corn bread and common fixings, 2 bits . . . white bread and chicken fixings, 3 bits." The original "bit" was a piece of coinage which resulted from chopping the Spanish cartwheel dollar into quarters and then dividing the quarters into two pieces or two bits, each worth twelve and one-half cents.

Despite the comparatively slow pace of the government occasioned partly

Park-Morrow, Women of the Mansion

Nancy Bates

by cumbersome transportation and inadequate communication, the executive and legislative officials moved steadily toward the formal declaration of statehood. The big day occurred on August 10, 1821 when President Monroe issued a proclamation declaring Missouri admitted into the Union. Governor McNair's term continued until the second state gubernatorial election named a new executive in August, 1824. Three months before McNair's term ended, his ninth child and sixth son, Lafayette Washington, was born on May 26. Since the families of the Spanish officials and the wife of the last territorial governor had frequent babies, it seems particularly appropriate that the first state Governor and his First Lady should welcome a new baby during their term of office. Mrs. McNair, who was thirty-seven when her service as first lady ended, had indeed set a perfect pattern of personal and civic service for those who would follow her in the state's executive mansions.

The second first family of the new state was well-accustomed to the duties of executive office, but by preference the new Governor was exceedingly withdrawn from the social amenities of the position. Frederick Bates, the second state governor, had served as territorial secretary and on several occasions as acting territorial governor during the absences of the men appointed to that office. Historians described the Governor as something of a recluse. The First

Lady could hardly have had time for extensive entertaining since her husband's term was cut short by his sudden death. Mrs. Bates was extremely young and, when she became first lady, had three children, ages one, three and four.

Nancy Opie Ball Bates was born in Virginia and moved with her family to St. Louis when she was thirteen. Her father, Colonel John S. Ball, later became a minister and helped found the Presbyterian Church at Troy, Missouri. On March 4, 1819, when she was not quite seventeen, she married Frederick Bates who was forty-one. A relative described this second First Lady of the state as small in stature, a "modest and unpretentious gentlewoman." Mrs. Bates also was said to be retiring and quiet.

Unlike the previous executive families who had lived in the heart of the St. Louis community, the Bates lived on a rural estate of one thousand acres on a Missouri River bluff in Bonhomme township, some twenty miles from St. Louis. The Bates' home, known as Thornhill, had a wide front and columned portico characteristic of the type found in Virginia – the birthplace of both the Governor and Mrs. Bates. When state affairs called him to St. Charles, Governor Bates had merely to step into a boat at his back door, cross the Missouri River and enter a waiting carriage for a short ride of three miles to the capital.

It was during the term of this reclusive Governor and his quiet, retiring wife that General Lafayette, hero of the Revolutionary War, chose to pay an official visit to St. Louis. The occasion resulted in a near social calamity for the young state. An account by John F. Darby in his publication of *Personal Recollections* tells of the preliminary attempt to provide a suitable reception.

> "When the city authorities found that General Lafayette was about to visit St. Louis, they, in those primitive days of honest municipal government, began to doubt their authority to appropriate money from the treasury to entertain their visitor. Dr. William Carr Lane, the mayor, in this emergency took his horse and rode all the way out to Governor Bates' farm . . . to beg the governor to come to town and receive General Lafayette, the expectation being that some of the moneyed men would advance the funds with which to entertain the general and that, if the governor would take part, they would afterwards get the state to make an appropriation to cover the expenses of the entertainment. Governor Bates refused to have anything to do with the matter. He said the state had made no appropriation to entertain General Lafayette and that he would take no part in any proceedings of any kind unless there had been money enough provided to entertain him in a manner becoming the dignity and character of the state. Dr. Lane returned from his visit to Governor Bates despondent, disheartened and almost discouraged."

In a personal memorandum the Governor was even more blunt. He noted that "they (the legislators) as well as myself, entertain for the General the most perfect respect, but truly he has had already sufficient evidences of the cordiality and good will which a free and enlightened people are always disposed to show their friends." And the Governor gave the gubernatorial door a final slam with the closing thought: "If he (Lafayette) personally looks for me at St. Charles or on the hills of Bon Homme – he would find me at neither place – for I have long since promised my family to visit some friends about that time."

If General Lafayette did attempt to impose himself on the reluctant executive, there is no hint of it in the official record of his visit. The city fathers of St. Louis came up with thirty-seven dollars from the city treasury. On the morning of April 29, 1825, as Lafayette arrived at the St. Louis riverfront, he was met by a borrowed carriage and horses and the General was taken to the spacious riverfront home of Pierre Chouteau. The state was represented unofficially by the first state governor, McNair, who was a member of the city reception committee.

Also a bit more hospitable than the chief executive of the state was the former territorial governor, General Clark. Notes kept by Lafayette's secretary tell of a visit to the Indian museum with Clark himself acting as host. It was recorded that Lafayette and his party were attracted to a displayed set of claws from a grizzly bear which the visitors thought must be the "most terrible of all the animals of the American continent." The climaxing event was a ball held for Lafayette at a St. Louis hotel. And all for thirty-seven dollars out of the city – not state – funds.

Three months after this event, on August 4, 1825, Governor Bates died of pleurisy. His young widow was left with the family's three young children and she was pregnant. The Bates' fourth child, Frederick, was born six months after his father's death. Unlike the misfortunes which were soon to confront Mrs. McNair, Nancy Opie Bates was without financial problems as a widow. She continued to live at Thornhill even after her marriage in 1831 to Dr. Robert C. Rubey. She was nearly seventy-five when she died.

With Governor Bates' death and Mrs. Bates' automatic abdication as first lady, Missouri's executive office was without a hostess. And the state remained in executive bachelorhood for the next seven years. The feminine vacancy occurred at a convenient time. The state soon was to move its headquarters up the Missouri River to the first combination capitol and executive mansion. The space set aside for executive living quarters in the new building appeared adequate for a single man but a wife and family would have found the quarters lacking a kitchen, among other conveniences.

Bates' successor in the office of governor was a one-legged shoemaker from Columbia, Missouri – Abraham J. Williams who had been serving as president pro tempore of the state senate. The executive office fell to Williams since the lieutenant-governor, the first in line, had resigned and moved out of the state. Official records show that Williams spent some time in St. Charles during his five-month tenure but the General Assembly was not in session and no outstanding event required the services of a first family. Williams called a special election for December, 1825 and in January, 1826, turned the state over to another bachelor – the fourth state governor, John Miller.

Plans for selecting a site for a permanent capital and constructing a capitol building were being made and carried out during the terms of the first four state governors of Missouri. The initial directive came during prestatehood days when Congress granted Missouri four sections of land to be used as a capital. A provision of the first state constitution specified that the capital city would be located on the Missouri River within forty miles of the mouth of the Osage River. Anticipating that the selection of a site and construction of a capitol would take time, the framers of the first constitution postponed until 1826 the actual date for removal of the government to its permanent location. Shortly after the first legislative session convened in St. Louis, a commission was appointed to pinpoint the site and the five commissioners reported in the spring of 1821. They apparently were uncertain whether the Congressional act required that the land must be selected from lots previously unclaimed – so-called public land – or whether grants from private landowners could be considered.

To protect the state's interest, the commission reported in the summer of 1821 the selection of four sections of public land south of the Missouri River – the eventual site of the capital. A letter was written by Governor McNair on July 3, 1821 informing the United States surveyor-general of the commission's selection and asking that this land be withheld from public sale until final action by the legislature. State records and newspaper accounts indicate the commissioners did not consider this selection as their final word. They asked for additional time to see if they could clear titles on two other possible sites which they thought were far superior. One was in the extreme northwestern corner of Cole County, just east of the mouth of the Moniteau River. This apparently was near the first county seat at Marion. The second alternative site, which the commissioners reported with the most enthusiasm, was in the area of a small village on the north bank of the Missouri – Cote Sans Dessein. By autumn of 1821, the commissioners actually recommended the Cote Sans Dessein location and noted that a private landowner had offered to donate 392 acres of the needed land.

No public accounts were kept of the final debate in the legislature so it is not clear what the deciding factor was that pushed the legislators away from the commissioners' favored area at Cote Sans Dessein. It may have been that further legal difficulties were feared because of clouded land titles. Whatever the motivation, the legislators made their final decision on New Year's Eve in 1821. The selection was 2,560 acres of land on the south bank of the Missouri River – the same site the commissioners had discredited as an area of badly broken bluffs and limited bottom land with the surrounding country "too poor to support any considerable population or extensive settlement." At the time of the selection, there was only one resident on the site – the owner of a dramshop

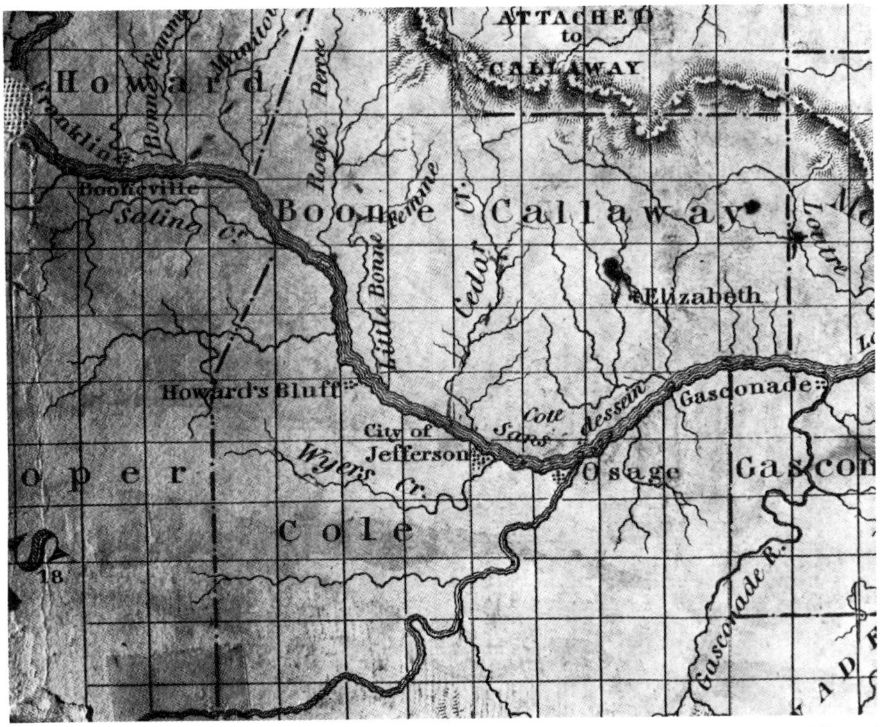

Beck, Gazetteer of Illinois and Missouri

Map drawn in 1823 showing location of Jefferson City on Missouri River in relation to other sites considered for the capital city

on the river bank for the accommodation of thirsty boatmen. A newspaper editor at Franklin was a bit more charitable and described the site as "a very handsome one." The editor observed that "the town will in all probability become a considerable place."

Thus, on New Year's Day, 1822, the site of a new state capital city was settled. The remaining jobs for the site commissioners were the platting of a new city and the acceptance of plans for a capitol building. A public sale of the first two hundred lots in the new community was set for the first Monday in May,

1823. Competition for the land apparently was limited for a later newspaper story reported that the lots sold very low – "some of the best for about $140 . . . payable in auditor's warrants and a long credit for two thirds of the amount."

More important for the executive of the state was the offering by the commissioners of a one-hundred dollar premium for the best plan for a state capitol. It is not known who planned the building, but public advertisements started appearing in Missouri newspapers in January, 1823 offering to the lowest bidder the construction of a brick building sixty feet long, forty feet wide and two stories high. The original plan called for six rooms and eight fireplaces – with the necessary doors and windows. Supervision of construction was turned over to three trustees, Josiah Ramsay Jr., John C. Gordon, and Adam Hope, all of them apparently residents of rural Cole County. The site for the building was a hilltop designated as the best location for the residence of future governors. Actually the building was planned as a home for executive families with the legislature located there temporarily until a permanent capitol could be constructed on the next hilltop to the west. Just the reverse situation resulted.

Winning contractor for construction of the first state capitol-mansion was Daniel Colgan who sublet the contract to James Dunnica of Kentucky. Dunnica later was paid $18,573 for his work. No plans of the building were preserved but a description was published in the first capital city newspaper which followed the state government from St. Charles to Jefferson City. This account appeared in the Jefferson City *Jeffersonian* of November 18, 1826:

> "THE GOVERNOR'S HOUSE – This stately edifice has been completed and ready for the reception of the legislature for several months. On Monday next, the two halls are to be, for the first time, occupied by the representatives of the state in General Assembly assembled. This house was only intended to be occupied by the legislature till a state house could be erected. It is a spacious and well constructed building; the workmanship it is said, is not to be surpassed in the state. It stands fronting the Missouri, on an eminence of two hundred feet above the level of its waters. Its dimensions are 60 feet by 40. A hall 12 feet wide passes through the centre and opens in front through a large Venetian door, and descends to the ground over seven large steps of hewn rock. There are, in this building, ten commodious rooms, two of which are very spacious; one below and one above, each occupying half the whole extent of the building. A stairway runs from the bottom to the top and opens through a sky-light into the ballastrade or large platform, surrounded with a railing, where a most beautiful prospect can be

Cole County Historical Society Museum

Architect's sketch of first state capitol-governor's residence in Jefferson City. Drawn after a study of early documents

> had for many miles up and down the river, as well as each way over the rugged hills of the surrounding country."

Accuracy of this account can only be presumed. Other meager facts gleaned from private letters further reveal that the House of Representatives met in the large room measuring 24 by 37 feet on the first floor of the building, and the state Senate in an identical room on the second floor. It also is presumed, from the original advertisements for bidders, that two chimneys and four fireplaces were located in both ends of the rectangular building. Other accounts vary concerning the half of the building not occupied by the legislature. The newspaper report above indicates eight smaller rooms, four on each floor. Another account stated that the first governor to move into the building used two rooms on the first floor as his apartment – indicating that the nonlegislative half of the building may have had only two rooms on each floor. This would fit better into the supposition that each end of the building had four fireplaces – two on the first and two on the second floor. Later improvements including the covering with lead of a flat area of the roof, the construction of a stable and a brick privy and the leveling and fencing of the grounds with cedar posts brought the total cost of the first state capitol-mansion to slightly over $20,000.00. A legislative observer of the time described the building as "neat and commodious." Apparently the best that could be said was that the first state building in the new City of Jefferson had a dignity of the sort that comes with a simplicity of construction. The building also was the first tangible symbol of a permanent state government in Missouri.

One of the first legislators to occupy the new structure, Dr. William Carr Lane from St. Louis County, wrote in a personal letter on November 28, 1826, the following observations concerning the new capital city: "... a place singularly compounded of Town-Hamlet-camp & wild woods ... a cluster of short steep hills, on the Missouri river, with deep ravines, – over a wide extent of which are scattered 3 Brick buildings (one of wh. is the Governor's house, & contains for the present both Governor & Legislature, & the other two, Half finished Taverns) – 2 small stone buildings & some 12 or 18 other buildings of one kind or another ... I took boarding at Major Ramsay's (no Kentuckian will willingly be less than a Major) – His wife a pretty woman ... I believe I pay $4.50 per week besides something for washing ... My pay being ... 2.25 per day ... We lodge in a cabin containing 3 beds, such as they are, some split bottom chairs ... The Table is well supplied – the boarders, some 40 or 50 in number, are civil, & I have no fault to find with my room mates ... I will not detain you with details, but sum up all in this – the business of Legislating does not please over much."

The legislature opened for the first time in the new capitol-mansion in mid-November, 1826 and Governor Miller by then apparently had moved his bachelor belongings into the executive quarters of the building. Records fail to note whether the first state building was located on one of the many Indian mounds found on the river bluffs throughout central Missouri. The disturbance of Indian bones and pottery was not such an unusual occurrence in those days as it was when the second capitol was built and comment was made concerning Indian burials on the site. However, the grounds of the first state building did adjoin the location of two strange relics believed to be connected with ceremonial observances of early Indian tribes. A later grading of the road beside the first capitol-mansion uncovered two wells filled with white sand. They were described as eight feet in diameter with the sand perfectly separated from the surrounding clay soil. Two early residents of the area who moved to the city in 1826 confirmed the presence of the sand wells and told how many citizens of the town hauled the sand away for their own use. Archeologists can only speculate that the sand probably was used in some ancient religious ritual of the Indians. But whatever the significance, the wells served to remind the reigning Missouri executives of the original landowners of the area of the Missouri Valley.

Chapter V

One historian has noted that Jefferson City – a city on a hill – cannot hide its face. But during the city's early years there were many legislators who wished they could hide its face and theirs too for selecting the site. The first lawmakers who deliberated on the location of a permanent capital acted wisely in specifying that it be located on the Missouri River and in the center of the state. These specifications were mandatory in view of transportation limited to river travel, horseback and stagecoach. The land selected for the capital was extremely broken between hills and valleys. About the only good remarks circulated concerning the new village were printed in early newspapers whose editors were anxious to project a favorable image to readers in other areas who might be prospective settlers. However, one outsider – the author of a gazetteer – very graciously noted a distinct advantage to the location of a capital city on an irregular site. "The politicians, when assembled there in the discharge of their delegated trust, and when walking from their quarters to the capitol, will be always kept in mind, practically, of the 'ups and downs' in political life and thereby acquire circumspection in the measure and cadence of their footsteps."

Sparsity of official records result in the presumption that the site of Jefferson City was chosen as a compromise to avoid entanglement with land speculators operating in other areas. But no sooner was the decision made than the state became enmeshed with the same speculators who quietly had filed claims, presumably fraudulent, on fifty-six lots in Jefferson City. The claims were cleared only after the state had threatened to take the land by eminent domain. The first lots in the city offered for public sale brought very low prices and mostly on credit. Thus, the early development of the new state community was impeded by disgruntled legislators who acted with great reluctance on funds to improve the state buildings and enlarge the city.

Shortly after the state government was moved from St. Charles to Jefferson City, the legislators authorized minimal improvements to the combined capitol-executive residence. By 1829, a total of $966.25 had been spent in adding lead to the roof, fencing the grounds with cedar posts and other improvements. A brick privy was constructed for $150.00. An appropriation of

$500.00 was voted for construction of a separate kitchen and a stable on the capitol grounds, but the commissioner in charge reported a year later that he did not regard the kitchen as necessary and used only $216.67 to build a stable. Thus, the bachelor governor had housing for his horse but apparently no place to cook, if he had been so disposed.

Accommodations for legislators and homes for new residents who naturally moved with the capital were mostly primitive. The first newspaper editor in Jefferson City, on June 24, 1826, wrote a story obviously slanted toward readers in other areas which noted that the site of Jefferson City was 1,200 miles from New Orleans, 125 from St. Louis, 120 from the junction of the Missouri and the Mississippi and 10 miles above the mouth of the Osage River. The editor mentioned that the first lots were sold at auction in May, 1823. "Previous to that period, the primitive wildness of the place was undisturbed except by one or two temporary cabins . . . Several springs of very fine water issue from the bluff and hills of the town, one of which supplies nearly all the citizens with water. About thirty families are now located here . . . The habitations now in use are generally made of logs neatly hewed; comfort without much cost is found within them."

Accounts by early residents noted that the capital city in 1826 was "but a struggling village, where Indians camped in close proximity, wolves howled around the doors at night." Game was plentiful and easily obtainable. Hunters merely stepped into their front yards to find deer. One old citizen of the community, Captain J. T. Rogers, recalled that his family meals in 1826 featured venison, bear meat, turkeys and wild honey. A note in the city newspaper in 1830 stated that meals at a Jefferson City hostelry could be obtained for seventy dollars a year. A typical central Missouri supper in the 1830s consisted of "pork chops, ham, eggs, Indian bread and butter, tea, coffee, milk, potatoes, preserved ginger and . . . an enormous tin dish of plovers, fricasseed."

Steamboats were rare in the early days and the waters of the Missouri River were dotted more commonly with Indian canoes, keelboats and French bateaux. Major J. S. Rollins of Columbia, in a speech made years later at a banquet in the state capitol, recalled his first visit to Jefferson City in 1831.

> "Jefferson City was at that time a small and insignificant village. These romantic hills were covered with primeval forests .. A small square brick structure . . . afforded the only accommodation for the officers of the state and the law makers as they wended their way biennially on horseback and on foot to the state capital . . . It was a lonesome journey then for our legislators, to undertake a trip from New Madrid, from Spring River, . . . over the Ozark Mountains, through a howling wilderness . . . It was the winter of the great snow

which laid upon the ground some fifteen or twenty inches deep, from December until the middle of March . . . We crossed the river upon the ice . . . The General Assembly was in session, the Senate holding its session in the second story, and the house of representatives on the ground floor, whilst the venerable governor, John Miller, resided in two rooms in the northwest corner of the capitol building, where he dispensed a genial and pleasant hospitality. Then, as now, our legislators were a social and frolicsome set. The hall of the house of representatives, was frequently used as a ball room, where inspired by the delightful music of the violin, the old and young joined merrily in the cotillion, the old Virginia reel and other old-fashioned dances, now almost out of date, and succeeded by the more fashionable modern round dances, the waltz, the schottische, the polka, the mazurka, the German, etc. These were primitive times, but a warm hospitality was universally prevalent, and honesty and fair dealing in private and public life, was the rule and not the exception . . .

"My second visit to the capital was in the summer of 1832 . . . We remained here several days, quartered with Gov. Miller in the old state house, in which he resided, enjoyed his old-fashioned and warm-hearted hospitality, and had a glorious time generally . . . "

That year, 1832, was the last of Governor Miller's seven years in office – a record of consecutive tenure which was to remain unbroken for more than a century. The personal appeal of Governor Miller must have been tremendous. A native of Virginia, he served four years as land registrar in Howard County – his only public office before being elected governor over two opponents in December, 1825. He was re-elected in 1828 to a full four-year term without opposition, the only time in history that a candidate for the state's highest office ran without challenge. Governor Miller was fifty years old at the end of his administration and was described by a contemporary as a "portly bachelor . . . an ordinary man of good common sense."

Although apparently well satisfied with his quarters in the first state building in Jefferson City, Governor Miller recognized the limitations of the accommodations. In a letter to his successor, Daniel Dunklin, Governor Miller wrote that he was preparing "to give you possession of the rooms I now occupy in the state house . . . You are right in the determination you have formed of not bringing on your family until you can provide a suitable residence for them." Governor Miller also offered to sell Dunklin the furniture used in the executive rooms at the capitol, including a "good high post bed – quite new – a secretary and book case of good quality – one set dining tables nearly as good as new –

16 chairs – half dozen Demi Johns that will be useful to you – one dozen tumblers – about 20 wine glasses of good quality – half dozen pitchers, together with many other articles which you will no doubt stand in need of . . ." Whether Governor Dunklin purchased these furnishings is not recorded, but the new executive did make use of the rooms in the statehouse for a short time.

True to his "determination," the new Governor moved immediately toward construction of a separate executive residence in which to house the sizeable Dunklin family. Three months after Governor Dunklin's election in August, 1832, the state legislature provided $5,000.00 for the purchase, lease or construction of a "house with the necessary out-buildings, in the City of Jefferson, suitable for, and adapted to, the accommodation of the governor of this state." In early January, 1833, advertisements began appearing in Missouri newspapers calling for plans for a new governor's house to be submitted by March 15, with the contract to be let to the lowest bidder on April 1, 1833.

A site on the same square, or block, as the first capitol-mansion was selected and work had started by fall. A note in a Jefferson City newspaper on October 18, 1833, stated that construction was underway but "owing to the ravages of Cholera, help was very hard to obtain and the work progressed slowly." Cholera was a serious plague of the time which had reached epidemic proportions in St. Louis the previous year. Evidently, the workmen recovered to continue construction of the governor's new home. A newspaper item on November 16, 1833 stated the building was in a "great state of forwardness, a portion of the wood work yet remaining to be done." The newspaper story observed that "this house will be as good as could be expected to be furnished, for the amount appropriated for its erection." It evidently was extremely modest because the next governor, only three years later, suggested that the state sell the house and buy or build a new one more suitable as an executive residence.

Records preserved years later describe the building as constructed of wood and stone with a two-story center section and one or one and one-half story wings on each side. Original plans called for a rectangular building 48 feet by 30 feet. The site was on the south half of the block containing the original capitol with the new building facing Main Street, later Capitol Avenue. An article listed as recollections of an oldtimer and included in papers preserved under a government work program nearly a century later contained the following details: "The structure was constructed of white native stone blocks about two feet square and one foot thick laid up like the present brick buildings. The four columns shown in the front were of circular cut and laid one upon another bottom to top." A letter written by the niece of a later governor described briefly the first floor of the building. Three front rooms were mentioned, one used by the governor's wife, a large middle room called the

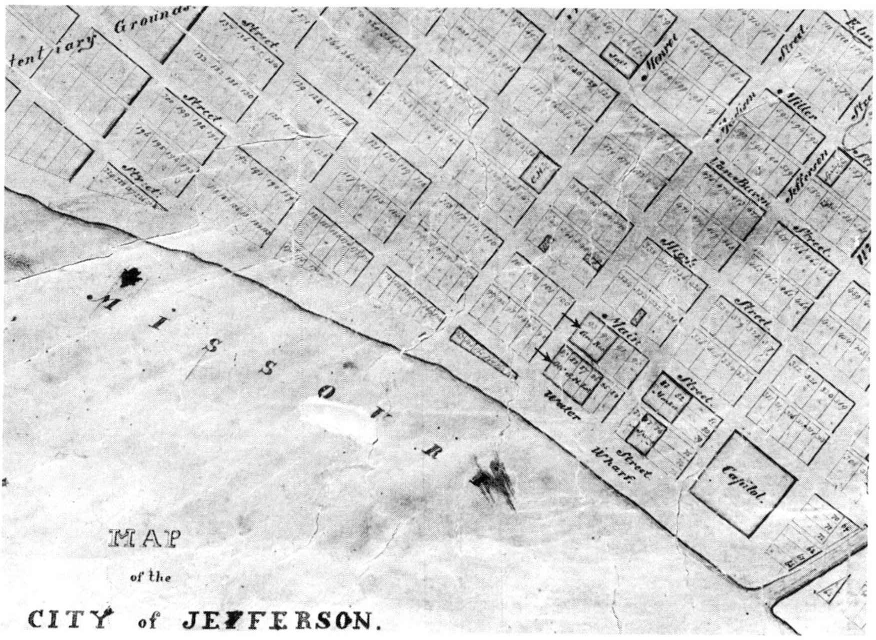

Official plat of Jefferson City in 1849, showing sites of first state capitol and first separate governor's residence in block between Main and Water Streets, two blocks east of capitol. Plat in office of Cole County Recorder Henry LePage

parlor which was entered from the porch and a third front room used by the governor as an office. The parlor was said to be much larger than the two adjoining rooms which evidently were located in the wings of the building. The three rooms were separated by folding doors which could be opened to make one long room. The kitchen was located in a separate small structure. This was the second building provided as a residence for the governor since Missouri had become a state and the first to be used exclusively by the executive families. A year after it was finished the legislature appropriated $1,318.50 to pay for furniture and $685.00 to grade the grounds and fence the yard.

Presumably the building was completed in time for Governor Dunklin to move his family from Potosi early in 1834. Mrs. Dunklin was at the time thirty-seven years old and most of the couple's six children had been born at the Dunklins' Washington County home. A great-granddaughter has described this first, First Lady to reign in the new state capital city as a woman of medium height, slender with black hair and eyes – very exquisite and dainty in her dress

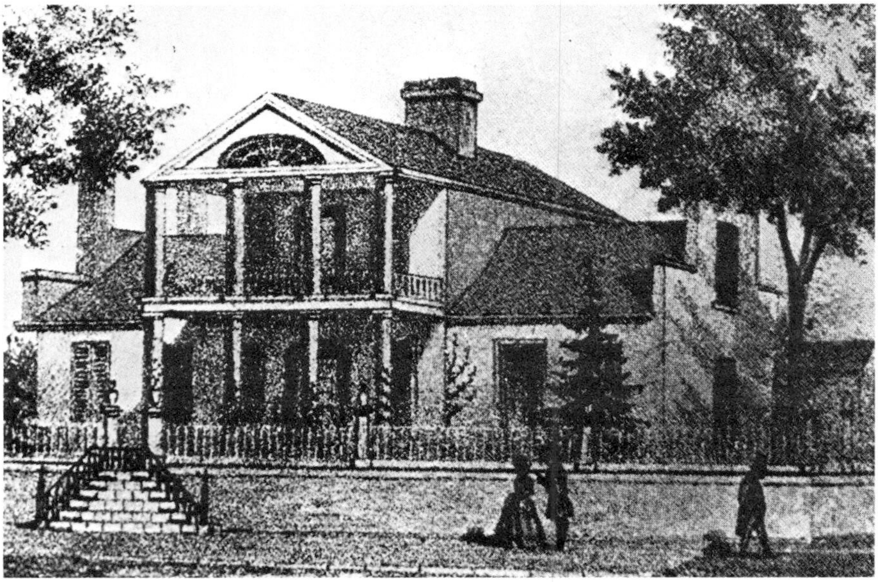

Park-Morrow, Women of the Mansion

Sketch, above, of first separate executive residence in Jefferson City. This was included among several sketches of old buildings in Jefferson City. It is not known whether the picture is an accurate representation of the building.

Drawing, below, of same executive residence. It is believed the drawing was executed from memory. Included in W.P.A. papers of Cole County, folder 4240, Western Historical Manuscripts

State Historical Society of Missouri

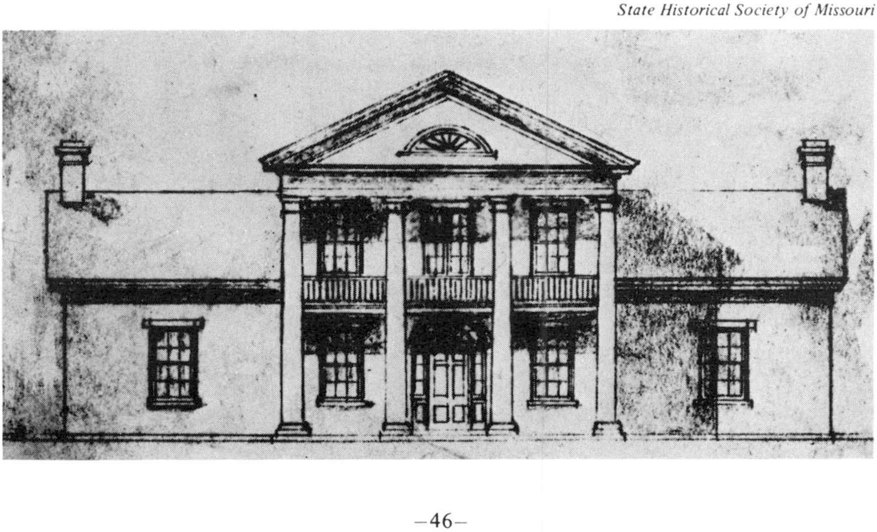

– with beautiful hands. Governor Dunklin had married his childhood sweetheart, Emily Pamelia Willis Haley, at her home in Kentucky in 1815. The Governor immediately brought his eighteen-year-old bride back to his property at the village of Mine-a-Breton near his tavern at Potosi. The Dunklins' first child, Mary W., was born on March 26, 1816. By the time Daniel Dunklin was elected lieutenant-governor in 1828 with the popular executive, John Miller, the Dunklin family included three daughters and one son. Descendants recalled that Emily Dunklin had more interest in family affairs than social activities and the concern of her children certainly occupied her hours while she served as the new official state hostess.

The first news about the Dunklin family recorded in a capital city newspaper concerned the death of a son, Henry, on August 2, 1834, at the age of five months and two weeks. This infant – the first child born to an executive family in Jefferson City – evidently had been born very shortly after the Governor moved his family into the new residence provided by the state. Another event chronicled by the city newspaper was the marriage of the Dunklins' oldest daughter, Mary W., on March 15, 1835. The romance had been pursued conveniently after the Dunklins' move to the capital city since the groom, Dr. Franklin Cannon of Cape Girardeau County, was serving in the Senate in the old statehouse situated in the backyard of the new governor's mansion. The brief newspaper item did not specify whether the marriage took place in the mansion but this could be presumed since home weddings were customary at the time and church facilities in the new capital city were extremely limited. The minister at the wedding was the Reverend Robert L. McAfee, a Presbyterian pastor who had been conducting services in the capitol building. The Presbyterian church played a prominent role in the Dunklin family life. Two younger daughters married Presbyterian ministers. Thus, Missouri's first, First Lady to reside in a separate executive residence built with state funds experienced during her reign the full cycle of family events – the birth, death and marriage of children.

There are no records of state social affairs during the Dunklins' term. The only event to gain attention was a near catastrophe at the capitol building which occurred a few months before the marriage of the Dunklin daughter. A crowd of state officials and city residents had gathered to mark the Eighth of January – an annual celebration of the anniversary of the Battle of New Orleans. A newspaper item told how some of the celebrants wrapped five pounds of gunpowder with string and set it off in front of the capitol. "Such a report was never heard before or since in the City of the Hills. It was distinctly heard at Fulton . . . the Legislature did no business for a week, for there was not glass enough in the city to refill the windows of the capitol and wagons had to be sent to neighboring towns to make out a supply." It was not recorded whether the blast damaged the governor's house. Since the capitol faced the river and the charge was placed in front of the building, the explosion certainly must have rolled with gusto up and down the Missouri.

It was from the vantage point of a boat on the river that most visitors viewed the new capital city, either in passing by or in approaching for a visit. One such traveler, Maximilian, Prince of Wied, in 1834 wrote that the village still was in its infancy, with buildings scattered and the ground covered with heaps of stone and high weeds "where cows and pigs roamed at liberty." Another traveler, who wrote a series of articles about Missouri which were printed in a Jefferson City newspaper in December, 1834, had this to record about the capital of the state:

> "It is eleven years since that spot was selected as the site of the new capitol . . . And it is nearly eight years since the Legislature first met here; still it is a small village, the surrounding country affording very little trade. Indeed there seems to be little to recommend the location except the fine building stone which is easily quarried from the bluffs upon which the town is to be built . . . And really nothing can look more beautifully white than this stone when well cut . . . It is to be regretted that the State House was not built of the same material, but such is our fondness for housing ourselves in brick that it is a wonder we do not wear earthen pans upon our heads, instead of beaver hats. Still this is a neat building of its kind, as is also the Governor's house, which stands near, where the present incumbent, Gov. Dunklin, lives, as hospitably as could be expected from his economical salary of $1500 a year."

Early executive families lived modestly unless they had private wealth and used it to enhance their official life. Records preserved in the papers of Governor Dunklin list purchases such as $2.81 for 2-1/2 bushels of apples, 80 cents for 8 pounds of sugar, 37 cents for a padlock and 50 cents for a chamber pot. These purchases were made by the Governor from a village merchant in late 1832 and early 1833, presumably before he had moved his family to Jefferson City and while he still was living in the executive quarters in the capitol building.

While travelers and visitors faulted the new capital city for its minimal growth, loyal local newspaper editors hammered away at an editorial campaign to beautify the capital area and to prod the legislators to do better by the official community. On August 22, 1835, the editor of the *Jeffersonian Republican* noted that the "improvement of this place during the last and present seasons has been very great . . . There have been built or are now building, four large two story Brick Store houses, which in point of style, size and convenience, would be no discredit to any western city – also some 7 or 8 dwelling houses – a large steam mill, ware houses, etc. . . . This ought to satisfy every person that Jefferson City never wanted anything but fair play to become a large town. The people are beginning to see through the slanders of such rival towns as wish and expect the Seat of Government through their abuses of Jefferson City." This was a reference to the specter of capital removal which was to haunt Jefferson City for nearly a century. Opportunists among the legislators played upon the original dissatisfaction over the site to nourish repeated efforts to remove the seat of government to a new location – and there were as many eager recipients as there were communities in the state. Governor Dunklin had done his best to lay the removal ghost during his first year in office by pushing through an appropriation for a new penitentiary located in Jefferson City. The

Emily Dunklin

Park-Morrow, Women of the Mansion

first sections of the state prison were built at the same time the governor's residence was under construction and the two facilities were only a few blocks apart.

Although not remembered for outstanding social events, the Dunklins apparently served satisfactorily until the Governor resigned three months before his term was over to accept a federal appointment. In October, 1836, Emily Dunklin and the couple's one surviving son and four unmarried daughters returned to their home near Potosi where they lived until a new estate was built by the Dunklins in 1841 near Pevely, Missouri and named "Maje." The name was said to have been taken from the first letter of the first name of the first four visitors to the new home. Governor Dunklin died at Maje in 1844 and Emily Dunklin died seven years later and was buried beside her husband on the estate grounds.

One of the illustrious names of Western history was added to the records of the Missouri mansion by the next first lady to serve in Jefferson City. The second hostess of the new governor's residence was Panthea Grant Boone Boggs, a granddaughter of Daniel Boone. The only picture of Mrs. Boggs shows a lady of seventy years with a face pinched by time. It would be far more romantic to erase the sunken cheeks and the set mouth and turn back to the image of a young girl of pioneer stock, born in Greenup County, Kentucky, who at twenty-one married an industrious young Missouri merchant and joined him for a life at New Harmony Mission near Kansas City where her husband carried on trade with the Osage and Kaw Indians.

The first child of Panthea Grant Boone and Lilburn W. Boggs was born at New Harmony Mission on August 22, 1824. The household at this time also presumably included Boggs' two sons, aged six and four, born to Boggs' first wife, Juliannah Bent, daughter of a well-known St. Louis jurist, Silas Bent. Juliannah had died on September 21, 1820, three months after her second son was born. By the time Panthea Boggs assumed the position of first lady in the fall of 1836, her family had increased to six children. The Boggs' second daughter was born November 30, 1836, just in time for the new first family to move into the executive residence in Jefferson City.

One of the first community-wide events which involved the Governor and his wife and their official home was the celebration of the Eighth of January during the Boggs' first year in office. A newspaper item told how "the evening of the 8th was embraced as a suitable opportunity by the people of this City and the members of the Legislature generally, to celebrate the anniversary of the glorious and ever memorable battle at New Orleans . . . The State House and Governor's House were illuminated from top to bottom . . . while the streets were rendered light as day, by sky rockets, the burning of tar and other combustibles . . . For three or four hours, an universal impulse of good feeling

Park-Morrow, Women of the Mansion

Panthea Boggs

prevailed all . .. By 11 o'clock universal silence prevailed."

Governor Boggs did not seem particularly smitten with the home provided by the state for he immediately suggested to the legislature that the house be sold and the proceeds used to build another executive residence "at some . . . more eligible point, less public and the grounds more extensive than those now afforded." The Governor received no response from this message and two years later, in November, 1838, he again suggested the residence be sold along with the ground and surrounding area. It was Boggs' idea to dispose of the entire site of the first capitol and the first separate governor's residence by dividing the area into building lots and selling them to private interests. It was providential that his plans failed for another governor, a century later, started long and expensive negotiations to buy back the privately owned parts of the rectangular block originally set aside by the state for the first capitol-mansion.

One occurrence which prompted Governor Boggs to make a second appeal for sale of the governor's house and grounds was the fire which destroyed the first capitol building. On Wednesday, November 15, 1837, at nine p.m., the fire started in the secretary of state's office on the second floor of the building. A newspaper account said the governor's residence was threatened but "prompt measures were taken by spreading wet blankets over the roof, to prevent the fire from taking." The newspaper said the absence of a high wind saved the governor's home and other private buildings. "The night was perfectly calm, with a very slight breeze . . . not even strong enough to communicate the flames to an adjoining log building eight feet distant." The destruction of the capitol was not considered a great loss and the stone and brick were sold at public auction two months later. However, the consumption of state and county records in the flames was a tragedy. The impact of the destruction of the records continued to be felt throughout history. A civic movement was started immediately for the purchase of fire buckets for every male resident of the capital city. A fire company was organized and plans adopted for the formation of a line of citizens from any future fire to the river. Buckets were to be filled at the river and passed along the line. State officials and legislators moved temporarily into a recently completed county courthouse and other buildings offered for the state's use.

Unfortunately, no public or private accounts were preserved which record the activities of the First Lady and her family during the excitement of the capitol fire. Panthea Boone Boggs undoubtedly helped prepare the wet blankets for the roof and also was busy calming her many children. The oldest of Governor Boggs' children at the time was nineteen-year-old Angus L. Boggs, the son of his first marriage. The youngest of his seven children by his second marriage was one-year-old Minerva Warner Boggs. Panthea Boone Boggs' eighth child was born in 1838 – a year after the capitol fire. Thus, the first two families to occupy the first separate executive residence built by the state both had sons born during their term of office in Missouri's capital.

Despite many demands resulting from a large family, the Boggs' administration was a busy and important one – socially as well as politically. A prominent Jefferson City resident, General William G. Minor, credited the Boggs with the first inaugural reception in Jefferson City. General Minor, in a newspaper interview, recalled that Governor Boggs extended an invitation to the public to call at the mansion and a "sort of informal reception was held." It was noted that no large gathering was possible since "the only room in the mansion in which the public was received was a room about forty feet square which would accommodate from 50 to 100 persons." General Minor also recalled that Governor and Mrs. Boggs introduced the custom of dining the members of the legislature in groups, taking them in alphabetical order and inviting only as many as could be comfortably seated. Again, unfortunately, neither the Boggses nor their legislative guests preserved a menu of these early state gatherings. State dinners, like family meals, presumably incorporated the most available meat and produce. Cows and hogs roamed freely through the capital city, turkeys were available at the markets for $1.00 each, chickens sold at $1.50 a dozen, eggs were slightly more than a penny apiece and butter was 20 cents a pound.

The Jefferson City Coffee House opened on the main street of the capital city in January, 1839, with such available items as champagne, wines, brandy, coffee, tea, tobacco, snuff, molasses, soap and candles. Legislative dinners given by the first family probably included purchases from the Coffee House as well as additional offerings from St. Louis since by 1839 the river trip had been shortened. A newspaper of the period made note of the improved river travel in an item that recalled that thirteen years previously only one steamboat arrived in the city during an entire year. "What a change," the item continued, "Instead of waiting 14 days for the return of a keel boat from St. Louis, we can go down and return in less than four days." And what a change for Panthea Boone Boggs compared with the first ladies under the Spanish regime who could replenish their pantries but once a year.

Despite Governor Boggs' repeated appeals for a new residence the only improvements found in state revenue records concerned funds for the papering and painting of the governor's house in 1838 at a cost of $296.25. In a final message to the legislature in November, 1840, Governor Boggs suggested the "propriety of causing the Governor's House to be supplied with suitable furniture." In January, 1841, a total of $1,500.00 was appropriated to buy furniture and $300.00 to repair the house and enclose the grounds. However, these expenditures could not have been made until after Governor Boggs and his family ended their tenure in the capital city and returned to their home in the frontier Jackson County village of Independence.

It was at their private home that, on May 6, 1842, an attempt was made to assassinate Governor Boggs. Mrs. Boggs still was seated at the supper table with several of her children when sounds of pistol fire were heard from a nearby room where the Governor was seated in front of a window reading a newspaper. Several balls from the load penetrated the back of the Governor's head and neck. Others passed close to his six-year-old daughter, Minerva, who stood near her father rocking the cradle containing the Boggs' infant daughter. The assassination attempt was believed to have been a result of the Governor's orders for expulsion of the Mormons from western areas of Missouri. However, no one ever was convicted. The Governor was treated by his brother, a Jackson County physician, and recovered to serve four years in the state Senate before he and his family moved to the Napa Valley in California. Panthea Boone Boggs again was called to a position of public service when her husband was appointed alcalde and thus became an important civilian official in northern California. Mrs. Boggs died on September 23, 1880 at the age of seventy-nine and was buried in the Napa Valley beside her husband.

The next administration in Jefferson City – the seventh since Missouri had become a state – was as personally tragic as it was politically noteworthy. Elected to succeed Governor Boggs was Thomas Reynolds, a young and able attorney who moved to Missouri after serving in high political office in Illinois, including terms as attorney-general and judge of the Illinois Supreme Court. Governor Reynolds was born in Kentucky in 1796. He moved to Illinois in his early twenties and immediately started a climb toward political success. In 1823, after he was elevated to chief justice of the Illinois Supreme Court, he returned to Fayette County, Kentucky and on September 2 married Eliza Ann Young. The couple's only child, Ambrose Dudley, was born in 1824. Reynolds' political acumen again was evidenced when he moved to Missouri in 1829 and after a

Eliza Ann Reynolds

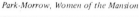

Park-Morrow, Women of the Mansion

residence of only three years was elected to the state legislature from Howard County. A biographer noted that as a speaker Reynolds rarely was excelled and "in canvassing the state for governor, but few were willing to encounter him."

Eliza Ann Reynolds, the new mistress of the governor's mansion and the fifth first lady of the state, evidently presided in a restrained although gracious manner. The Reynoldses were said to have planned an informal inaugural reception with guests invited at "early candle-lighting," but no refreshments were served. A descendant wrote that the First Lady was "a meticulous housekeeper and devoted mother." During the Reynolds' regime, the governor's residence was said to have been "resplendent with Mrs. Reynolds' mahogany furniture, coin silver, fine linen and bric-a-brac." The lovely furniture was threatened on December 4, 1841 – the first year of the Reynolds' administration – when a fire swept the governor's residence. The flames, which were said to have originated from a defect in one of the chimneys, had gained considerable headway by the time the bucket brigade was formed. A newspaper account said the flames were spread by a strong wind but the "virtue of water in copious streams" soon had the fire under control. A month earlier a fire had caused extensive damage at the state penitentiary and again, as it had done following the capitol fire, the city improved its equipment by purchasing three fire ladders and two fire hooks.

Jefferson City at the time of the Reynolds' term had grown to a community of some eleven hundred residents and more than one hundred buildings. Two major "public houses" on the main street, the City Hotel and the National Hotel, served as stops for the stages which had upgraded transportation for legislators and visitors. A steam ferry boat, referred to by a newspaper as a "matter of amusement and utility worthy of notice," assisted travelers in crossing the Missouri River from the northern part of the state. A typical excursion of the time was a steamboat ride to a nearby farm or community for a picnic of barbecued venison. Another civic improvement of the early 1840s was the reopening of the Rising Sun Hotel by Major Alfred Basye. This hostelry was one of the first public houses built in Jefferson City shortly after the legislators occupied the first capitol building. The hotel faced the river and was perched on a high bluff across the street east from the site of the first capitol and the grounds of the executive residence.

In the summer of 1843, items concerning a decline in Governor Reynolds' health began appearing in city newspaper columns. On December 21, 1843, a newspaper observed that "Gov. Reynolds is again in a very feeble state of health." Early in the year, 1844, the same newspaper noted that the Governor's health was "declining rather than improving." On Friday, February 9, 1844, shortly after breakfast, the Governor sent for a rifle to be brought to his office in the executive residence. He placed the muzzle against his forehead, wrapped strong twine around the trigger and tying the other end to his thumb, discharged the weapon. Passersby, hearing the report, rushed into the house and found the young executive dead. A letter on a nearby table was addressed to a friend, William G. Minor. The note said: "I have labored to discharge my duty faithfully . . . but this has not protected me for the last 12 months from the slanders and abuse of my enemies, which has rendered my life a burden to me." The Governor's funeral was held the next day, Saturday, February 10. A large procession formed in the yard of the executive residence and proceeded to a nearby city cemetery. Citizens of the community, by public agreement, wore crepe on their left sleeves for thirty days following the Governor's death.

A political contemporary wrote that Governor Reynolds' prospects at the time of his death "were greater than those of any man in the state." The same biographer observed that many of the Governor's friends blamed his death on domestic troubles. Others blamed melancholy due to his ill health. Only scant public mention was made of Mrs. Reynolds. A brief newspaper item a week after the funeral noted that "the health of Mrs. Reynolds which was much impaired by the death of her lamented husband, Governor Reynolds, is much improved."

On May 15, 1844, the only son of the late Governor and Mrs. Reynolds, Ambrose Dudley Reynolds, married Frances De Wilton Basye, the seventh child of Major Basye, owner of the Rising Sun Hotel. The wedding occurred only a few months after the Reynolds' administration had ended so abruptly and tragically. Mrs. Reynolds, according to a family genealogical account, moved from the executive residence to Platte County and eventually remarried. Later in life she was afflicted with a lingering illness which prompted Ambrose Reynolds to leave his family to care for his mother. The separation was said to have become permanent and the Reynolds' only son, following the death of Mrs. Reynolds in January, 1869, was reported living as a recluse in southwest Missouri. Thus ended the public accounting of the family of the young chief executive of the state.

The Governor's suicide forced attention, justifiably or not, on the possibility of domestic disharmony which never before had been publicly acknowledged concerning the first families of Missouri. Previous executives had died in office under questionable circumstances such as the Spanish Lieutenant-Governor De Leyba and the melancholy territorial Governor Meriwether Lewis. But it was the first time the first lady of the state had been portrayed as contributing negatively to her husband's executive life.

Chapter VI

A political dynasty was founded in Missouri's executive office on February 9, 1844 as Meredith Miles Marmaduke was administered the oath as governor and Lavinia Sappington Marmaduke became the first lady of the state. A change of administration cannot be delayed by emotion and even as the funeral cortege of the late Governor Reynolds moved toward the cemetery in the capital city a new regime took over in the capitol building. Marmaduke had served as lieutenant-governor and thus stepped up to complete the nine months remaining in Reynolds' term. It was through the family of the new Governor's wife, Lavinia, that the lines of the political dynasty can be traced. The lines actually reached back into the executive office of Kentucky through Mrs. Marmaduke's mother who was the sister of the Kentucky governor, John Breathitt. Three of Lavinia Marmaduke's sisters were to marry the man destined to reign as Missouri's Civil War governor. Her son was to be elected as the twenty-fifth governor of the state – the only time in history a father and son were to serve in Missouri's highest office. And two of Mrs. Marmaduke's granddaughters were to succeed to the position as official hostess of the governor's mansion.

The figure at the foundation of all this was born near Franklin, Tennessee on September 22, 1807. Ten years later, Lavinia Sappington moved to Missouri with her parents, Dr. John Sappington and Jane Breathitt Sappington. The family eventually settled in Arrow Rock in Saline County. Family records show that Dr. Sappington carried out an extensive practice with sick calls extending to Jefferson City on the east and Lexington on the west. It was during this time that Dr. Sappington gained fame by introducing quinine as a remedy for malaria.

In 1824, a young engineer who was engaged in trade with Santa Fe camped for a while during a trip to the West on a farm belonging to Dr. Sappington. This incident was reputed to be the start of a romance between the engineer, M. M. Marmaduke, and Dr. Sappington's daughter, Lavinia. The two were married two years later, on January 4, 1826, at the Sappington home known as Fox Castle. The Marmadukes also set up housekeeping near Arrow Rock.

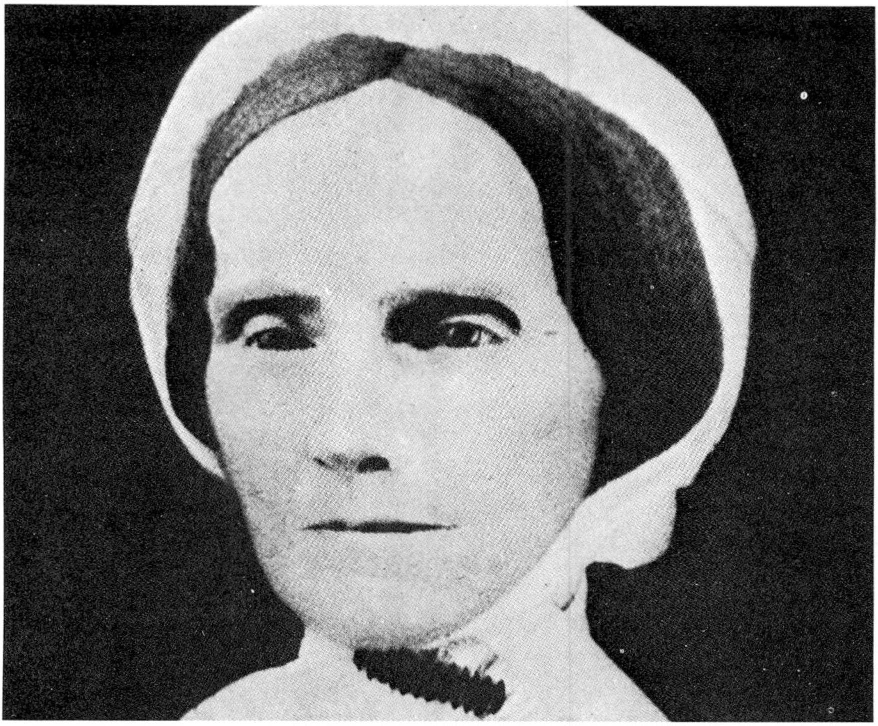

Park-Morrow, Women of the Mansion

Lavinia Marmaduke

As was customary at this period in history, the interests and concerns of Lavinia Sappington Marmaduke were primarily limited to her family whose size soon was enough to keep her well occupied. The Marmadukes had three daughters and seven sons and all but one of the sons survived infancy. Mrs. Marmaduke was described as quiet but possessing the strength of character found in a calm nature. Friends were said to remark on the sight of the small, fragile mother surrounded by her six stalwart sons. There are no records available to indicate whether Mrs. Marmaduke actually moved her family to Jefferson City during her husband's brief reign as governor. Such a move would have been difficult since her eighth child was not quite two years old. Official entertainment no doubt was curtailed following Governor Reynolds' suicide and no account of social functions in the governor's residence was published in the newspapers of the capital city. But whether her service at the state capital was daily or occasional, the entry of her name on state records was sufficient to mark the start of the Sappington-Marmaduke dynasty.

Mrs. Marmaduke's death some forty years after her service as first lady of Missouri was to precede by only a few months the deaths of two of her daughters and by only two years the death of her son in the executive Mansion in Jefferson City.

With the end of the administration of M. M. Marmaduke in November, 1844, a thirty-eight-year-old bachelor, John Cummins Edwards, assumed the state's highest office as the state's youngest elected governor. For the first time the new executive residence in Jefferson City was without a first lady. To fill the vacancy, Mrs. Ivy Dixon Edwards, who had married the Governor's brother, E. Livingston Edwards, served as official hostess for state dinners or receptions. One record stated that Governor Edwards held a reception on the occasion of his inaugural but no refreshments were served. A report to the legislature at the close of his term indicated that Governor Edwards frequently entertained visitors from throughout the state and he may have continued the legislative dinners started by Governor Boggs. Mrs. Edwards evidently divided her time between assisting at state affairs and looking after her own home several blocks away in Jefferson City. One major social function away from the capital which Governor Edwards attended was the wedding of Emily Smith Dunklin, daughter of the former governor, to Faulkland H. Martin, on April 15, 1846. The ceremony took place on the Dunklin family estate, Maje, south of St. Louis with Governor Edwards serving as best man for Martin who was secretary of state at the time.

An incident involving Governor Edwards was recalled years later by a Jefferson City youngster who attended a private school located across the street east from the governor's house. The story, which portrayed the executive as a man with fixed ideas of conduct, was told in a series of reminiscences by Dr. R. E. Young, a Jefferson City physician.

> "One of the most frequent games at school was shinny . . . Once as Governor Edwards was passing, a rock struck by one of the boys hit him on the chest. He went up to the boy, and tapping him lightly on the head, told him he should be more careful. The boy ran home and told his father and grown brother that the governor had struck him with his cane. There was trouble at once for in those days governors were not thought to be made of any better stuff than the ordinary mortal. The incident was in a fair way to end in a duel when less hot headed men took hold of the matter and it was amicably adjusted."

Although a bachelor, Governor Edwards was concerned about the condition of the executive residence and set about repairing the building, even out of his own pocket. In 1845, the legislature gave him $350.00 for repairs to the residence and grounds. The money also was to be used for "removing privy and the old kitchen." Later records indicate the kitchen was not torn down until funds were available four years later for construction of a new one. In 1847, the General Assembly approved $100.00 to repair the furniture belonging to the residence. In his valedictory message to the legislature in December, 1848, the executive noted his unsuccessful efforts to get sufficient money for repairs and new furniture. He stressed that he had used his own money and left some bills unpaid to do the work he felt was essential. "The house itself is in much better condition than it was four years ago, the roof having been made tight and the cellars dry. It is now deemed a healthy residence, and if furnished, would be comfortable enough. The rooms with smoking chimneys have been supplied with stoves, and these ought to be retained for the use of the House."

Governor Edwards also urged that most of the furniture should be sold, noting some pieces had been on hand fifteen or sixteen years. "Of many things, essential to the use of a family, the house has been for years almost wholly destitute," he continued. "To expect the Governor to furnish the House out of his own private funds is out of the question. To do this, and extend a little hospitality to visitors from different parts of the State, a matter expected of him, would consume more than a governor's income. No man in medium circumstances can do this without reducing himself to beggary and want; and no rich man should be required to do it . . ."

As had his predecessors, Edwards solved the problem of scanty furniture and of more scanty state funds by supplementing the state quarters with his own furniture, some of which he left for the use of his successors. Tradition credits Governor Edwards with having a sideboard made for the state residence which featured a large star carved in the front panel and unusual circular, enclosed shelves at each end. The work was done locally, perhaps by a cabinetmaker such as Mathias Wallendorf who had opened a shop near the capitol building. Within the next four years, the legislature was to make several sizeable appropriations for furniture and repairs to the executive residence, but the only record of a refund made to Governor Edwards was $120.00 approved the next year after his term expired.

Shortly after the end of his administration, the Governor "caught the gold fever" and left Missouri for California. He lived five years as a lonely rancher before he caught a fever of another sort and married a dark-eyed French girl, Emma Jeanne Catherine Richard. She was about nineteen and he was forty-seven. The couple had eleven children. Two daughters have recorded the romance of Governor Edwards and his young wife. Emma Richard Edwards, according to the family records, was born January 8, 1834 in New Orleans. Her parents, Madame Catherine and Monsieur Etienne Richard, were born in Alsace-Lorraine and French was the only language of their home and of their neighbors in the New Orleans French Quarter. When the daughter was about ten she was enrolled in a private school opened by a French nobleman and his wife near New Orleans. The weekly trip to and from school occasioned a carriage ride to the banks of the Mississippi and a rowboat ride across the river to a waiting carriage sent by the school.

When Emma Richard was sixteen, her parents were invited by a family friend to move to Stockton near the California gold fields. In the middle of preparations for the move, Etienne Richard died suddenly. His widow and daughter finished packing and boarded a boat for the trip through the Isthmus of Panama to San Francisco. The arrival of Madame Richard and her young daughter was said to have created great excitement in Stockton, a frontier mining center. Emma Richard and John Edwards are believed to have met at a ball or reception in Stockton. After a well-chaperoned courtship in keeping with French tradition, Madame Richard consented to the marriage and the ceremony took place early in May, 1854. The couple moved to Governor Edwards' 360-acre ranch where the children were born. Emma Richard Edwards died on November 29, 1925, at the age of ninety-one and was buried beside her husband

Sideboard of Governor Edwards

in the San Joaquin Valley – the adopted home of the former Missouri Governor and of the dark-eyed *jeune fille* who became his wife too late to serve as the state's first lady.

In Jefferson City, a new first lady was serving as hostess of the state residence which had benefited from generous responses to Governor Edwards' appeals for funds. In March, 1849, a few months after Governor Edwards left the capital, the legislature appropriated $2,000.00 for repairs to the residence and outbuildings and for the purchase of new furniture. This was the most money for the governor's residence approved at one time by the General Assembly during the fifteen years since the structure had been built at a cost of $5000.00. The Assembly directed that all the old furniture, except what the executive family might want, be sold at auction and new purchased. The governor also was empowered to build a new kitchen on the site of the old one. The new structure was to be built of brick, "one story high and thirty-two feet long by sixteen feet in width, the wall to be nine inches thick, with a brick partition wall across the center, with a stack chimney in said wall." There was no indication as to whether the new kitchen was attached to the executive residence. The French style of old St. Louis and a practice common in Virginia and Kentucky was to have cooking done in a separate structure in the backyard of a home. A more American style was to have the kitchen, a long, narrow room, attached to the back of the house and this may have been the plan for the executive quarters since only one wall was mentioned in the specifications set by the legislature.

Presiding over the refurbished executive residence was a hostess of Southern birth who was said to have been related to the famous Langhorne sisters of Virginia – Lady Nancy Astor and Mrs. Charles Dana Gibson. The new hostess was Nancy Harris Roberts King, wife of Missouri's tenth governor, Austin Augustus King. She was a native of Virginia who met her young lawyer-husband in 1827 while visiting relatives in Tennessee. She was twenty-one years old at the time and family tradition tells that she was twitted by her widowed mother and friends about bringing home a husband. It was perhaps the doting mother who supposedly said, "Nancy, you are so beautiful you ought to marry a prince." A few months later that same year, Nancy was married in Jackson, Tennessee and said in a letter, "I have done better than marry a prince, I have married a King." The couple's first child, Walter, was born in Tennessee in 1828. Shortly after their second child, a daughter, Frances, was born in November, 1830, the couple moved to Columbia, Missouri, where Austin King immediately launched a political career with terms in the state legislature and on the circuit bench of Ray County where he moved his family in 1837.

Descended from the finest families of the Old South, Nancy King evidenced personal convictions of unusual strength for women of her day.

Park-Morrow, Women of the Mansion

Nancy King

Family records show that during the years when the law prohibited educating Negroes, Mrs. King built a schoolhouse on the Kings' Ray County property where she taught the children of slaves to read and write. The schoolhouse remained standing for many years until it and the family home near Richmond were destroyed by fire. Nancy Roberts King was forty-two when her husband was elected governor – older than her predecessors. All her eight children were born prior to the move to the capital city and all but one son, who had drowned at the age of six, and an older married daughter apparently accompanied their parents to Jefferson City late in 1848. A historical recounting of the social life of Missouri's first families noted that the Kings "gave splendid entertainments *with refreshments.*"

In January, 1849, shortly after Governor King's inaugural, the state began to experience an epidemic of cholera, that most dread disease of the time. By

May, Jefferson City newspapers noted the disease was prevalent in the central Missouri area. In the issue of May 12, 1849, the Jefferson City *Inquirer* carried the first word of a disaster which was to result in countless acts of great charity and in charges by residents of other areas of incidents of selfishness among the citizens of the capital city. The steamer Monroe docked at the city wharf on May 10 with two passengers dead and several dying of cholera. The newspaper stated that "men, women and children lay promiscuously on the cabin floor; some just attacked, some in the jaws of death." The newspaper said most of the officers of the boat deserted, "leaving the stricken passengers and crew to the care of the people of the city." Vacant houses and the Episcopal and Presbyterian churches were turned into hospitals. There were 52 deaths among the 150 passengers on board the steamer and another two deaths were recorded among local residents. An item in the May 19 issue of the newspaper denied charges made in St. Louis that citizens were guilty of selfish acts, such as seizure of baggage to pay hotel bills of stricken passengers.

City newspapers failed to note the situation of the executive family at the time although both the churches involved were located across the street from the governor's residence. The First Lady no doubt had anxious moments concerning the health of her husband and children. Her charitable nature, evidenced by her concern with the education of slaves, must have been deeply touched by the pitiable plight of the many travelers, young and old. By July the epidemic had subsided and life in the capital community must have returned to normal. However, the Kings were to witness another epidemic during their administration.

Cholera again was prevalent in the summer and fall of 1851 and the victims included the state's Attorney-General William A. Robards. By the time of this second epidemic, two of the King children had left the executive residence for a trip to the California gold fields. The Governor accompanied his sons as far as Ray County where they evidently joined one of the frequent caravans which started along the Oregon and Santa Fe trails from western Missouri. The two venturesome sons were Walter, who was twenty-two, and a younger brother, probably William, who was eighteen. The three youngest of the Governor's sons, Edward, Thomas and Austin Jr., were enrolled in the little common school of the capital city – the community's first venture in free public education. The older daughter, Frances, was married and the Kings' other child, Bettie, undoubtedly was enrolled in one of the many private seminaries open to girls at the time such as the Female Academy in Columbia which her father helped to organize.

The reign of Nancy King as first lady of Missouri ended early in 1853 as executive inaugurals were for the first time moved from November or December of the election year to January of the following year. The King family returned to their farm near Richmond and four years later, on October 2, 1857, Mrs. King died in her Ray County home. On August 10, 1858, Governor King married Martha Anthony Woodson in Kingston, Missouri. They had two daughters, Nannie who was born in 1860 and died in infancy, and Mary Belle, born in January, 1862.

Missouri's early years of statehood were characterized by the service of Southern belles as first ladies. The years at the midway point of the nineteenth century were no exception as the mantle of state hostess passed between first ladies both born in Virginia. Succeeding Nancy King in the executive residence in January, 1853 was Martha Head Price, a native of Orange County, Virginia. The new First Lady was to display to an even greater degree the courage which saw her predecessor flout the law concerning education of Negroes. The life of Martha Price was to encompass such responsibilities as the superintendency of a large farm while her husband was fighting a war with Mexico, the direction of her family on a flight to Texas while her husband fought the cause of the South and the survival of a shipwreck while enroute with her children to Mexico to join her husband in exile. The story of Martha Price is reminiscent of the life of the First Lady of Spanish colonial days who experienced capture and imprisonment by pirates while on a trip up the Mississippi River to her home in St. Louis.

Family tradition places the meeting of Martha Head and Sterling Price at a party given by mutual friends at Chariton a short time after the parents of both had moved to Missouri from Virginia. The two were married at the Head family home in Randolph County on May 14, 1833. Both the bride and groom were twenty-three years old when they set up housekeeping at Keytesville where Sterling operated a mercantile business. After a few years they moved to a farm on Bowling Green Prairie in Chariton County and later built a large home which they named Val Verde. It was this 400-acre farm that Martha Price had to oversee, along with their four young children, when Sterling Price left in 1846 to fight in the Mexican War. Family records note that she served during General Price's two-year absence with "great prudence and skill" as manager of the large farm, a role rare to women of the time. A newspaper item in October, 1848 hailed the General's return as a hero "beloved by his soldiers, respected by his fellow citizens, and with laurels encircled around his brow that will perpetually bloom in the affections of his countrymen."

The warmth of General Price's heroic return evidently had not cooled by the time he became a candidate for governor in 1852. He was elected despite a campaign curtailed by the illness of his wife and son. A letter written by a friend at the time prompted a newspaper editor to publicly exonerate General Price for his failure to canvass the state. The editor noted that the "lady of Gen. Price for some time past, was not expected to survive, and that his eldest son was also very sick . . . " Indeed, he would have been censurable had he left home, the editor concluded. General Price's popularity stood him in greater stead during the campaign than did the public appeal of another hero, General William Clark, who some thirty years earlier curtailed his campaign to remain by his wife's bedside and lost a bid to serve as Missouri's first state governor. Mrs. Price was still recuperating but evidently was sufficiently strong to move with her children into the executive residence for the inaugural ceremonies in January, 1853.

Park-Morrow, Women of the Mansion

Martha Price

A large reception, termed by some an inaugural ball, was held by the new first family and attended by hundreds including friends and relatives from Chariton and Howard Counties. One of the first formal entertainments planned by capital city residents for the new first family probably was held in the mansion of Thomas Lawson Price, the first mayor of Jefferson City and a prominent businessman of the time. According to Jefferson City legend, it was an unbroken custom for many years for the incoming governor and his wife to be received first in the Price home. Although bearing the same name, the two Price families were not directly related until several years later when the

Governor's son, Celsus, married Thomas Lawson Price's daughter, Celeste. Celsus was only eleven years old when his parents first moved to the capital city. An older brother, Edwin, was seventeen; a younger brother, Heber, was nine and the only surviving sister, Stella, was six. To help her aunt attend the duties of official hostess and look after the Price baby, Quintus, the Governor's niece was invited to live in the executive residence. A letter written by the girl, Elizabeth Price, provides an intimate glimpse inside the second home built for Missouri's first families as it stood in the spring of 1853. The letter was addressed to a friend in her home town, Brunswick, Missouri.

> "You know I never was in the habit of writing on the Sabath, and today I thought I would make an exception. I came into Uncles office after breakfast and read one chapter in my Bible – afterward the pen, ink and paper, had such an attraction for me I could not resist writing to you. There are three front rooms to this house – one is Aunts the next is the parlour – which you enter off a large porch – the last is the office in which I am sitting. Uncle has not been to St. Louis to get furniture so the house is furnished just as ex-governor King left it. This room has a very pretty carpet on the floor corresponding with the other two rooms – they are furnished very much alike, and have folding doors between so if they wanted to they could throw open the doors and make one long room. The end rooms are a little smawler than the middle room. I will not give you a very minute discription now – but wait until it is furnished anew, for I think it will then be worth discribing."

The room used as the governor's office where the letter writer struggled with her spelling evidently was located in one of the two wings that flanked the two-story center portion of the governor's residence. The reference to the anticipated buying of furniture tied in with an appropriation, $1,500.00, made available by the legislature to buy furniture and repair the building and grounds. This was the second sizeable appropriation within four years for new furniture. The Assembly also continued during the Price administration the biennial allotment of $250.00 started in 1850 for upkeep of the executive residence. This sum was increased to $500.00 during the last two years of the Price regime.

While the General Assembly was becoming more generous with money for furniture and repairs, it still was necessary for the first family to pay most of the expenses of their state home out of the executive's salary. General Price was successful in getting an increase from $2,000.00 to $2,500.00 a year, but records show he refused to accept the higher amount during his term. He also requested salary increases for other state officials, noting that "house rent, servant hire, provisions and all other expenses necessary to the support of a family have increased at least two-folds in this city within the last 10 years."

Costs of entertaining also came out of the governor's salary and the niece, in her letter, mentioned the daily social life of the First Lady. Observing that Mrs. Price's health "was improving slowly," the niece said: "Most every body in Jefferson have called on us, at least all the young ladies and a good many married ones, last week we went out calling - and intend going out again tomorrow." At one point in her letter, the girl mentioned she had interrupted her writing to watch the passing of the Martha Jewett, a steamboat which traveled the Missouri River at that time. "There is a lot enclosed belonging to the Governor's house," she wrote, "that Uncle lets his horses run in, it is one side of a hill and slants down most to the river - it is now very green and pretty, it has some fruit trees in it, and we are going to get a nice seat put there for us, and then I expect to spend a good deal of my time looking at the boats." In a postscript, the Governor's niece wrote that "Uncle is going to take us out jugging soon . . . It is some way of catching fish . . . I like to fish very much but think this will be the most interesting way I have ever tried."

Descendants of Martha Head Price described the First Lady as a "queenly woman . . . symbolizing what a real lady should be . . . tall, very erect." She was said to have shown the same graciousness and charm to the humblest person that she did to those of position or wealth. Mrs. Price's charitable nature was evidenced in November, 1855 during a disaster which reached into many of the homes of the capital city. The occasion was planned as a celebration to welcome the first train to arrive on the newly completed tracks of the Pacific Railroad. City streets were decorated, a dinner was planned at the capitol and the First Lady had invited a group of women to the governor's residence to visit while they awaited the train's arrival scheduled for midafternoon. The time for the arrival passed and a formal postponement of the celebration was announced. It was not until early the next day that a boat arrived with the news that the bridge across the Gasconade River had collapsed with the weight of the train. Nine cars, all except the last one, fell some thirty feet into the river. Thirty-one persons, many of them civic leaders from St. Louis and other communities, died in the wreckage. Public buildings in the capital were turned into temporary hospitals or morgues. It was said that Governor and Mrs. Price joined in ministering to the injured and comforting the bereaved.

A year after this disaster, on December 5, 1856, the Prices' seventh child, a son named Athol, was born in the executive residence and a month later the Governor's term of office ended and they returned to their farm home, Val Verde. Athol died shortly before his fourth birthday and friends said the Prices were particularly stricken by the loss of this child of their middle age. One other child, their first daughter, had lived to be only fifteen months old.

Mrs. Price was left with the care of only three children when her two oldest sons joined their father in the Confederate Army. She moved with her younger children to Texas during the Civil War and, at its conclusion, joined General Price in Mexico. The General had obtained a land grant from Emperor Maximilian and laid out a colony he called Carlotta where he hoped to establish a permanent settlement peopled with exiles of the Confederate cause. In an early morning fog, the ship carrying Mrs. Price and her children to Mexico was wrecked. The passengers were saved but most of the cargo was lost, including the piano of nineteen-year-old Stella Price and all the furniture of the family, some of which no doubt had been used by the Prices in Missouri's executive residence. The passengers later boarded another vessel and sailed again for Vera Cruz. Mrs. Price wrote a friend that General Price had been waiting anxiouslyfor three weeks. "He heard of our shipwreck six days after the occurrence," she wrote, "but the accounts were so various that he did not know what to believe. His anxiety became so great that he had a severe attack of sickness." She said her husband was "so much reduced that I could hardly recognize him." However, in a display of amazing resilience, Mrs. Price concluded her letter with a cheerful observation. "Our prospects for a pleasant society at Carlotta are good .... I think that if no unforeseen accident occurs the Americans will do well and most of them be comfortably settled in a few years."

Events did not fulfill Mrs. Price's optimistic predictions. The General's personal health continued to worsen along with the political health of the Americans' friend, Emperor Maximilian. After seven months, Mrs. Price left Mexico with her children and her ailing husband for the return to Missouri. In early January, 1867, the wedding of the family's son, Celsus Price, occurred at the Thomas Lawson Price mansion in Jefferson City, but the General was unable to attend. In late summer Mrs. Price made a final effort to abate her husband's illness with a trip to a health resort. The trip was futile and on Sunday, September 29, 1867, the former Governor died in St. Louis. The family's new daughter-in-law, Celeste, and her newborn baby died that same day. Three years later, Martha Head Price, at the age of fifty-nine years, ten months and eight days, died at the home of her oldest son.

Another Missourian turned exile in Mexico was the man who followed General Price in the executive residence in Jefferson City -- Trusten Polk. The inaugural of Governor Polk on January 5, 1857, started a series of events which saw four governors serving within one year. The changes came so swiftly that the citizens of the capital city barely had time to pay a courtesy call on one first lady before she was succeeded by another.

When the Polks took office, they gave a reception and supper for state officials and city residents. One official wrote in later years that the

Park-Morrow, Women of the Mansion

Elizabeth Polk

entertainment was on a scale that "had never been seen in Jefferson City . . . the viands were furnished and the table spread by a St. Louis caterer." Mrs. Polk, described as a "most charming and brilliant woman," presided at the table and "was the life of the assemblage." Mrs. Polk was the first hostess of the state of Missouri who was not born in the South or Midwest. Three of the earlier first ladies were Kentuckians by birth and Mrs. Polk's two immediate predecessors came to Missouri from Virginia. Although the cause of the South was to dominate her later years, the early life of Elizabeth Newberry Skinner Polk was spent in Windsor, Connecticut. She moved to St. Louis with her family in 1826 when she was seven. On December 26, 1837, she married Trusten Polk, a twenty-six-year-old St. Louis lawyer. Their fifth child and only son was born in August, 1856, the same year his father was a candidate for governor. This son lived less than four years.

There is some question as to whether the Polk children actually had time to complete the move to Jefferson City. Eight days after his inaugural, the state legislature elected Governor Polk to the United States Senate and he resigned as governor on February 27, 1857. The Polks' fifty-three-day term was destined to be the shortest in history. The Governor's service in his new Senate seat also was brief for he withdrew from the sessions in 1861 to join the Confederate military service. He eventually was expelled from the Senate for his activities. A grandson recalled that Mrs. Polk, the Connecticut-born first lady, was banished from St. Louis for giving aid and encouragement to the Southern cause and during her absence the Polks' furniture and the Governor's extensive library were seized. The property was restored after the war and the Polk family regathered in St. Louis where Mrs. Polk lived until shortly before the turn of the century.

The third occupant of Missouri's executive residence during the busy year of 1857 was Hancock Lee Jackson who stepped up from lieutenant-governor when Polk resigned. Special attention most certainly was given to preparations for Jackson's inaugural because of an event which was rumored to have caused a delay in the inaugural ceremonies for Governor Polk. A St. Louis newspaper said the House and Senate were in joint session, the gallery full of ladies in "grand and breathless expectation" when there was an "awful and awkward pause." The St. Louis paper blamed the delay on a fruitless search

Ursley Jackson

Park-Morrow, Women of the Mansion

through capitol offices for a Bible to be used for administration of the oath. The paper charged that the nearest Bible was found at the penitentiary. A Jefferson City newspaper branded the story of the Bible shortage in the capitol as "false and malicious." Regardless of the truth, there no doubt was special attention paid to the availability of a Bible for Governor Hancock Jackson's inaugural the next month.

The lives of Hancock Lee Jackson and his wife —Ursley Oldham Jackson — touched the history of Missouri only briefly. Hancock Jackson and the new First Lady of Missouri were married on March 8, 1821 in their native state of Kentucky. The groom had visited Missouri two years earlier and evidently was impressed with the prospects of the area. Shortly after the couple's first son was born in January, 1822, the family moved first to Howard County and then to the southeast corner of Randolph County, Missouri, where he operated a large farm. All of the Jacksons' eleven children were born and at least three of them were married by the time he assumed the executive office. Although the Governor's name sounds as if it should head the muster role for the cause of the South, his public activities in Missouri apparently were concluded about the time the civil conflict began. Following his inaugural late in February, Governor Jackson called a special election for August and in October, 1857 a new governor was installed.

During her husband's eight-month term there were no published accounts of official entertainment in the capital city by Ursley Jackson. There are no records to confirm that she moved their family from the Randolph County farm home. The distance from the farm to Jefferson City was not too great for occasional trips and the condition of the executive residence was not too enticing to a propsective hostess. The Assembly had increased the biennial repair funds to $500.00 for a two-year period, but later statements indicate the money had done little to keep the twenty-three-year-old home in livable condition. After his term ended, Governor Jackson continued in public service briefly as a federal marshal for the western district of Missouri. A final bid for state office came in 1860 when Hancock Jackson made an unsuccessful campaign against his cousin, Claiborne Fox Jackson, in that year's gubernatorial race. This contest ended Hancock Jackson's public life and the family's private life in Missouri was closed five years later when they moved to Oregon.

Missouri's fourth governor during 1857 was to be the last executive to serve a full term before the Civil War. Robert Marcellus Stewart was a bachelor and, as one writer noted, a "Bourbon in the full sense of the word." An official state biographer described him as "tall and handsome, with dark hair, though inclined to slovenliness; a stranger to thrift but not to alcohol." An account of official inaugural functions through the years stated that Stewart entertained in "his own peculiar style." Stewart was inaugurated on Thursday and the next day, October 23, he hosted a celebration for state employees and friends. A Jefferson City newspaper in a story headlined "Sad Accident" told how a clerk of the House was badly hurt when he fell sixty feet down the bluff near the capitol and landed on the railroad tracks. The story said the clerk "was at the Governor's levee and at a late hour left to go to bed." The capitol in 1857 was the structure built after fire destroyed the original capitol and the new structure was located on a hill immediately west of the governor's residence. A painting of the capital city at the time of Governor Stewart's administration shows the newer capitol dominating the entire countryside as it was meant to do. Jefferson City by then had grown to a community of some two thousand residents. Rail service had been completed and communications improved with the opening of daily reports on the Missouri River Telegraph. City markets offered bacon at 10 to 14 cents a pound and butter at 12½ to 20 cents a pound. A bill introduced in the General Assembly proposed to raise the pay of legislators from $3.00 to $5.00 a day.

Legends and anecdotes mushroomed around the state's fourteenth governor whom some described as the "most brilliant as well as the most eccentric statesman who ever served as chief executive." Stories were told about a liberal use of the Governor's power of pardon including the pardoning of all women convicts and their employment at the executive residence where they "robbed and pillaged at their heart's content." Many years after his term an outstate Missouri newspaper carried a series of reminiscences concerning the Stewart administration. The newspaper stated: "Every Missourian over fifty knows of the time when the governor rode his horse up the steps of the executive mansion and ordered a peck of oats to be served in the piano, declaring that Dobbin, having accomplished a far better day's work than his master, deserved as respectful service at the hands of the state." This incident was the most enduring legend to survive the administration although exact details of serving the oats have been disputed, with other accounts claiming the horse was served from a fireplace mantel and another story of a sideboard being used. Regardless of where the horse dined, its hoofprints remained visible for years in the wooden steps of the executive residence as tangible evidence of the escapade.

The governor's residence that played host to the horse was undergoing major renovations inside and out. Soon after he moved into the home, Governor Stewart obtained a special appropriation of $500.00 for repairs to the building and grounds. This supplemented the $500.00 already appropriated for the 1857-58 biennium. Again in 1858, he obtained another appropriation of $1,000.00 to continue the work. A letter written to the editor of a Jefferson City newspaper by a visitor to the capital city in April, 1858 noted "the Governor's house, so long a disgrace to the state, is being fixed around, and the lovely spot rescued from offensive degeneracy." This was the second major refurbishing since Governor Edwards' demands had resulted in higher appropriations. Strangely, the two governors who worked the hardest to upgrade the state quarters both lived in the building as bachelors. Perhaps the absence of a family to fill the rooms of the executive residence made its faults more visible.

One lesser known anecdote of the Stewart administration was an outgrowth - at least in part - of the Governor's bachelorhood. This romantic legend was preserved in a scrapbook of Emile Karst, former French consul in St. Louis. The incident, evidently, was printed in a St. Louis newspaper by a newspaperman also involved. The account states:

> "When Bob Stewart of St. Joseph was governor, in 1858 or 1859, the writer (then a reporter) visited Jefferson City in the interest of his paper for an interview with Gov. Bob. He met there Mr. Emile Karst, then French consul at St. Louis and a most respected and eminent citizen, who had visited Jefferson City to obtain a pardon for a young Frenchman who had been sent to the penitentiary for a minor offense. For some days we were unable to find Gov. Bob, who was on one of his periodical toots, and the governor's secretary, learning from me that Mr. Karst was one of the most eminent violinists in the country, asked us to spend the evening in the governor's mansion, and have Karst to bring his violin. Karst had played one or two airs in his own inimitable manner, and Gov. Bob silently stole out of his hole and applauded the performer. Without waiting for an introduction, the governor said to Karst 'You can do me the greatest favor that any man in the United States can render to a governor in this state.' The governor's mansion was the then well-known white house on the location of the present capitol (mansion) grounds, but closer to the street. Said the governor: 'On the opposite side of the street lives a very fascinating young widow whom I have tried to convince that I am a musician; I will take my violin and sit on the porch and go through the motions,while you sit inside of the window and play two or three airs for me.' Their places taken, Karst's violin spoke gently to the air, and in a short time the window on the opposite side was raised, the dim outline of a face was seen, and by the time Karst had finished the piece two white hands were gently applauding. Another air followed, and again there was applause, and Gov. Bob, rising and bowing returned to the room and said to Karst: 'I do not know who you are or what you want, but if it is anything in the state of Missouri that is within the gift of the governor, it is yours.' Karst took a large package of papers from his pocket, stated he desired a pardon of the young Frenchman, and

had various recommendations. Stewart impatiently interrupted him by saying: 'I said you could have all there is in the state of Missouri,' and turned to his secretary, saying: 'Go immediately to the secretary of state – never mind if you have to wake him from his slumbers – and have a pardon prepared and the seal of the state attached, and bring it here immediately'; and thus Karst fiddled a prisoner out of the penitentiary."

State Historical Society of Missouri

Jefferson City in 1859

This and other such incidents of the Stewart regime must have occurred before the Governor went to New York in the spring of 1859. He brought back with him two nieces to serve as hostesses in the executive residence during the last two years of his term. Hopefully the Governor's conduct was more circumspect around his nieces. They were nineteen-year-old Elizabeth Westcott and her seventeen-year-old sister, Annie, daughters of the Governor's sister, Mrs. Emily Stewart Westcott. On a visit to the girls' home in Truxton, New York – the same town where the Governor was born – Stewart obtained the mother's consent for the nieces to return to Missouri – a great adventure for the girls. Elizabeth in later years wrote the following account of their trip to Missouri:

"How well I remember when Uncle was bringing us to the State he loved, calling it by every endearing title and enumerating its advantages. Nor can I describe my surprise when I beheld the city itself. Except the Capitol Building, Executive Mansion, the State Penitentiary, and a few dwellings, not an imposing building met our view. Hotels were not even medium. Though on acquaintance I am bound to say the McCarty House, though ramshackle to the eye, did serve some of the best meals ever. The venison roasts, buffalo tongues, fried prairie chicken and quail, not mentioning other things, can never be duplicated . . .

"The street leading to the Mansion in 1859 was without sidewalks – merely a washed-out gully. The Mansion, as they called it, was like thousands of houses in other cities, without the more modern conveniences. The neglected yard was partly atoned for by two galleries of exquisitely choice plants, the Governor's private collection.

"Our room opened on the upper gallery. It was large and the walls were hand-painted with the shield of the State in each corner and with the United States flag in colors in the center of the ceiling. The mahogany bedstead had an immense canopy lined with scarlet silk. The head-board was adorned with a golden eagle holding the lace mosquito bar in his talons and looking royal in the hanging-lamp light."

There are no records of state social affairs at which the two young girls from New York were called on to preside in the Missouri executive residence. Two major events which occurred after their arrival in Jefferson City in which they may have been involved were the visits to Missouri of the Prince of Wales, later King Edward VII of England, who attended a large reception in St. Louis, and Stephen A. Douglas, who made a campaign speech in Jefferson City in October, 1860. During that same year, according to family records, Elizabeth Westcott met John Severance, a civil engineer employed in the construction of a railroad in Missouri, and the two were married. The Severances, along with the younger niece, Annie, and the Governor lived in St. Joseph at the end of Stewart's administration in January, 1861. Ten years later, the Governor died while staying at the home of Bertram Heim and his wife, a German couple who had worked as his housekeepers in Jefferson City. He was buried at Mount Mora cemetery in St. Joseph and relatives soon noted the presence of a mock orange bush mysteriously growing at one side of the grave. It was concluded that the bush was planted by one of Stewart's "sweethearts." At least, this was the account of the bush's origin handed down to following generations who remembered sprinkling the Governor's grave with the white blossoms each spring.

Before he left the capital city, Governor Stewart set the stage for the eventual erection of a new governor's residence. In both his major messages to the General Assembly, Stewart appealed for a new building. "As it cannot be completed during my term of office," he stated in his first biennial address, "I feel no delicacy in saying that a new Governor's Mansion is greatly needed. The present edifice, besides being illy constructed and a very inconvenient dwelling, cannot much longer be made tenantable, even by repairs. The outhouses are also in a state of dilapidation. Altogether the present buildings are unsuitable and inadequate to the purposes for which they were intended, and by no means creditable to this great and wealthy State." In his final message on January 3, 1861, he reminded the legislature of the condition of the executive residence and urged that provisions be made for a "new and substantial edifice." Within two months bills were passed by the General Assembly and signed by the governor appropriating $20,000.00 for a new mansion and $2,500.00 to furnish it. But other events, already taking shape in the nation, were to preclude the expenditure of these funds and the money never was used for the purposed for which it was intended.

Chapter VII

Men fight war on the battlefields. Their women stay home and face different conflicts – the turmoils of fatherless, brotherless and, frequently, bereaved families. This truism of soldier-wives of all ages was particularly applicable to the wives of Missouri's governors during the Civil War years. Two of the first ladies of Missouri buried their governor-husbands during the war and, a short time later, the wives themselves died - all before peace returned to the state. The Civil War obviously divided the nation. In Missouri, as perhaps nowhere else, the war divided the state – not only its citizens, but its elected officials. All the wives of these officials suffered extreme hardships.

The year 1861 started in surface harmony in Missouri as the administration of the bachelor Governor Stewart ended in January and Claiborne Fox Jackson assumed the executive office. The residential prospects of the first family looked bright with an appropriation voted for construction of a new executive mansion. The Jackson administration opened with fanfare and celebration presided over by the new first lady, Eliza Whitsett Jackson, described as a woman of personal charm who took pride in meeting the demands made upon her. And the demands were many including the social requirements of her position and the duties of a mother to ten children. Eliza Jackson was the oldest daughter of Dr. John Sappington, the physician of Arrow Rock famous for his pioneering use of quinine for fever. She was born in Tennessee in 1806 and moved with her parents to Missouri in 1817. A few years after the move she married Alonzo Pearson, a store owner in Chariton. This unfortunate union ended officially in 1831 after the state legislature approved a special divorce bill – the procedure for legal divorce at the time. The legislative act awarded the couple's five children and all the family property to Mrs. Pearson.

Only a few months after this painful personal experience, Eliza Sappington Pearson helped in preparations for a wedding in the Sappington home. On February 17, 1831, a younger sister, eighteen-year-old Jane Sappington, married Claiborne Jackson who was at the time a partner in a general store in Franklin. Jane died five months after her wedding. Two years later, the Sappington home was the scene of another wedding when Jackson married another of the doctor's daughters, Louisa Catherine, also eighteen years old on her wedding day. Louisa was killed in a runaway accident on May 9, 1838 and a month later her third son died. Later that year, the twice-widowed Jackson returned to Fox Castle, the Sappington family home, to ask for the hand of Eliza. The doctor is credited with the reply: "You can take her, but don't come back after the old woman." Eliza Pearson married Claiborne Jackson on November 27, 1838 and assumed the care of her sister's boys – two-year-old John and four-year-old William S., in addition to the two boys and three girls of her own previous marriage. It must have taken great personal courage to undertake a union with a man for whom she was third choice combined with the trauma of her own previous unsuccessful marital experience. And added courage was to be demanded in later years when she was required to leave her home and remove her family to a primitive settlement in another state.

At the time of the marriage of Eliza and Claiborne Jackson, the latter was completing the first of his six terms in the General Assembly which included four years as speaker of the House and one term as state senator. The Jacksons had three children of their own by the time he made his first unsuccessful bid for the governor's office in 1848. Jackson's inaugural as governor on January 3, 1861 and Eliza's accession as first lady re-established, although briefly, the Sappington-Marmaduke dynasty in the executive mansion. This was the dynasty started by another Sappington daughter, Lavinia, when her husband, M.M. Marmaduke, was inaugurated seventeen years earlier. Family correspondence indicates that Mrs. Jackson, unlike her sister, spent little time in the executive residence in Jefferson City. A letter written by the Governor from the capital on June 3, 1861 addressed to his wife at their home made these observations on the unrest:

> "My position here is a most difficult one to say the least of it. If the people of the State were only united I should fear nothing, but unfortunately they are, to some extent, divided . . . It is my duty to remain at my post, and I shall do so let what may come. I should be very happy indeed to have you here with me & things may so change in a few days that I will send for you."

Things did change but not in such a way as to cause the First Lady to come to the capital city. Mrs. Jackson was soon to leave Missouri never to return to the state much less to the executive residence in Jefferson City. Nine days after the Governor's letter was written to his wife, Jackson and other state officers packed the public records. The next day, June 13, 1861, the officers evacuated by river steamer to Boonville moving ahead of the anticipated landing of Federal soldiers. On July 30, a special convention in Jefferson City declared the office of governor vacant.

Jackson, meanwhile, made arrangements for his family to leave Missouri during the hostilities. Land had been purchased in Red River County, Texas and the family moved there. The following account of Mrs. Jackson's life in Texas was written by a granddaughter based on information supplied by her mother, Louisa Jane Jackson Lamb, the second child of Governor and Mrs. Eliza Jackson:

> "A large central cottage (was) built, where Mrs. Jackson lived and where the dining room and kitchen were maintained. Small cottages surrounded it, where the daughters and daughters-in-law, with their children, lived, all eating at the central dining room . . .
>
> "Beyond the family cottages were cruder ones, if that be possible, where the twenty picked slaves brought from Missouri were housed. No slave was forced to go, but of the many who volunteered to go, twenty were selected as best fitted for the ordeals of the journey and their ability to do the tasks of frontier life.
>
> "The location was dismal, surrounded by canebrakes, often invaded by Indians, and chills and fever were most prevalent. There Mrs. Jackson ministered to her large family, day and night. She visited the sick, encouraged the homesick ones, and shared with the younger women the anguish of fear for the safety of the loved ones at war. Gardens were planted, materials woven, lasts made on which to make shoes from the hometanned hides. . .
>
> "Privations were many, keenly felt yet bravely met by these cultured ladies who had known nothing but the finer things of life. From there Mrs. Jackson was called to the bedside of her husband at the Pulaski House, Arkansas, opposite Little Rock, where he died. The trip was a very hard one, the shock of the husband's death a crushing one, but she returned to the Texas homestead where she felt she was so needed. In July she was smitten with a congestive chill. Lacking ice, medicines and other necessities, she did not recover. She was buried at midnight in a pine casket carried by her negroes; and by the light of pine-knot torches she was laid in alien soil."

The death of Governor Jackson occurred on December 6, 1862. On March 23, 1864, his son, Claiborne F. Jackson Jr., died in the service of the Confederate Army and was buried in or near Laredo, Texas. Four months later, on July 5, 1864, Mrs. Jackson, the displaced and dispossessed first lady, died. At the conclusion of the war, the bodies of Governor and Mrs. Jackson were moved to the Sappington cemetery in Saline County, Missouri. However, the grave of

Park-Morrow, Women of the Mansion

Eliza Jackson

their soldier son was unmarked and his body could not be found for removal.

A story of the orphaned family's return to Missouri from the Red River Valley also has been preserved as told by a son-in-law, Dr. C. L. Lamb, who was among the group making the trip. He recalled how harness was made of home-tanned hides. "On rainy days the traces would stretch until they were longer than the lines, putting the horses out of reach of the driver. Then would come the hot sunshine when the traces would shrink until the horses would be so close to the vehicle they could not pull. In homespun pants, which had also suffered from sun and rain, the menfolk of the party, all six feet and over, presented a sight wholly without sartorial equal."

Few dates are available to reconstruct Mrs. Jackson's final two years in Arkansas and Texas. In May, 1863, she still was in Little Rock following her husband's death. She wrote a letter at that time, addressed to "My Dear Son," commenting on recent battles of the Civil War. She observed that "yesterday's dispatches say we have whipped the Yankees again at Vicksburg amongst them tho they had about five to one when the attack began and that Stonewall Jackson had died of the wound he received in his last battle; his arm was amputated but it did not save his life – another great loss to our service." Mrs. Jackson continued to assess the progress of the war and comment on propsects of victory in a military style rather amazing for a woman born to the life of a Southern lady. She also noted that a representative had called on her "with an order or request from Gov. Reynolds for all the funds, papers, transportation or stock that belonged to the State of Mo." She said in her letter that she told the representative she "had no funds in my possession except some silver coin, about the amt. of your Pa's salary which had been reserved for that purpose." Thus, the executive reins of at least one side of the state of Missouri were changing hands.

When Governor Jackson died in December, 1862, the man elected as his lieutenant-governor, Thomas Caute Reynolds, declared himself the legal governor of Missouri. Gathering what he could find of the state papers in Arkansas, Reynolds moved his exiled government from place to place until November, 1863, when he established a rebel Missouri capital in Marshall, Texas – a town of some two thousand persons located near the head of navigation of the Red River and Caddo Lake.

Sometime in November or December, Reynolds leased a home for use as a governor's mansion. A copy of the lease shows he agreed to pay $225.00 a month in Confederate treasury notes for the house, grounds and some of the

Building used as Missouri Confederate capitol in Marshall, Texas. This building is believed to be similar to the one used as an executive residence in Marshall which had been remodeled when photographed in later years.

State Historical Society of Missouri

furniture. This house at the time was a well-built one-story frame cottage which many years later was enlarged into a Victorian house of porches and gables. The original house leased by Governor Reynolds featured such niceties as parquet floors. Reynolds felt he was so well-established with his pocket government which included an acting secretary of state and adjutant general, an aide and several clerks, that he sent for his wife. She arrived from the East in late December. It was said Mrs. Reynolds displayed a great amount of ingenuity in getting the aid of a Union gunboat to help her cross the Mississippi River on her way to the Confederate capital of Missouri.

The new Confederate first lady of Missouri, Heloise Marie Reynolds, was a native of Gibraltar where her American father, Horatio Sprague, operated a mercantile business and served for many years as United States consul. Heloise and Thomas C. Reynolds met while he was in Madrid serving as secretary to the United States legation in Spain. They married in Gibraltar November 28, 1848 or 1849 when she was about twenty-one and he was about twenty-eight. The couple moved to St. Louis in March, 1850 and Reynolds was appointed in 1853 as a United States district attorney, an office he held for four years. It was during this time that he fought a duel with B. Gratz Brown – a man who later was to serve as the undisputed governor of Missouri. The argument between Reynolds and Brown concerned a newspaper item supposedly written by Brown.

Arrangements for the affair of honor erupted into a secondary quarrel over the distance to be involved. Brown wanted to use rifles at eighty yards but Reynolds objected since he had poor vision and couldn't see beyond thirty yards. Final stipulations called for pistols at twelve paces. The affair took place on an island or sandbar in the Mississippi River. Reynolds was not hurt but Brown was hit in the leg. The bone was split at the knee joint and Brown walked with a limp throughout his life. One account told how Reynolds, on his return home, found "his brave wife suffering greatly, yet fully resolved to bear the worst. She believed in fighting duels when duels were necessary, and like the spartan matron would have buckled on her husband's armor and bidden him to go forth to fight and return on his shield or come not back dishonored."

It was this "spartan" matron who traveled through a country torn with civil war to fulfill her rather hollow position as first lady of an exiled Missouri government in Texas. She arrived in Marshall in December, 1863. Although the situation seemed to have called for little in the way of celebrations or entertainments, older citizens of the Texas town were to recall "a number of social events" held in the Confederate mansion of Missouri. Governor Reynolds seemed to be a person beholden to the civilities of less strenuous times. In a reminiscence of the Confederate state government, Senator George G. Vest, in later years, recalled an incident involving Governor Reynolds and his pocket government when it was "dodging about in the bush down in the Ozarks." As Vest told the story to a St. Louis newspaper reporter:

> "Claib Jackson had gone off in disgust and Reynolds was the Acting Governor, establishing the seat of government wherever Sterling Price's army stopped over night. Even in those days Reynolds was punctilious and polished as circumstances would permit. Vest says that one day he went down to the farm house that was doing service as the executive mansion at that particular time. He had received an intimation that Governor Reynolds wanted to see him, and he walked in wearing a pair of top boots and a blouse and very little else. The Governor received him with considerable dignity, and from time to time looked at his outfit rather critically. However, the evening passed along, and when supper time came the Governor and the guest sat down to a meal which Senator Vest says made his thoughts go back to the days of flapjacks at home. When they had finished the meal the Governor began on his visitor's attire.
>
> "'Vest,' said he, 'you ought to be more particular about your personal appearnace.'
>
> "The visitor explained that under the exigencies of the times he couldn't respond to a dinner invitation in a dress suit. After chatting awhile the Governor said, 'Vest, you've been talking about me.'
>
> "The visitor expressed surprise at such an assertion and denied its truth promptly and emphatically.
>
> "Reynolds drew out of his pocket a memorandum book, evidently kept with great nicety, ran down the index until he found V-Vest, and opened to the pages indicated. Then he read a complete record of some flippant remarks which Vest had made on an occasion weeks before which the author had entirely forgotten. The record contained the date, place, witnesses and words of the conversation. This was too much for Vest.
>
> "'Yes,' said he, explosively, 'I did say that – every word of it. I think you are going around here putting on too many airs with your little old one-horse Confederate State government, carrying your commission in your hat and the great seal of Missouri in your saddle-bags. Put that in your memorandum book if you want to.'"

In the autumn of 1864, Reynolds left Texas to join General Sterling Price, the former governor of Missouri, on an ill-fated campaign to Missouri. It was said Reynolds hoped the campaign might result in his delayed inaugural in Jefferson

City. A reinforced Federal garrison forced the Confederates to bypass the Missouri capital and, after a final defeat at Westport, the army fled toward the South and Reynolds returned to his fugitive capital.

Following the final surrender of the Southern forces in May, 1865, Reynolds sent his wife to stay again with relatives and joined other Confederate exiles in Mexico. A letter written by Reynolds from Vera Cruz to Jefferson Davis in Liverpool, England, told of the exiled executive's various jobs in Mexico, the latest as superintendent of an English railroad for a salary of $5,000.00 a year. Reynolds stated in that letter, written on September 30, 1868, that he hoped to send for his wife to join him in Mexico. However, it is doubtful she made the trip as Reynolds returned to St. Louis in the spring of 1869. A Jefferson City newspaper, in an item printed on May 26, 1869, noted that "one by one the Mexican exiles have returned. First came Gen. Price," the newspaper continued, "then Shelby and Polk, and last week's *Republican* announces the return to St. Louis of an old citizen, who, in 1860, was elected Lieut. Governor of Missouri. Whatever opponents may say of his political predilections, they at least must give him sincerity and self-sacrifice." One of Governor Reynolds' first actions in St. Louis was to return the state seal to the executive office in Jefferson City. This apparently was the seal taken from the capitol when Governor Jackson evacuated to Boonville in 1861.

Three years after the Confederate Governor and Mrs. Reynolds had re-established their home in St. Louis and started toward re-establishment of their economic security, Mrs. Reynolds died in a painful accident. Her clothes were ignited by a spark while she was sleeping before a fire in an upstairs bedroom. The barking of a pet dog attracted a servant girl and the girl's screams brought a passerby to help wrap Mrs. Reynolds in a rug. However, the burns were too extensive and she died early the next day, January 25, 1872. A capital city news story of the tragedy recalled that "Mrs. Reynolds, with the Governor, passed the exciting winter of 1860-61 in this city. She left among the extensive acquaintances then formed, most pleasant impressions. Since the war, we have frequently heard from ex-Confederates warm eulogies of her benefactions and charities to ill and wounded sufferers in the 'lost cause.'" Mrs. Reynolds, who had no children, was forty-four at the time of the fatal accident.

In the spring of 1879, Governor Reynolds married Mattie Jones, daughter of Captain Isaac H. Jones of Crescent Hill, Missouri. While still on their honeymoon, they visited Jefferson City and were serenaded by a group of friends – a form of special acclaim. The serenaders were invited inside the boarding house and "handsomely rewarded" by the Reynoldses for their disturbance. On March 28, 1887, the sixty-five-year-old Reynolds wrote a letter to friends concerning his failing health and his fear that he might become a burden to his wife. Two days later he fell or jumped eighty feet down an elevator shaft in a St. Louis business building and was killed instantly. He was the second Thomas Reynolds to serve Missouri in an executive capacity and he was the second Governor Reynolds to die violently.

Thomas Caute Reynolds' death caused no state executive changes – as had the death in office of the first Governor Reynolds – since the Confederate officials long before had been replaced by a provisional governor and lieutenant-governor selected by a special state convention. Hamilton Rowan Gamble, a St.

Park-Morrow, Women of the Mansion

Caroline Gamble

Louis attorney and former member of the state Supreme Court, was chosen provisional governor in July, 1861. Ironically, Hamilton Gamble and the provisional first lady, the executive couple selected to stablize Missouri within the Union, both were born in southern states. Their marriage took place at the family homestead of the bride, Caroline Lane Coalter, in Columbia, South Carolina, on November 8, 1827. Gamble had served Missouri in various offices through the years, starting in 1824 as secretary of state under Governor Bates. While sitting as presiding judge during the famous Dred Scott case, Gamble voted in favor of the slave. Ill health forced his resignation from the state's highest court in 1854 and he moved his family to Norristown, Pennsylvania. Although still not strong physically, he acceded to an appeal from Missouri to serve as a member of the special convention which later placed him in the governor's office.

Family records show that the Gambles reopened a home in St. Louis where Mrs. Gamble stayed except when rare special occasions required a trip to the state capital. Even had she moved to the executive residence in Jefferson City it is doubtful there would have been social activities during those tumultuous days of the Civil War era. The couple's children were well beyond infancy when Gamble was chosen provisional executive – the oldest, Hamilton, was twenty-four; their only daughter, Mary, was eighteen and the youngest was sixteen-year-old David. Mrs. Gamble's main concern was the health of her husband. It probably was pressure from his family that contributed to Gamble's decision to submit his resignation as provisional governor in June, 1863. But equally strong pressure from his colleagues caused him to withdraw the resignation. Six months later the Governor died. He had broken his arm and his age and ill health contributed to his failure to recover. A St. Louis newspaper in a special eulogy observed that the Governor at the time of his call to office, "gave up his family and friends to serve a state which had cherished and honored him." He died on January 31, 1864. Mrs. Gamble died in June of the same year.

Missouri's executive home during these years was not at all fulfilling the legislative plans for the building. Originally, the General Assembly had approved construction of the house to provide a comfortable residence for executive families. It was neither a family residence nor comfortable. The last family had moved out four years before the war. The Assembly obviously agreed that the house was no longer suitable since an appropriation had been voted for construction of a new mansion. But use of this appropriation – like most other peace-time projects – had been superceded by the war.

Information concerning the state executive residence was scanty during the Civil War. State officials were occupied with more important matters. No appropriation was requested or considered. The only information available is a brief reference made by Albert Cotsworth, a musician who moved to Jefferson City before the Civil War when his mother was employed to teach music at a seminary for girls. Professor Cotsworth recalled the executive residence during the Civil War as a "low-storied building with many wings and embowered in trees and furnished with that richness of velvet carpets, venetian mirrors, and lace and brocade curtains hanging from lambrequins and held back by heavy cords and fastened to supports screwed into the casing, wide fireplaces and . . . superb 'antiques' . . . Each morning we watched guardmount in front of the Mansion – a sort of improvised plaza made in the street."

Park-Morrow, Women of the Mansion

Olivia Hall

Professor Cotsworth also recalled a marriage in the executive residence. He said as the bride "passed one of the open fireplaces the flutter of her tarlatan dress caught fire and a very near tragedy was prevented only by the presence of mind of the groom" who put out the flames. There was no information as to the identity of the bride. The only executive marriage on record during the war years was the wedding in June, 1864 of Olivia Oliver, daughter of the provisional secretary of state, and Willard Preble Hall, the provisional lieutenant-governor who became chief executive following Governor Gamble's sudden death. Newspaper notices of the marriage gave no indication as to where the ceremony was held. One relative observed that Judge and Mrs. Mordecai Oliver, parents of the bride, were people of "means and prestige" and the marriage of their daughter elsewhere than her own home did not seem in keeping with family traditions. However, the Olivers were only temporary residents of the capital city and the executive mansion seems a more likely setting for the wedding of the Governor.

"Ollie" Oliver was Governor Hall's second wife. He first married, in 1847, Anne Elizabeth Richardson in St. Joseph. The first Mrs. Hall accompanied her husband to Washington when he served three terms in Congress. Letters to her family in Missouri told of her meeting the wife of President Polk and of her viewing the impressive flowers and greenhouses at the White House. Four children were born to Anne Elizabeth Hall but only three sons survived their mother who died in 1862 while her husband was serving the provisional government in Jefferson City. The second Mrs. Hall evidently was the only first lady who lived in Jefferson City during the war years. A niece recalled Ollie Hall as a "most fascinating woman; tall, with dark, lustrous eyes, willowy figure and possessing an abounding interest in life and a zest for all its activities." Ollie Hall was nineteen when she married Governor Hall – a forty-four-year-old widower. The second Mrs. Hall and the Governor had three children – a daughter, Emma, and a son, Stephen L., both of whom later moved to California, and another son who died young. Mrs. Ollie Hall lived sixty years beyond the end of her tenure in the state executive residence and later, after the death of Governor Hall, married Alfred F. Batt in Kansas City.

In late 1864, as the administration of the last provisional Governor and First Lady was ending, the Civil War also was ending within the borders of Missouri. In January, 1865, a newly elected governor was sworn into office and a first family moved in as fulltime occupants of the executive residence – the first family to live in the house since the close of the Sterling Price administration in 1857. Executive entertainment also was resumed as the new governor, Thomas C. Fletcher, and the new first lady, Mary Clarissa, held a large reception on January 23, 1865. A newspaper story of the event said it was the "social occasion of the season." In response to invitations very generally given, the newspaper continued, "members of the General Assembly, State Officers and sojourners of our city at an early hour began to assemble at the mansion and they continued to drop in until eleven o'clock, by which time the signs of an ebb tide were observable . . . Judging from signs of the times . . . with partners balancing in the most approved style, we suspect that many of the crowd didn't go home till morning . . . We do know . . . that everybody was pleased with the Governor and his estimable lady."

With the postwar renewal of official social functions in Jefferson City, the life of Missouri's First Lady resembled more the role played by the state hostesses of previous years. Actually, there were incidents in the story of Mrs. Fletcher's family that reached back to the state's earlier history. Mary Clarissa, "Clara," Fletcher was one of the few governors' wives who was born in Missouri as was Mrs. McNair – the first, first lady to serve following statehood. Mrs. Fletcher's father, Captain John W. Honey, had married three times. His first marriage was to Mary Antoinette Labbadie, youngest daughter of Silvester Labbadie Sr., a successful merchant of early St. Louis. He evidently was the same Mr. Labbadie who was accompanying the wife and family of the Spanish Governor Cruzat from New Orleans to St. Louis when they were captured by river pirates and later released for ransom. The marriage of Mary Antoinette, the merchant's daughter, to John Honey ended in divorce after five years. Mr. Honey, who later became a steamboat captain, married a third time to Mary Seaborn Austin whose family was prominent in the history of Texas.

John and Mary Seaborn Honey were living in Herculaneum in 1827. Their

Mary Clarissa Fletcher

Park-Morrow, Women of the Mansion

close friends and neighbors were Clement and Margaret Fletcher. A son was born to the Fletchers in January of that year and when a daughter was born to the Honeys a few weeks later, the two children were betrothed in their infancy. On April 16, 1851, when they were twenty-four years old, Thomas C. Fletcher and Clara Honey were married. Descriptions by friends, and a painting, portray Clara Fletcher as romantic in appearance as was the story of her background. She was said to be small and poised and simply but beautifully dressed. Her dark hair was worn parted in the middle and brushed back smoothly.

The Fletchers moved to the executive residence in Jefferson City shortly after they were reunited following the Governor's service in the Union Army. Making the trip to the capital with their parents were the Fletchers' two teen-age children, Ella and Edwin Lewis. A young man whose mother conducted dancing classes in Jefferson City at the time recalled the two Fletcher children at those classes. "She (Ella) was a dark-eyed and dark-haired beauty, knew her charms and of course had all the attention her heart could wish." The young man told how Mrs. Fletcher came to the occasional parties of the classes and "it did not seem to jar on her Methodist creed to do so, although we were told that that body of believers called dancing "wicked."

Although Mrs. Fletcher's creed gave way before her children's dancing parties, she was extremely temperate in her hospitality as first lady. Even before her marriage, she was a leader of a group known as Daughters of Temperance. Family records stated that wine was kept at the mansion during the Fletchers' administration, but the First Lady "never dispensed any of it."

Three events of state and national impact occurred during the Fletchers' term. On January 11, 1865, only days after his inauguration, Governor Fletcher signed an emancipation proclamation, declaring that "henceforth and forever, no person within the limits of the State shall . . . Know any master but God." Thus, Missouri became the first slave state to officially renounce slavery. In April, General Lee surrendered to General Grant and the Governor immediately proclaimed April 15, 1865 as a day of thanksgiving and public worship to mark the victories of the Federal army. This day of thanksgiving turned out to be a vastly different day and the public worship was rededicated when word arrived of the assassination of President Lincoln the previous night. Later, Fletcher issued another proclamation setting aside June 1, 1865 as a day of "fasting, humiliation and prayer throughout the state . . . as expression of sorrow over the assassination of the late loved and honored Chief Magistrate."

Governor Fletcher's term also coincided with a period of great upheaval in Missouri politics when more than eight hundred judges, sheriffs and other officials were thrown out of office. Authority for these ousters came from a constitutional convention which met in St. Louis in 1865. The same convention drafted a loyalty oath which prohibited many citizens from voting and many lawyers and ministers from practicing their professions because they refused to sign the oath. It was Governor Fletcher's responsibility to find replacements to fill the hundreds of vacant offices and to enforce new voter registration provisions. All these events must have reflected on the conduct of affairs in the governor's residence in Jefferson City.

Fletcher was the first Republican governor to be elected in Missouri and the last governor to be elected to a four-year term for more than a decade after the Civil War. At the close of his term in January, 1869, the Fletchers moved into an imposing new home in St. Louis where he practiced law for several years. Joseph Washington McClurg, a widowed merchant from Linn Creek, moved into the executive office in the capitol and installed his twenty-two-year-old daughter, Frances Ann, as his hostess in the nearby executive residence. McClurg was serving in Congress when he was elected to a two-year term as governor and his daughter patterned her entertainments in the Missouri capital city after the White House receptions she attended with her father in the nation's capital city. It apparently was an adaptation of Washington social customs that prompted "Fannie" McClurg to announce that she would be "at home" to callers on Tuesday of each week. However, the Tuesday-only affairs were relaxed when one of her new friends in the less formal society of Jefferson City asked good-naturedly if she was only "at home" one day a week.

Frances McClurg was the first governor's daughter to inherit the title and duties of official state hostess since Missouri had become a state. Her mother, an older brother and a baby sister all had died about 1861. Governor McClurg had married Mary C. Johnson, a native of Virginia, on October 18, 1841 in Ste. Genevieve, Missouri. The Governor had returned from Texas for the ceremony – a trip which covered 1,200 miles – on the back of a mule. In 1852, after an excursion to the gold fields in California, McClurg moved his wife and four young children to Linn Creek where he started a highly successful mercantile business and where four more children were born. In 1862, following the death of his wife and two children, McClurg started his political career and was elected to the first of three terms in Congress.

Apparently several of the younger McClurg children moved with their father into the executive residence in Jefferson City. An older sister, Emma, already was married but there were three boys and one other sister younger than the mansion hostess. Two of the brothers, James and Marshall, were remembered years later as ardent fans of the croquet court set up on the mansion lawn. One resident said the church affiliation of the first family caused the game to be dubbed "Presbyterian billiards." The champion players, however, were the Governor's daughter, Fannie, and the Governor's secretary, Charles Draper. The two had first met at Governor McClurg's inaugural reception and were frequent companions at the croquet court and on horseback rides through the Cole

County hills. They were married shortly after the close of McClurg's term. A daughter of the hostess, in recalling her mother's life in Jefferson City, told how her mother would watch from the windows of the executive residence as young Charlie Draper walked to the capitol in the morning and how she would listen for his whistle as he walked home late at night.

Thus, the young hostess' days were filled with personal interludes as well as public responsibilities. A happy combination of the two apparently was an entertainment held by the Governor and his daughter on New Year's day. It was customary at the time for all the young men of the town to call at the homes of their lady friends. Fannie McClurg had instructed Aunt Hettie, the mansion cook, to prepare roast turkey, ham, pickles, jellies and "other substantial and appetizing viands." The young gentlemen, years later, remembered their relief when they arrived and saw the bountiful buffet after a tiring afternoon of cake and wine. Food they were served by the McClurgs, but wine they were not. Governor McClurg had taken a strong public stand against the use of alcohol and immediately banished it from his own table. One newspaper editor pointed out that McClurg was the only Missouri governor during the nineteenth century who ever recommended passage of a bill absolutely prohibiting the sale of intoxicants. What a change in the residence that still bore the hoofprints of a horse ridden by a former governor who wanted Dobbin served oats in the best state style.

Governor McClurg also was very strict about accepting gifts during his term of office. According to a story recalled by relatives years later, a grand piano was delivered to the executive residence one day as a present from the company. The young hostess played the piano all afternoon and later cried when the Governor came home and ordered the piano returned. Fannie remembered the incident as the only time she begged her father to compromise his principles.

Governor McClurg's administration primarily was concerned with many more serious problems than the gift of the grand piano. It was a period of continued controversies resulting from the recent Civil War. During McClurg's first year in office, the former Confederate governor of the state, Thomas C. Reynolds, returned the state seal to the Missouri capitol. In a note accompanying the seal, Reynolds wrote: "Although of no official value, yet it is still interesting as a relic of the time when Civil War had not yet divided the Missourians. May its return be an augury of the speedy oblivion of past strife."

In February, 1869, leaders in the state women's sufferage movement came to Jefferson City to petition the legislature. The women were received in the mansion by Governor McClurg who signed their petition. One of these leaders was Mrs. John S. Phelps of Springfield, wife of a prominent attorney who later would succeed to the state executive office.

During McClurg's second year in the capital city, the fifteenth amendment to the United States Constitution was adopted giving Negroes the right to vote. A story in a Jefferson City newspaper on April 6, 1870 told of the observance in the Missouri capital:

> "The celebration of the ratification of the 15th amendment on Monday last will long be remembered. As was natural, the negroes were joyous but were orderly and quiet. About two hundred of them marched through the streets, preceded by a band of music .... Addresses were delivered at the Presbyterian Church and Governor's mansion, by Rev. Mr. Whitaker and Gov. McClurg."

An era had ended and a new one had opened not only for political affairs of the state but also for the residence provided for Missouri's governors. The state's first families soon would be housed in a spacious new building more deserving of the title of executive Mansion.

Chapter VIII

The City of Jefferson – a community conceived by the state and mostly built by the state – was nearing its half-century mark in 1870. The town's population had increased in the years since it was founded from one or two families to nearly five thousand individuals. Progress had been impeded by the disenchantment of the legislators with the site selection combined with the inherent distrust of anything political felt by residents in a basically agrarian area. But progress was made. Railroad transportation was improved to the point where a train trip from St. Louis took only six to seven hours. One Jefferson City merchant, in the interest of his line of stoves, noted the changes made by 1870 in an advertisement placed in a capital city newspaper: "People long ago must have had an inconvenient time of it. Just think, no railroads, no steamers, no gas, no friction matches, no telegraph, no sewing machines, no Charter Oak Cooking Stoves."

Residential development of the capital city was widely scattered among the hills. Several major farmsteads were operated within a mile or two of the capitol building. Streets in the city were lighted with coal-oil lamps on wooden poles. Boarding houses and hotels were numerous for the accommodation of legislators and other transient state employees and visitors. Across the street from the governor's residence, a new hotel, the Schmidt, was under construction in the late 1860s. The state capitol building on its site on the river bluff west of the mansion was thirty years old but its exterior was well preserved. An armory had been constructed south of the capitol where Civil War relics, including cannon balls, captured muskets and battle flags, were displayed. Breweries were the major industry of the capital city with two large installations producing some ten thousand barrels of beer a year.

But there were two conditions which were occasioning frequent editorial protest. An item printed in a city newspaper in 1869 referred to the first of these conditions. The writer said it was a "positive disgrace" that the members of the legislature and numerous other strangers "who throng the streets of the capital of Missouri every winter, should, during their daily walk to the State

House and other places in the heart of the city, find their progress impeded by filthy, wallowing porkers, and by hungry cows hunting for some garbage to eat."

Another major cause for editorial complaint was the condition of the governor's residence. A note published in 1868 stated bluntly: "That old rookery, known as the Governor's mansion, presents such a slushy appearance that a gentleman mistook it for a soap and candle manufactory a few days since." State officials also were calling for a new building. Governor Fletcher in his closing message to the General Assembly in January, 1869 stressed that the "house provided by the state as a residence for the Governor is dilapidated in every part and cannot longer be made comfortable." Fletcher recalled that $20,000.00 for a new mansion had been appropriated in 1861, but "the financial condition of the State was such at the time I came into office, that I was unwilling to use the appropriation, and it was transferred to the Interest Fund." The next executive, Governor McClurg, also used his parting message to renew the appeal for a new governor's residence. "The present mansion," McClurg told the legislators, "is antiquated, dilapidated and uncomfortable; unsuited to the age and inadequate to the reasonable requirements of the public."

Governor McClurg's remarks were made as he left office in January, 1871 and a new executive, B. Gratz Brown, took the oath as governor. The Brown family, including the new first lady, was on hand for the inaugural ceremonies but soon returned to their home in St. Louis. A month later, on February 10, the Browns opened the old mansion long enough to hold a reception. A Jefferson City newspaper commented that the "Governor's levee . . . was a throughly-Democratic and good old-fashioned affair." The newspaper noted that "All classes were there: the matron and her daughter; the millionaire and the mechanic . . . The host and hostess had the rare tact of making all enjoy themselves. The supper was all that could be wished for, and our only regret was that the mansion was too small for the hospitality of the host to be displayed to its full advantage." In the same newspaper, a lengthy editorial repeated appeals for a new executive residence. The editorial stated that many residents of the city had not attended the Browns' party "from fear of the danger that might result if there was a crowd in the rooms above."

But even as the editorial was published legislators were responding to pressures for a new mansion. A bill had been introduced in the General Assembly on January 4, 1871 by Cole County Representative John F. Wielandy calling for an appropriation of $50,000.00 for a new executive residence. Twenty-five hundred dollars of the appropriation was earmarked for advertising and fees of the architect. The governor, auditor and treasurer were named as a board of commissioners with authority to contract for the construction on "grounds owned by the state, adjoining the present residence of the governor." This site was the same location on the river bluff where the first combination capitol-governor's residence had been constructed nearly fifty years earlier. The Wielandy bill passed and was signed into law on March 18, 1871, two days before the Assembly adjourned.

Advertisements for plans began appearing in newspapers with the notice that architects' proposals had to be received by the state by April 10, 1871. The day following the deadline, Governor Brown and Major Samuel Hays, the state treasurer, met in the Planters' House in St. Louis to review the plans. The third commissioner, General D.M. Draper, state auditor, had not arrived at the start of

Bryan, Missouri's Contribution to American Architecture

George Ingham Barnett, from a painting by Chester Harding

the meeting. Architects listed in Jefferson City newspapers as having submitted plans included Patrick Walsh, John S. Thomas, Barnett and Piquenard, Adolphus Drulding, Randolph Brothers, Thomas Brady, Desborne & McNamara, G. W. Osborn and A. Grable. Several of the architects were present at the St. Louis hotel to explain their plans and the Governor pointed out defects such as location of rooms and width of halls. A newspaper account of the meeting said "some amusement was caused by the discovery that one of the plans offered was not provided with chimneys."

Plans submitted by the St. Louis firm of Barnett and Piquenard were selected by the state officials. The choice, thus, associated with the new structure two of the outstanding architects of the time. Alfred Piquenard later was the architect for the capitol of Illinois and died in 1876 before it was finished. The other partner, George Ingham Barnett, was considered a leader in his profession not only in Missouri but throughout the West. He was a native of England where he received his early training. Mr. Barnett was the exclusive architect for the many structures erected in St. Louis by Henry Shaw, including work at the world-famous Missouri Botanical Garden. One historian noted that Mr. Barnett was reputed to be the ablest architect of the classical school in the country. "He had no use for modern innovations and style, such as low ceilings, small windows and dwarfed door-ways. His buildings, whether public or private, always showed in their treatment what is characteristic of the educated architect, namely, character, expression and proportion." It was generally agreed in later years that Mr. Barnett was the partner primarily responsible for the plans for Missouri's new executive residence in Jefferson City.

A month after the plans were selected, a contract for construction of the building was awarded to Gottlieb Martin of Jefferson City on his bid of $56,500.00. Mr. Martin, only a few months earlier, had completed a new public school building in Jefferson City which featured the same mansard-style roof planned for the new mansion. Mr. Martin was one of eight contractors who submitted bids and all but one exceeded the $47,500.00 maximum originally specified by the legislature for the cost of the building.

Work started immediately. The alley bisecting the mansion grounds, east to west, was closed so the new building would not have to be confined to the northern half of the block. Newspaper items noted the progress of the contruction and mentioned that stone mouldings for the exterior were "dressed by private citizens" and other parts of the stonework were done at the state penitentiary. In mid-December, the building was nearing completion. The ornamental iron railing on the roof was in place when on December 13, 1871, a slight setback occurred. A newspaper story revealed that the granite columns donated by Governor Brown for the front portico had arrived and "after being placed on the ground were found to be nine inches short of the desired length." The newspaper concluded that the miscalculation was "an unlucky mistake, but will deter the work but little." Material for the columns had come from the granite quarry owned by the Governor in Iron County. The gift by the Browns of the four pink pillars was to start a custom of each first family presenting some lasting gift as a memento of the administration.

As the finishing touches were added, glowing descriptions of the structure appeared in print. The original plans had specified a three-story building, 66 feet and 6 inches square, placed 75 feet from Madison Street, which it faced, and 200 feet from Main Street, later Capitol Avenue. The design called for a stone basement extending eight feet above the ground. The first story was planned to be eighteen feet in height and the second story fifteen feet. The roof, named for the French architect Francois Mansart who popularized this type of garret with sloping sides, was to be thirteen feet high. Superstructure of the building was red brick with dressed stone used in the corners and for the window sills and door frames. A portico was placed in the front with large bay windows on the north (river) and south sides. The style of architecture was described as Mediterranean or French-Italian. Other outstanding exterior features, in addition to the granite columns, were the hand-carved walnut doors at the front entrance which weighed nearly one ton each.

Inside the building gray Napoleon marble fireplaces were built in rooms on the first two floors using material reportedly produced in Greene County, Missouri. A graceful stairway, with a railing hand carved from walnut, wound upward from the first floor foyer uncluttered by visible supports. This outstanding interior feature was soon to become renowned as one of the most beautiful stairways of its kind in the nation. Hardware on doors throughout the building was fashioned of German silver. The basement contained the kitchen, laundry, storeroom and boiler. On the first floor were the reception parlors, library and dining room all with sliding doors to be opened for accommodation of crowds and closed for better heating. The second floor contained seven bedrooms. Six more bedrooms and a billiard hall, later used as a ballroom, were on the third floor.

Final costs of the building, as listed in state auditor's reports, amounted to $74,960.00 which presumably included the furnishings. An extra appropriation voted in December, 1871 provided $15,000.00 for carpets and furniture and to buy from private ownership a small lot on the Main Street side of the mansion block.

Furniture was purchased from a St. Louis firm for the first-floor parlor and library and for one major bedroom on the second floor. A description of the furniture in bills presented the state reflect the elegant style of the period, as well as prices in the 1870s. For the grand reception rooms to the right of the massive front doors, the Browns bought two Grand Duchess sofas, two large easy chairs covered in scarlet Irish silk poplin, four smaller easy chairs and a mirror with a gilt frame – all costing $850.00. For the library, purchases included a walnut and gilt bookcase, $130.00; a French-style desk in walnut, $70.00; a library table with an inlaid top, $65.00; a mirror with a walnut and gilt frame measuring fifty inches by sixty inches, $175.00; two sofas, four chairs and a rocker. Total cost of the original furnishings for the library was $721.00. In one upstairs bedroom, presumably that occupied by the Governor and First Lady, a set in birdseye maple and walnut, including a bedstead, dressing case and washstand, was purchased at a cost of $240.00. Also bought for the major bedroom were a rocker, chair, table and lounge. For the windows, purchases included lace curtains measuring four and one-half yards long on the first floor, lambrequins and cornices. The total cost per window averaged nearly $100.00 on the first floor.

On December 30, 1871, construction was finished and final touches were being added to the state's proud new building. The city fire apparatus was driven to the river bank and hose brought over the bluff to fill two cisterns which supplied the Mansion with water. A capital city newsman observed the filling of the cisterns and reported the "performance was splendid."

The state's first family had been completely dispossessed since late October. On Friday, October 27, 1871, razing of the old mansion had started. A city newspaper noted the executive residence built in 1833-34 "has served well the purpose for which it was intended; . . . many scenes of festivity, many occasions of sadness and many deep political intrigues have taken place beneath the roof while in its chambers have been heard the soft words of love and fierce denunciations of hate. But the many and varied changes . . . the proud position we occupy in the Union, all rendered necessary the erection of a new, larger and more beautiful edifice – one more in keeping with the present age – for the abode of the Governor of our great and growing state." Materials from the old mansion were offered at public auction while some of the supplies from the dismantling were used in construction work at the state penitentiary.

There are no records to indicate that the first family occupied the old state residence very long following the inaugural levee in February, 1871. The General Assembly adjourned in late March and executive entertaining at that time was confined largely to the periods when legislatures were in session. It may have been that the Governor's sister, Eliza Brown, who came to Jefferson City from Kentucky remained to act as her brother's hostess until the old mansion was torn down. The first lady, Mary Gunn Brown, was expecting her sixth child and moved to the family farm near Ironton close to the quarry where the pillars for the new Mansion were produced. Several members of the Brown family were quite sick in the fall and Mrs. Calvin Gunn, widowed mother of the First Lady, had gone to the Iron County home to help care for them. It was while on this visit to the Brown farm that Mrs. Gunn died in September, 1871. Her body was returned to Jefferson City and the funeral was held at the old mansion on Wednesday, September 13, 1871 – the last public function before the building was demolished.

During the two months between the destruction of the old executive residence and completion of the new Mansion, some of the Brown family could conveniently have occupied one of the three new brick houses constructed in 1871 under the Governor's direction on property originally owned by the First Lady's family. These row houses, across the street east of the new Mansion, were built on the site of the home where Mary Gunn Brown was born in 1842. Her

Park-Morrow, Women of the Mansion

Mary Brown

father, Calvin Gunn, had moved to Jefferson City as state printer in the summer of 1826 while the first combination executive residence-capitol was under construction.

Stories were told of Mary Gunn, as a girl, throwing mud balls and sailing boats on a pond near her home. It was the front gate of this home – so close to the heart of state government activity – that figured in the meeting of the editor's daughter and B. Gratz Brown, then a thirty-two-year-old state senator. A romantic legend related by relatives tells how sixteen-year-old Mary was swinging on the gate in the spring of 1858 when Senator Brown walked past. He was said to be so attracted to the girl that a companion who knew the Gunn family offered to take him back and introduce them. About three months later, on August 17, 1858, they were married in the Gunn family home. The couple lived in St. Louis where Brown had a law office and was a writer and later editor of a St. Louis newspaper.

It was in their St. Louis home that Mrs. Brown remained with their four children while her husband was serving as a United States senator. At the close of his term in Washington, the Browns were both in poor health and they opened the farm home in Iron County for a year of rest and recuperation. Political activities brought them back to St. Louis in the summer of 1869 where their fifth child was born and Brown laid the groundwork for a campaign which was to lead to his successful candidacy for governor and his nomination as an unsuccessful candidate for vice-president of the United States.

January 20, 1872 was moving day for members of Missouri's first family as they occupied the resplendent new building which befitted its designation as the executive Mansion of Missouri. There still was some final finishing to be done but the building was sufficient for its debut into city, state and even international social circles. The first function held in the new Mansion was a noon reception on January 23, 1872 for the Grand Duke Alexis of Russia who was touring the United States and had just completed a buffalo hunt. The Duke and his party arrived in Jefferson City about 9:30 a.m. on a train said to be rented for his trip at $3,500.00 a day. The visiting dignitaries were met at the station and the Duke was driven to the capitol building in a carriage loaned by a Jefferson City undertaker and drawn by four white horses. Governor Brown escorted the Duke to the Mansion for a luncheon attended by state officers, supreme court judges, legislators and city officials and their wives. The meal was described as "unostentatious and unpretending, yet rare and brilliant in itself and all its surroundings." Assisting the First Lady were the Governor's sister and her own sister, Elizabeth Gunn who had been a member of the executive household since the death of her mother the previous year. The Duke was described as over six feet tall, with blond hair and whiskers "a la militaire." At 3 p.m. the visitors walked across the street to the Madison House and received callers for an hour. The Madison was located on the site of the Schmidt Hotel which was destroyed by fire only a few years after it opened. The visitors' train left the capital city about 4 p.m. and the first family started immediately preparing for a public reception to be held twenty-four hours later.

On Wednesday night, January 24, 1872, Missouri's new Mansion was opened formally with the public invited to a ball "with refreshments." Ladies throughout the state ordered dresses weeks in advance and reported descriptions of their gowns to local newspapers. The columns soon were crowded in an undeclared contest for the most sumptuous ball dress of the year. Favored fabrics were silk and satin, tarlatans and tulle with trains and berthas trimmed with Valenciennes lace. Hairdressers were so busy that many ladies reportedly slept upright for several nights to protect their elaborate coiffures. On the night of the ball, the sliding doors of the Mansion all were pushed back making the first floor appear as one large room. The following description of the affair was printed several years later in a Jefferson City newspaper:

> "It was a most brilliant gathering. The Mansion itself was beautiful in its new and handsome furnishings. The ladies shone like a Louis XV salon, with high, light puffs of hair and nodding plumes, while the brass buttons and epaulettes of the State Guards outdid themselves and made their wearers look small in comparison. There passed through the parlors that night most of the notable men of the State, the judges and many of the eminent lawyers attendant upon the Supreme Court; Major Rollins of Columbia, with his courtly manners; the gray-haired Alfred Morrison of Howard, who was State Treasurer when Claiborne F. Jackson was Governor; Judge Miller with his snowy hair, who knew everybody in the State, above and below ground, and others; yes, others, for the great house was packed from the front door to the roof.
>
> "When supper was served, the guests mounted not only the grand stairway to the second story but the narrow one to the third, and here the long tables were loaded with delicacies of the season. Everything that St. Louis caterers could supply was there, but the thing most mentioned was a pyramid of spitted snipe; and the mob, from the gracious, graceful guests of the first floor became a pushing crowd on the narrow stair and doorway, not so much to eat as to see the much-talked-of feast.
>
> "The middle of the hallways where they crossed each other was divided off for dancing, but the crowd was too great for it to be either beautiful or pleasant.
>
> "As the evening wore away, tired lines were showing in the Governor's face and about his eyes. The opening ball had been successful in every way, but he was glad when at last he could bid his guests good night and retire for the rest his turbulent term demanded."

Within two weeks, the first family started a schedule of less spectacular state social affairs, such as small dinners for all members of the state Senate and House of Representatives – a custom started some thirty-five years earlier but suspended by the war years. The legislators were entertained in groups of thirty, again invited in alphabetical order.

Perhaps it was at one of the legislative dinners that guests experienced the results of the apprenticeship of ten-year-old Gratz K. Brown who had been presented a new set of carpentry tools by his father, the Governor. It seems the youngster had practiced with his saw on the dining room chairs. The changes wrought by the boy went unnoticed until guests were seated for a state banquet. Most of the chairs, according to the family legend, had at least one shortened leg causing the chairs and occupants to roll about disconcertingly.

Another anecdote recalled by children of the first family concerned a return train trip from St. Louis. The First Lady was accompanied by her infant daughter, the baby's nurse and others of the family's five children. At one stop, the mother suggested the nurse take the baby off the train for a walk to soothe its fretfulness. The train pulled away from the station while the nurse with the baby still was walking. The conductor, described as a family man himself, responded to a distraught mother's appeals and prevailed on the engineer to back the train five miles to pick up the missing passengers.

One of the better-known stories concerning the young family and the new Mansion occurred as the father-Governor was walking toward the capitol with the former United States Senator John B. Henderson. Responding to some impulse which occurs to parents, the Governor paused to look back at the Mansion. He was horrified to see his young children running around the mansard roof of the building, secured only by the iron grillwork. Governor Brown, according to the legend, turned to Henderson and suggested he go on to the capitol "while I go back and spank the children."

Other occurrences at the Mansion of necessity resulted from the political happenings of the state which are never far removed from the conversation and concern of the first family. One such event – unique in history – was the reaction of friends and associates to Governor Brown's nomination in the spring of 1872 as a candidate for vice-president on the Liberal Republican ticket which was headed by New York newspaperman Horace Greeley. A week after the nominating convention a Jefferson City newspaper noted that a crowd had gathered at the Madison House across from the Mansion to celebrate the nomination. Also joining the celebrants was a brass band led by Antoine Thaute of the capital city. "At half past 9 o'clock the crowd, led by the band, marched to the Executive Mansion. Gov. Brown was called for and came forward and delivered the most appropriate and well-timed speech we ever heard."

The ticket of Greeley and Brown lost in the national elections, although the gubernatorial candidate backed by the combined forces of the Liberal Republicans and Democrats won in the state. In January, 1873, the Governor closed his term and the Brown family moved back to St. Louis. It seems particularly appropriate that the first, First Lady to occupy Missouri's magnificant new Mansion with the mansard roof should have been the first governor's wife to be born in Jefferson City. Governor Brown continued the practice of law until he died in 1885. The family's eighth and youngest child was five years old at the time. Mary Hansome Gunn Brown, whose social activities as state hostess were frequently curtailed by ill health, outlived her husband by only three years.

A minister's daughter, Virginia Juliet Lard Woodson, was the first hostess of the state privileged to live during her husband's entire administration in the new Mansion. Governors' terms were limited at that time to two years and Mary Gunn Brown was able to spend only one year in the newly finished residence. There were similarities of life in the Mansion during the Brown and Woodson administrations. The Browns had a houseful of their own youngsters and liberally extended the hospitality of the Mansion to relatives. The Woodsons had only one daughter at the time of their residence in the capital city but they were equally generous with invitations to relatives to join them in the Mansion. And the Woodson administration was to make the first entries in the record book of marriages and births occurring in the new executive residence.

"Jennie" Woodson, the first lady of the new administration, was only twenty-six when she moved her family to the capital. She was the third wife of Governor Woodson who at fifty-three was the same age as her father. Silas Woodson and Jennie Lard were married in Kentucky on December 27, 1866 and moved immediately to St. Joseph, Missouri, where he practiced law. The groom had purchased the home just outside St. Joseph built by the bride's father, the Reverend Moses E. Lard who had moved to Kentucky during the Civil War. Governor Woodson's only child by his previous marriages had died in 1865, so it was just the bride and groom who occupied the large house.

On January 8, 1873, the Woodsons held their inaugural reception in the executive Mansion in Jefferson City. A family letter said a St. Louis caterer spent one week prior to the affair in the basement kitchen of the Mansion. The banquet table extended the full length of the dining room and was described as a "marvel of confectionery art and floral decoration." Members of the receiving line included the Governor and First Lady and Miss Cornelia Shannon, a ward of the Governor and sister-in-law of Mrs. Woodson. A newspaper account detailed Mrs. Woodson's dress as "a handsome brocade silk of a beautiful color, known as gaslight green, whose mingling and shimmering shades almost dazzled the eye." The item added that the dress had a heavy train and a lace collar. The First Lady's hair was arranged "in puffs and curls, its only ornament being a pink plume. Thus attired," the story continued, "Mrs. Woodson, who is naturally a very handsome woman, and blessed with youth and perfect health, beamed on her guests and was superlatively lovely." The newspaper story added that a brass and string band played and guests danced – "waltzing, scottishing recklessly about . . . until long after the noon of night."

Cornelia Shannon was just one of a family of relatives of the First Lady who accompanied the Woodsons to Jefferson City. Also moving with them were Dr. and Mrs. R.D. Shannon and their two daughters, including eight-year-old

Carey who later recorded her memories of the caterers working in the basement and other preparations for the inaugural reception. Carey said her favorite position during the opening reception and many state entertainments was seated beside the bronze statue of a lady which for years adorned the newel post at the foot of the grand stairway.

Dr. Shannon, whose medical education had been generously underwritten by Governor Woodson, was married to Mrs. Woodson's sister. He served on the Governor's staff and they lived in the executive residence in the capital city until an increasing family necessitated a search for other quarters. This increase was the addition of two more daughters, twins Cornelia and Mary, who were born on June 30, 1873. These were the first babies born in the new Mansion and the first births in the state's executive residence in Jefferson City since Athol Price was born in the old residence in December, 1856.

The month before the appearance of the twins, Dr. Shannon's sister, Cornelia, was married in the Mansion. A description of the ceremony was

Virginia Woodson and sister, Mrs. R. D. Shannon

Park-Morrow, Women of the Mansion

published in the *Central Magazine* of St. Louis, as follows:

> "The beautiful and accomplished belle of our State Capital, Miss Cornelia Shannon, daughter of President Shannon of the Missouri State University, and ward of Governor Woodson, was married at Jefferson City, on Thursday morning, May first, 1873, to Mr. William Newton White of Columbia, Missouri.
>
> "The wedding ceremony was performed by the Reverend J.W. Mountjoy of Paris, Mo., at the Executive Mansion, His Excellency, Governor Woodson, giving the bride away.
>
> "A grand reception, presided over by the hostess, Mrs. Woodson, followed, which was attended by the elite of Missouri.
>
> "The bride was attired in a white silk dress with court train, the waist cut decollete and trimmed with a vine of orange blossoms. A magnificent point-lace veil confined with a wreath of bridal flowers, descended almost to the floor, partially concealing the exquisitely molded neck and arms of the fair bride, who looked as charming as the first May blossom.
>
> "We wish the happy couple a long and prosperous life and hope their union will be a bond of love, welcome as the May day on which it began."

This first wedding in the new Mansion came at the conclusion of a series of social events at which Miss Shannon assisted the First Lady. Capital city newspaper columns carried almost weekly accounts of receptions which occasionally were open to the general public. These regular events ended in mid-March at the close of the legislative session and the summer months were devoted to less formal entertainments such as picnics for the many young friends of the Woodsons – both those who lived with them at the Mansion and relatives who visited. The frequency of the social events planned by the First Lady prompted one newspaper editor to observe that though Mrs. Woodson was a member of the Campbellite Church and the daughter of a minister, "all this did not prevent her from having any number of balls at the Executive Mansion." A family friend stated that Governor Woodson spent twice the amount of his state salary to supplement the costs of living and entertaining at the Mansion.

During a summertime lull, Mrs. Woodson turned her seemingly unlimited energies to directing additional work on the Mansion grounds. In May, 1873, a professional gardener was employed to supervise the landscaping which included planting a flower garden and the addition of a summerhouse on the southeast corner of the grounds. Two other events connected with the new Mansion and its construction had occurred earlier that year. Late in February – only one year after the Mansion was finished – the contractor, Gottlieb Martin, died. A newspaper account stated Mr. Martin, a native of Germany, had moved to Jefferson City in 1865 as superintendent of a large manufacturing firm. In 1870, he went into the construction business. His work included the new city public school building, a new Cole County jail and then the new state executive residence. The same newspaper issue, on March 5, 1873, carried another story which told of an "unprecedented phenomena" at the Mansion. The story related how the "chandeliers, the door knobs, the railways for the doors, and the stair carpet rods emit flashes and give shocks which are accompanied by reports whenever touched." The amazed reporter observed that he was confident the phenomena, which was first noticed in February, was the result of natural causes. "Nevertheless, people would like to have our savants settle the difficulty. What makes the Executive Mansion a grand electrical battery? Let some wise body rise and explain."

A week later, the newspaper readers were provided an explanation. Some unidentified "wise body" said the phenomena was not entirely new but occurred mostly in homes having soft and heavy carpets. It was caused, the newspaper stated, by the friction of feet in passing over the carpet. "In some instances, the quantity of electricity thus generated is sufficient to give a slight shock to a person taking hold of a metallic door knob, and to light gas, if it turned on and the tip of the finger held close to the burner." The newspaper editor failed to chronicle whether any member of the executive family had tested the gas-lighting ability of their fingers. Such a test could have been made since gas pipes and fixtures were installed throughout the Mansion and gas service was available in the capital city by the winter of 1873.

With the start of their second year in office in January, 1874, the Woodsons reopened a social season which included a masque ball with the First Lady dressed as Queen of the Night in a black silk robe and coronet of moons and stars in her hair. Also attending the Mansion parties was a battalion of the St. Louis guards in full-dress uniforms. Assisting the First Lady in the early months of 1874 was another relative invited to make her home in the state's executive residence, Miss Ellen Woodson, orphaned daughter of the Governor's brother. It was a repeat performance of the Woodsons' first year – a young relative moves to the Mansion, assists at state social functions and marries.

Ellen Woodson was born on a Kentucky plantation as the youngest of nine children. Her father, Wade Netherland Woodson, died on a trip to California and, a short time later, her mother was fatally burned when sparks from a meadow fire ignited her dress. Following this double tragedy, the younger children were taken to Missouri to live with a married sister. Silas Woodson, while tending to his brother's estate, was enchanted with the child Ellen and adopted her. Later, Ellen moved to Missouri's executive residence to assist the First Lady who was near her own age. Noted for her keen wit and quick repartee, Ellen soon had many suitors knocking on the Mansion's massive front doors. A widower from Kentucky brought his three motherless children to help plead his cause. A statesman from Washington sent a special message asking her to move to the nation's capital. But Ellen's choice was a young newspaper editor from Boonville who frequented the capitol as assistant secretary to the Senate.

George Frame, also a native of Kentucky, won the heart of the Governor's niece and their wedding took place in the Presbyterian Church in Jefferson City on December 29, 1874. The bride wore a gown of ivory satin trimmed with lace and was escorted to the altar by the groom and preceded by Governor and Mrs. Woodson. Among the newspapermen who were listed as guests at the wedding was Eugene Field, also an admirer of the bride. In a newspaper story about the bride's return to Jefferson City, Field wrote: "a more beautiful, lovable woman never ornamented society. The sweetness of her character beams in her lovely face and glows from her eyes, unusually blue-blue eyes fringed by black lashes, black as her raven hair."

A few days after Ellen's wedding, the Woodsons ended their tenure in the new Mansion and moved back to their rural home near St. Joseph where the First Lady gave birth to twins – a boy named for his father, and a girl named for her mother. The twins were born on June 18, 1875 – two years after their twin cousins were born in the Mansion. Following the Governor's death in 1896, Mrs. Woodson moved to Kansas City where she died at the home of a daughter on January 25, 1907.

During its first three years, Missouri's new executive residence had been the scene of an unprecedented number of social events, including the reception of a foreign dignitary, and had been the backdrop for a full range of human events, including two births and two marriages. Furnishings presumably were completed during the Brown administration and landscaping was undertaken by the Woodsons. Thus, when Mary Barr Hardin started her reign as first lady in January, 1875 the state's newest official building apparently was in superb condition. It was during the Hardin administration, 1875 and 1876, that the state legislature started biennial appropriations of $1,000.00 a year to pay for "current expenses." This presumably recognized the tremendous cost formerly borne by the first family for the buying of food and paying extra servants to assist at the numerous state receptions. Mention was made in the records of the Woodson family of a butler and cook, Addison Green and his sister, Jennie Green, who continued to live in the Mansion with the changing administrations. Many such Mansion employees were to preside in the back rooms throughout the years and, although seldom mentioned in official records, they were to become an integral part of the official building.

Mary Hardin, the third hostess to serve in the new Mansion, instituted a reign of austerity which was quite a contrast to the schedule of her predecessor who, although a minister's daughter, was a devotee of dancing and fun. Speculation concerning the Hardins' plans even appeared in print two months before his inaugural when a capital city newspaper reporter pondered: "Will our next Governor permit dancing at the mansion? is the question of the hour with metropolitan belles and beaux." Obviously, word of Mrs. Hardin's strict adherence to the code of her Baptist faith had preceded her to Jefferson City and the Governor seemed in complete agreement with his wife's views. When he was asked to promise certain concessions when he became governor, Hardin replied: "There is only one pledge that I will make to be fulfilled when I get to be Governor. I pledge that there shall be no masquerade balls at the mansion." Whether the Governor considered masquerades as symbolic of all frivolity or whether he had a special aversion to masks is not known, but it is known that his promise was fulfilled. Although the "belles and beaux" may have been disappointed, the older visitors to the Mansion were impressed with the degree of education of the new First Lady.

Born in Kentucky, Mary Barr Jenkins had moved with her family to Boone County, Missouri, in 1835 and in the fall of 1842 when she was eighteen years old, she graduated from Bonne Femme Academy, a private Boone County educational facility. An account of a school exhibition in 1841 mentioned how Mary Jenkins read from a Greek testament and from Cicero "with extraordinary ease and lucid diction." Also listed as a student of the academy was Charles H. Hardin who married Mary Jenkins on May 16, 1844. A tribute written by the groom on his wedding day had these words for the bride: ". . . a lady of intelligence, refinement and special literary taste and accomplishment. She has written much, both poetry and prose, but having an aversion to an appearance in public . . . little of either has appeared in print."

For many years, the Hardins lived on a farm where Mrs. Hardin spent many weeks alone while her husband was in Jefferson City as a member of the House of Representatives from Callaway County. Mary Hardin's loneliness, combined with her devotion to writing, is reflected in her diary for those years in which she meticulously set down the number and description of the garments she laundered and the number of candles she moulded each day. Recipes also were recorded including the following for Sally Lunn – a type of cake popular at the time: "1 pt. new milk, 2 eggs, piece of butter size of hen's egg, 1 table spoonful of fresh yeast, 3 pts. flour. Make a very soft dough, rise in a buttered pan and bake like a cake. Split it open and pour over melted butter." Perhaps Sally Lunn and others of her recorded recipes such as mince pie and cornstarch cake became favorites for the table of the executive family in the Mansion twenty years later. However, the First Lady's culinary skills gave way to professional service for the inaugural events in Jefferson City.

Governor and Mrs. Hardin moved into the Mansion early in January, 1875 and their introduction to the society of the capital city was an informal New Year's reception. Following the swearing-in ceremony in the capitol building on January 12, the Hardins held a large formal reception in the Mansion. A newspaper account stated "the beauty and fashion and talent of the state" were represented among the crowd. "The supper was furnished by Pezolt of St. Louis; the tables were tastefully decorated and fairly groaned under the weight of good things."

There is no indication through journals of the period that Mrs. Hardin had regular receptions at the Mansion but she was active in charitable, civic and religious undertakings such as assisting in a drive to collect clothing and provisions for the underprivileged. She helped direct a group of capital city women in an appeal for funds and articles to display at the national centennial celebration held in Philadelphia in 1876. One of the best-remembered events of the Hardin administration was a special day of prayer proclaimed by the Governor at the height of an infestation of grasshoppers which were devastating crops throughout the state. A biographer recorded that Governor Hardin had received an anonymous letter suggesting a day of prayer. He shared the letter with his wife who immediately and earnestly concurred in the request. The special day of fasting and prayer was held on June 3, 1875. Rain broke the drought the next day and within two weeks the pests were reported to have vanished from the state.

A vivacious contrast to her reserved aunt during the Hardin administration was provided by the Governor's niece, Fannie Hardin, a former student at Stephens College in Columbia. The first family's religious code evidently was not applied to their young charge, for Fannie made a mark as a belle of Jefferson City. She was included in the guest list of dances and parties given by the leading families. She still was well-remembered in the capital city four years later when she was married in Mexico, Missouri to a St. Louis attorney. Fannie probably was present to assist in the welcome to the Mansion of Jefferson Davis who toured the country during 1875.

The leader of the Confederacy was one of two important visitors who came to the Missouri capital during the Hardin administration. The first was King Kalakaua of the Sandwich or Hawaiian Islands who was traveling cross-country by train. The King, described as dark and rather corpulent with a very pleasing contenance, arrived in Jefferson City in late January, 1875 and made appearances before the House and Senate. There is no indication that he was received at the executive Mansion before he returned to his train in the late afternoon. School children of the city, who were dismissed to see the King, acted as his escort back to the depot. In the fall of that year, 1875, the second visitor to Jefferson City, Jefferson Davis arrived. Mr. Davis came by train in early September and stayed overnight at the Mansion before continuing his trip to Kansas City. His schedule included a serenade by citizens and a ride through the city in a carriage provided by Burr McCarty, operator of one of the city's outstanding hotels. During the carriage ride, Mr. Davis stopped at the capital city fairgrounds and at the national cemetery where he viewed the monument to the Federal soldiers massacred by Confederate guerrillas at Centralia.

At the close of the Hardin administration, a St. Louis newspaper correspondent noted that the Mansion "has been the most homelike place on earth." The story observed that Mrs. Hardin was a strict Baptist and "I dare say nothing has occurred in her house during the whole two years that could make her pastor bat his eye with the slightest disapproval." The simplicity of the First Lady, bordering on severity, is reflected in her portrait believed to have been painted by George Caleb Bingham who served as adjutant general during

Mary Hardin, a copy of her portrait in Mansion

Governor Hardin's administration. Her dark hair, parted in the middle, was drawn tightly to the nape of her neck. But the hair merely served as a background for the piercing, intelligent black eyes. This painting of Mrs. Hardin was moved to the Missouri Mansion some sixty years after the Hardin administration. It originally had hung in Hardin College in Mexico, an institution founded by the Governor as a continuation of educational philanthropies started by members of his family who were active in the opening of William Jewell College at Liberty, Missouri, named for the Governor's uncle.

At the conclusion of the Governor's term in January, 1877, the Hardins moved to their farm, Forest Home, about three miles north of Mexico, Missouri. The Governor renewed his law practice briefly in partnership with his brother-in-law, William H. Kennan of Mexico, but devoted most of his time to the farm operation and the promotion of Hardin College. In 1884, the Hardins gave a plot of land to the city of Mexico and it still was in operation as a municipal park nearly a century later. In April, 1888, Mrs. Hardin went into mourning following the death of her niece and namesake, sixteen-year-old Mary Hardin Kennan of Mexico. Four years later the Governor died and the next year, 1893, Mrs. Hardin's sister, Mrs. Kennan, died. Relatives said Mrs. Hardin's mourning was continuous. She divided her time between residence in the Ringo Hotel in Mexico and the home of her late sister. A niece, Mrs. Florence Kennan Mason, recalled that Mrs. Hardin constantly wore black and never was seen without a little black lace cap on her head and needlework, the Bible or a Greek prayer book in her lap. Mrs. Hardin died in Mexico on September 27, 1904 and was buried beside her husband's grave at the Jewell family cemetery in Columbia, Missouri.

Some unfortunate family circumstance prevented the position of first lady of the state from being officially assumed by one of the outstanding Missouri women of the nineteenth century. Following Governor Hardin into office was John S. Phelps, a Springfield lawyer who entered the executive position after eighteen years of notable service in Missouri's congressional delegation. As his hostess, Governor Phelps brought to the Mansion his oldest daughter who fulfilled her role superbly. Most official records attribute Mrs. Phelps' absence from the Mansion to ill health. However, there were accounts of her presence at social and cultural events in other cities while Governor Phelps was in the Mansion and her death a year after the start of her husband's term was described at the time as as a surprise. It seems more accurate to assume that Mrs. Phelps' decision to remain in Springfield resulted from an estrangement between the Governor and his wife.

Mary Whitney Phelps was born in Maine, the daughter of a sea captain who died in a storm when she was quite young. She married John S. Phelps, a young Connecticut attorney, on April 30, 1837, when she was twenty-five years old.

That fall, the Phelpses moved to Greene County, Missouri, where they purchased a small lot with the groom's first meager earnings. During her husband's absence practicing law, Mary Phelps had a log cabin built on the lot and completed its furnishings as a surprise to her husband when he returned. It was in this log cabin that the first of the Phelps' babies was born. The couple had five children but only two – a boy and girl – lived beyond early childhood.

Mrs. Phelps' penchant for adventure, even at the risk of bodily harm, was illustrated by her eagerness to ride the Butterfield stage in a wild dash through Missouri. John Butterfield was racing with the mail across country from California. In the fall of 1859, Butterfield, who was a friend of Congressman Phelps, reached Springfield and stopped at the Phelps' home. He invited Mrs. Phelps to ride with him to Tipton where the stage would connect with the railroad. Mrs. Phelps, then in her mid-forties, eagerly gathered up a few belongings and her thirteen-year-old daughter and joined Butterfield. In a recounting of the adventure years later, the daughter remembered that "between Springfield and the first relay station my mother and I bounced around the driver's seat, holding each other to keep on board." The daughter noted that at the stop to change horses Mrs. Phelps joined the mail sacks inside the coach. At Tipton, the mail and passengers quickly changed to a railroad mail car for the journey to St. Louis where Mrs. Phelps and her daughter ended their part of the trip.

Two years after the ride with Butterfield, the daughter was assigned to the more confining life of a private-school student while the mother turned her attention to the wounded of two major Civil War battles. The first of the battles, Wilson's Creek, resulted in a charitable deed which gained Mrs. Phelps a permanent place in Civil War history. Nathaniel Lyon, the Union general, was killed at Wilson's Creek and in the confusion the defeated Union troops left his body on the battlefield. Later, the General's body again was left behind when the troops left Springfield for Rolla. Hearing of the oversight, Mrs. Phelps obtained the body, placed it in a wooden coffin and zinc case and had it buried temporarily in her garden to guard against vandalism. It eventually was removed from her garden and taken to Connecticut for burial.

The battle of Wilson's Creek occurred in August, 1861. Nearly a year later, a second battle, Pea Ridge, occurred south of Springfield in Arkansas. Mrs. Phelps accompanied her husband to the scene of the fierce three-day fighting. She is said to have torn her clothing into bandages as she cared for the wounded of both armies. Another of her notable activities was the opening in Springfield of an orphanage for children of both Union and Confederate soldiers. Congress, probably encouraged by Mrs. Phelps' friend, President Lincoln, had voted $20,000.00 for Mrs. Phelps' many services and she used the money to start the orphanage which at one time housed some two hundred and fifty children. At the close of the war, Mrs. Phelps located families to take the younger children and found jobs for her older charges. She redirected her energies to the family's one-thousand acre farm on Kickapoo Prairie in Greene County and to superintending the making of cheeses which were widely acclaimed by friends who received them as gifts.

In February, 1876, Mrs. Phelps suffered the first of a series of misfortunes. She was a passenger on an ocean vessel, the City of Panama, when she fell through three open hatchways, a distance of twenty feet. Her fall was broken partially by soft cargo but her right arm was shattered. She was said to have been on her way home from the West coast at the time of the accident. Her husband was elected governor in November of that year and in January, 1877, he took the oath of office at the state capital and held an inaugural reception in the Mansion.

Assisting Governor Phelps at the Mansion was Mrs. Mary Phelps Montgomery – the daughter who at thirteen rode on the Butterfield stage. Mrs. Montgomery's service as her mother's stand-in won high praise in all published accounts of her frequent receptions and state dinners. One newspaper story of executive entertainments during Mrs. Montgomery's reign described a banquet which certainly would have not been excelled in variety or splendor by any banquet served to the society of the nation's capital or even in royal circles of Europe. Whether this lavish entertainment was customary for Governor Phelps or whether it merely was the special service provided for his inaugural reception is not told by the newspaper. The item originally was printed in the Kansas City *Journal of Commerce* on February 2, 1877:

> "Jefferson City, Jan. 30 (1877) – Since governors were deemed necessary to the proper sailing of the Ship of State, there have been receptions and receptions. Missouri has not been exceptional in this regard, but has maintained an enviable position among the sisterhood . . .
>
> "Governor Phelps with the queenly Mrs. Montgomery to preside over the household, opens auspiciously and gives promise of a brilliancy never before attained . . . The governor is dressed in the conventional party black and smiles benignantly on all who seize his outstretched hand . . .
>
> "In the rear of the reception parlors a sumptuous feast is spread – a wide table near fifty feet long . . . .Twenty ornamented cakes, all of elegant designs and as tempting to the palate as to the eye, citrons, almonds, Chinese fruits, Charlotte de Russe, Bauraux, Flavareux, Polonaise, Chartreux, Bisquite Glasse, boned turkey, patty progreces and other delicious and ornamental dishes add to the

scene of beauty. Ice creams of a dozen delicate flavors are molded into swans, doves, dolphins, bouquets of flowers and other comely forms. The solids are roast ham . . .buffalo tongue, roast turkey, oysters on the shell with citron, and fried oysters, stewed oysters, chicken salad, chicken magnes, broiled quail and all kinds of game save venison, which is interdicted by law."

Governor Phelps and his daughter held receptions during the legislative session every other week on Friday night. Announcements would be made in the House and Senate and in the newspapers with invitations extended to the general public. The affairs would start about 8 p.m. and include dancing all evening with food served about 10 p.m., including the "dainties, delicacies and substantials of the season." If all the dinners were equal to the one described in the Kansas City newspaper, Governor Phelps must have contributed liberally from his private funds since legislative allotments still were set at $1,000.00 a year for "current expenses" of the Mansion. Prices of food, of course, were modest compared to later markets with oysters, a favorite of the banquet table, selling raw in Jefferson City at the time for twenty-five cents a dozen. Personal expenses of the Mansion hostess also must have been considerable since her wardrobe was constantly on public display. One of Mrs. Montgomery's gowns worn at a Mansion party reflects the lavish yardage of ball dresses in the late 1870s. The dress, fashioned of lavender taffeta, featured two skirts, one long and one shorter overskirt, and a jacket with a high neck and three quarter length sleeves.

Between legislative sessions, Governor Phelps maintained a busy social schedule with dinners for supreme court judges and other state officials, New Year's Day receptions so customary at the time, and special events for the visits of relatives from the East coast and for touring notables from other states, such as General Augustus C. Dodge of Iowa who had served with Governor Phelps in Congress. Also apparently living in the Mansion were the two daughters of the hostess, Mary and Antoinette. The Governor's son-in-law, Colonel J.B. Montgomery, was a regular visitor between business trips. Another addition to the executive household made his inaugural appearance shortly before Governor Phelps' first Christmas in office. The new Mansion resident was a baby boy, Russell Montgomery, born to the state's hostess on December 17, 1877. A brief birth notice in a Jefferson City newspaper stated: "Another little cherub at the mansion salutes his excellency as grandpa."

The new baby – first grandson of a governor to be born in the new Mansion – was only a few weeks old when Governor Phelps received an urgent call to his home in Springfield. The Governor and his daughter left immediately by train but before their arrival, Mary Whitney Phelps, the first lady, died. She succumbed on January 25, 1878 to pneumonia which developed suddenly from a cold. Following the shipboard accident in 1876, Mrs. Phelps had fallen again in 1877 while attending a lecture in St. Louis. It was said her balance was imperfect owing to her previous injury and she had tripped over a defective sidewalk. She again had broken her arm, but there was no indication that she had been invalided by the two accidents. A Jefferson City newspaper termed her death a "sad and unexpected event." A eulogy printed in a Springfield paper following the funeral said of the First Lady: "Her impulses were noble and generous; her charity as diffuse as the sun, and many good men and women are today scattered through the world who were saved from degradation if not death by her." A bequest in the will of Governor Phelps, who died in 1886, set aside money for a monument in the Springfield cemetery to the memory of his wife and their three children who died in infancy.

With the close of Governor Phelps' administration in 1881, the first decade of Missouri's new Mansion neared an end. These years had encompassed scenes of numerous state entertainments where the lavish ball gowns and ornate coiffures of lady guests had evoked comparisons with the court of Louis XV – the court where Missouri's first, First Lady danced prior to the start of her reign in another executive "mansion" on the banks of the Missouri River.

Chapter IX

Missouri's post-Civil-War era with its turbulence over voting rights and loyalty oaths had passed. Bitterness had eased by the early 1880s to the point where refugees in exile returned to their homes and the former president of the Confederacy toured Missouri visiting briefly in the proud new executive Mansion. State finances had recovered to permit construction of this building to replace a badly worn relic of prewar years and to serve as a symbol of social rehabilitation. Life in the new executive residence had completed a decade singularly free from personal disruptions. It was a time of marriages and births and elaborate entertainments. But this period of tranquility was soon to end as one element of lawlessness which lingered from the Civil War intruded into Mansion life and necessitated, probably for the first time, a special bodyguard for the executive family. Before another decade was to pass, two unexpected deaths in the Mansion were to plunge the capital city and the state into deep mourning and disrupt the period of postwar serenity.

Missouri's Mansion was ten years old in 1882. The latest residents were Thomas T. and Caroline Crittenden who had assumed the position of governor and first lady a year earlier. It was the Crittendens who were to experience the first postwar troubles. The opening months of their administration, however, were devoted to less serious matters such as the need for major renovations at the Mansion. Ten years is a comparatively youthful age for a building but requests for major repairs were presented the legislators by Governor Crittenden in his first biennial message. In the years ahead, such requests were to become almost routine with each new administration and, more to the point, with each new first lady who moved into the Mansion. These requests, often viewed as excessive by more conservative legislators, apparently result from two major factors. First, a building such as an official state residence is in more constant use by larger crowds than a private home and costs of upkeep obviously are higher. A second less obvious factor behind the appropriation requests is the periodic change of occupants. The faults of a structure always are more obvious to the unaccustomed eye of a new tenant. Shortcomings of a building tend to fade with familiarity. In later years, the requests for repair funds were to become larger and the urgency of needs greater. Too frequently the first family understandably confined the work of its administration to the noticeable surface needs of the huge building. Less obvious but equally needed repairs on the foundation and inner structure of the Mansion were overlooked or delayed.

During the administration of Governor Phelps the legislature approved $2,500.00 to buy kitchen furniture and supplies, fix the kitchen range and repair water fixtures and an extra $5,000.00 for painting and "refitting" the Mansion. The General Assembly appropriated $13,000.00 during the Crittendens' term, 1881-1885, for repainting, refurnishing and repairs to the building and improvements to the grounds. In his appeal for the funds, Governor Crittenden told the legislature:

> "The Executive Mansion was erected in 1872-73. Some parts of the building have never been repaired. As a matter of economy, and to preserve the building in a condition worthy of the State and of the purpose for which it was built, and to protect it from immediate decay, it should be properly and thoroughly repaired without delay. It should be painted inside and outside. The blackened and stained condition of the outside of the walls mars the appearance of the handsome structure. The plumbing is in a defective condition and almost entirely useless, and if not soon wholly renovated and reconstructed will render the house unpleasant and even unhealthy. The roof requires early attention. The guttering and spouting are in a disordered condition. The lightning rods and iron railings should be repaired or replaced. The permanent tubs in the laundry are so decayed that they have become useless and offensive. New pumps are needed in the cisterns. I urge upon the Legislature the necessity of giving this matter immediate attention. No State has an executive mansion superior to it in architectural beauty, or better adapted to the purpose for which it was so generously erected. I suggest that the repairs be made under the direction of the Governor and Warden of the Penitentiary."

After the General Assembly generously responded to Governor Crittenden's appeal, he noted in his closing message to the legislators that the Mansion was in excellent condition and "is now one of the handsomest Executive Mansions in the United States, which has been as carefully managed and preserved by the better part of the executive office as if it had been her individual property."

This "better part of the executive office" was the Kentucky-born First

Park-Morrow, Women of the Mansion

Caroline Crittenden

Lady and mother of four children who supervised the extensive Mansion repairs during the Crittenden administration. Caroline Wheeler Jackson Crittenden was introduced to her future husband by a mutual friend, John M. Harlan of Kentucky who later was a justice of the United States Supreme Court. Caroline and Thomas Crittenden were married in Frankfort, Kentucky on November 13, 1856. The ceremony was held in the Capitol Hostel of Frankfort, a hotel that boasted a ballroom on springs for whatever advantage such an arrangement might offer. The home of the bride's widowed mother in Frankfort later became the site of a new Kentucky state capitol.

One year after their marriage, when Caroline Crittenden was eighteen the couple moved to Lexington, Missouri. The groom had studied law in the office of his uncle, John J. Crittenden, one-time governor of Kentucky and twice

United States attorney-general. They made the trip from Louisville to St. Louis by boat, then to Hermann, Missouri by railroad and again by a Missouri River boat from Hermann to Lexington. This was in 1857 and the sentiments which were to lead to the Civil War already were affecting many communities. In an autobiography, Crittenden noted there was only a handful of "active Union men" at Lexington. Soon after he and his bride were established, it became known that the young lawyer from Kentucky also could be counted with the Union men. "My life was bitterly sought by a band of young desperadoes," the Governor wrote, "I had to escape from Lexington at night in a passing steamboat going to St. Louis."

Mrs. Crittenden had left Lexington for a visit to Kentucky a short time before her husband made his hasty departure and on November 28, 1859 her first child, Henry Huston, was born at the home of a sister. Despite her southern heritage, Mrs. Crittenden strongly supported her husband in his stand with the Union. Members of her family recalled how she and another young wife traveled in an army ambulance with a military escort to visit their husbands who were officers with the Seventh Missouri Cavalry. A second son, Thomas T. Jr., was born during the war at the home of the same sister who by then had moved to Illinois.

In 1864, Crittenden served briefly as attorney-general in the provisional state government before he moved to Warrensburg to re-establish a family home and law practice. The same sentiment that forced the Crittendens out of Lexington was involved in a postwar incident that placed the Governor again in danger. General Frank P. Blair Jr., former leader of Union forces, had come to Warrensburg to make a speech and was a guest of the Crittendens. During his address, an attempt was made on Blair's life. The would-be assassin was killed but in the commotion the speaker's stand was knocked down. Repairs were made hastily by Colonel Crittenden and other former Civil War officers who were present and Blair continued his address.

The Crittendens maintained their home in Warrensburg although Mrs. Crittenden occasionally went with her husband to the nation's capital during his two terms in Congress in the 1870s. The family by then included three sons and one daughter, Caroline Allen. The daughter, "Carrie," moved with her parents to Jefferson City on January 1, 1881. Also a part of the new executive household were two Negro servants, Ruthy Miller, who continued for several years as the Mansion cook, and David Glenn, the butler and driver of the carriage who later in life became well-known in Mexico as a cook on the private cars of leading railway offícals of that country.

Newspaper stories throughout the state heralded the arrival of Mrs. Crittenden as Missouri's new first lady. Although the pace of entertaining at the Mansion during the tenure of Governor Phelps' daughter could hardly have been more lively, reporters wrote that the "social atmosphere of the State Capital will, no doubt, be much enlivened after the inauguration of the new Governor." Mrs. Crittenden, the stories noted, "is a Kentucky lady and was reared up in the best society of that State." The first social event recorded in the newspapers was a reception held for fifteen hundred persons on January 26, 1881. The news item added that there was no dancing and no refreshments were served. Another brief newspaper notice informed the ladies of the capital city that Mrs. Crittenden, assisted by two nieces who were guests at the Mansion, "will receive on Thursdays." Besides the "at homes" for ladies, the Crittendens continued the customary receptions on New Year's Day.

A major social affair was a party given by the Crittendens on November 13, 1881 to celebrate their twenty-fifth wedding anniversary. The occasion was described in the customary profuse newspaper style as "the most brilliant gathering ever witnessed at the mansion." A side event of the anniversary celebration was recorded in another column of the same newspaper. That item told how a convict working at the Mansion took suitcases of guests and, after rifling the contents, threw them in the Missouri River. Thus, it was confirmed that inmates of the nearby state penitentiary were used to help in upkeep and service at the Mansion, a practice that was to continue for many years.

Shortly after the anniversary party, a period of extreme tension prevailed at the Mansion. The Governor had solicited sizeable rewards for the capture and conviction of Jesse and Frank James, leaders of one of the many lawless gangs that roamed the state as an aftermath of the Civil War. The Governor's son, Henry Huston Crittenden, wrote in later years that the first family as a result of the campaign against the James boys received many anonymous letters threatening bodily harm and warning of a possible kidnaping of Carrie, the young daughter. During the height of this tension, a heavily armed and rough-looking man appeared at the front door of the Mansion and pushed his way past David Glenn, the butler who also served as Carrie's bodyguard. Mrs. Crittenden heard the commotion from the upstairs and quietly sent for the town marshal. The intruder was arrested and it was determined he was a mentally-unstable coal miner from Callaway County who had just returned from the West. The purpose of his invasion of the Mansion was never clear.

Climactic events in the Governor's campaign against the James gang occurred in the spring and fall of 1882. In April, Jesse James was shot and killed in his hideaway home in St. Joseph. Early in October, Frank James, the older brother of the outlaw pair, arrived in Jefferson City in the middle of the night and registered under an assumed name at the McCarty House, the hotel famous for its food and hospitality. On October 5, 1882, Frank surrendered his famous gun before an assemblage of state officials and newspapermen who had received a mysterious summons to hurry to the Governor's office. Later that evening, an open house was held with hundreds of townspeople flocking to the hotel to view the famous outlaw. A newspaper story mentioned that "among the later callers were Gov. Crittenden and wife, who in taking a walk, dropped in for a few moments and had a social chat." One account of Frank James' day in Jefferson City, told years later by a relative of the hotel owner, mentioned a visit by the outlaw to the Mansion. This visit must have occurred in great secrecy, perhaps as a preliminary to the formal surrender in the Governor's office. Early the next day, Frank James was taken to Independence to await trial.

Five days before Christmas, the Governor and the First Lady suffered a personal tragedy which served again as a reminder that residency in the state executive Mansion provides no immunity from life's sorrows. The condition of Carrie Allen Crittenden, the first family's only daughter, had become critical from the effects of diphtheria. She died on the evening of December 20, 1882 at the age of nine years. Her last words, according to her brother, were spoken to her bodyguard, chauffeur and faithful friend, David Glenn. "Drive on, David, I see the angels," she said.

Funeral services were held at the Mansion amid Christmas decorations already put in place and burial was at a city cemetery. The Crittendens thoughtfully suggested that no children attend the funeral to guard against possible spread of the disease. Governor Crittenden later wrote the words to a ballad, "My Child," and dedicated it to his wife. Music was written by Milton Wellings and the song was published in St. Louis in 1883. Carrie's death was the first in the new Mansion and she was the first child of an executive family to die in Jefferson City in many years – the last apparently being the infant son of Governor and Mrs. Dunklin in the old residence in 1834.

Before the end of her executive service in 1885, Mrs. Crittenden was responsible for a lasting gift to the Christian Church in Jefferson City of which she was a faithful member. Although reared in the Presbyterian faith himself, Governor Crittenden, according to a later recounting of the story, readily consented to his wife's scheme to get a new bell for her "poor little Campbellite Church." The First Lady sent for her close friend, Judge John W. Henry, a member of the state Supreme Court who "frequently indulged in a friendly game of poker with kindred spirits," mostly state officials. Mrs. Crittenden explained that her church needed a loud-sounding bell to remind the membership its presence was needed to fill the empty pews and "hear the true doctrine, as expounded by Alexander Campbell, David Proctor and Brother T.P. Haley." Noted for her disdain of artificiality, Mrs. Crittenden came directly to the point.

"Judge Henry," she said, "I want you men in that poker game to buy a bell for our church." The judge readily and understandably consented and consulted with his friends. They agreed to set aside all "jack pots" for that purpose. It was said a sizeable sum was realized. The bell soon rang clear and long on Sunday mornings summoning the congregation which chattered enthusiastically about the "religiously inclined gentlemen" who had kindly donated the bell. It was said that Judge Henry later told Mrs. Crittenden, in another of their private conversations, that "every time I walk anywhere in the streets of Jefferson City and hear the ding..dong . . ding . . dong of that bell, it sounds exactly as though it was saying Jack . . pot . . Jack . . pot!" The bell probably still was ringing its sound with the double meaning when the Crittendens ended their stay at the executive Mansion and moved to Kansas City where they maintaned their home except for four years when the Governor served as consul-general in Mexico City. The Governor died in Kansas City in 1909 and his wife died in the same city on January 27, 1917 at the age of seventy-seven.

Missouri's next governor, John S. Marmaduke, was the fourth bachelor to serve in Jefferson City and the first to reside in the new Mansion. His administration marked the culmination of the gubernatorial dynasty which had seen three members of the same family assume Missouri's executive office. Governor John S. was the son of former Governor M.M. Marmaduke and the nephew by marriage of Governor Claiborne Fox Jackson. The three administrations served as a tangible bridge of the Civil War period in Missouri and the roles played by the three Governors in that conflict point up the paradoxes of human events.

Governor M.M. Marmaduke who served as governor in 1844 was a slaveholder and a large landowner but he stood with the Union in the Civil War. Governor Jackson who successively married three of Mrs. Marmaduke's sisters did all within his power to align Missouri with the Southern cause and, when he failed, fled the state to head a refugee Confederate government. The last of the triumvirate of this dynasty, John S. Marmaduke, was a graduate of West Point and an officer in the United States army. But, as the lines were drawn early in the Civil War, the young officer chose the cause of the South – despite his father's loyalty to the Union. He fought with distinction and rose to the rank of major general in the Confederate army. John S. Marmaduke's election as governor also symbolized the ebb of animosities which followed the war – he was the first leader of the Confederate cause to be elevated to the highest office in Missouri.

To act as official hostess, Governor John S. Marmaduke invited his widowed niece, Mrs. Lalla Marmaduke Nelson, to serve by his side in the Mansion. Mrs. Nelson, in a letter written many years later, recalled that she and her uncle moved into an "immaculately kept house, for Mrs. Crittenden was a notably fine housekeeper and homemaker." Mrs. Nelson also recalled that the Mansion, even after the efforts of preceding executive families, still was only partly furnished. Mrs. Nelson said the Crittendens had used a lot of their own belongings, which, when moved out, left noticeable gaps. The legislature during John S. Marmaduke's term provided an average of $4,750.00 a year for all expenses of running the Mansion, paying the staff, repairs to the building, buying furniture and improving the grounds. One structural change made by Governor Marmaduke was the addition of glass doors to the front entrance of the residence. He frequently used the reception hall or foyer for his living room but found it considerably darkened by the heavy walnut doors which had to be closed in cold weather. The Governor had pine doors fitted with glass panels so they could keep out the cold and let in some light.

Lalla Nelson, the new hostess, came to the Mansion as a thirty-year-old widow with a seven-year-old son. The hostess' husband, Arthur W. Nelson, had died in 1880 in a runaway accident on the couple's large cattle farm in Cooper County. The marriage of Lalla Marmaduke and Arthur Nelson created a link with the future of the gubernatorial position just as the Marmaduke family connected with the past. Arthur Nelson's sister, Mrs. Margaret Nelson Stephens, was to serve as an outstanding hostess in the Mansion at the turn of the century.

The new hostess barely had moved into the executive residence before the Marmaduke family suffered a series of family deaths. On Saturday, February 14, 1885 the Governor's mother and Missouri's former first lady, Mrs. Lavinia Sappington Marmaduke, died at her home in Marshall, Missouri following a prolonged illness. At the time of her funeral, two daughters were sick and unable to attend. These sisters of the Governor, Mrs. Sarah Marmaduke Yerby and Mrs. Jane Marmaduke Harwood, both died within the next five months. A short time after the burial of Mrs. Marmaduke the following letter to the editor was printed in a Platte City newspaper and reprinted in a capital city newspaper. It was signed with the initials "T.W.P." – presumably T. W. Park whose son was to serve later in the state's executive office.

> "The death of Mrs. M.M. Marmaduke, the venerable mother of the Governor, John S. Marmaduke, recalls an incident that has not yet appeared in print, and which illustrates the gentler and more reverential phase of our soldier-governor's character. I trust that I violate none of the proprieties in relating it.
>
> "Immediately after the nomination of Gen. Marmaduke sort of an impromptu levee was held at the capitol at which he received the congratulations of a dozen or more of his warm personal friends. His election being assured, the suggestion was playfully made by several of the gentlemen that the general ought to marry as it would hardly be appropriate that the mansion should be without a mistress.
>
> "'Ah, the mistress has already been chosen,' said the general.
>
> "'Who is she?' 'Is she handsome?' 'Where does she live?' came

in rapid interrogatories.

"'I will tell you gentlemen. She is to me the most beautiful woman on earth, and is as gifted and lovable as she is beautiful. She is not without experience in the art of graceful presiding, and has an intellect I reverence. You will not be ashamed of her, gentlemen. It is my mother.'

"But the beloved mother did not live to preside a second time over the executive mansion of our state."

Under the circumstances of the family deaths, social affairs of the Mansion were greatly subdued. One of the few receptions honored the visit in early July, 1885 of General P.G.T. Beauregard who served as the Governor's commanding officer in the Civil War. The Mansion hostess, Lalla Nelson, primarily devoted her time to supervision of the large state residence and the care of her young son. Both of these subjects of her concern, the Mansion and her son, figured prominently in her marriage at the end of her first year as official state hostess. The ceremony was scheduled for 10 a.m. on December 3, 1885 in the reception parlors. The Mansion hostess was to become the bride of Robert W. Cary, a real estate dealer from Kansas City. Guests were limited to close family and friends and the highest ranking state officials.

Shortly before the ceremony was to start, the bride's young son was overcome with doubts concerning "the man" who was going to take his mother away from him. His mother found the boy in tears on the back porch of the Mansion. But the youngster was reassured and his tears were dried in time for the first strains of the wedding march. The ceremony was performed by the Reverend J.J. Wilkes of Boonville assisted by the Reverend Dr. John Gierlow of Grace Episcopal Church in Jefferson City. Following an elaborate wedding breakfast, the bride and groom left for their home in Kansas City. The little boy of the back porch episode, Arthur W. Nelson, was to attempt in later years to return to the executive residence but lost the race for governor in 1924. Eight years after that campaign, his life ended tragically when his fishing boat overturned and he drowned in the newly formed Lake of the Ozarks.

Miss Iola Harwood of Kansas City, daughter of the Governor's late sister, moved into the Mansion to replace her cousin as the state's official hostess. Lalla Nelson's marriage seemed to close the Governor's period of mourning and the next two years of his administration were highlighted with receptions and the customary "at homes" for the ladies of the capital city held by Miss Harwood, assisted by Mrs. Darwin W. Marmaduke whose husband, the brother of the Governor, had been appointed warden of the state penitentiary. One of the first big social affairs and evidently Miss Harwood's debut as hostess was a military reception given in mid-March, 1886. Many paragraphs in newspaper accounts of the reception concerned the art collection of Governor Marmaduke which included two steel engravings, "Stump Speaking" and "The County Election," by the Missouri artist George Caleb Bingham. It was noted that one of the engravings depicted an election scene in Saline County "where all the progenitors of the Marmaduke-Sappington family have lived and flourished since the territory of Missouri was organized." It also was noted that many portraits of former governors had been moved to the Mansion from the executive office in the capitol. Miss Harwood, the hostess, most frequently dressed for official social events in black silk, perhaps in respect to the recent death of her mother.

Outstanding on the Mansion social calendar during the administration of the bachelor executive was a series of Christmas parties for Governor Marmaduke's many young nieces and nephews and for all the youngsters of the capital city. The first of these was held in December, 1885 with some fifty-five children attending. Governor Marmaduke, according to printed reports of the party, "entered into the spirit of the occasion with a zest and cordiality unlooked for in a confirmed bachelor way up in his fifties." The second young people's reception was held in December, 1886 with the guests numbering nearly one hundred and fifty. Invitations were out for the third annual party in December, 1887 but had to be hastily recalled and the party cancelled. Governor Marmaduke was seriously ill with pneumonia. The Governor had resisted postponement of the children's affair but yielded at the insistence of his physician. At 9:37 on the night of December 28, 1887 – the evening originally set for the party – Governor Marmaduke died. An item in a Jefferson City newspaper described the Mansion:

> "The reception room yet bore the marks of gay decoration of flowers which made a strong contrast with the sorrowing friends assembled. From the dining room, the visitor could hear the sobs of Edward Craddock and his wife, Ophelia, the colored servants of the governor, both war relics of the family. This was the only noise to break the awful stillness, save now and then the noiseless approach of the governor's niece, Miss Iola Harwood, or his sister-in-law, Mrs. D. W. Marmaduke. . . .
>
> "Yesterday, the little children of the city, having learned of the governor's illness, gathered up a great quantity of beautiful flowers and dispatched a messenger with this floral offering . . . .
>
> "The sick chamber is the southeast corner room over the library. It is quite a spacious bedroom and has been occupied by the governor ever since he took possession of the mansion. The furniture is simple, consisting of a bed, stand, book case and writing desk. The room is at the head of the great stairway . . . ."

The funeral was held at the Mansion with many areas of the city draped in mourning. Bad weather caused the family to change plans to take the body to the famed Sappington cemetery where most of the Governor's family was buried. The internment was held instead at a Jefferson City cemetery near the grave of Governor Thomas Reynolds whose suicide some forty years earlier had elevated Governor Marmaduke's father to the state executive office.

Jefferson City by 1887 had served as the seat of Missouri's state government for more than sixty years. The population of the city had reached eight thousand, rather evenly divided between native-born Americans and immigrants from Germany who started arriving in central Missouri in the late 1830s and early 1840s. Electricity came to the city in 1887 and a year later a single light was installed in the front yard of the Mansion. Original regulations provided that the electricity would be turned on at candlelight and off at one in the morning. Capital city newspapers, in the spring of 1888, revived a campaign for removal of the "village cow" whose favorite rendezvous was said to be in front of the Mansion. In compliance, the city council on May 23, 1888 passed by a vote of five to two an ordinance prohibiting horses, mules, asses, cattle, hogs, sheep, goats and geese from running at large. The ordinance did not mention any special restraints for legislators.

It also was in the spring of 1888 that Missouri's new executive family held its first reception in the capital city. The lieutenant-governor, A.P. Morehouse, assumed office immediately but no official gatherings at the Mansion were held during the first four months following the state funeral of Governor Marmaduke. Mrs. Morehouse was no stranger to the capital city having visited frequently from her home at Maryville during her husband's two terms in the legislature and his nearly three years as lieutenant-governor. Although born in Indiana, Mrs. Morehouse, then Mattie McFadden, moved with her family as an infant to Lexington, Missouri. She was married in Lexington on January 10, 1865 to Governor Morehouse who was a former schoolteacher and lawyer. She was forty-nine years old when she assumed the role of the state's official hostess and, early in 1888, moved into the Mansion with her two teen-aged daughters, Nannie and Anna, and her son, Edwin "Ned" V., about ten.

The Morehouses' first state reception was held on April 10, 1888, in honor of the Imperial Club, a prominent social organization in the capital city. As was popular at the time, the party was planned around a color, this time pink, with the same hue carried out in food and decorations. Mrs. Morehouse's black silk party dress was trimmed with pink and her daughter, Nannie, wore a dress of rose pink faille, "decollete and sleeveless, tied at the shoulders with knots of ribbons." A band played for dancing and a banquet of "all the choice delicacies of the season" was served in the Mansion dining room. Other small parties were given for the Governor's debutante daughters while the son's entertainment was mostly confined to the billiard room on the third floor.

A New Year's reception closed the Morehouse administration. An article in a Kansas City newspaper, written in retrospect, described Mrs. Morehouse as a "quiet, unostentatious mistress of the Executive Mansion, beloved for her hospitality and charitableness." Mrs. Morehouse was not in office long enough to carry out any major changes in the Mansion, but one account credits her with renovating several pieces of "fine old furniture," including a canopied bed which had been shunted to the third floor. This possibly was the same bed which later was to be known as the Prince of Wales bed and whose acquisition and origin was to be much in dispute.

Governor Morehouse retired from public life after he left Jefferson City and confined his work to the management of farms in Nodaway County. On September 23, 1891 – two years after he left office – he took his own life

Martha Morehouse

Park-Morrow, Women of the Mansion

during a delirium reportedly resulting from a sunstroke. Mrs. Morehouse and her younger daughter had left a few days earlier to visit in Lexington. The older daughter, Nannie, and her brother had remained at home. The Governor slashed his throat with his knife and died quickly. The younger daughter, Anna, also died suddenly six years later and Mrs. Morehouse's health, which had started to decline with the Governor's suicide, continued to worsen. She died on January 10, 1900 at the home of a Maryville physician where she had gone for medical treatment.

January was a significant month in the life of the state's next official hostess, Jane Perry Francis. She was born in January, 1855. She married David Rowland Francis in January, 1876 and in January, 1889, at the age of thirty-four, she became first lady of Missouri. Jane Francis' experiences as a young girl and more recently as wife of the mayor of St. Louis had given her excellent training for her duties in the state capital. She was educated in France and studied architecture in Germany before her marriage. During the four years prior to his election as governor, her husband had served in the highest office of the state's largest city and many guests in state and national political positions had been welcomed in the Francis' home.

By the time the Francises packed for their move to Jefferson City, their family included six sons – the oldest twelve and the youngest three months. A newspaper reporter described the boys as "splendid specimens of miniature manhood." The oldest of the boys, John D. Perry Francis, was present for his father's inaugural speech in the capitol. Afterward he joined the line of well-wishers and when it came his turn, the boy stepped up with outstretched hand to congratulate his father on a fine speech. His father was surprised for a moment, then extremely moved and despite the crowd he stooped down and kissed his young son.

A special train reserved for the occasion had brought the new first family to the capital along with a large delegation of relatives. At a prearranged hour, the incoming Governor and Mrs. Francis were driven from the train to the Mansion for breakfast with the outgoing Governor and First Lady and a brief tour of their new home. Inaugural day, January 14, 1889, conformed to the pattern of bad weather which was the traditional dismal climatic format of many of these state ceremonies. Thus, the new First Lady viewed the capital community for the first time through sleet and drenching rain. The capital society had greatly anticipated the opening of the Francis' administration and in rather forthright style, one editor wrote:

> "It had been the custom during many years for the new governor to throw open the Mansion for a brilliant ball and magnificent supper. Gov. Phelps was the last to observe this

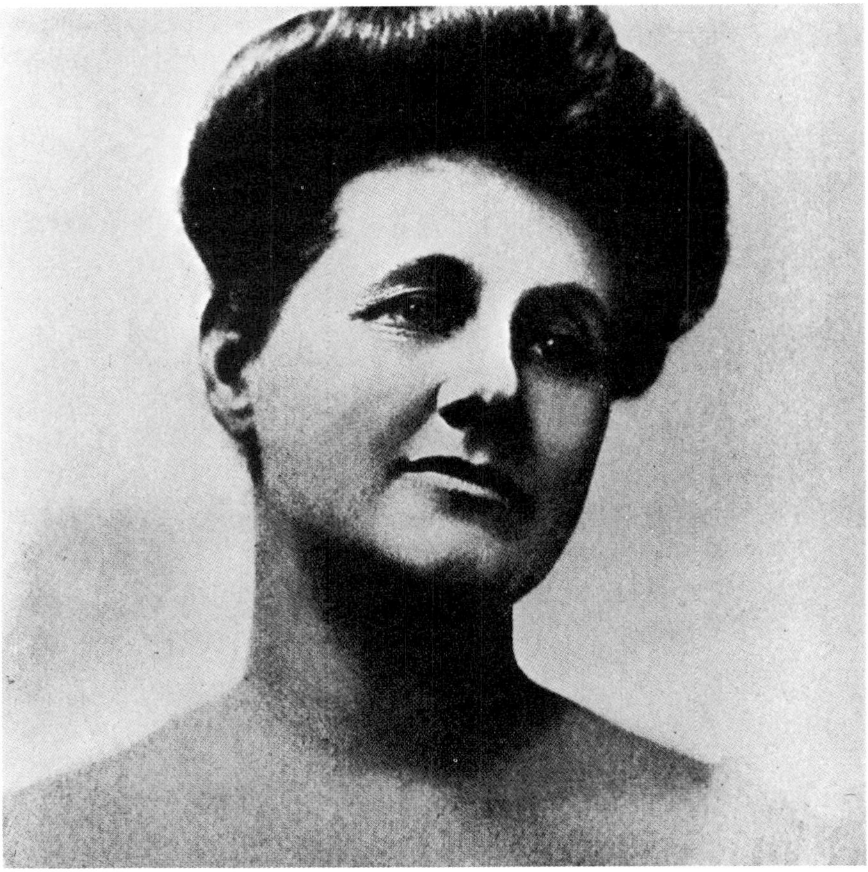

Park-Morrow, Women of the Mansion

Jane Francis

exquisite amenity, Gov. Crittenden claiming he had had no proper time in which to prepare such a spread. Gov. Marmaduke went into office less ostentatiously than any governor Missouri ever had; he not only gave no supper and no ball, but did not even issue invitations to the legislature. His first evening in office was celebrated only by a few friends, including some members of the general assembly and their wives, who paid their respects to the governor in a way. But something more seems to be expected of Gov. Francis."

Governor and Mrs. Francis did have a reception, described as an informal affair from eight to eleven on inaugural night. There was a band and dancing but no mention was made of refreshments. Mrs. Francis greeted the state guests in a sleeveless black velvet gown with a low neckline. There was no comment concerning the affair in city newspapers so it is uncertain whether it satisfied the editorial expectations. By early March, the Francis family was established in the Mansion. Mrs. Francis selected the bedrooms facing the east or front of the Mansion for the family's use instead of the north or riverside rooms. She pointed out that the sun never shone on the north rooms and at night the state residence presented a "dark, unhospitable front to the city" when the east rooms were not inhabited.

It didn't take the new hostess long to survey the condition of her new home. By mid-March, 1889, a special legislative committee was appointed to determine the needs. It was found the carpets were in holes, furniture was scant in most of the first-floor rooms, window shutters were off the hinges and the building was in need of painting and papering. Even the front doorbell wasn't working. The committee recommended an appropriation of $12,000.00 to pay for new furniture and repair work. The money also was to be used to connect the Mansion with the new city water system which had started operations the previous year and with the recently completed electric plant at the state penitentiary. New chandeliers were recommended as the executive residence added electricity to its interior lighting facilities. A steam or hot-water furnace was recommended to replace four old furnaces. It was not indicated when the four furnaces were installed but the Mansion apparently had a central heating system when it was constructed since a boiler was mentioned as being located in the basement. The committee's recommendation was trimmed to $11,000.00 before it was passed by the General Assembly and the First Lady and her children moved back to St. Louis to make room for the carpenters and painters.

Late in November, 1889, as the family returned, newspapers throughout the state published lengthy accounts of the renovation. The brick exterior had received a new coat of deep red paint. Inside, the entrance hall was decorated in shades of green. A structural change designed by Mrs. Francis was the addition of two small windows at the darkest end of the nook under the grand stairway. This little corner was reserved by Mrs. Francis as a private area for the mistress of the Mansion and it was to be so used by many first ladies to follow her in the executive residence. In the back parlor, or music room, a new Steinway grand had replaced an older piano described as a Steck which could no longer be played. A legend as told to Mrs. Francis blamed a strolling tuner with tuning the old piano "too high and it stopped short never to go again." Draperies of uncut velvet and rich velours were hung throughout the first-floor rooms.

On the second floor, the decorative touches included numerous bear, fox and deer skins placed on the floors in most of the bedrooms. Also of note was the "new and most modern" plumbing installed in the second-floor bathroom.

On the third floor, the famous billiard table was repaired. The origin of this table is clouded but its permanency and prestige were to increase through the years. A story handed down by official families attributes the acquisition of this table to Governor John S. Marmaduke and it certainly seems a normal purchase for a bachelor executive. But regardless of the origin, the table was used to relieve the frustrations or perhaps even enhance the political plans of a century of state officials and legislators.

Suden's Souvenir of Jefferson City

Missouri Mansion in 1891

The Francises gave a series of parties to permit guests to inspect the new decorations. One of the outstanding events was a reception on January 20, 1891 to celebrate the Francis' fifteenth wedding anniversary. Flowers were ordered from St. Louis, two orchestras played and a "course supper" was served to five hundred persons.

During several months of her reign, Mrs. Francis was not well and the family butler, according to his own account, would carry the First Lady downstairs to greet guests from a chair and then carry her back to her bedroom. Also recalled by the butler, Philip Jordan, were picnics on the nearby Moreau River. Mrs. Francis in a high cart driven by the Mansion coachman would lead the excursion to the river, followed by a hay wagon loaded with the Francis boys and finally the family dogs, Queenie, Bill and Calamity. Undoubtedly the family goat remained at home, where it served to torment at least one visitor. A St. Louis legislator, Representative Dennis Ryan, had a grievance against the goat and drafted a bill to require it to be restrained at all times. However, his lawmaking attempts were thwarted by a fellow representative who stole the proposed bill and fed it to the goat. The legislator's grievance was detailed in a story printed in a St. Louis newspaper:

> "The grievance Ryan had against the goat resulted from an encounter he had with it while calling on the governor one dark night. After entering the grounds he encountered the goat and mistook it for a dog. Ryan placed his hand on the goat's back and talked soothingly to it, but it quickly resented the familiarity of the St. Louis man and a vigorous bunt in the ribs revealed to Ryan that he was at the mercy of the billy goat. He started to run, closely pursued by the goat. After stumbling over various obstacles Ryan reached the fence at the end of the cliff and clambered on top, where he hung until the timely arrival of a friend who rescued him from his perilous position. He didn't attend the mansion reception that night, and it isn't strange that he should have a grievance against Gov. Francis' goat."

Following the pattern of her predecessors, Mrs. Francis played an important role, not only during her husband's gubernatorial years but in his political future. The effect of this influence was the subject of an unusual amount of written comment at the time. Newspapers in Columbia publicly praised the First Lady for her assistance in passage of legislation proposed by her husband for the University of Missouri. On another occasion, in the spring of 1892, friends had called at the Mansion to persuade Governor Francis to run for the United States Senate. The Governor listened, but before he replied he summoned his wife to the library. The proposition was repeated and the First Lady was asked for her opinion. She reminded the Governor of his growing family and their sons' needs of a father's attention to give them the right start in life. "I think it would be small compensation to my husband and myself in our old age," Mrs. Francis was quoted as replying, "to know that he had represented Missouri in the United States Senate, if it had brought disastrous results to our sons." She concluded that she was opposed to further political office until the Governor's family duties had been discharged.

Three years later when Governor Francis was prevailed upon to serve briefly as Secretary of Interior in the cabinet of President Cleveland, he moved his entire family to Washington for the year of his appointment. The Governor also held other positions of importance, including president of the Louisiana Purchase Exposition in St. Louis in 1904, but he did not reactivate his political interests until his youngest son had reached maturity. In 1924, the Francises were wintering in San Antonio, Texas when Mrs. Francis suffered a heart attack. She died on March 20 at the age of sixty-nine.

The involvement of Mrs. Francis served to establish Missouri's first ladies within the public spotlight as definite influences on the administration. This trend had been developing during the post-Civil-War years. The war years had so separated executive families that those first ladies had devoted their energies toward protecting their property and their families, frequently in exile. One outstanding example of the public advancement of governors' wives following the war occurred when Mrs. Hardin was recognized for her influence in the issuance of the famous grasshopper plague proclamation. A newspaper eulogy at the time of the death of another postwar first lady, Mrs. Morehouse, recalled how she, as mistress of the Mansion, "performed her part in such a way as to win wide popularity and to add no little to her husband's strength as a political factor." The public acknowledgement of Mrs. Francis' influence on pending legislation and on her husband's political plans placed first ladies firmly on a level of political importance that was to continue and strengthen within the twentieth century.

Missouri's last first lady to complete her term within the nineteenth century, Sarah Louise Stone, was the second state hostess to be born in Cole, the capital city county. The other Cole Countian was Mary Gunn Brown, daughter of the state printer and first hostess of the new Mansion. It would not seem unusual if many governors' wives were natives of central Missouri since Jefferson City was the hub of state political activity. To that city hundreds of young men traveled each year, some to stay in legislative positions others to visit briefly on errands with the executive or judicial offices of state government. Young ladies of the city and surrounding areas were introduced to the aspiring young politicians and frequent marriages would seem logical. But such sequence was the exception – at least as far as marriages involving future chief executives. Only three Cole Countians were to serve as mansion hostesses during the first one hundred and fifty years of the history of Missouri as a state.

Mrs. Stone, who frequently used the nickname "Lula," was born on a large Cole County farm seven miles from Jefferson City. Her parents, William Kimbrough Winston and Catherine Dixon Winston, were descendants of several outstanding families among the original settlers of central Missouri. These settlers came primarily from the more southern states of Kentucky, Tennessee, Virginia and the Carolinas. Twenty-one-year-old Sarah Louise Winston and William Joel Stone, a young attorney from Vernon County, were married at the

Winston farm on April 2, 1874 and immediately established their home in Nevada, Missouri.

On January 9, 1893, shortly before noon, Governor Stone took the oath as chief executive of the state. That same day, shortly after noon, the new first family moved into the Mansion and Sarah Louise Stone prepared for "Trial Number One," as her daughter later termed it. Evidently, the informal expectation that a new first family would hold a large reception on inaugural night had changed by now into an established tradition. Extensive entertainment within hours after assuming complete charge of a new home and a staff of servants seems an extreme challenge. But the demand was to be met by all succeeding first ladies. Mabel Stone, one of the two young daughters of the first family, wrote that the burden of such an undertaking was lifted, in her mother's case, as soon as she took her place that evening by the side of her beloved husband. This overwhelming sense of achievement must be the same personal reward for all

Sarah Louise Stone

Park-Morrow, Women of the Mansion

first ladies as they climax inaugural day with an elaborate reception, dance and buffet.

Another major challenge was literally to fall into the lap of the new hostess very shortly after the inaugural reception. According to a recounting of the event, the Stones had scheduled one of a series of receptions during the legislative session. The table was set for a very formal dinner in the long dining room. Shortly before the guests arrived, a water pipe broke in the ceiling and the table was deluged. Mrs. Stone, in a calm fashion which was said to be very characteristic, quieted the hysterical servants and crowded the tables into the dry end of the room. Dinner was served on time while the hostess did her best to direct attention away from the dripping and disfigured ceiling.

Social events during the Stone administration were just as numerous but apparently more reserved than the affairs planned by either her predecessor or successor in the Mansion. Parties included the customary dinners for state officials and less formal gatherings for Cole County friends or guests of the three Stone children – Kimbrough, a college student, and the girls, Mabel and Mildred. The daughter, Mabel, wrote that no matter how large or small, how formal or informal the event, the First Lady's "gracious, quiet manner, so tactful and so genuinely hospitable, made everyone feel that here indeed was a gentlewoman whose heart was in tune with her fellowman." Mrs. Stone's resourcefulness and her attention to the countryside of her birth, resulted in unusual floral arrangements for one party. While on a drive into the surrounding hills, Mrs. Stone noticed the pink clover blooming abundantly. She sent the coachman and her daughter back to gather the wild flowers and the fragrant blooms were used throughout the Mansion for a luncheon that day.

Two months after the Stones moved into the Mansion, one of the rare burglaries occurred in the executive residence. On Friday night, March 3, 1893, a marauder broke into the building and rifled the Governor's trousers, taking his gold watch and about five dollars in change. Also missing were three rings belonging to Miss Katherine Turner, the Governor's niece. Several bottles of wine were emptied in the dining room. A newspaper story of the occurrence said none of the family was disturbed and the burglary was not discovered until the next morning when both the front and side doors of the Mansion were found to be open. There was no additional information made public about possible arrests or recovery of the stolen items. The young lady who lost her rings was compensated with a new ring later that year when the Stones had a party to announce the engagement of Miss Turner to Judge O. M. Spencer of Columbia.

During the second year of their administration, in 1894, the Stones held a military reception on New Year's Day honoring members of the Governor's staff in their elaborate uniforms. This occasion was to be continued for many years with Mrs. Stone credited with its origin. An orchestra always was engaged for important receptions and parties and it played from the nook under the grand stairway behind a bank of palms. There was dancing on the entire first floor and in the large square hall on the second floor. It was the era of the waltzes, two-steps, schottisches and polkas and such square dances as the lancers, parisian and quadrille. Governor and Mrs. Stone always were available for the Virginia reel.

Appropriations for the Mansion had increased steadily with an average of $3,750.00 a year made available just for current expenses during the Stone administration. Although the state funds were earmarked to pay wages of servants, the Mansion staff for a time did not include a housekeeper and Mrs. Stone did her own shopping at capital city markets. This changed, however, after Governor Stone hired Alex Slater, a Negro from Fulton, Missouri, who took over the marketing. Alex, who was to remain as a most trusted friend of several administrations, also had charge of the handsome black riding horses used frequently by the Governor and his daughter, Mabel. The horses must have been important to the Governor for one of the first special appropriations approved by the General Assembly was an item of $1,500.00 to tear down the old and build new stables on the Mansion grounds. There was as yet no need for garages. Another special appropriation of $4,000.00 was provided for repairs during 1893 and 1894 which would take care of the broken pipes which caused the deluge in the dining room.

Despite the extensive redecorating by Mrs. Francis, Governor Stone suggested that more major work was needed. In his second biennial message during his final year, Governor Stone noted that the Mansion, as a semi-public building, is "frequently thronged by large numbers of people and the use to which its furnishings is subjected makes it necessary that it should be replaced every seven or eight years." The repairs he urged were to be funded and completed during the tenure of his successor.

The close of the Stone administration did not bring an end to Mrs. Stone's service to her husband's political career. She and her two daughters spent many months in Europe after they left the Mansion but returned to Missouri before Governor Stone was elected to the United States Senate in 1903. He twice was re-elected and died in Washington during his third term in 1918. Mrs. Stone died fifteen years later at the age of eighty. The Stone family had made at least one return visit to Jefferson City in the summer of 1904 when the younger daughter, Mildred, was married to John George Parkinson of St. Joseph and the wedding reception was held at the state's executive residence. This affair was the result of a special invitation from a sympathetic hostess who understood the desires of a girl who was too young for such an event during the years she knew the Mansion as her home and her mother as its hostess.

Chapter X

It was 1897 and the people of Missouri soon were to witness the opening of a new century for the first time since the granting of statehood. At the start of the nineteenth century, the area of Missouri was part of Spanish territory. A rapid series of events in the early 1800s changed the territory from Spanish to French and then to United States ownership. By 1820, residents were electing their first executive officers and a year later, statehood became official. The capital was moved from St. Louis to St. Charles and then to the City of Jefferson. Two separate residences were constructed on the Missouri River bluff to house the state's executive family – the first in 1833 and the latest in 1871. And in January, 1897, the last first family to serve during the nineteenth century, Governor and Mrs. Lon Vest Stephens, took office for a term which would extend into the twentieth century.

Governor Stephens' inaugural climaxed two other events which were to carry the capital city into the new century on a note of jubilation. During the same election in November, 1896 that elevated Stephens to the executive chair, voters throughout the state balloted on another question most vital to Jefferson City. The question concerned the move of the capital city to Sedalia – a proposal which had plagued Jefferson City for years, depressing all phases of municipal growth. The issue was defeated by a two-to-one vote and the capitol building and executive Mansion seemed secure on the sites originally chosen for them.

Another event which occasioned a major community celebration occurred on May 22, 1895 when ground was broken for a new bridge across the Missouri River. Previously, travel to areas in the northern half of the state took a circuitous rail route through St. Louis or Kansas City or there were crossings by ferryboat when river and weather permitted. But the new bridge, built with funds donated by city businessmen, provided the first reliable and quick access to and from the capital city to areas north of the river. This was soon to prove an even more vital link as automobiles replaced horses and carriages for private travel and motorbuses replaced stagecoaches for the public.

Missouri Mansion with gazebo. Sketch, showing building on north or river side, was one of several buildings on a poster published in 1896 as part of effort to defeat proposed removal of the capital to Sedalia. Copy of poster in possession of David L. Bryan of Jefferson City

Missouri's new first lady, Margaret Nelson Stephens, entered the Mansion at a time when the city and even the state and nation were at a peak of festivity and frivolity. It was the height of the Gay Nineties and Margaret Stephens, a daughter of great wealth and high social position, was an ideal hostess for the time. She excelled at elaborate entertainments and the Stephenses had the private means to supplement the state funds available for such affairs. The First Lady was tall, with golden brown hair and hazel eyes – the ideal model for the lavish gowns of the time and she had new dresses, frequently imported from France, to wear for most major occasions at the Mansion. A visitor who strayed from a crowd touring the Mansion was discovered by the First Lady going through her closets. Mistaking Mrs. Stephens for another of the visitors, the intruder remarked: "There's enough silk waists and things in there to supply everybody here and they're mighty fine, too." Thus, it was a happy happenstance that brought Mrs. Lon Vest Stephens to the Mansion for the administration which was to close the Gay Nineties and open the new century.

The Stephenses already were residents of Jefferson City when he was nominated in August, 1896. Lawrence Vest, more often called "Lon" V. Stephens, first was appointed state treasurer in 1890 and later elected to a four-year term. During that time, he and Mrs. Stephens built an ornate, three-story home on what was then Main Street, later Capitol Avenue, in Jefferson City. It was from this home, known as Ivy Terrace, that the First Lady moved a few blocks west to assume her duties as the state hostess. The Stephens' first six months in office were comparatively quiet; social activities were curtailed because of illness and redecorations. Governor and Mrs. Stephens were both sick during the November election and as soon as the ballots were counted they left for Hot Springs, Arkansas – a favorite spa of the period. They returned just long enough for completion of the legislative session and the start of extensive repairs in the Mansion.

Governor Stone had left office with an appeal for money for renovations and new furniture and the General Assembly, in response, provided $7,000.00 for the work which started in the spring of 1897. Most of the money, $5,446.00, was paid to a St. Louis firm, Comstock Furniture Company, while a St. Louis decorator, Charles B. Gallup, planned the work. Another sizeable amount, $222.40, was spent for new china since the Mansion table service at the opening of the Stephens' administration was not adequate for a party of twelve if all ate from matching plates.

By late June, 1897, most of the work was finished and again newspaper articles acclaiming the beauty of the Mansion appeared throughout the state, much as they did during the Francis' administration. Again the stories told of dark, rich fabrics and furniture. The theme, described as First or Early Empire, was carried out in wallpaper and draperies. The walls of the library to the left of the entrance hall were covered with tapestry of royal purple and gold with draperies of heavy gold French velour. Dark oak furniture was upholstered in leather. On the walls were portraits of many of Missouri's governors of the nineteenth century, including the lifesize painting of B. Gratz Brown. The darkness of the library was relieved in the double reception parlors where all woodwork and furniture had been repainted ivory as they were in the Francis' administration. Rugs throughout the reception hall and drawing rooms were green with a design of deep pink rosebuds. The dining room was decorated in dark blue and gold. A French paper which was a reproduction of the Gobelin tapestries famous during the reign of Louis XIV was hung on the dining room walls.

On the second floor, the bedroom of Governor and Mrs. Stephens, to the right at the head of the stairway, was decorated in light blue with all other guest rooms done in the first-floor colors of green, rose and gold. A room considered by one newspaper writer as the "most interesting of all" was the northwest guest room. This room, the writer stated, "contains the bedroom suite that occupied the 'state' chamber in the old Mansion before the war, and consists of an elegant old mahogany four-poster bed, dressing table with large mirror, washstand and wardrobe." The newspaper story noted that the room "was fitted up to preserve the quaintness of the furnishings." Draperies and hangings for the bed were made of English linen, printed from English blocks 150 years old.

As the residence reopened, a calendar of social events was planned by the First Lady which was unequaled if not unprecedented in the history of the Mansion with the mansard roof. At the start of their second year in office, the Stephenses held a military reception on New Year's Day, a continuance of the custom evidently inaugurated by Mrs. Stone. The major social event of 1898 was a musicale with Mrs. Grace Van Studdiford, a nationally known light opera singer, as the star guest. Also present from St. Louis was Henry M. Blossom Jr., who later wrote the lyrics for such comic operas as "The Slim Princess" and "The Red Mill." Invitations were shaped like musical instruments. A dessert table was centered with a floral harp and cakes shaped like musical instruments were served. A buffet supper included such offerings as bouillon, cold turkey, ham, sweetbread croquettes, oyster patties, chicken salad and beaten biscuits. A unique event was held on February 24, 1899 when the Stephenses entertained two hundred members of the General Assembly and visitors at a Ball Masque. Governor Stephens, a normally dignified executive-type, wore a flashy plaid costume with a red stovepipe hat and carried a china pug dog. Mrs. Stephens appeared as a Gibson Military Girl wearing a red velvet coat, a sword and a cocked hat with a feather.

Perhaps the most elaborate party was held on October 5, 1900 in celebration of the Stephens' wedding anniversary. The size of the party in the Mansion was quite a contrast to the small family ceremony held twenty years earlier when Lon Stephens married Margaret Nelson and guests were limited to immediate relatives. The ceremony was held in the home of James M. Nelson, the father of the bride and a Boonville banker. Mrs. Stephens was born in Cooper County where her grandfather, Jacob F. Wyan, had settled as a pioneer in the early 1820s. The magnificent homes of Mrs. Stephens' family were showplaces in Boonville and nearby rural areas. One of these homes, the residence of the First Lady's sister, Mrs. Nadine Nelson Leonard, still was occupied by a descendant more than a century later. The home, known as Ravenswood Farm, was near Belair, Missouri.

Mrs. Stephens' dress for her twentieth anniversary party in the Mansion was described as a Marie Antoinette gown of champagne brocade printed with pink roses and violet asters. The bodice of this gown was copied by the artist, J. W. Cunningham of St. Louis, when he was commissioned by women throughout Missouri to paint a full-length oil portrait of Mrs. Stephens. It was said the artist preferred the anniversary dress because it was lower cut at the neckline than the inaugural gown which was copied for the skirt of the portrait figure. This inaugural dress was fashioned of blue and silver brocade with a high neckline and long, tight sleeves of shirred white chiffon. The full skirt was trimmed in bands of jeweled braid. Mrs. Stephens posed for one week for the portrait and occupied herself during the sittings by reading a book entitled, *When Knighthood Was in Flower.* Mrs. Stephens' portrait, which cost about five hundred

Margaret Stephens

Park-Morrow, Women of the Mansion

dollars, was the first painting of a first lady to be hung in the Mansion. It started a tradition which later was to be regularly observed – the tradition of having portraits painted of each state hostess and placed in the first-floor rooms.

Mansion hospitality during the Stephens' administration was not reserved exclusively for the adult officialdom of the state. Two causes close to the First Lady – children and church – also occupied important places on her calendar. On December 26, 1899 invitations were sent to eight hundred children and five hundred of them responded to attend a special Mansion Christmas party. A newspaper description mentioned two little girls given their first dolls which "gladdened their wan, pinched faces, and will ever cause them to look upon Mrs. Stephens as an angel of beneficence." The Methodist Church of the capital city also benefitted from the benevolence of Mrs. Stephens who served as president of a committee to raise funds for a new church building. She raised $2,000.00 from friends and by special benefits held at the Mansion, such as musicales and auctions. One of these events, a baby show, was held in the fall of 1900 in the front yard of the Mansion. A major attraction, in addition to electric lights, was a new fountain installed in the yard during the Stephens' administration. In recognition of the First Lady's efforts combined with a generous contribution from the Governor, a marble slab with the inscription "Margaret Nelson Stephens Chapel" was placed in the vestibule of the new church.

Mrs. Stephens' concern with humanity resulted in the only note of criticism published during her reign. One editor thought Mrs. Stephens appealed too frequently for action by the Governor in behalf of inmates of the state penitentiary. During the early part of the administration, mothers, wives, sisters and even young children of prisoners flocked to the Mansion to solicit Mrs. Stephens' sympathy. This soon affected the First Lady's health and for a while Mrs. Stephens' cousin and companion at the Mansion, Anna Salter Birch, would pretend she was the first lady and receive the prisoners' relatives. Finally, the Mansion butler had to turn away such visitors. However, Mrs. Stephens continued her frequent trips to the prison particularly at Christmastime when the Governor appeared to personally issue holiday pardons. On one occasion, a woman prisoner gave birth to triplet girls and Mrs. Stephens, at the mother's request, selected names for the babies, Ethel, Edna and Katherine, for three of the First Lady's friends.

Beside visits to the prison, Mrs. Stephens took frequent rides around the capital city to call on friends and she and the Governor went riding many evenings after his day ended at the capitol. The main vehicle used was a Victoria with gold harness, a gift from relatives. Also used was a drag and a spider with rubber wheels. But the most remarkable form of recreation and possible transportation were the bicycles, one each for the Governor and Mrs. Stephens. A newspaper made note that the first family could be seen after dark riding along the driveways of the Mansion grounds on their bicycles. The news story proclaimed that "Gov. Stephens is the first and only governor who is a wheelman."

Although amply endowed with wealth and social position, Mrs. Stephens' life as first lady and as an individual was not without concerns and sorrows. In the spring of 1898, a page in Mrs. Stephens' diary, which she had kept faithfully since she was eleven years old, was headed with the word "War." She recounted the events, starting with the sinking of the American battleship, The Maine, which led to the Spanish-American War. Trains filled with soldiers going south passed through the city daily, she noted, and "the entire City of Jefferson, it does seem, goes down to greet them." More personal was the sorrow felt by the First Lady, and mentioned in her diary, concerning the fact that her marriage was childless. The void was filled somewhat by a cousin and later a niece who lived constantly with the first family. Also part of the executive household was a series of family dogs. One pet, Fritz, was killed by a circus wolf during a visit to Hot Springs and a favorite of Mrs. Stephens, Nellie Bly, died after swallowing a seven-inch hat pin.

The greatest sorrow during the Stephens' administration was the sudden death from pneumonia of Governor Stephens' niece, Martha, daughter of Mr. and Mrs. Speed Stephens of Boonville. The girl had been married several months earlier to Edward G. Rolwing of Charleston, Missouri. The Governor and Mrs. Stephens had prepared for the final reception of their administration, a military ball scheduled for New Year's Day, 1901, but the affair was cancelled as the Stephenses left for the funeral.

On January 12, 1901, the Stephenses moved back to Ivy Terrace, their private residence in the capital city, where they lived for a year and a half until they made their final move to St. Louis. After Governor Stephens' death in 1923, Mrs. Stephens, on March 26, 1928, married John W. Johnson of St. Petersburg, Florida. He was twenty-nine and she was sixty-eight. A year later, on April 17, 1929, she died of a heart attack at her winter home in Florida and was buried beside the Governor in Boonville. Thus ended the public service of a First Lady who helped convey the state across two centuries atop a series of elaborate official entertainments in Missouri's Mansion with the mansard roof.

If a great musician were called upon to set down as an operatic score the story of Missouri first families through the years, the resulting work would be a series of contrasting melodies – some gay and light, some slow and somber. Each administration would have a central melody setting out the main tone of the years and each would have undertones reflecting the contrasting tempos of the executive life. The main melody of the Stephens' administration would be gay and light with a counterpoint of somber notes representing the First Lady's concern with those less fortunate. The musical score of the next administration

Park-Morrow, Women of the Mansion

Mary Dockery

would be built around a more quiet and reserved central melody.

The successor to Mrs. Stephens was Mary Elizabeth Dockery, the wife of Alexander Monroe Dockery. The new First Lady, who was rather tall with dark hair and eyes, was in her early fifties when she moved into the Mansion in January, 1901. She had a heart condition which forced her to limit her activities as the state's hostess. Also accounting for the quiet reserve of Mrs. Dockery was a series of family tragedies which marred her early married life. The Dockery wedding was in 1869 and in the years that followed the couple had eight children. Six of the children died as babies; a daughter, Lena, died at seven and "little Alex" died when he was three. Such personal bereavements surpassed even the losses of Missouri's executive families during the Spanish regime when infantile deaths were not uncommon as the result of the primitive medical facilities. One friend observed that the "serenity and calm" of Mrs. Dockery was remarkable resulting as it did from such sorrows.

As might be expected, Mrs. Dockery turned her attention more and more to her husband's life and needs. When Dockery was elected to Congress for the first of eight terms in 1882, Mrs. Dockery moved her home to the national capital. A Washington newspaper noted that Mrs. Dockery "is so devoted to her husband that she remains in Washington until Congress adjourns, no matter how long it lasts." A biographer wrote that Mrs. Dockery "lived for the husband she loved." She was said to have read every newspaper published in Dockery's congressional district in Missouri and thus advised her husband on the needs of his constituents. The Dockerys lived in a Washington hotel during most of his sixteen years in Congress and returned to Missouri in the spring of 1899 when Dockery announced as a candidate for governor.

In mid-January, 1901, the Dockerys came to Jefferson City to prepare the Mansion for the inaugural. They had visited the state's executive residence for a few days following Dockery's election in November and had arranged with the Stephenses for rehiring of members of the household staff. Among the relatives accompanying the new first family for the inaugural were two of Mrs. Dockery's sisters and three nieces. One of the nieces, Mrs. Robert Motley of Bowling Green, Missouri, later wrote of her memories of the occasion. The executive party had gathered at the Madison House, across the street from the Mansion. Mrs. Dockery had received the keys from Mrs. Stephens when she noticed that the day was Friday. In deference to a personal superstition, Mrs. Dockery decided to stay another night in the hotel and let her sisters go ahead and take possession of the executive residence. She moved in on Saturday morning – a less ominous day for a move, according to her beliefs. The ball given the night of the inaugural on Monday, January 14, 1901 was widely attended because of the years of congressional service by the Governor. Mrs. Dockery's inaugural gown was fashioned of green brocaded satin, trimmed in narrow chiffon ruffles edged with green satin ribbon. The gown had a high neck and long sleeves.

Because of Mrs. Dockery's fragile health, social events at the Mansion were reduced in size although not in frequency. It was said that "few weeks passed that the doors of the house of Mrs. Dockery were not thrown open to small parties of young and old." The last public appearance of the First Lady was at a dinner for Miss Bessie Clarke of Jefferson City and Earl Chittenden of St. Louis on December 18, 1902, two days before the two were married. Although her guests didn't notice, the First Lady was not well and in two weeks her condition worsened. Preparations were being made for the traditional New Year's Day reception and military ball. Mrs. Dockery insisted that the decorating continue and while she was extremely ill in her bedroom on the second floor, workmen put up the usual military bunting and flags on the first floor. Guests had started arriving in the city before the affair finally was cancelled. A heart specialist was called from St. Louis but the First Lady failed to respond and died on the very day set for the reception – January 1, 1903. The military decorations became a background for her funeral which was held in the Mansion with the casket placed in the large reception parlor.

All of the ministers of the capital city joined in conducting the service with Mrs. Dockery's own Methodist minister, the Reverend C. E. Patillo, giving the memorial message. Mrs. Dockery was buried in Chillicothe the next day beside the graves of her children. A Chillicothe newspaper, in a front-page story of several columns, reviewed the life of the First Lady whose father, Greenup Bird, had been cashier of the Chillicothe Savings Association. Mrs. Dockery was born in Liberty, Missouri in 1849. Her family moved to Chillicothe in 1865 where she and Mr. Dockery were married. In 1874, the couple moved to Gallatin and Mr. Dockery opened a medical office for a brief practice of his profession before he was elected to Congress. In summation, the Chillicothe newspaper in its eulogy stated: "Possessed of an unusual degree of womanly sagacity and good judgement, she was always the confidante and advisor of her husband who held her opinion in high regard."

Mrs. Dockery was the first governor's wife to die in the state executive Mansion and the first, first lady to die since Mrs. Phelps succumbed to pneumonia at her home in Springfield. Mrs. Dockery's death was the third within an executive family in the new Mansion – the others being young Carrie Crittenden on December 20, 1882 and Governor John S. Marmaduke on December 28, 1887. All three deaths occurred during the Christmas season.

Missouri's Mansion was without a hostess only briefly following the state funeral. Governor Dockery prevailed on his executive clerk, Al Morrow, and his wife, Kate, to move into the state residence so that Mrs. Morrow could superintend whatever social affairs would be necessary during the two years remaining in his term. This no doubt was of great solace to the Governor and it was a uniquely fortunate move for the Mansion. Mrs. Morrow was deeply interested in the history of the building and its occupants and was gifted with the ability to gather and record the information. Her collection of data which was published several years later had been accumulated during the years her husband served as clerk to successive executives, starting with Governor Stone.

Social requirements of the hostess necessarily were limited in deference to the late First Lady and Mrs. Morrow turned her attention at the outset of her residence toward needed repairs. The General Assembly in the spring of 1903 provided an extra $10,000.00 for improvements. Most of the money was used for the first major structural change in the exterior of the Mansion – the addition of a porte-cochere at the south door. This carriage entrance proved quite a boon to hostesses. The south door entered from the porte-cochere led to a hall where guests could go up a back stairway to the second floor to leave their wraps and then make their formal entrance down the grand stairway. This method of entrance avoided many drafts into the building which resulted from the constant opening of the front doors. The first guests to use the new addition attended a prenuptial party for Miss Frances Cook, daughter of Secretary of

State and Mrs. Sam B. Cook of Jefferson City. Another change made under the direction of Mrs. Morrow was the replacement of the pine front doors installed by Governor John S. Marmaduke with more handsome oak doors fitted with beveled plate glass panels.

Many official entertainments were necessitated by the Louisiana Purchase Exposition which started in St. Louis in April, 1904. And in June of that year Mrs. Morrow assisted the Governor in opening the Mansion for the wedding reception of Mildred Stone, daughter of the former governor and then United

State Historical Society of Missouri

Mansion with porte-cochere, about 1906. Photograph of a post card in papers of Joseph Wingate Folk, folder 5, Western Historical Manuscripts

States Senator and Mrs. William J. Stone, and John George Parkinson of St. Joseph. Thus, the young bride was permitted to return for this most important event to the home where she played as a girl while her mother served as first lady. That same fall, the bride's mother, on a return visit to Jefferson City, was being entertained again in the Mansion when the meal was interrupted by the delivery of a telegram. Governor Dockery read the news that the Missouri Building at the St. Louis exposition had been destroyed by fire. Mrs. Morrow recalled how Mrs. Stone, although assuring her host that she hoped there had been no great harm to the contents of the building, said she would be just as happy if the portrait of Mr. Stone had been destroyed. It was part of the collection of governors' portraits loaned to the exposition. However, a later inventory showed none of the portraits was harmed and the painting of Governor Stone was to be returned until it was replaced some years later with a painting more to the liking of the Stone family.

At the close of the fair, the furnishings of the Missouri Building which were saved from the fire were divided among various state buildings and institutions. The Mansion, as a result, received several pieces of gold-leaf furniture and a Louis XV bed and dresser. The delicate gold-leaf benches and chairs were discolored by water and smoke but later were refinished and placed in the reception parlors where they remained through the years as a major attraction among the Mansion furnishings.

On Sunday, January 8, 1905, Governor Dockery opened his residence to its new occupants for the next four years – Governor-elect and Mrs. Joseph W. Folk. The outgoing Governor entertained the new first family at dinner Sunday night and at a final breakfast Monday morning on inaugural day. This was one of the first records of an inaugural-eve dinner involving the outgoing and incoming first families. Such a Sunday night event later was to become traditional with the change of administrations.

The inaugural ceremony in 1905 provided an outstanding example of the range in ages of men and women who held the position of Missouri's first family. Governor Dockery, who was nearly sixty and had white hair, stood near the incoming Governor who had reached the minimum legal age of thirty-five only a short time before he was elected. Gertrude Folk, the new first lady, was thirty-two on inaugural day – one of the youngest state hostesses to serve in the new Mansion. Mrs. Folk admitted in her memoirs that "youth is a great asset when there is discretion back of it." But she later was aware that her age, combined with a background as the daughter of conservative parents in a little southern town, caused her some hardships in her new life in state politics. Gertrude Glass Folk, the daughter of Thomas E. Glass, a druggist, and Governor Folk both were born in Brownsville, Tennessee. In 1896, Joe Folk returned from St. Louis where he was practicing law to marry his childhood sweetheart in a ceremony which united two of the oldest families of west Tennessee. They set up housekeeping in St. Louis where the groom continued the legal career which resulted in his successful race for governor.

During the gubernatorial campaign, Mrs. Folk recalled that she had received frequent requests from newspapers for a photograph of herself. She had denied all requests, despite a mild admonition from her husband, since she had been taught that "no real lady would permit her picture to appear in a newspaper." She was convinced that a later incident was the result of her uncooperative attitude. She had been invited to a celebration at the New York

Building at the St. Louis exposition honoring Alice Roosevelt who also was to be a guest. Getting in and out of a hansom cab, which was her means of transportation to the fairgrounds, was an athletic feat and a most ungraceful one. "As I alighted from the cab in the attitude of the Grecian bend, in my frills and furbelows," Mrs. Folk wrote, "to my horror I saw innumerable cameras focused on me and there was nothing to do but submit. When this horrible creature bearing my name appeared in the Sunday paper the following day, I feared my husband's chance for election was jeopardized."

The new governor, Joseph Folk, had made many enemies because of a forceful exposure of corrupt practices in the municipal government of St. Louis and because of further investigations of misconduct in the legislature. But Mrs. Folk, due to her naivete concerning politics, was unaware of such feelings and

Gertrude Folk

Park-Morrow, Women of the Mansion

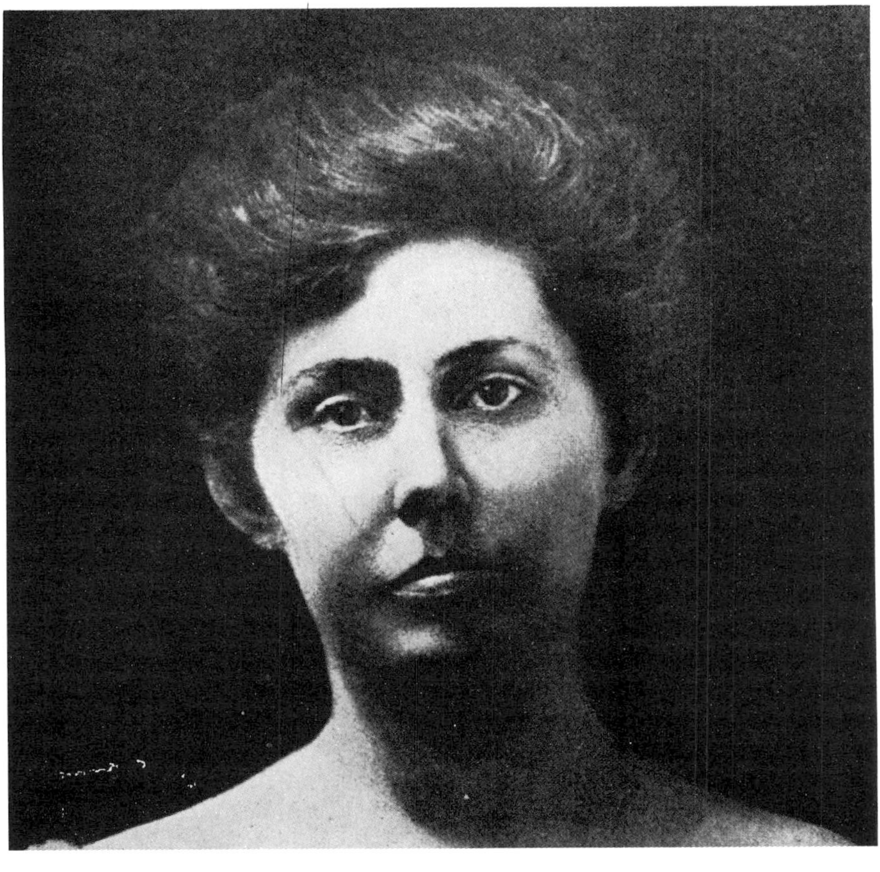

considered everyone her friend. This indifference of the First Lady to political activities was a matter of concern to a biographer, Louis G. Geiger, who studied the Governor's career. Mr. Geiger observed that Mrs. Folk was a "gifted and charming woman" whose intelligence was indirectly recognized by a newspaperman who once asked if she wrote her husband's speeches. It was a matter of speculation whether the Governor failed to see the possibilities of family teamwork, which was to be a marked characteristic of later state administrations, or whether the Governor wished to preserve his home as the one spot which politics did not penetrate. Whatever the reason, Mrs. Folk confined her activities to the social side of the executive office and to organization of a music club in the capital city. Her main contribution to her husband's few evenings at home was to play the Governor's favorite melodies on the Mansion piano.

Major Mansion events of the Folk administration were the affairs by then considered traditional – a gala inaugural ball at the outset of a term, annual Christmas Trees for the young people of the capital city and military receptions on each New Year's Day. Mrs. Folk's outstanding memory of the crowded inaugural ball was the finding of her new high-heeled slippers in a corner of the drawing room where they had been discarded at the height of the evening. Mrs. Folk gathered her young guests for the annual Christmas party by inviting the children of her friends and asking that each bring a child of less fortunate circumstances. Presents included dolls and dishes for the girls and false faces and firecrackers for the boys.

One of the sadder aspects of her position was the handling of appeals from relatives of convicts seeking pardons for sons, fathers or husbands. Mrs. Folk recalled how one mother pushed past the butler and prostrated herself at the First Lady's feet begging for the life of her son who was to be hanged at dawn the next day. Another woman forced her way into the Mansion saying she would kill herself on the porch if the Governor did not give her son a pardon. Most touching were the children who appeared at the Mansion seeking Christmas pardons for their fathers. Mrs. Folk found these experiences "most harrowing" but considered them "out of my sphere." These were the same tribulations that had so affected the health of Mrs. Lon Stephens and would continue to plague the ladies of the Mansion until a parole board was established and governors were relieved of such responsibilities.

The year 1905, the Folks' first year in office, was perhaps the most eventful of their four years in the capital city. A concurrent political dispute resulted from the election controversy between Thomas K. Niedringhaus and Richard C. Kerens, both seeking the Republican nomination to the United States Senate. The wives of both candidates had set up social headquarters in separate hotels in Jefferson City. Mrs. Folk, in a demonstration of her unconcern with political proprieties, delighted in visiting each headquarters for tea, presupposing, and rightly so, that she was equally welcome at both places.

It was the same Mrs. Niedringhaus who upset a social practice the First Lady attempted to introduce at the Mansion. Prior to one of her weekly "at home" gatherings, Mrs. Folk instructed York, the butler, to greet the guests at the door and then announce them formally by calling their names at the door of the reception room. The system was extremely brief in duration since the first guest to arrive was Mrs. Niedringhaus. Mrs. Folk recalled the horrified expression on the butler's face when he tried to read the name on the calling card. The guest was kept standing at the door while the butler stared and stammered. He finally dropped the card and Mrs. Niedringhaus took charge of the occasion by walking past the distraught butler and introducing herself to the amused hostess. Mrs. Folk said she "thereupon decided it was best to leave the announcement of guests to the White House and Diplomatic Department."

A major fire, the first in the new Mansion, also occurred during the Folks' eventful first year. The fire started in the chimney of the fireplace in the first-floor reception hall and spread to the bedrooms above. Guests who were occupying the bedrooms sounded the alarm. Governor Folk, working in his night clothes, threw the contents of 100 tubes of fire dust on the flames and checked the blaze until the volunteer firemen arrived. A large mirror over the fireplace, the white marble fireplace itself and furniture, including an antique walnut secretary, in the second-floor bedrooms were among the articles lost. One Mansion guide, escorting tourists through the executive residence in later years, decided to change her reference to the one piece of furniture lost in the fire. The guide had noticed the agitation of guests when she mentioned the fire had destroyed "an old secretary on the second floor."

A visit of the Morning Choral Club of St. Louis scheduled for the day following the fire had to be cancelled. The first family and their guests moved across the street to the Madison House where the Folks remained for several weeks. Architects called in to survey the damage said the fire apparently spread after Mrs. Folk attempted to create a cheery atmosphere in the foyer by having a fire started in the fireplace. The architects estimated the loss at $4,000.00 to the building and $11,000.00 to the carpets and furniture. There was $32,000.00 worth of insurance on the Mansion and contents at the time.

With the fire insurance money and $18,000.00 appropriated during the Folks' four-year term, the First Lady carried out extensive redecorating projects. She brought out of storage the gold-leaf furniture from the St. Louis exposition and had it refinished for the reception parlors. The front hall fireplace was duplicated in walnut. Tapestry, which Mrs. Folk thought would "never have to be replaced," was hung on the dining room walls and a walnut archway was removed from the middle of the room. This was the last evidence remaining to indicate that the dining room originally had sliding walnut doors which could be closed to divide the area into two smaller rooms, each with a fireplace. The doors had been taken down sometime prior to Mrs. Folk's renovation projects. In keeping with her talents and interest, Mrs. Folk bought a new Steinway baby grand piano. Funds to hire a night watchman were provided by the next General Assembly, apparently to guard against future disasters.

The legislature had been increasingly considerate through the years regarding appropriations for Mansion expenses. During the Folks' term, the appropriations included $2,000.00 a year for current expenses, including salaries, and an average of $250.00 a year for the grounds. Additional amounts were provided for redecorations and refurnishings of the Mansion. Although the members of the staff of the executive residence were paid little in cash, they had "toting" priviliges which meant the Folks' grocery purchases had to cover food, not only for the Governor's table, but for the five families of the staff members. A fowl or a roast seldom reappeared on the executive table, not matter how little was consumed at the first meal. This "toting" practice resulted in a menu change which shattered the First Lady's plan for her final breakfast in the Mansion. On inaugural eve, Mrs. Folk served turkey with the anticipation that it would be followed by turkey hash, one of her favorites, for breakfast on inaugural day. Bacon and eggs were served instead and when questioned the butler replied: "We thought you was goin' way, so we just ate the turkey up." A member of the executive office staff estimated that Governor Folk's expenditures while in office exceeded his income from the state by some $3,000.00 to $4,000.00 a year. The deficit was offset at the end of his term by income from a series of Chautauqua lectures – a popular way at the time for civil servants to balance their bank accounts.

Several years after his term in Jefferson City, the Folks moved to Washington, D.C., where they were living when Mr. Folk died in 1923 while on a trip to New York. Mrs. Folk returned to Brownsville and the Governor's body was buried in that Tennessee town of their birth. She still was living in Brownsville when she died nearly thirty years later of a cerebral hemorrhage. Paradoxically, Mrs. Folk became interested in politics during later years. In August, 1933, she wrote to a friend who was active in national politics. "Isn't this an era of rapid changes . . . I wish I were a real part of it," she said in commenting on the administration of Franklin Roosevelt. She noted that she had a position in the women's division of the NRA, one of the New Deal recovery programs. This was the candidate's wife who once had refused to have her picture in the newspaper during her husband's campaign for the governor's office in Jefferson City.

On January 11, 1909 – a day of an historic blizzard and zero temperatures in the Missouri capital city – Governor and Mrs. Folk made their final inaugural trip from the executive Mansion to the state capitol. At this inaugural ceremony, there was no contrast of young and old, for both the outgoing and incoming governors were extremely youthful. Governor Folk was thirty-nine and the new official, Governor Herbert S. Hadley, was thirty-six. The new first lady, Agnes Lee Hadley, was the same age her predecessor had been on inaugural day – thirty-two. Thousands of visitors crowded the city to witness the installation of the first Republican governor to take office since post-Civil War days. The storm that swept the Governors with snow during their ride to the capitol in an open Victoria was unabated for the inaugural ball. Snow blew into the Mansion as each of the some ten thousand guests was admitted. Mrs. Hadley recalled how her gloves soon became torn with the prolonged handshaking and when she took them off her hand began to bleed, staining the front of her white satin inaugural gown. Later, a more accomplished politician advised her in the art of handshaking – grip quickly and first.

On the day following the inaugural, Mrs. Hadley moved her family from a private residence they had occupied during the four previous years when the Governor was state attorney-general. And, for the first time since the Stone family was in residence twelve years earlier, there were children of an executive family in the Mansion. The Hadley children, at the time of the move, were Herbert S. Jr., age two; Henrietta, age four, and John M., age six. As expected, presence of the young children resulted in many unique situations such as the time the First Lady found her youngsters enjoying a Sunday morning football game in the first-floor reception hall with a religious leader of the time – Bishop Daniel Tuttle of the Episcopal Church. The older Hadley children were enrolled in the city's public schools but during one cold winter, a private tutor was employed to teach classes in an improvised schoolroom on the third floor of the Mansion. Later, a dancing teacher was engaged to instruct the youngsters of the first family and a number of their friends in two-steps and waltzes and in proper party manners. The youngsters performed on the third floor in the original billiard room more frequently used as a ballroom in recent years and the scene of dancing by many older and more accomplished guests.

For family bedrooms, Mrs. Hadley chose for herself the north middle room with a bay window and a northeast room was turned into the nursery. The Governor, for health reasons, moved into the southeast bedroom which had a fire escape outside the south window. He slept one winter on a porch built on the landing of the fire escape. The Governor in 1906, during his term as attorney-general, had suffered two attacks of pleurisy which prompted several doctors to caution him that a gubernatorial campaign might prove fatal. However, a family physician, Dr. W. A. Clark of Jefferson City, had suggested that a person with Governor Hadley's active mind could never be well nor happy on the sidelines and, in the doctor's judgment, it would be better to lose his life pursuing his destiny.

Park-Morrow, Women of the Mansion

Agnes Hadley

Governor Hadley's health also resulted in the "house-raising" of an executive retreat which figured prominently in state entertaining. This took place after the Hadleys, during their first year in office, had continued their annual trip to Estes Park in Colorado. The Governor spent most of his vacation worrying about state affairs in Missouri so when the family returned they bought a 125-acre farm six miles west of the capital city. Timber was cut from the thirty acres of virgin woodland and sawed for a log house. The "house-raising" was accomplished in one day through the labors of some sixty friends of the first family including four judges of the state supreme court – James D. Fox, Henry Lamm, W. W. Graves and John C. Brown. Other helpers included state and city officials and farmer-neighbors. At noon, the volunteers were served barbecued beef and lamb which had been cooking under the trees most of the previous night. Later, many of the volunteers were guests at the frequent parties held in the log cabin. On one such occasion, after a supper party, a violent rainstorm made the roads impassable. The Governor brought cots from the loft and Missouri's first family and their official guests spent the night in the log cabin. The farm, which was cared for by a tenant, was a boon to the executive dinner table. The First Lady counted 600 Plymouth Rock chickens served during one year at Mansion meals. On another occasion, a noted singer of the day, Lillian Nordica, was in the capital city for a performance. On the morning after the concert, Mrs. Hadley sent a gift to the singer's private railroad car – a basket of fresh eggs from the executive farm.

As a social schedule, Mrs. Hadley conformed largely to the customs established by her predecessors – the annual Christmas Trees for children and "at home" teas for ladies of the city on Monday afternoons. It was for the first "at home" that Mrs. Hadley, with complete faith in the chimney repaired by Mrs. Folk, had a fire lighted in the ominous front-hall fireplace. The house immediately was filled with smoke and the fire had to be carried out to the yard, smoke, embers and all. Mrs. Hadley fortunately escaped a major blaze which had resulted from her predecessor's introduction to the same fireplace.

Other entries in the Hadleys' social calendar were connected with visiting officials and notables from other states. The arrival of one such visitor, William Jennings Bryan, the powerful orator and former presidential nominee, illustrated the unique problems confronted by a Republican governor serving with other elected officials who were mostly Democrats. Prior to the arrival of Bryan, a rivalry had developed between the Governor and Democratic officials as to who would entertain the visitor. Governor Hadley sent his secretary, Charles H. Thompson, to the train to "capture" Bryan. Thompson decided the "Great Commoner" was more likely to be riding on a day coach. While the committee from the legislature inspected the Pullman passengers, Thompson recalled that he "snatched Mr. Bryan off the day coach and carried him off to the Executive Mansion to spend the evening as the guest of the Republican governor." During the visit, the young Hadley children climbed on his knees to listen to stories Mr. Bryan was so skilled at telling.

More taxing on the ingenuity of the First Lady were the many unexpected guests at the Mansion. One noon, fifteen men missed a train for Kansas City and accepted the Governor's invitation to lunch. Mrs. Hadley's only recourse was to appropriate the lunch the Mansion employees had prepared for their own meal in the kitchen – bacon and greens. This was supplemented with ham and eggs, bread, butter and coffee. This incident was early in Mrs. Hadley's reign and resulted in the opening of a Mansion pantry stocked to resemble a small grocery.

Governor Hadley was a congenial host and thoroughly enjoyed guests at his table. Equally important was his love of sports and hunting. He enlisted a group of friends to buy a farm adjoining his executive retreat and organize a golf club. This venture resulted in the formation of the Jefferson City Country Club which, when dining facilities were added later, played a major role as the scene of many affairs of state. The Governor's hunting grounds were the Cole County hills around the capital city and his companions were the leading sportsmen of the community. Many of these men were members with the Governor of the Painted Rock Club which had a clubhouse on the nearby Osage River. Their annual major hunt in the autumn culminated in a dinner in the Mansion which unqestionably was unequalled by previous Mansion banquets and certainly not excelled by subsequent executive dinners. The menu, as recorded by Mrs. Hadley in her personal daybook, was as follows:

"Oyster Cocktail, Crisped Crackers, Olives, Celery

— — —

"Roast Quail, Roast Wild Turkey, Cranberry Jelly
Creamed Potatoes, Peas, Beaten Biscuts

— — —

"Roast Possum, Roast Coon with Sweet Potatoes
Turnips, Applesauce, Corn Breads

— — —

"Squirrel Stew, Fried Rabbit, Escalloped Tomatoes, Soda Biscuit

— — —

"Roast Saddle of Venison, Roast Wild Duck, Fruit Salad
with French Dressing, Salt-rising Bread

— — —

"Pumpkin Pie, Cheese, Nuts, Coffee"

Perhaps a similar meal was served the Hadleys when they attended a national governors' conference in 1912 in Richmond, Virginia. The conference guests were invited to breakfast at the executive mansion of the state. That meal featured game brought by the Chickahominy Indians as their yearly offering to the governor – a custom remaining from colonial days. An earlier governors' conference had been held in Kentucky where the Hadleys were guests in Frankfort of the three sisters of B. Gratz Brown in the boyhood home of the executive who built Missouri's Mansion with the mansard roof.

Historic changes were made by the legislature during the tenure of Mrs. Hadley in the finances provided for the Mansion, its operation and upkeep. An appropriation bill signed in June, 1909 stipulated for the first time that the $5,000.00 earmarked for current expenses during 1909 and 1910 could be used to help pay for the meals of Mansion employees. Board costs for the five staff members for one month were figured at $12.00 each or a total of $60.00 a month. In another unprecedented provision, the legislature appropriated money to pay for an executive vehicle. The Hadley account books again carefully recorded the expenditure of $490.00 for a surrey ordered from the Columbus Buggy Company and $375.00 for a team of horses purchased from Henry Andrae who served at the time as warden of the penitentiary and for years operated a stable in the capital city.

Mrs. Hadley's precision in the Mansion accounts was remarkable since her only background for the bookkeeping duties was employment before her marriage as a reporter for *The Kansas City Star* and, thus, affiliation with a profession whose members are not noted for attention to personal finances. Agnes Lee, the daughter of a Kansas City grain broker, Charles Lee, was born in Kansas City on March 27, 1876. She graduated from the University of Kansas in Lawrence where she worked briefly on the *Lawrence Journal.* She married Herbert S. Hadley, the young prosecuting attorney of Jackson County, in a ceremony in Kansas City on October 8, 1901. The groom set up separate bank accounts for himself and his wife. All went well until Mr. Hadley arrived home one night to be greeted by his young wife's confession that she was overdrawn at the bank by $64.40. Instead of the impatient reprimand expected by Mrs. Hadley, the young lawyer replied: "Well, I wouldn't give a damn for a wife who couldn't overdraw her bank account." However, they shared a joint bank account thereafter, as Hadley advanced from county prosecutor, to state attorney-general and to the governor's office. A biographer noted that Mrs. Hadley was keenly interested in politics and served as a "constant inspiration" to her husband throughout his early political life and his service as governor of Missouri. At the close of his administration in Jefferson City, the Hadleys moved to Colorado for the Governor's health. They returned to Missouri when the Governor was named chancellor of Washington University in St. Louis. He still was serving in that position when he died in 1927. Mrs. Hadley married Henry J. Haskell, an editor of *The Kansas City Star,* in 1931. They just had celebrated the fifteenth anniversary of their wedding when she died on February 4, 1946.

It was in the early part of the Hadleys' second year in the state executive office that the major event of their administration occurred. The First Lady recalled that she was writing letters in her bedroom about six o'clock on Sunday evening, February 5, 1911 when there was a sudden stroke of lightning which she thought at first might have hit the Mansion. She continued her writing until some time later she heard cries of alarm. A flame had been seen trickling from the dome of the capitol building. A night of confusion followed. Inmates of the penitentiary joined with state executives and city residents in fighting the fire. Calls for fire apparatus were phoned to nearby communities, but the flames had too much of a start and spread rapidly.

Lights in the Mansion soon went out and the First Lady and the childrens'

Missouri capitol burns. This building faced east toward the back of the executive Mansion.

nurse wrapped John, Henrietta and the baby, Herbert, in blankets and they all sat during the rest of the night on the window sills of the west bathroom watching while flames destroyed the capitol. The Governor assisted other state officials in efforts to save official documents but for weeks neighbors found papers bearing the state seal blown into streets and vacant lots. The legislature, which was in session, met temporarily in the Supreme Court building and in the hall of St. Peter's school – both buildings across the street from the capitol grounds. Later, a temporary capitol was built and used during construction of the new statehouse.

Thus, for the second time in the history of the state, a first lady watched with her children while Missouri's capitol burned. In 1837, Panthea Boone Boggs probably had more duties on the occasion of the first capitol fire when it was necessary to put wet blankets on the roof of the executive residence to prevent the spread of flames. Both Mrs. Boggs and Mrs. Hadley had the care of small children during the height of the fires. Both capitol fires left state officials and legislators without quarters. The resulting reconstruction in the twentieth century secured – permanently – the capitol building on its historic site chosen in the early nineteenth century. Jefferson City citizens cheered the turn of the first spade for the new capitol as the end of the prolonged capital removal agitation.

Chapter XI

Tuesday, May 6, 1913 was a pivotal day for Missouri's Mansion with the mansard roof and the executive families which had occupied it for more than forty years. On this day, construction of the state's multi-million dollar capitol – the third in Jefferson City – was started. With the digging was buried the threat of capital removal which had appeared in varying strengths throughout the years since the site was chosen on the Missouri River bluffs of Cole County. The end of this agitation also formally secured the location of the Mansion and preserved for the future this home for the state's executive families built on the site of the first capitol building in Jefferson City.

Occupying the Mansion during most of the capitol construction period was the state's newest hostess – Mrs. Elizabeth Terrell Myers Major. It was a singularly momentous occasion for those of superstitious inclinations when Mrs. Major and the governor, Elliott W. Major, assumed their role as first family. Inaugural day that year of 1913 fell on January 13. Mrs. Major said she walked into the Mansion with courage in her heart but not a single charm or rabbit's foot in her pocket. The inaugural ceremony had been held in a temporary building erected on the south capitol grounds to provide interim housing for executive and legislative officials.

Mrs. Major's introduction to Mansion life started as it did for all first ladies of recent years with the extreme challenge of occupying a different home and meeting an unfamiliar staff shortly after noon and preparing for an elaborately formal inaugural ball set to open a few hours later. Added to the myriad of expected details was the flurry of questions such as "Where are you going to put me?" from the two Major daughters, Micca and Elizabeth, and "When do we eat?" from the Major son, Elliott Jr. The physical move to the Mansion for the Majors was shortened, as it was for the Hadleys, by the fact that both families had occupied private homes in Jefferson City during the four years prior to the gubernatorial installations when the husbands served as attorney-general. That was the first state-wide office held by Governor Major who previously had been a member of the state Senate. He and Mrs. Major had been married on June 14, 1887 at the home of her parents, Ovid A. and Micca Shaw Myers, near

Edgewood, Missouri. Governor Major, a native of Lincoln County, and Mrs. Major, a native of Pike County, both had attended schools in Pike County. He later had studied law in the office of Champ Clark in Bowling Green where Mrs. Major attended Pike College. For a short time after their marriage, they had lived in Frankford and in 1888 settled in Bowling Green where they were living when he was elected attorney-general in 1908.

Most vivid in Mrs. Major's memories of her opening days in the Mansion was her first "at home." The affair happened to come during a period of springlike weather which occasionally occurs in January. Guests arrived in such numbers that the butler had no time to close the doors between arrivals so he resorted to merely standing erect beside a wide-open entrance. Friends of the First Lady, observing his idle role, sent him to the dining room where his services were in greater need and they took his place by the front doors in case they should need to be closed. Mrs. Major observed that this seemed to set the keynote of informality which she strove to follow during the next four years. Small groups were entertained sometimes as often as twice a week with the evening concluded by dancing on the third floor.

A description by Mrs. Major of the annual military balls which by then were traditional provides details of the procedure for these formal New Year affairs. After guests gathered on the first floor, martial music would start and officers of the National Guard would appear at the landing of the circular stairway and march down the stairs according to rank. Mrs. Major admitted she had trouble identifying the insignia on the uniforms and resolved her dilemma by addressing as "Colonel" any officer whose proper rank was in doubt.

Entertaining visiting dignitaries also occupied an important role in the Mansion social schedule. Mrs. Major particularly recalled two episodes resulting from such visits. On one occasion United States Senator J. Hamilton Lewis of Illinois was in Jefferson City and the Governor called on him at the Madison House to extend an invitation to spend the night at the Mansion. Dispensing with the formality of even a paper sack, the Senator stuffed his pajamas under his arm and walked across the street to the executive residence. The next morning he refused offers of assistance and made the return trip to the hotel with his pajamas draped over his arm. On another occasion, Governor and Mrs. James Hayes of Arkansas were Mansion guests. During the evening, Mrs. Major recalled that the neighboring Governor appropriately played the "Arkansas Traveller" while executive guests joined in a lively square dance. Another distinguished visitor was Champ Clark who was a Pike County neighbor of the Majors. Clark was serving at the time as speaker of the United States House of Representatives, the first Missourian to hold that office. Mrs. Major on the occasion held an informal evening reception for the Clarks' daughter, Genevieve, who soon was to be married.

Park-Morrow, Women of the Mansion

Elizabeth Major

While the walls of the magnificent new capitol continued to grow taller, Mrs. Major obtained funds for major changes in the exterior of the Mansion and grounds. A screened porch was added to the second floor at the back of the building. Electric light posts were placed along the driveway and in the dark corners of the grounds. The driveway itself was graded, resurfaced and curbing installed.

At the conclusion of the Major administration, Kelly Pool, a newspaper editor at Centralia who later was to become a notable capital city journalist, published a tribute to the First Lady, praising her "rare good sense and . . . beautiful poise." The editor said, "the democracy of the humble country home in Pike County is the democracy of Mrs. Major in the Mansion." Mrs. Major's service also could be described as providing a quiet foil for the extremely busy administration of Governor Major. During his four years, among other accomplishments, the flag designed by Mrs. Elizabeth Watkins Oliver of Cape Girardeau was adopted as the official state banner. And of great importance to a governor's wife, a board of pardons and parole was created, thus ending the parade of inmate relatives whose dramatic appeals had so tormented first ladies through the years. At the end of his administration, Governor and Mrs. Major moved to St. Louis where he practiced law. She had returned to Pike County for a visit when she died in a Bowling Green hotel on November 8, 1941.

Many state problems cannot be settled during one administration and are carried over for the next chief executive. In the case of the incoming governor in January, 1917, it was an international problem which had started during the Major administration and culminated within the next four years. This was the war in Europe. The full impact of the conflict was felt in Missouri's Mansion during the term of Major's successor, Governor Frederick Dozier Gardner. The entrance of the United States into World War I not only affected the social life of the state's first family but a member of that family saw duty overseas.

Wartime problems, however, were far from the mind of the new first lady, Jeannette Vosburgh Gardner, early in the year 1917 when at noon Monday, January 8, she watched her husband take his oath as governor. Although both born in other states, Governor and Mrs. Gardner were residents of St. Louis when he was elected to Missouri's highest executive office. Governor Gardner had moved to St. Louis from Tennessee to serve as office boy in a coffin company of which he later became president. Mrs. Gardner, a native of New York, moved to Missouri at an early age when her father, Jacob Vosburgh, also entered the manufacturing business. They were married in St. Louis on October 10, 1896.

The inaugural ceremony for Governor Gardner originally was to be held in the Museum Hall of the new capitol which was nearing completion, but the day turned out to be unusually mild and, at the last minute, the incoming executive directed that a platform be erected on the south steps of the new capitol. Work still was underway on the platform when guests started to assemble but the ceremony opened on schedule. The mild temperatures were a drastic but welcome contrast to the blustery weather which literally had blown many previous first families into the capitol and Mansion.

At the climax of the inaugural festivities, the new First Lady took her historic position in the receiving line of the inaugural ball of the Gardner administration. Her gown was made of silver cloth with the bodice, front panel and train cut from cream-colored satin embroidered with silver flowers and decorated with rhinestones. Mrs. Gardner soon was faced with the same painful experience that had confronted Mrs. Hadley – a throbbing and nearly crushed hand. Again a veteran politician came to the rescue. "You take hold first, lady," he advised Mrs. Gardner, "or they will wring it off." Mrs. Gardner said the way he used the word "wring" was so suggestive of the barnyard that she shuddered at the mental image provoked.

Three orchestras played for the guests including the Gus Haenschen group which was well-known later for a radio program of showboat music. The evening was enlivened – quite by accident – by the serving of champagne. Weeks before the affair the Governor had decreed that no liquor was to be served at official

Jeannette Gardner

State Historical Society of Missouri

functions in the Mansion and caterers had ordered quantities of sparkling grape juice. But an uninformed St. Louis friend sent champagne as a gift. The servants made no distinction between the grape juice and its royal cousin, pouring from whichever bottle was handy. Mrs. Gardner soon discovered the mistake but countenanced the continued service in discreet silence. She recalled how little comedies were enacted every time a fresh tray was brought into a room. Faces beamed with anticipation and then the first taste was followed by a happy smile or a resigned frown.

Mansion renovations gained Mrs. Gardner's immediate attention and one major structural change had the full support of the Governor. Money for the improvement was written into an appropriation bill after one weekend when the Mansion was crowded with guests. There was only one large bathroom on the second floor, other than a small bath accessible only from one guest bedroom. And the demands on the central bath were heavy. Mrs. Gardner recalled how family members and guests would appear frequently in the central hall and glance hopefully at the bathroom door. Soon, everyone would leave his bedroom door ajar and listen for the departure of the bathroom occupant. "Often two or three persons would come tumbling into the hall at the same time on signal from the bathroom door," Mrs. Gardner said. Most of the family and guests played the game in good humor except the Governor. He ordered another bath installed adjoining his room and funds were included in the regular appropriation in 1917.

Mrs. Gardner also supervised a project to restore the wood in the winding stairway to its original rich walnut. Other repairs were needed and several legislative wives who had been guests at the Mansion volunteered to help lobby their husbands. As a result, a special appropriation of $30,000.00 was passed. However, the work of the ladies' lobby went down to defeat at the hands of the Governor who vetoed the funds.

Two other additions, one material and one personal, were made by Mrs. Gardner – changes which were to remain part of Mansion life for years to come. The first was a playhouse built for young Janet Gardner on the river terrace below the dining room porch. The second addition was a new Mansion chauffeur, Arthur Hardiman, whose service to the state's executive family was to continue over nearly half a century. Automobiles were becoming more commonplace by World War I but harness and a stable were still listed as items to be repaired by Mansion appropriation funds while the Gardners were in office.

Following the inaugural ball, a series of smaller parties for ladies of the capital city, legislators and visitors from Missouri and other states, dotted the Mansion schedule during the early months of 1917. War still seemed remote until one night when the former governor, William J. Stone, who was serving at the time as chairman of the United States Senate Foreign Relations Committee, was a guest in the Mansion. Early in the evening a telegram arrived for the

Senator from Washington, D.C. Mrs. Gardner didn't know it at the time but the telegram informed Senator Stone that the United States had severed diplomatic relations with Germany. The First Lady recalled how Senator Stone's face paled as he read the message. Excusing himself, he walked slowly up the winding staircase to his room. He paused midway and "with a tragic sweep of his hand, ran his fingers through his long hair." This was the last time Mrs. Gardner and the other guests present at the Mansion were to see the Senator alive. A year later his body was returned to Jefferson City. Senator Stone had died in Washington, D.C. on April 14, 1918 following a paralytic stroke. His body lay in state in the Missouri capitol. Stores and schools closed and thousands passed the bier of the man whom a large floral tribute described as "The Noblest Roman of Them All."

During the interval between the Senator's long walk up the Mansion stairway and the return of his body to the capitol, war had come to the United States and to the home of Missouri's first family. The Gardners had three children. At the time the United States entered the war, William was eighteen and a student at the University of Missouri in Columbia; Dozier at fourteen was a student at Smith Academy in St. Louis, and the youngest, Janet, was just barely ten and had classes with a private tutor, Miss Helen Green. None of the youngsters appeared at first to be of an age to be drawn into the conflict. The older son changed that. Although barred from enlistment, he pleaded with his father for help in entering some form of service. It was arranged that William and twenty-four other University students would form an ambulance unit and, following brief training, they sailed for France on June 23, 1917.

Mrs. Gardner quickly involved herself in home-front efforts. Perhaps as never before in history, the wife of a Missouri governor became publicly active in war campaigns. She was a recruiting agent in the Navy's "Pledge A Man" effort to raise twelve hundred men for the fleet. Various appeals were published throughout the state under Mrs. Gardner's signature. The First Lady helped sell War Savings Stamps in front of the St. Louis Post Office and personally offered a fifty-dollar bond to the school child writing the best essay on Liberty Bonds. Women and children of the capital city came to the Mansion once a week to knit and Mrs. Gardner went frequently to the Red Cross sewing room to cut and roll bandages.

These efforts were not without humorous sidelights. One such incident occurred when Marie Dressler, the great comedienne, came to Jefferson City in behalf of the Third Liberty Loan. Miss Dressler was a guest at the Mansion for tea when she suddenly jumped from her chair and ran out the front door shouting after a departing guest. Mrs. Gardner remembered her astonishment when the grand woman of the stage retrieved a tea napkin that the guest had unwittingly tucked into her sleeve.

Even the Mansion yard was channeled into the war effort as the Governor and First Lady plowed the first war garden in Missouri. The event, of course, was highly publicized to encourage similar efforts. The Mansion garden produced onions, lettuce, peas and other vegetables and a flock of chickens tended by the Governor provided eggs for the Mansion table. Food conservation or "Hooverizing" as it was called also came to the Mansion. Meat was served only at the dinner meal four times a week and cornbread frequently was substituted for wheat bread.

Christmas, 1918, was a climactic period for victory celebrations following the Armistice. Earlier in December, Mrs. Gardner had gone to New York to meet the ship, Rochambeau, carrying William and his University classmates home from their six-month duty with the ambulance service. The return of her son as well as sons of friends made the annual Mansion Christmas Tree for children a particularly joyous occasion. Preserved by the First Lady as a memento of that year was a Christmas greeting card from General John J. Pershing, a native Missourian who had commanded the American Expeditionary Force. His card said merely: "With peace on earth I send my Christmas greetings to you – Paris, 1918."

Two national issues, prohibition and women's suffrage, occupied the time and efforts of the First Lady in the postwar year, 1919. The Governor on February 17, 1919 signed the resolution passed by the Missouri legislature ratifying the Eighteenth Amendment. During the intervening weeks before the law prohibiting the sale of liquor went into effect, "farewell" parties throughout the state and nation were frequent and riotous. Even the Mansion felt the pressure of impending prohibition when one of the prison inmates employed at the Mansion disappeared from his detail with a bottle of Mrs. Gardner's perfume and the Governor's hair tonic. The First Lady said the man evidently "couldn't stand the thought of finishing his time and being released in a bone-dry world." The trusty was captured several miles from the city, very drunk and very sick.

The second national issue of concern in 1918 was the movement to permit women to vote. It was while attending a suffrage meeting in Sedalia that a Missouri governor's wife, perhaps for the first time, made a speech at a public meeting. Governor Gardner had concluded his talk and the leaders of the meeting called on Mrs. Gardner for a few words. She assured them she shared her husband's views on the suffrage issue and then concluded her remarks with the observation: "I have never made a political speech. I never intend to make one. If I have gotten my husband any votes, it has not been by talking but by keeping still." This incident was in 1917 and the Missouri Assembly bypassed the suffrage issue that year. However, political thought changed during the war years as women filled unprecedented positions in commercial and industrial services. On April 5, 1919, Governor Gardner signed a bill to permit women in Missouri to vote for president. Leaders of the suffrage movement were invited to the Mansion for a luncheon following the signing ceremony. Mrs. Gardner recalled how intrigued her daughter, Janet, was by the costume affected by the leaders – a mannish-cut black coat and skirt, a white shirt with a high collar, black bow tie and black silk sailor hat.

Severe styles of the suffragettes, however, were to be eclipsed by a change in dress and manners soon to sweep the nation. Society in 1919 was on the edge of the Roaring Twenties – the era of the flapper with short dresses and bright cheeks and the time of such lively dances as the Black Bottom and Charleston. The incoming first lady of Missouri, Hortense Cullers Hyde, selected an inaugural gown of metallic cloth with a lace overdress which reflected the start of flapper styles. It hung straight from the shoulders and was ankle length. It probably was the first time an inaugural gown did not brush the floor when a new hostess made her first public appearance. Inaugural ceremonies for the new governor, Arthur M. Hyde, made one further concession to the times. Inaugural crowds had grown larger through the years and the Mansion had grown older so the inevitable resulted. The Hydes held two inaugural balls – one in the traditional setting of the Mansion and a simultaneous dance in the rotunda of the new capitol building. An orchestra played in each place.

The Gardners stayed in Jefferson City to take part in the festivities and Mrs. Gardner again wore her inaugural gown of satin, which was heavily embroidered and floor length, reminiscent of prewar styles. Following the ceremonies, the Gardners returned to St. Louis where he renewed his business interests and they both continued politically active. He was appointed by Franklin D. Roosevelt to a presidential advisory council and served briefly before his death in 1933. Mrs. Gardner was co-chairman of a committee of St. Louisans who worked for the re-election of President Roosevelt in 1936 and the next year was a member of the social service commission for St. Louis. She died on June 4, 1943 of complications following surgery.

The general aura of festivity surrounding the executive inaugural soon was replaced by serious conservatism, emanating from a governor who, as the second Republican to hold the state's highest office since post-Civil-War days, might be expected to strive for reduced expenditures. Financial records of the Hyde administration show that the Governor personally paid the food bills for the Mansion and demanded immediate receipts which he carefully filed. One of the first major food items purchased by the new executive family was a twenty-pound country ham obtained from a Jefferson City delicatessen for $13.45. Daily food costs as recorded in the Hyde records were extremely conservative. Meat purchases during a Christmas season included: a hen, $1.50; beef roast, 60 cents; steak, 30 cents; pork roast, 90 cents; and veal roast, 90 cents. Other food prices at the time were bacon at 50 cents a pound and eggs at 27 cents a dozen.

Park-Morrow, Women of the Mansion

Hortense Hyde

Mrs. Hyde was not in good health during the first two years of her residence and social affairs at the Mansion were limited. However, she was able to meet the challenges of major redecorations. She was advised by members of the Capitol Decoration Commission which was created to supervise the final artistic touches in the new capitol. Arthur A. Kocian, a St. Louis art dealer and secretary of the commission, made it possible for Mrs. Hyde to make outstanding additions to the Mansion furnishings. These were six more pieces of the gold-leaf furniture used in the major reception room. Innumerable letters were written by Mrs. Hyde to companies throughout the nation with pictures of the existing furniture and inquiries as to whether it could be copied. Finally, Mr. Kocian sent photographs to a St. Louis firm with which he was working in the reframing of many of the governors' pictures in the Mansion. The Northern Picture Frame Company of Chicago, which was contacted by the St. Louis firm, carved, gilded and upholstered four arm chairs and two side chairs. Total cost was $1,500.00. With the added pieces, the double reception parlors were completely furnished with the gold-leaf furniture which continued throughout the years to be a major attraction to visitors.

This project was a particular labor of love for Mrs. Hyde. Since her first visits to the Missouri Mansion, including an inaugural-eve dinner. Mrs. Hyde had mused over a memory twinge caused by the gold furniture. Later, when the original pieces were being prepared for reupholstering, the whole story was revealed by the canvas beneath the old coverings. On the canvas was written: "Bought for the Missouri Building, St. Louis Exposition, 1904." It was at this exposition that Governor and Mrs. Hyde had spent several days of their honeymoon following their wedding in Trenton on October 19, 1904. Governor and Mrs. Hyde were born only a few miles apart – he in Princeton and she in the farm home of her parents, Charles H. and Cornelia Adkisson Cullers, located between Princeton and Trenton. The Governor attended College and law school in other states and, then returned to Missouri to practice law with his father. Following their wedding trip to St. Louis, the young couple lived in Princeton where Governor Hyde served as mayor for one term. In 1915, he moved his legal practice, his automobile sales business and his family to Trenton.

An incident immediately following the wedding ceremony of Governor and Mrs. Hyde was indicative of his reaction to frivolity. A story in a Grundy County newspaper detailed how the groom's fellow Elks had unhitched the horse and pulled the carriage and the newlyweds to the railroad station themselves. Upon arrival at the station a speech was demanded of the groom. "Even under the nervous strain of recent matrimony," the newspaper story continued, the groom was not without his "wits and tongue." Mr. Hyde was quoted as replying to his friends: "'Gentlemen, there is an injunction in Holy Writ – or if it is not there, it ought to be – which I think is applicable to this occasion. It is "Lord, let they servant depart in peace."'" The newlyweds did depart for the St. Louis fair where one of their first stops was a visit to the Missouri Building with its French gold-leaf furniture.

Two altogether coincidental happenings expedited the redecorations carried out in the Mansion by Mrs. Hyde. When the new hostess first occupied her second-floor bedroom, she was obsessed with the idea of a fire in the bedroom fireplace. She had the chimney examined and it was pronounced safe. Fires burned several times that winter in the First Lady's bedroom. However, workmen later found cracks in the flue and the cheery fireplace fires came to an end. The Hydes spent the second summer in the Mansion with the fireplaces torn apart and the marble mantles removed while the chimneys were rebuilt.

A second incident served to confirm the urgency of the need for new wiring in the executive residence. Supplies had been ordered for the work when the Hydes had to leave for a convention in St. Louis. Their nine-year-old daughter, Caroline, was left in the Mansion with a friend. As Mrs. Hyde recalled the incident, lightning from an electrical storm struck the northwest side of the Mansion, shattering the glass in the back porches. Caroline was ironing doll clothes near one of the windows and was knocked across the room but was not injured. Guards patrolled the building for several hours while workmen traced an odor of burning wood. The cause was found in a back bedroom where the oak mounting around the ceiling light had ignited and burned briefly before it died out. The rewiring was carried out immediately.

Recarpeting originally was planned only in the reception parlors, but the legislature requested Mrs. Hyde to continue the project throughout the Mansion. Some four hundred and twenty yards were required of one pattern which was used in the foyer, on the grand stairway and the second-floor parlor. Among the special items purchased by Mrs. Hyde was a Steinway grand piano in mahogany and a Victrola. For the extensive repairs and current expenses at the Mansion, the General Assembly provided $20,000.00 during the first two years of Mrs. Hyde's reign and $23,000.00 during the second two years.

For the first time, appropriations for the Mansion did not mention funds for the maintenance of stables although repairs to the garage were specified. Automobiles were phasing out horse-drawn vehicles as a means of executive transportation. Cars evidently had been available to the first families of at least four administrations but horses still were used for pleasure rides. Governor Hyde, who had operated an automobile sales business before his election, was particularly aware of the advantages of motorized transportation.

A state-wide furor developed during the second year of Mrs. Hyde's residence in the Mansion. The dispute was politically motivated and was directed toward the First Lady. The hubbub became public knowledge when one Missouri newspaper accused Mrs. Hyde of ordering the removal of all the portraits of Democratic governors from the Mansion because "the sight of them set her nerves on edge." It was one of the few times that a first lady was made a part of political byplay.

Mrs. Hyde herself set the record straight in an account written several years later. The shuffling of the governors' portraits in 1922 started when the state fair at Sedalia borrowed them for an exhibit. This attracted attention to their varying sizes and types – some oils, some etchings and some done in pen and ink. The next year, before the pictures were rehung, the General Assembly directed the Capitol Decorating Commission to have them all copied in oil and then the legislators decided they should be hung in the new capitol. Mrs. Hyde concurred because she felt it was a wiser place for the pictures since the capitol was fireproof and more accessible to the public. Also, the extreme weight of some of the portraits was dangerous for the Mansion walls. A more enlightened newspaper countered the attack on the First Lady by pointing out that the removal had been ordered by the Assembly. The defending writer accused the first editor of a "wrongful and insulting attack upon Mrs. Hyde."

An incident which occurred during the height of the editorial exchange about the portraits seemed to completely exonerate the First Lady. Another large picture had been hung near the front door of the Mansion to replace the portrait of Governor Francis. One night the Mansion echoed with the sound of a crash in the front hall. The night guard ran toward the noise and the Governor hurried down the grand stairway with a gun. The racket had resulted when the picture had fallen, striking the radiator. An arm was knocked off an antique settee and the picture was on the floor in pieces.

During 1923, the redecorating was completed and Mrs. Hyde stepped up the pace of social activities in the Mansion. A series of Wednesday afternoon teas was held for legislative wives and daughters and dinners for the lawmakers. The annual military balls were continued for officers of the National Guard. To protect the new carpets, tarpaulins were placed on the floors for events which involved dancing. In the fall of 1924, Mrs. Hyde again had to curtail her calendar. She was involved in an automobile accident which left her with painful injuries and required several months of convalescence. The injuries prevented Mrs. Hyde from taking the role written for her in the pageant presented on October 6, 1924 at the formal dedication of the new capitol.

Mrs. Hyde recalled that the pageant dramatizing Missouri's history was held at night on the steps of the new building and was a splended success – until it rained. "Rain at the wrong time was as typical of our beloved state as anything in the pageant," Mrs. Hyde observed. This reaction was illustrative of the First Lady's many gracious attempts to find something beneficial in all happenings. Although not present for the ceremonies, Mrs. Hyde was able to entertain many of the notables gathered for the occasion, including four former first ladies invited to a noon luncheon.

In complete contrast to the dedicated Governor and the reserved state hostess, was the young lady of the Mansion for the years 1921 through 1925. This was the daughter of the first family, Caroline, who completely disregarded the need for dignified conduct by playing ball and roly-poly, a type of blindman's buff, in the reception hall and other of the Mansion's many spacious rooms. Caroline who was nine years old started her residence with an incident remembered years later by both the First Lady and her daughter. It seems the pre-inaugural dinner given by Mrs. Gardner for her successor had to be held on the second floor because of preparations for the inaugural ball on the first floor. It was discovered that the butler had forgotten the napkins. Caroline, attempting to reassure her hostess, cleared the air with one statement. Using her best adult manners, Caroline suggested that Mrs. Gardner shouldn't be upset because the Hyde family didn't ever use napkins anyway.

A final singular test of Mrs. Hyde's abilities as state hostess came during

St. Louis Post-Dispatch

First Ladies who attended dedication of new capitol. Left to right, Mrs. Elliott W. Major, Mrs. Joseph W. Folk, Mrs. Arthur M. Hyde, Mrs. Frederick D. Gardner, Mrs. Herbert S. Hadley

the last military ball of the Hyde administration in January, 1925. As the day neared, Governor Hyde became sick with a sore throat. Impatient with his illness, the Governor insisted that plans for the reception proceed. It was agreed that the ball would be held if the host would remain in bed. Mrs. Hyde spent the day receiving guests and running up the stairs to make sure the Governor was following orders. The Governor was true to his word and Mrs. Hyde carried out their last major social event by herself. Shortly after the end of their four years in the state's capital city, the Hydes moved to the national capital where he served from 1929 to 1933 as Secretary of Agriculture in the administration of President Herbert Hoover. Governor Hyde died in 1947. Ten years later, Mrs. Hyde moved to the Virgin Islands where her daughter was living. Mrs. Hyde died in her home at Frederiksted, St. Croix, Virgin Islands on September 4, 1962.

It still was the raucous Roaring Twenties when Mrs. Hyde handed the keys and responsibility of the executive Mansion to her successor – Nelle Tuckley Baker. The incoming First Lady was a native "Jeffercitian" – the second governor's wife to be born in the capital city and the third Cole Countian to serve as hostess of the Mansion. Mrs. Baker was born in Jefferson City in 1880, the daughter of Richard Sayers and Elisabeth K. Tuckley. She married Sam A. Baker on June 1, 1904 while he was principal of the Jefferson City High School. They continued their home in the capital city as the Governor advanced from principal to superintendent of the city schools and, in 1918, to election as state superintendent of schools.

Mrs. Baker's gown for the inaugural festivities on January 12, 1925 was a strict example of the styles of that period – a short shift, fashioned of white chiffon encrusted with silver and crystal beads. The inaugural ball for the first time was moved completely to the capitol rotunda with only the afternoon reception held in the Mansion. The same arrangement was to be used for the annual military balls of the Baker administration – afternoon receptions in the Mansion and evening receptions and dancing in the capitol. Missouri's continued population growth and the modernizing of transportation facilities during the half century since the new Mansion opened had resulted in ever-increasing crowds at major state functions. Thus, the executive residence was losing its regal position as the sole site of state social affairs. Dances on the third floor, high above the nearby Missouri River, eventually were to become a memory of years past.

Another tie with the previous century ended when Sam A. Baker defeated Dr. Arthur W. Nelson in the gubernatorial race in 1924. Arthur Nelson was the son of Lalla Marmaduke Nelson who had served as hostess in the Mansion for her bachelor uncle, Governor John S. Marmaduke. Nelson's campaign as the Democratic nominee for governor was the final link of the Sappington-Marmaduke dynasty of the nineteenth century with state political life.

Traditions had slowly evolved to provide a social guide for first ladies and Mrs. Baker adopted the pattern of past administrations – "at homes" for wives of legislators and of state officials and periodic dinners for members of the General Assembly. Also continued were the teas in the Mansion as capital city members of the Daughters of the American Revolution gathered annually to celebrate Washington's Birthday. Periodic parties were held for members of the city music club started by Mrs. Folk. Perhaps it was the large size of parties given at the Mansion which caused guests to forget occasionally that they were dining in a home – not a restaurant. Mrs. Baker recalled how one state guest summoned a waiter to inform him firmly that he had ordered buttermilk with his meal. First ladies often had felt they were supervising a hotel but this was one of the few incidents in which a guest attempted to adjust the dinner menu to suit his personal taste.

Along with an accepted pattern of social affairs, a household staff also had become a part of the Mansion traditions as key people remained through the changes of administration. One of these staff members, Barbara Pohlman, had started her service as housekeeper for Mrs. Hadley and remained to provide vital continuity for Mrs. Major, Mrs. Gardner and Mrs. Hyde. She, however, was able to stay only long enough to help Mrs. Baker get settled in the Mansion before

Nelle Baker

Park-Morrow, Women of the Mansion

she had to leave her position because of sickness in her family. An innovation in the Mansion staff ordered by the Bakers was the reassignment of prison labor to yard work and occasional housecleaning rather than the use of prisoners for daily duties within the household.

Two structural changes made by Mrs. Baker in the state executive residence were the installation of doors to the first and second floor back porches. French doors were installed between the dining room and the first-floor porch along the west side of the Mansion. Another set of doors was placed in the large northwest bedroom to the porch on the second floor which previously had to be entered through the housekeeper's bedroom. The third-floor ballroom, although decreasing in use for major state functions, still was an important part of the building and Mrs. Baker had the huge area completely renovated. Appropriations were made by the legislature in one lump sum for the first time, combining funds for current expenses and repairs into one item. These budgets amounted to $20,000.00 for 1925 and 1926, the first two years the Bakers served as first family, and $25,000.00 for the 1927-28 biennium.

Mary Elisabeth Baker, a high-school student, succeeded Caroline Hyde as the only child of the reigning executive family and, thus, THE young lady of the Mansion. Mary Elisabeth fortunately was able to take part in two major weddings which were high points of the Bakers' residency and the first such ceremonies to be held in the Mansion in forty years. Ironically, the previous wedding in December, 1885 involved Lalla Marmaduke Nelson, the mother of the man Governor Baker had defeated in the gubernatorial race. The first ceremony invited to the Mansion by the Bakers was the marriage of Miss Margaret Reavis of Jefferson City and Herbert Kimes of Cameron, Missouri. Miss Reavis was the twenty-one-year-old daughter of George Reavis who was the state director of vocational education at the time. The wedding was held at 11 a.m., June 24, 1925, in front of the fireplace in the reception parlor which had become known as the Gold Room because of the graceful gold-leaf furniture. Some fifty friends and relatives were guests and Mary Elisabeth Baker and Lillian Tweedie of Jefferson City were attendants for the bride who had selected a color scheme of blue and maize. The rail of the grand stairway – that magnificent entranceway for a bride – was completely wrapped in smilax and roses.

A year later, on June 26, 1926, the second wedding of the Baker administration took place in the Mansion. It was a much larger evening affair involving Mary Todd Gentry, daughter of the then Attorney-General and Mrs. North Todd Gentry, and H. K. Hannah Jr., of Odessa, Missouri. Miss Gentry chose blue and pink for her decorations and again used the marble mantle of the Gold Room as a background for the ceremonial altar. The young lady of the Mansion, Mary Elisabeth, served this time as a candle lighter. Governor and Mrs. Baker – on each occasion – entertained the brides, their parents and their bridal attendants at dinner the evening before the weddings. One sidelight of the Gentry-Hannah ceremony was a slight mishap as the bride hurried up the grand stairway to change into her traveling clothes. The traditional bouquet-throwing was disrupted when the flowers caught in a chandelier high above the many outstretched hands. The heroine was a household maid who dislodged the bouquet with a wall brush. The catching of the flowers became so anticlimactic that the identity of the recipient was quickly forgotten.

An event of international importance served as a keynote of a new era and a closing chapter of the Baker administration. On June 18, 1927, the First Lady accompanied her daughter and the Governor to St. Louis for two days of ceremonies marking the return of Charles A. Lindbergh. During the previous months, the young pilot had made his memorable nonstop flight across the ocean to Paris. Parades, receptions and a banquet were part of the welcome planned for the aviator. The First Lady shared a banquet table with Mrs. Charles A. Lindbergh, mother of the honored guest. A commission as a colonel in the Missouri National Guard presented by Governor Baker was later to become part of the Lindbergh trophies displayed in the Jefferson Memorial Building in St. Louis.

The wake of the aviator's famous little plane, the Spirit of St. Louis, served to sweep away the final remnants of the Roaring Twenties and mark a new era, not only in transportation but in social and economic conduct of the state and nation. Governor Baker had made one brief air trip, perhaps the first state executive to use this means of transportation, and his daughter in July, 1928 made a flight from St. Louis to Jefferson City in fifty-five minutes – a record time.

A few months after the end of Governor Baker's term in January, 1929, he suffered a paralytic stroke and was an invalid until his death four years later. Mrs. Baker remained in Jefferson City, sharing a home with her daughter, until 1942 when Mary Elisabeth's work occasioned a move to Columbia for ten years. In 1952, the two returned to the capital city where they were living when Mrs. Baker died on November 19, 1966 after an illness of one month.

Chapter XII

More than one hundred years had passed since Marguerite Susanne de Reilhe McNair, the accomplished daughter of a French family, assumed her role in St. Louis as wife of the first state governor. The passage of time had brought historic changes to the dimensions of the position of first lady. Improvements in transportation contributed to the increased demands placed on a governor's wife as official hostess. The development of train travel, then the automobiles and, in the 1920s, more frequent use of airplanes brought a wider range of visitors to the doors of the executive residence in the capital city. Official guests did not stay as long but they came more frequently. Arrival of a foreign dignitary was not the rarity in the twentieth century that it was in the 1870s when the Grand Duke Alexis of Russia helped dedicate the state's magnificent new Mansion.

Also affecting the scope of activities of Missouri's first ladies was the enfranchisement of women following World War I. Women voters were to become an increasingly important political factor; they had to be reckoned with at the polls. The wife of a candidate for governor could be a measurable political asset. In the years ahead it would make good political sense for a candidate's wife to form a team with her husband in campaigning the state and the teamwork would continue in the Mansion.

Another factor in the changing role of executive wives was the influence of a presidential first lady, Eleanor Roosevelt, with her unparalleled pattern of social involvement. Coincidentally, it was a distant relative of President Franklin Delano Roosevelt who inaugurated a change in the role of Missouri's first lady. Frances Delano Caulfield, better known as "Fannie," assumed her position as first lady of Missouri in 1929 while her cousin was still governor of New York. Fannie Caulfield, a former St. Louis County schoolteacher, was born in Des Moines, Iowa but her family moved to Cuba, Missouri when she was an infant. She was the second wife of Henry S. Caulfield, a St. Louis attorney. In 1897, he had married Miss Adele Lopez who died one year later. In 1902, Henry Caulfield and Fannie Allice Delano were married in her family home in Cuba. He served one term in Congress before Republican leaders approached him with the idea of a state-wide race.

Although her predecessor, Mrs. Baker, had assisted her husband in the clerical work required by a campaign, Mrs. Caulfield apparently was the first governor's wife to accompany her candidate-husband on his campaign trips about the state. Such tours had not been undertaken in the early years of statehood because of the limited facilities for transportation. In the last half of the nineteenth century, campaign excursions by a wife were not recommended due to the hardships of travel. But again improvements changed the pattern. Just as better roads, new automobiles and airplanes brought more visitors to the capital city, the better facilities removed obstacles to travel by a candidate's wife.

Mrs. Caulfield admitted her campaign trips were "strenuous and grueling" but found at least one lasting benefit. She recalled that she entered the executive Mansion with a feeling that she knew the state and its people "rather thoroughly." Another innovation of recent years which was a part of Governor Caulfield's inauguration in 1929 was the broadcasting of the ceremonies by Radio Station WOS. This pioneer radio venture had started operations a few years earlier with broadcasts sent out from a studio in the dome of the new capitol.

The fashions of the 1920s – simple, austere lines and short skirts – again were reflected in the inaugural gown of Mrs. Caulfield. Her dress was made of slate blue chiffon velvet, accented with a back panel lined with pale pink satin. Also present for the inaugural were the previous first ladies who served the state in the 1920s, Mrs. Hyde and Mrs. Baker, both wearing their inaugural gowns with their short skirts and straight lines. Tradition gave way to safety precautions for the staging of the inaugural festivities which were completely removed from the Mansion for the first time. A newspaper story noted that "the innovation of holding the governor's reception in the capitol building, put into effect this year, was decided upon on account of the condition of the winding stairway in the executive mansion . . . it was considered too dangerous to trust so large a crowd upon it." The inaugural ball had been moved to the capitol four years earlier.

Extremely bad weather, an unfortunate talisman of the past, covered the state with sleet on inaugural day and nearly resulted in another baby being born in the Mansion. The Caulfields' oldest daughter, Elizabeth Barksdale, and her husband were forced to stay overnight until chains could be brought on the morning train to replenish the exhausted supply at capital city garages. The day after the Barksdales returned to St. Louis the first grandchild of Missouri's new executive family – Henry Caulfield Barksdale – was born. The Caulfields' second daughter and her husband, Frances and Lucian Galena, also were present and helped lead the inaugural procession at the opening of the ball. The Caulfields' eighteen-year-old son, John, was home temporarily from college and their youngest daughter, fifteen-year-old Jane, was visiting from a private girls' school in St. Louis for the period of the inaugural ceremonies. The only young children in the executive residence during the Caulfield administration was the new grandson, who "signed" the guest register in the Mansion when he was three months old and a second grandson, Clarence, born to the Barksdales before the Caulfield term ended.

Frances Caulfield

Park-Morrow, Women of the Mansion

The new First Lady, like all her predecessors in Jefferson City, faced the immediate post-inaugural problems of becoming acclimated to her new role and her new home. Mrs. Caulfield recalled and soon agreed with a statement by Governor Hyde that life in the Mansion could be compared with "keeping house in a convention hall." The staff included a male cook, Harris, who later was replaced by a Negro woman, two maids and the chauffeur. The position of housekeeper was vacant so Mrs. Caulfield assumed the responsibilities for setting out daily assignments for the staff, for holding morning conferences with the cook and making daily trips to the markets. Her first social undertakings were the traditional dinners for legislators and afternoon teas for legislative wives and ladies of the capital city. All the state senators were invited to the first of the legislative dinners and places were set for thirty-four guests who were served a formal meal of three courses. Trestles and table tops were brought from the basement and made into a long table extending the length of the entire dining room. The twenty-three high-back chairs of the regular dining room furniture were supplemented by folding chairs. Mrs. Caulfield remarked that it was the first stag dinner her husband had ever held.

Some four hundred women from St. Louis, Columbia and Jefferson City attended the opening "at home" tea in late February. They were served coffee, cake, candy, cookies and cranberry frappe made in the huge freezers in the Mansion basement. Mrs. Caulfield had been impressed with the many facilities available in the Mansion which were not found in the ordinary kitchen, such as the freezers, a pantry for preparing pastries and a special machine for making beaten biscuits.

A highlight of the Caulfields' first spring in the Mansion was the entertainment of foreign ambassadors who were attending Journalism Week activities at the University of Missouri in Columbia. Guests included the Japanese ambassador and his wife, the Mexican ambassador and his wife and some fifty others invited for breakfast early in May, 1929. In personal notes, Mrs. Caulfield wrote that the "Japanese minister is talkative and jolly and the Mexican minister serious and so polite and courteous." She observed that "everybody liked Mrs. Debuchi (the Japanese ambassador's wife) . . . she is a doll, so tiny and gentle." Mrs. Caulfield recalled how the Japanese ambassador commented on the brownness of the Missouri countryside at the time. He quite seriously suggested that the Governor "must do something about that." The breakfast reminded Mrs. Caulfield of parties in the nation's capital which she attended while the Governor was in Congress. She observed that "Jefferson City and its social and political problems were but Washington in a smaller sphere and simpler form."

It soon became obvious to Mrs. Caulfield that she would have to make a firm decision on just how the Mansion would be used; she would have to strike a delicate balance between the state's need for a building to serve as the home of the first family and as a semipublic state-owned structure. This conflict of purposes was a problem that had plagued most first ladies because of the many demands for use of the Mansion, submitted by officials of numerous state conferences and meetings, particularly those involving women. Mrs. Caulfield made the decision for her administration early during her four-year term and noted her thoughts in her diary. She wrote that she decided against lending the Mansion "just as a public site for large affairs." Any function involving the Mansion, she decided, should have either the Governor or Mrs. Caulfield as host. Other demands which Mrs. Caulfield found annoying, even to the point of rudeness, were the frequent requests to use her name and the Mansion to promote various causes. One woman insisted on coming to a private party at the Mansion to sell artificial flowers to guests.

A personal pleasure which Mrs. Caulfield was able to pursue actively at the Mansion was the planting of flowers, particularly "old-fashioned blooms" such as iris. Bulbs were brought from her own yard in St. Louis and planted in a garden on the riverside of the Mansion. Stepping stones also were placed to form a walk down the terraces on the river bluff. Mrs. Caulfield recalled how she and the Governor would sit on the stone steps on hot summer nights and watch the lights of automobiles traveling roads across the river in Callaway County. Another hobby, in addition to gardening, for which Mrs. Caulfield was widely known, was the collecting of maps, an interest she inherited from her father. Her collection included maps of treasure islands and charts of transoceanic flights. One map was dated 1650. In a more personal note, the First Lady observed that life in the Mansion required a wardrobe of dressier clothes than were necessary in her previous life as a St. Louis housewife. A seamstress would charge three dollars and fifteen cents a day and a dress would be finished in a maximum of a day and one half.

At the end of the legislative session, the first appropriations were available and Mrs. Caulfield planned needed repairs, inside and outside. The funds provided for the 1929-30 biennium included $25,000.00 for current expenses and $15,000.00 for repairs and equipment. Identical appropriations were approved for the Caulfields' last two years in the Mansion. A major project directed by Mrs. Caulfield was the modernization of the Mansion kitchen. A new electric range replaced the wood cookstove and an electric refrigerator was installed in place of the icebox. A new bathroom with pink tiles on the walls and floor was constructed where there had been a large closet in Mrs. Caulfield's second-floor bedroom on the north or riverside of the Mansion.

Two items reminiscent of the past which were included in the repair schedule were recovering of the billiard table in the third-floor ballroom and renovation of a neglected summerhouse on the edge of the river bluff. The billiard table, of course, was the same one believed to have been purchased and left in the Mansion by the bachelor-governor, John S. Marmaduke. Origin of the summerhouse was clouded although it was known to have been built by 1896. Plans for a summerhouse, or gazebo, were announced in 1873 during the administration of Mrs. Jennie Woodson but there was no confirmation that it was completed. Had it been built in that period it would be more than fifty years old, a remarkably long time for such a structure to remain after constant exposure to the weather.

Mrs. Caulfield said chickens had roosted in the quaint lattice summerhouse in recent years, but she utilized materials left from an interior project and had the house cleaned and painted a soft green. The Japanese-style roof was repaired and stone laid for a floor. This structure was used frequently by Mrs. Caulfield for summer breakfasts. She described it as having two openings for doors, one of which faced the river. It was furnished with a round white wooden table and wooden chairs. Mrs. Caulfield noted in her diary that the "chair that faces the river is the 'company' seat on account of the beautiful outlook."

Mrs. Caulfield recognized the potential danger from old unused cisterns on the Mansion grounds. To guard against mishaps, she had the metal covers welded shut and padlocked. Mrs. Caulfield observed following the cistern project that "it is so easy here . . . I have only to see a thing needs mending and say I want it fixed and it is fixed. I hope I do not let it spoil me for regular life."

About midway in her four-year tenure, Mrs. Caulfield wrote a series of stories about life in the Mansion and they were printed in a publication known as the *Missouri Ruralist* which had a large farm circulation. This literary venture was unprecedented in the undertakings of a first lady of Missouri and one to be recalled later when Mrs. Caulfield's illustrious relative, the nation's First Lady, published a series of columns under the title of *My Day*. Mrs. Caulfield gave her readers an intimate look into Mansion life and the less publicized ways the residence was used by the Governor. She wrote that "when the Governor is trying to be very quiet and work on a speech without interruption, he comes over to the Mansion. There are so many big rooms that he can always find a quiet spot." She also noted that she spent a part of each day reading letters and writing replies. Crank, anonymous criticisms were torn up and put in the scrap basket. "No one but the basket and I are the wiser."

Mrs. Caulfield's creative interests were extended into the art field later in life. In 1956, some twenty years after she left Jefferson City, Mrs. Caulfield won second prize for a painting she entered in a show for amateur artists. Governor and Mrs. Caulfield had reopened their family home in St. Louis after his administration and they still were living in that residence when she died on February 10, 1961 at the age of eighty-five.

A notation on the last page of Mrs. Caulfield's guest register at the

Mansion included the signatures on December 2, 1932 of Guy B. and Eleanora Gabbert Park, the governor-elect and the incoming first lady of Missouri. The Parks were taking an introductory tour of the huge residence that soon was to be their official home for four years. The change of administrations in January, 1933 came at a time when the nation was in the depth of a financial depression. It was a period of bank failures and bread lines. Missouri's capital city, with its economy stablized around the state government, was not as depressed as urban areas with their massive unemployment. But economies were necessary and the Mansion budget was trimmed.

During the previous administration, the General Assembly had appropriated $40,000.00 covering a two-year period for expenses and repairs at the Mansion. For the years of 1933 and 1934, the legislature provided a Mansion budget of $14,500.00 with the governor's capitol office sharing in the repair funds. Thus, the new first lady, Mrs. Park, faced residency in a huge home with very little money available to pay for its operation and upkeep. Among the new items which Mrs. Park felt could be afforded under the reduced allotment were new curtains. However, her plans met with temporary disapproval from the Governor who objected, not to the cost, but to the amount of material involved. Mrs. Park recalled that curtains for one bedroom in the Mansion with its high ceilings required "just about as much material as for our whole house at home."

This "home" referred to by the new First Lady was in Platte City where, prior to their move to Jefferson City, Mrs. Park lived as a housewife, Governor Guy B. Park served as circuit judge and their daughter and only child, Henrietta, held a position as English teacher in the Platte City high school. Governor and Mrs. Park, both natives of Platte County, Missouri, had met while she attended Gaylord Institute, a private school in Platte City which was directed by the Governor's mother. The First Lady often remarked that she "got the only man out of a girls' school." They were married November 16, 1909 at the home of her parents, Mr. and Mrs. Michael Gabbert near Weston. Their home in Platte City was closed on Sunday, January 8, 1933 as the Parks traveled to Jefferson City to be overnight guests of the Caulfields in the executive Mansion. The occasion also saw a changing of Mansion pets as the Caulfield dog, a wire-haired fox terrier, gave up his official position to "Judge," the Parks' police dog. "Judge" had caused a major preinaugural stir in the capital city when he escaped from the truck that brought him to the Mansion ahead of the Parks. Quite a crowd had joined in the chase before "Judge" finally was cornered near the capitol.

Monday, January 9, 1933 was one of those rare inaugural days which was warmed by a bright sun. Following the oath taking in the capitol at the traditional high noon, the two first families returned to the Mansion for a final lunch before the Caulfields left in the afternoon for St. Louis. Protocol for the change of first families in the Mansion was not as firmly fixed as the procedure for the change of governors. Generally, the incoming family would be invited to the Mansion on inaugural eve and would stay as overnight guests. Occasionally, the outgoing family would remain, either in the Mansion or in a nearby hotel, to attend the inaugural ball. But both the "before" and "after" arrangements of each family varied, apparently according to the preferences of the individuals involved.

Members of the household staff at the Mansion also varied with the families in residence. The Parks brought with them their own cook, Ada Boyd, who had prepared the Governor's favorite southern dishes at Platte City. One of Ada Boyd's first tasks in Jefferson City was to help Mrs. Park renovate the beaten-biscuit machine in the basement kitchen of the Mansion. As soon as Mrs. Park spotted the machine, she knew it would have to be put to use for her family. She posted her own biscuit recipe to be used during her administration and to remain for the guidance of later Mansion cooks and first ladies. Other members of the previous household staff employed by the Caulfields were retained. And during the Parks' term, Barbara Pohlman, the veteran housekeeper who first helped Mrs. Hadley in 1909, returned to the executive staff. A few key household servants, such as Barbara, provided the only continuity through the changing of official residents and this proved a great help to a new first lady during her period of adjustment. Actually, inaugural day was less trying for the Mansion hostess following the move of major inaugural festivities, including the state reception and ball, to the capitol.

Mrs. Park's ball gown in 1933 marked the formal end of the Roaring Twenties as she, for the first time in four inaugurals, selected a form-fitting, floor-length dress, contrasted to the shorter styles of her immediate predecessors. Mrs. Park's gown was made of heavy white crepe trimmed with wide bands of bugle beads. The new First Lady immediately launched a schedule of the traditional social events. She opened her social service with a Thursday "at home" ten days after she moved to the Mansion. It was attended by nearly five hundred guests including wives of legislators and state officials. Members of the General Assembly were entertained at the customary series of stag dinners.

Assisting at the Mansion social events during Mrs. Park's first year, 1933, was twenty-two-year-old Henrietta whose life was immediately reshaped by her change of residences. Soon after her move to Jefferson City, the executive daughter met a young man from St. Louis, J. Marvin Krause. In November of the inaugural year they were married. It was the first wedding in the Mansion with the mansard roof involving the daughter of a governor who was in office at the time. The last previous wedding of a governor's daughter, according to available records, involved the oldest daughter of Governor Dunklin, Mary W. Dunklin, who was married in 1835 in the old mansion – the second executive residence

Park-Morrow, Women of the Mansion

Eleanora Park, in her inaugural gown

built by the state in Jefferson City.

Henrietta Park followed the path taken by other Mansion brides – a dramatic entrance on the arm of the Governor, a slow walk down the historic walnut stairway and across the first-floor reception hall into the Gold Room. The white marble fireplace of the Gold Room served as a background for the ceremony. The gown of the bride was fashioned of white satin brocade with a train four feet long. The only attendant was the bride's cousin, Miss Margaret Gow, who wore gold moire. To carry out the bridal traditions, Mrs. Stephen B. Hunter, wife of the director of the state penal board, had provided Henrietta with a lucky sixpence for the toe of her white satin slippers. In the dining room, the bride and groom cut their wedding cake which weighed 220 pounds and was four and one-half feet high.

The ceremony was performed on November 16, 1933, the twenty-fourth anniversary of the marriage of the bride's parents, Governor and Mrs. Park. Following a trip to Mexico, the newlyweds lived in St. Louis where, a year later, an executive grandson, Guy Park Krause, was born. Just as in the preceding administration, a grandson was a frequent and honored guest in Missouri's Mansion. There are natural advantages to being the grandchild of a governor and one such advantage was the present to the new executive baby of a baseball autographed by Dizzy Dean, pitching star of the St. Louis Cardinals, as a souvenir of the 1934 World Series.

Little information is ever found in public records of the special problems of a new governor in adjusting to his move into the state Mansion. One problem encountered by Governor Park concerned his first attempt to use the historic old billiard table on the third floor. He searched the entire Mansion for the billiard balls, even looking in the refrigerator in the basement. The cues too were missing. A newspaper story was published concerning his search and immediate offers for new billiard equipment were extended. A twelve-ounce cue actually was sent to the Governor.

Special requests for personal favors filled the Governor's mail and one such letter also concerned the Mansion. The writer from St. Louis, evidently impressed with accounts of the Park-Krause wedding, asked the Governor to marry the writer of the letter and his fiancee in the Mansion. The writer explained that he had "never accomplished anything of great note" but apparently felt that a marriage in Missouri's executive Mansion would give him a place in history. Another special request to the Governor came from Hollywood asking that Shirley Temple, a child movie star who was a favorite of the time, be appointed to his staff of honorary colonels. The Governor rejected both the request for the marriage in the Mansion and for the appointment for Miss Temple. Governor Park wrote that he felt colonels on his staff should be personal friends or should be important residents of Missouri.

Although travel was curtailed during the depression, Mrs. Park did her share of entertaining notable visitors to the state and to the Mansion. Both President Roosevelt and Mrs. Roosevelt visited Missouri on separate occasions but their trips did not include Jefferson City. On November 14, 1934, Mrs. Roosevelt was in St. Louis for a conference on mobilization of human needs and the state's First Lady joined the nation's First Lady at the speaker's table. In the

St. Louis Post-Dispatch

Governors' wives attending National Governors' Conference in Missouri, 1936. Left to right, seated, Mrs. George Perry, wife of the governor of Virginia; Mrs. Robert L. Cochran, wife of the governor of Nebraska; Mrs. Guy B. Park of Missouri; Mrs. Hjalmar Jolman Petersen, wife of the governor of Minnesota. Standing, Mrs. James E. Berry, wife of the lieutenant-governor of Oklahoma; Mrs. H. W. Nice, wife of the governor of Maryland; Mrs. C. A. Hardee, wife of the former governor of Florida who was secretary of the Conference; Mrs. Paul V. McNutt, wife of the governor of Indiana; Mrs. Stanley C. Wilson, wife of the former governor of Vermont who was treasurer of the Conference

fall of 1936, Governor and Mrs. Park were in Hannibal to meet the President who was an honored guest at the dedication of the Mark Twain Memorial Bridge. Earlier that year, on February 22, 1936, a member of the President's cabinet, Postmaster-General James Farley visited in the Mansion while he was in the capital city to speak to a state convention of Young Democrats.

A major event during the Park administration occurred in November, 1936 when governors of eighteen states and many of their wives came to Missouri to attend the twenty-eighth annual National Governors' Conference – the first visit of that group to the state. Governor Paul V. McNutt of Indiana served as chairman of the conference. Among the state executives who sent their regrets was Governor Alfred M. Landon of Kansas who a few days before the conference was defeated as the Republican presidential candidate. The opening session of the three-day conference was held on November 16, 1936, in the Hotel Coronado in St. Louis. The agenda for that day, in addition to the business meetings, included a sightseeing trip through St. Louis and a dinner at the Hotel Jefferson.

On Tuesday, November 17, the governors and their parties rode on a special train which arrived in Jefferson City at noon. The group of some seventy persons took part in a motorcade through the business district before the visitors were driven to the Missouri Hotel. A business session was held in the Senate chamber in the capitol in the afternoon. Planes were available to fly the visitors to the Lake of the Ozarks and Bagnell Dam, a new recreational area which had been developed south of the capital city. All the visitors were special guests of Governor and Mrs. Park at the Mansion for a formal reception from 4 to 5:30 p.m., prior to a banquet at the Missouri Hotel. The onference was concluded in Kansas City where the governors were taken by their special train for final business sessions, extensive bus tours of the city and a banquet on Wednesday night at the Hotel Muehlebach.

Each of Missouri's first ladies has left in the executive residence physical reminders of her life and service in the Mansion. Some she received merely in the name of the state; others carried an imprint of her own personality. Mrs. Park in 1933 received as a gift to the state and to the Mansion a set of twelve service plates from the state department of the American Legion Auxiliary. Each plate carried a different print commemorating the founding and early exploits of the United States Navy. Also for the dining room, Mrs. Park furnished new pieces to complete the set of sterling flat silver in the Mount Vernon pattern and had the old pieces refinished. An antique silver coffee urn was found in the basement coalbin where it apparently had been stored by a thoughtless Mansion employee and Mrs. Park had it refinished and restored to use in the dining room.

A more personal gift to the Mansion was Mrs. Park's portrait painted by Richard E. Miller of St. Louis and New York and financed by the Governor's staff of honorary colonels. The portrait was formally presented on April 8, 1934 and was hung in the Mansion with those of other first ladies, starting with Mrs. Lon Vest Stephens. Also during the Park administration state funds were made available to have the portrait of a former first lady, Mrs. Joseph W. Folk, painted. It later was added to the Mansion collection.

Mrs. Park's most outstanding contribution was the publication of a book, *Women of the Mansion,* which she helped compile to preserve a history of the state's executive residences and the ladies who lived and served in them. Mrs. Park started formulating plans for the book during a return trip to Platte City after a preinaugural visit to the Mansion. The germ of this literary undertaking came from Mrs. Kate Morrow who had been connected with state executive life for many years and served as hostess in the Mansion following the death of Mrs. Dockery. The two ladies spent many months researching and editing the book which consisted of 435 pages and was published in 1936. It was a unique and rewarding effort to preserve the story of first ladies since Missouri had become a state. It was thought the volume would assist future hostesses in identifying the many meaningful pieces of furniture in the Mansion. It also was intended as a guide to the origin of social customs and traditions as they developed through the years. One biographer wrote that Eleanora Park, through her study and research, came to have a unique attachment for the Missouri Mansion and for all its furnishings and *objets d'art.*

When his term was over, Governor and Mrs. Park returned to Platte City and the family home they had built in 1915. Mrs. Park continued to live there after the Governor died in 1946 until she suffered a stroke in 1966 and moved to Columbia, Missouri where her daughter was living. Mrs. Park still was residing in Columbia in 1969. Although withdrawn socially, Mrs. Park remained alert and interested in articles and letters, particularly those reminiscent of her days in the state's executive Mansion.

During the closing weeks of his administration, Governor Park had started negotiations which were to add to the Mansion grounds. Perhaps the motivation for his effort was a letter written in 1935 by a St. Louis resident complaining about the unsightly condition of the area between the Mansion and the capitol. Small lots in the Mansion block had been sold through the years to private owners. These sales mostly had taken place in the early days of the capital city when legislators looked to the revenue from land sales to finance state construction projects. Most of the eastern half of the Mansion block where the second executive residence was located and the land where the first capitol and new Mansion were constructed had been retained by the state through the years. But lots fronting on Capitol Avenue and along Jefferson Street in the western half of the block had been parceled off for private dwellings and small business houses. The first large lot on Capitol Avenue was repurchased by the state on November 25, 1936 for $31,000.00. Negotiations for the others were completed within the next three months for additional expenditures of $57,000.00. It was a laudable project and in the years immediately ahead, future first ladies and civic organizations would combine their efforts to turn the area into a quaint park and garden.

This start on the repossession of the Mansion grounds literally laid the groundwork for a major reconstruction of the sixty-five-year-old residence of Missouri governors – the most extensive ever undertaken. There had been other redecorations, such as the work of Mrs. Francis in 1889 and the elaborate project of Mrs. Stephens in 1897. There had been a few changes in the exterior of the building – a porte-cochere constructed during the term of Governor Dockery in

1904 and a second-floor back porch added by Mrs. Major in 1915. But there had been no major structural renewals and suggestions already were heard in the 1920s for razing of the Mansion and building a modern home for Missouri's executive families. This movement was thwarted by the financial depression of the 1930s and, thus, it was to the Mansion with the mansard roof that a new first family was to move in January, 1937. The new residents were Governor-elect Lloyd C. Stark and the incoming first lady, Katherine Lemoine Perkins Stark.

A week prior to the inaugural date, a major ice storm covered the state. Roads in many sections were impassable and power and communication lines were broken. In Louisiana, Missouri, the private home of the Starks was without lights or heat and the two children of the first family-elect, three-year-old Mary "Molly" Murray Spotswood Stark, and two-year-old Katherine Lemoine Stark, were sent to St. Louis by train to stay with their grandmother. Antique furniture, which was to be used to supplement the furnishings in the Mansion, was carried gingerly down ice-covered steps and loaded into trucks for the hazardous drive to the capital city. The move was completed without mishap and the Starks, responding to the invitation of the Parks, arrived at the Mansion on inaugural eve.

Inaugural day on January 11, 1937 started very early for the Starks as the minister of the Grace Episcopal Church in Jefferson City, the Reverend Wilbur D. Ruggles, arrived at the Mansion to serve communion to the new executive family. This was planned, Mrs. Stark recalled, "to prepare us for the great tasks that lay ahead." The practice of opening the day with a religious service was to be adopted by later first families as part of the customary inaugural events. Other parts of the ceremonies for the Starks were conducted in the by-then traditional setting – legislators and state officials seated in the rotunda, honorary colonels in uniform lining the curved double stairway leading from the rotunda to the second floor and the inaugural platform arranged at the top of the stairways directly in front of the door to the governor's reception room. Despite several uneasy minutes, Episcopal Bishop William Scarlett arrived on time over the ice-covered roads from St. Louis to deliver the invocation. The University of Missouri band played the Star-Spangled Banner and two-year-old Katherine Stark joined in the "Sail, Baby, Sail" – the only song she knew.

Traditions for inaugural afternoon and night, which would be observed in the years to come, were established by the start of the Stark administration – an afternoon reception at the Mansion for the honorary colonels and their wives; a larger, formal inaugural reception for state officials in the governor's reception room in the capitol climaxed by the Grand March led by the new Governor and First Lady down the curved stairway to the rotunda floor to signal the start of the inaugural ball. Mrs. Stark wore the white Alencon lace gown, trimmed with pearls, which she had first worn six years earlier for her wedding. The dress, sleeveless with a scoop neckline, was cut along form-fitting lines relieved at the knees with a slight flare which formed a short train in the back. She carried a bouquet of orchids from the Missouri Botanical Garden in St. Louis which traditionally provided orchids each year for the Veiled Prophet Queen.

It was the St. Louis Botanical Garden which indirectly resulted in the introduction of Governor Stark and the First Lady. Mrs. Stark, who was born in St. Louis on March 23, 1901, had studied landscape architecture and gardening at the Botanical Garden after her college studies were interrupted by illness. She also taught botany to occupational therapy students. Friends in St. Louis were planning a dinner to which they had invited the Governor who was at that time head of the Stark Brothers Nurseries at Louisiana, Missouri. The friends selected Katherine Perkins as a dinner partner for Governor Stark because she shared the Governor's interest in horticulture. Mrs. Stark recalled that the Governor made an excuse to write down her name and address in order to ship her some apples. They were married on November 23, 1931 at the home of her parents, Mr. and Mrs. Albert Thompson Perkins in St. Louis County and lived in Louisiana until he was elected governor.

Post-inaugural Tuesday is the Day of Reckoning for all first ladies. The previous first lady has left with the inaugural crowds and the new mistress of the Mansion is alone with her huge new home. But, as in past years, it was the continuity of staff which eased the change for Mrs. Stark. Raymond Carter, the white-haired chauffeur, had served the state's first families for some ten years. Barbara Pohlman, as housekeeper, had been the bulwark of the staff through several administrations. The cook already was acquainted with the machine that turned out the beaten biscuits. Mrs. Stark herself assumed daily direction of the staff which included the designation of the next set of net glass curtains to be washed – a task done one window at a time in a year-round cycle. When the last set of curtains was finished, the first was ready for washing again.

To assist in keeping household accounts, Mrs. Stark ordered all food for personal meals, paid by the Governor out of his own funds, from one grocery store and provisions for official dinners, paid by the state, from a second store. The problems arose, however, concerning borderline cases such as hash from a turkey left from a state dinner. Despite all the meticulous planning by the First Lady and advice from the experienced staff members, miscalculations did occur. Mrs. Stark recalled an occasion when guests had assembled in the library for her first official luncheon. At the last minute, the butler took her aside and whispered that there were too few places set. She had forgotten to count the Governor and herself.

Later, Mrs. Stark was witness to a mishap at a White House party that made her miscalculation slight in comparison. The First Lady accompanied the

Governor and their cousins, Mr. and Mrs. Edwin Stark, to Washington for one of the famous Gridiron dinners given by the Washington press corps. Mrs. Roosevelt invited the "Gridiron widows" to a simultaneous dinner party at the White House. At the start of the ladies' meal, bouillon was served from white pitchers. Coffee was poured from identical enamel pitchers with the next course. Waiters later picked up the wrong pitchers and several guests, who had received refills for half-empty cups of coffee, finished their meal drinking a strange mixture of half coffee, half bouillon.

Through the years, the demands of social correspondence, of keeping expense accounts and supervising redecorations had placed an ever-increasing burden on the First Lady. After a two-year struggle to keep apace, Mrs. Stark

Katherine Stark, a copy of her portrait in Mansion

received approval for a personal secretary and Miss Dorothy Hetlage was hired for the position. Miss Hetlage previously had been secretary to the director of the St. Louis Art Museum. This position of personal secretary was to be continued and her assistance was considered as vital as the work of any other key staff member. Mrs. Stark also was assisted at Mansion social functions by Mrs. Nelle T. Lashley who was filling a new position as hostess at the state capitol building. Men students at Lincoln University in Jefferson City were hired as temporary help for major state dinners and a special detail of trusties from the penitentiary arrived daily for heavy cleaning and yard work.

Urgent needs for Mansion rehabilitation became obvious to the Starks soon after they were settled in the state residence. Previous first families had been equally aware of the demands but a world war and more recently a nationwide depression had forced postponement of funds for all but emergency repairs. A survey of the shortcomings of the building showed that windows had loosened through the years and rags had to be stuffed in the frames to keep out wintry blasts. Buckets were frequently rushed to the third floor to catch drips from a leaky roof. The basement kitchen was flooded on occasion and infested with rats. A dumbwaiter to bring food from the basement to the dining room was too small and too slow to get very much food to the table while it was hot. The graceful curving stairway was deemed unsafe after bearing the tread of thousands of people during its sixty-five years of service to state visitors and brides. Temporary braces had to be put under the stairway before the Starks felt secure in using it for their military reception on inaugural day.

A state architect, Ray Voskamp, was called to the Mansion to estimate minimum costs and then the appropriation chairmen of the House and Senate were asked to inspect the premises and help arrive at a reasonable allotment. A timely bit of silent lobbying was done by Mrs. Stark entirely by coincidence. She was sick with the flu when the legislators were conducted through her bedroom and they found a forlorn first lady in the middle of a huge bed deeply muffled against drafts from the rag-stuffed windows. The House chairman immediately burst forth with the opinion that he thought at least fifty thousand dollars was needed to do the work. That was exactly the figure estimated by the architect but previously unannounced. The General Assembly actually appropriated $45,000.00 for material, supplies and labor, plus another $10,000.00 for furnishings and equipment. That was more than the entire appropriation for original construction of the Mansion in 1871.

An interior decorator, Adrian Lamb of St. Louis, donated his services and worked closely with the state architect. The Starks continued to live in the Mansion during the remodeling, despite disruptions involved, such as stepping from joist to joist when the floor was torn out in the upstairs hall. The Mansion daughters again were sent to St. Louis to the care of their grandmother, Mrs.

Albert T. Perkins. When the Governor and Mrs. Stark had to be absent, the Governor's legal secretary and his wife, Mr. and Mrs. J. D. James, moved in to supervise the work. While the first floor was the center of active remodeling, the Starks moved their dining room to the second floor. Waiters, stepping carefully around scaffolds and carpenters' horses, carried the food from the dumbwaiter, up the winding stairway to be served. Later, when the dumbwaiter was torn out, meals had to be carried from the basement up two flights.

It was the food service area which underwent the biggest renovation. A new two-story wing was added to the south side of the Mansion in the vicinity of the porte-cochere which was removed. A new kitchen was built on the first-floor level of the wing with a garage underneath. The kitchen was a light airy room, measuring twenty by thirty feet. White cabinets with metal tops at working height extended around the walls of about two-thirds of the room. A charcoal broiler, an unusual appliance for the time, was installed next to the stove. Also in the kitchen was a board connected with a new buzzer system, with metal tabs indicating front door, library, or any room in which a ring would originate. This new wing which for the first time removed the kitchen from the basement resulted in a permanent structural change to the exterior of the Mansion.

A butler's pantry with cork-topped cabinets for quiet handling of plates and a small stove for last-minute warming was built into the space occupied by the original dumbwaiter. In the dining room, a second large French door, matching the doors to the porch installed by Mrs. Baker, was built to replace a window. Bronze chandeliers of English eighteenth-century style were hung to complement the tapestry on the walls.

Other additions to the dining room which were uniquely a part of the Stark administration were the antlered heads of two large deer, favored trophies of the Governor. The First Lady, unlike other wives confronted with such startling wall ornaments, said they were hung with her complete approval since she had similar hunting trophies among the eight or ten additional heads on the walls of the third floor.

Other structural renovations on the first floor included the bracing of the stairway. Steel shafts were fastened into the wall leaving the stairway curve unmarred by posts from the floor. And the bronze lady lost her place of honor on the newel post of the stairway. The large statue, which contained lights in the upraised arms, was a period piece installed when the Mansion was built and appeared overly ornate in the trend toward greater simplicity. This was the sturdy lady who had saved many youngsters from a harder bump on the floor at the end of a slide down the stairway. She also had served as a companion for Mansion residents who sat beside the lady on the post to watch state receptions which they were too young to attend.

On the second floor, a five-foot slice was taken off the hall to provide closets for surrounding rooms where guests previously depended on old-fashioned wardrobes. As the wall was rearranged, a new door was cut to provide a direct outlet to the hall from the northeast bedroom which previously was entered only through an adjoining bedroom. The third floor was redecorated in red, white and blue. The historic billiard table was centered under a dome light at one end of the large room while a ping-pong table of more recent vintage was placed at the other end of the room under another dome light. A room off the recreation area was panelled with pine and lined with cabinets and shelves for housing pieces of Missouriana and the guns of the Governor who used the room as a study.

Throughout the building heating pipes were placed within the walls, window frames were rebuilt and Venetian blinds hung in windows. New electric wiring was installed and new telephones with an intercom system added. Unused fireplaces were sealed to further add to the success of a new heating system. Many layers of wallpaper were removed and the downstairs walls were covered with canvas and painted. A parquet floor of black walnut was laid in the front hall and in the recessed alcove under the curve of the stairway. New bois-de-rose carpeting was added to the other first-floor areas and extended up the stairway and on the second-floor hall.

Three new crystal chandeliers with hundreds of sparkling prisms, were hung in the first-floor reception hall. Shortly after they were in place, Mrs. Stark was horrified to see one swaying dizzily on its chain. The cause was the "Big Apple," a dance craze of the period, being performed by young John Stark and his friends on the third floor. Mrs. Stark observed that a dance by that name certainly was appropriate for the son of a nurseryman, but it was not a safe tempo for the chandelier. She reluctantly had to request more sedate dancing by the young guests. John was the youngest of two sons born to Governor Stark's first wife, Margaret Pearson Stickney, who died in 1930. The older boy, Lloyd Stickney, was married at the time his father was governor. It was the brother, John, who played Santa for his little sisters at Christmas, actually making an entrance from one of the large Mansion fireplaces.

A change which caused a major stir in the capital community was the use of white paint to cover the original red brick of the exterior of the executive residence. When the first shock subsided, it was noted that the white provided a contrast for the pink granite pillars donated by the original residents, Governor and Mrs. B. Gratz Brown. Another major exterior project was the renewing of the five thousand square feet of Mansion roof.

Hebert Hare of Kansas City, a landscape architect, donated his services in the rearrangement of the Mansion grounds – a project which included the removal of the historic old summerhouse on the river bluff. A rose garden was planted on the level with the Mansion while a promenade and elaborate rock garden were arranged on the hillside. A retaining wall was built using rocks selected from a creek bed in Ralls County. One of the prisoners who helped in the project seemed to take particular care in his work, prompting the First Lady to stop and congratulate the man on his craftsmanship. He replied that "every man in his lifetime wants to do one masterpiece and this is mine."

At this time, the land repurchase project was completed as lots in the southwest quarter of the Mansion block were bought back from private owners. This was the reclamation effort started by Governor Park a few months before he left office. Arrangements also were completed for assistance in renovating the area by the Works Progress Administration – a rehabilitation program started by the federal government during the depression. A sunken garden was arranged and a shelter house, in pergola style, constructed along with terraces and walkways. Throughout the grounds some three thousand plantings, including mature trees forty and fifty feet high, were donated by the Governor and Mrs. Stark as reflections of their professional interest in horticulture. Sundials, benches and birdbaths were donated by garden clubs throughout the state. As the yard work was completed another relic of the past gave way to progress – the stables were removed from the Mansion yard where they had stood to shelter for many years the only means of transportation available for executive families.

One ominous sight on the newly beautified Mansion grounds was the presence of an armed guard protecting the Stark children. This reflected an intrusion of serious political matters into the life of the executive family. It was a time of upheaval in the state as attempts were undertaken to break the political machine which had controlled Kansas City for more than a decade with inroads into state politics. Letters were received threatening the lives of the Stark children and officers from the state highway patrol were called to the Mansion to provide constant surveillance for the girls. Mrs. Stark said the "children never knew what it was to run and play freely on the lawn or in their playhouse out back."

One other tragic intrusion on the Mansion grounds occurred on the night of a disastrous fire which destroyed the Madison House – a hotel favored by official state guests and the scene of many top-level political conferences. The Madison was located across the street south of the Mansion and predated the executive residence by only a few months. As the flames quickly consumed the building, a Mansion guard was rushed to the scene with ladders to help rescue guests from windows of upper floors. The Mansion yard was used to store all the equipment from the hotel beauty shop. Mrs. Stark observed that the hair dryers, et cetera, on the front lawn presented a rather ludicrous sight in the midst of all the tragedy.

With the massive renovation of the Mansion completed, Mrs. Stark turned her attention to a traditional project – sitting for her portrait which was to be a gift from the Governor's staff of honorary colonels. Charles F. Galt of St. Louis, who had painted other first ladies, was selected for the commission. Sittings proved strenuous since the Stark daughters were sick at the time and the First Lady constantly was called to their room. She remarked later that the artist achieved "remarkably serene results" under the circumstances. Mrs. Stark also noted that no portrait of Mrs. David R. Francis had been placed in the Mansion and she interested the Francis' children in the project. Mr. Galt painted a portrait from a photograph taken while the former First Lady was in the Mansion. The portraits of both Mrs. Stark and Mrs. Francis were presented in the same ceremony. Later, Henry Haskell of Kansas City, the second husband of Mrs. Agnes Hadley, employed Mr. Galt to paint a larger picture to replace a small one in the Mansion and the new portrait of Mrs. Haskell was dedicated at a second reception held by the Starks. Mr. Haskell, editor of *The Kansas City Star*, had been a close friend of both Governor and Mrs. Hadley and he and Mrs. Hadley were married in 1931, four years after the Governor's death.

The unveiling of Mrs. Stark's portrait was a reminder to the executive family of a very personal tragedy. The First Lady was expecting her third child at the time she was posing for the painting. The Starks' daughter, Susan Spotswood Stark, was born in a St. Louis hospital late in October, 1938, but lived only eleven days. This was the first baby born to a first family since Missouri's executives moved into the new Mansion in 1872.

As January of 1941 and a change of administrations approached, a period of major and vital rehabilitation of the Missouri Mansion ended. The executive residence had survived the first demands for its destruction. But these demands were to be renewed as the Mansion became the center of a national controversy within the next twenty years.

Chapter XIII

A century of legal precedents was shattered by a political dispute in 1941. Inaugural ceremonies were delayed more than a month while a controversy raged regarding elections returns. During early years of statehood, the regular inaugurals were held in November or December, but when Governor Sterling Price took the oath in 1853, the ceremony was held on January 3 – the first inaugural to occur in the year following the general elections. Then, the 1875 constitution set inaugurals for the second Monday in January. It was not a particularly advantageous time as dramatized by all too frequent storms of ice, sleet and/or snow, but it was the time set by law and the January date had been dutifully observed except during the Civil War. However, the legal requirements were disrupted by a political wrangle of unprecedented proportions which followed the general election in November, 1940. Democratic leaders were demanding a vote recount after the first returns showed their gubernatorial candidate had lost by a slim margin. Forty-four days were consumed before any settlement was reached and a new governor was admitted to the capitol and a new first lady to the Mansion.

It was the last Wednesday in February, 1941 that the inaugural was held and Forrest C. Donnell, a Republican, assumed Missouri's executive office and Hilda Hays Donnell became the new state hostess. Although the new First Lady consistently had remained aloof from politics, she had been an active observer of the prolonged election contest, particularly the arguments before the state supreme court. Mrs. Donnell never seemed to doubt that her husband's election would be affirmed. She had packed at least one bag shortly before the original inaugural date in January had been cancelled. This long-packed suitcase was among the trunks and boxes which filled the back seat of their car on inaugural eve, February 25, 1941, as the Donnells drove to Jefferson City with two highway patrol cars acting as escorts and their son, John Lanier Donnell, acting as chauffeur.

Governor Stark, who had not supported the election contest of his own party, and Mrs. Stark had remained in residence during the delay and were on hand to welcome the new first family to the Mansion. Preliminary inaugural festivities opened Tuesday night with a dinner at the Jefferson City Country Club given by friends of the Donnells. The two official families breakfasted together in the Mansion prior to the start of the parade on inaugural day held in traditional bitter cold and snow. Shortly after the inaugural service, the Starks left for their home in Louisiana where they lived until 1946 when they bought a stock farm of some one thousand acres near Eolia, Missouri. In 1969, they still were living on "Aberdeen Farms" in a brick house which was more than one hundred years old.

A significant part of the oath-taking ceremony for Governor Donnell was the use of two Bibles, one held by his father, John Cary Donnell of Kansas City, and one by his son, John, a law student at Washington University in St. Louis. Both books were bound in white and were the childhood Bibles of the Donnells. Although the Bibles were identical, they obviously were presented in separate ceremonies since Governor Donnell grew up in northwest Missouri and Mrs. Donnell spent her childhood in Lancaster in northeast Missouri. The First Lady's parents, Mr. and Mrs. Frank P. Hays, moved to St. Louis when she was twelve and she attended private schools in St. Louis and Baltimore, Maryland. She and Governor Donnell met after she had traveled following her schooling and then returned to St. Louis to help her mother with younger members of the large Hays family. The Donnells were married on January 29, 1913 in a ceremony in the Hays home. Mrs. Donnell still had her wedding dress packed away in her St. Louis County home twenty-seven years later when her husband made his first bid for statewide office – the race for governor. Mrs. Donnell had remained out of the "public eye" by choice, but she traveled with the Governor during the campaign and occasionally attended the special schools conducted by party leaders for women voters.

Inaugural day for the Donnells followed the schedule by then considered traditional – military reception in the Mansion, state reception in the capitol and the grand march down the circular staircase from the second floor to the capitol rotunda opening the formal inaugural ball. After the transfer of the keys, Mrs. Donnell faced the awesome task of presiding over the imposing executive Mansion. Fortunately, the veteran staff member, Barbara Pohlman, remained as the housekeeper to help Mrs. Donnell adjust to her new home and her new role. Secretarial duties were assumed by Miss Virginia Henwood, a long-time resident of Jefferson City who was well-acquainted with many residents of the city, both those of the general public and members of leading political families. She helped Mrs. Donnell with the customary social schedule which included dinners for state officials and legislators and teas for women of the city. Mrs. Donnell set Tuesday for weekly "at homes," or informal calling hours when city women and legislative wives came to the Mansion without special invitation to meet the resident First Lady.

Photo by Herb Weitman, Courtesy Gov. and Mrs. Forrest C. Donnell

Hilda Donnell, a copy of her portrait in Mansion

Although Mrs. Donnell adhered to the anticipated social calendar, she broke with custom in her personal habits. Much to the surprise of Jefferson City merchants, Mrs. Donnell went personally to the markets to shop for her groceries. A story recounted by a newspaper writer told how Mrs. Donnell, shortly after the inaugural, entered a downtown market and looked over the stock of groceries and meats while she waited for a clerk. When she had made her purchases, the clerk asked about the address for delivery. She, without pause, said the bundles were to be sent to her home, the executive Mansion. The flustered clerk, realizing he had been waiting on the Governor's wife, was informed by Mrs. Donnell that she hoped on her next trip to the market she wouldn't be waited on out of turn or given any other special attention.

This marketing incident firmly established the new First Lady in her favored role of a quiet, unassuming housewife – even though her home address had been changed from Webster Groves in St. Louis County to the state's executive Mansion in Jefferson City. Her interests were her home and her garden and she presided over both with great simplicity. She made it plain, when asked, that politics was her husband's business; her business was to welcome all who came to her door – regardless of their party affiliations. As evidence of this attitude, Mrs. Donnell had made personal appeals to St. Louis newspapers asking that stories be published explaining that "everybody is welcome to the inaugural." She was afraid someone might hesitate to attend without an invitation.

One of the first distinguished visitors to stay with the Donnells overnight in the Mansion was Mrs. Ruth Bryan Owen Rohde who was on tour to describe her experiences as United States minister to Denmark. She was the first woman ever appointed as head of a United States diplomatic post. It was not Mrs. Rohde's first visit to Missouri's executive residence although she hardly could remember an earlier trip in the 1890s with her parents, Mr. and Mrs. William Jennings Bryan. It was on that occasion that the very young girl disrupted a reception planned for her parents by Governor and Mrs. Lon Vest Stephens. It seems Ruth wanted to attend the party and her mother had to delay joining the receiving line until members of the staff were sent upstairs to distract the willful child.

On December 7, 1941, one month after Mrs. Rohde's visit and ten months after Governor Donnell took office, social plans as well as state functions had to be abruptly curtailed. The Japanese had bombed Pearl Harbor and the United States was plunged into the second World War. Governor and Mrs. Donnell immediately sent out notices cancelling the customary open house at the Mansion on New Year's Day, "due to the fact that our country is at War." The annual state fair at Sedalia eventually was cancelled. The nation went on "war time," later known as daylight saving time, and the lights on the capitol dome were extinguished for the duration. Five German cannon, relics of World War I which were displayed on the capitol grounds, were sold by the state as contributions to the drive for scrap metal.

Rationing of sugar, tires, meat and gasoline were imposed on all families. Trips to the capital city and the Mansion by business and social groups throughout the state had to be sharply reduced as a result of the travel restrictions. Governor Donnell appealed to all Missourians to observe a voluntary speed limit of thirty-five miles an hour to conserve rubber and, on at least one occasion, he rearranged a trip to Kansas City using the state car and went by train instead.

As her social schedule was restricted, Mrs. Donnell opened the Mansion to assist several wartime activities. In January, 1942, some six hundred Cole County women were invited to the executive residence for an explanation of Red Cross activities and modeling of uniforms worn by volunteers. A majority of the women signed up for duty. Even before the United States actively entered the hostilities, the Donnells had shared their first Thanksgiving in the Mansion with two servicemen from Fort Leonard Wood, a major army installation located south of the capital near Waynesville. One of the soldiers, Howard C. Hartwig of Grosse Point, Michigan, was spending his first Thanksgiving away from his family and he said later, "It was the nearest thing to a big dinner at home that I can think of." The Donnells also invited four soldiers to stay at the Mansion during wartime Christmases when several hundred soldiers were guests of the city.

One outstanding event of the Donnells' term resulted directly from the war. The Grand Duchess Charlotte of Luxembourg had been forced into exile by German invaders and had moved her family to Quebec. In 1943, a tour of the United States by the Grand Duchess was planned by the United States State Department and she was scheduled to arrive in St. Louis on April 4. The next day the Duchess and her party were entertained by Governor and Mrs. Donnell at a dinner at the Chase Hotel. Also as a part of her schedule, the Duchess, accompanied by St. Louis Mayor and Mrs. William Dee Becker and Mrs. Donnell, toured the zoo and other attractions in Forest Park. She was greeted at the zoo entrance by a Great Kudu antelope, dressed for the royal visitor in a white vest, straw hat, dark trousers and a bow tie.

On May 3, 1943, the Donnells relaxed their restricted social activities for the occasion of the unveiling of the First Lady's portrait. Mrs. Donnell's portrait had been painted by the same artist favored by many executive wives, Charles F. Galt of St. Louis. He portrayed Mrs. Donnell in her inaugural gown of shell pink brocade which had a silver lame trim. The gown was fashioned with a full skirt, puffed sleeves and a sweetheart neckline. The previous summer, former Governor and Mrs. Arthur M. Hyde had been luncheon guests of the Donnells and brought with them to the Mansion a portrait of Mrs. Hyde painted by Mr. Galt. This project had been interrupted in the 1920s when Mrs. Hyde was residing in the Mansion. She explained that the artist selected at that time died suddenly before he could start the portrait and later Mrs. Hyde was unable to pose because of injuries received in an automobile accident. So the project was suspended for some twenty years – a delay Mrs. Hyde thought later was not in the best interests of a first lady hoping to appear as young as possible.

Food restrictions presented problems to all housewives during World War II and Mrs. Donnell was no exception. It was recalled how the capital city experienced a turkey shortage in 1943 and when Mrs. Donnell went shopping for her holiday dinner the scarcity of the traditional bird caused the butcher to "shake his head sidewise." Mrs. Donnell replied in her customary unassuming manner: "So, we'll have chicken." The less-traditional bird was shared by the Donnells' son, John, who had graduated from law school in February, 1943 and had started his own law practice in St. Louis. Visits with their children were one pleasurable activity that the first family still could pursue during the war years. And two most memorable occasions were the christening of their grandchildren, Elizabeth Donnell Rogers in March, 1942, and Richard Donnell Rogers in November, 1944. Both ceremonies were held in the Gold Room of the Mansion for the children of the Donnells' daughter, Ruth, who lived in St. Louis.

Another religious ceremony held in the Gold Room during the Donnells' term was a wedding involving two young friends of the executive family. On September 18, 1943, Miss Rosemary Booth of Kirksville was married to Karl William Dahlem. She worked as a secretary in state selective service headquarters in Jefferson City and Mr. Dahlem was secretary to Governor Donnell. The wedding was held at four p.m. with the service performed by the Reverend William A. Dahlem of Dalton, Missouri, father of the groom. The bride wore her mother's wedding dress of white mull and lace fashioned with a high collar and leg-o-mutton sleeves. A reception for some one hundred guests was held in the dining room following the ceremony.

On September 21, 1943, a state constitutional convention opened sessions and the increased activity at the capitol enabled Mrs. Donnell to schedule open houses and receptions to welcome the convention members and wives. The "con coners" worked exactly one year and, before adjournment, set February 27, 1945 as the date for submission of the new constitution proposed to replace the one written in 1875. The special election, which favored the new document, did not occur until after the Donnells had completed their service in Jefferson City and a new governor and first lady were installed in office.

The gubernatorial inaugural in January, 1945 marked a decade of name similarities in the governor's residence – first the Parks, followed by the Starks and then Phil M. Donnelly of Lebanon succeeded Governor Donnell. It was the first time in history that the difference of only one letter represented a change of personnel in the executive Mansion. It also was the first time a war had outlasted one entire gubernatorial administration.

The prolonged conflict in Europe and in the Pacific continued to drain from civilian life such things as cigarettes and gasoline, meat and sugar, and clothing, particularly less essential items as elaborate ball gowns and accessories usually selected by a first lady preparing for inaugural ceremonies. As a result, Missouri's new hostess in 1945, Juanita McFadden Donnelly, had purchased sufficient yardage of satin in a color variously described as aqua or April green and a friend made the satin into an evening dress and matching bag. Mrs.

Donnelly did her own work sewing on pearl beads to trim the gown.

This sewing project was reflective not only of wartime shortages but also of Mrs. Donnelly's conservative tastes. Missouri's new First Lady was devoted to her family and to the consuming hobby of flower gardening – both interests in which her personal handwork was essential. Mrs. Donnelly was born in Paducah, Kentucky and moved to Missouri where her father entered the clothing business. She and Governor Donnelly attended high school together in Lebanon, but her family had moved to Maplewood by the time they were married on May 22, 1915. The couple immediately established a home in Lebanon and Governor

Juanita Donnelly, a copy of her portrait in Mansion

Courtesy Mrs. Phil M. Donnelly

Donnelly started a political career in city and county offices followed by twenty-two years in the state General Assembly.

Juanita Donnelly had visited the capital city and the Missouri executive residence many times as a legislator's wife and had stayed overnight in the Mansion as a guest of the Starks. But viewing the executive Mansion as a visitor is far different from entering it as the future hostess. To help as much as possible, the Donnells invited the Donnellys as their guests in the Mansion on two different occasions between the general election and the inaugural. On the second visit, staff members were called in for introductions and each promised to remain in his position. In later reflection, Mrs. Donnelly said she often wondered "what a governor's wife would do without a Barbara (Pohlman, the housekeeper) to tell her so many things about the house and the customs of the Mansion." Also remaining was the veteran chauffeur, Arthur Hardiman.

A third and final visit was on inaugural eve when the Governor-elect and incoming First Lady, and their son, David, and two Donnelly nieces, Miss Ann Donnelly and Mrs. J. D. Butts, were guests for a family dinner and an overnight stay prior to the next day's activities. Again wartime pallor was in evidence. The glitter of the traditional uniforms of the honorary colonels was missing from the festivities. Governor Donnelly had decreed that his colonels would wear only special arm bands to designate their position. As soon as the ceremonies were concluded at the capitol, Governor and Mrs. Donnell left Jefferson City to prepare for a move to Washington where he was to serve six years as United States Senator from Missouri. At the conclusion of his term in Washington, the Governor returned to his law office in St. Louis, and, in 1969, he and Mrs. Donnell still were living in St. Louis and he still maintained his practice there.

On Wednesday, January 9, 1945 – the day after Governor Donnelly's inaugural – Mrs. Donnelly's plans for acquainting herself with her new home and position were shattered when news arrived that her mother had fallen only hours after her return home from Jefferson City. She had broken her hip and was taken to a hospital in Springfield, Missouri where she died within five days. Two years later, Mrs. Donnelly's father died after a similar accident. He had broken his hip while visiting his daughter and Governor Donnelly in the Mansion and lived only ten weeks.

First ladies through the years had agreed that the daily arrival of fresh flowers sent to the Mansion compensated partly for the many disadvantages of life in the state executive residence. Mrs. Donnelly, with her interest in gardening, found particular pleasure in the flowers sent from hothouses at two prison farms located near the capital city. One of the disadvantages of Mansion life which Mrs. Donnelly encountered very early during her residence was the number of abusive telephone calls received by a first family. Mrs. Donnelly said the first such call she received came from a young woman who refused to identify herself until Mrs. Donnelly came to the telephone. The caller then asked the First Lady if she were going to open the state residence to soldiers and their wives who wanted to live in the Mansion. When Mrs. Donnelly tried to explain that such a request was impossible, the caller became insulting. "After that I did not answer the telephone until I knew who was calling."

Other difficulties resulted from the perpetual conflict over use of the Mansion as a home and as a public building. Mrs. Donnelly soon found chains were necessary on all outside doors. "Otherwise people would just open the doors and walk in and the governor and his family would never have any privacy." As had many of her predecessors, Mrs. Donnelly formulated rules for visits and tours. She decided the Mansion would not be shown to children under high-school age and tours were limited to thirty-five persons. Guiding of tour groups was handled by Mrs. Helen Ruthven Fogle who was employed by Mrs. Donnelly as her personal secretary. Also a part of the rules was the restriction that visitors were admitted only on appointment made by telephone or letter. There still were problems. On one occasion, Mrs. Donnelly had made arrangements to entertain about two hundred members of a church group – one thousand responded to the invitation.

Frailties and vagaries of Mansion personnel also led to problems. An afternoon luncheon was an outstanding example. A new houseboy was to serve for the first time as a replacement for a more experienced prisoner who had been paroled. Mrs. Donnelly spent hours coaching him. But he became confused by the crowd and carried out all his instructions exactly in reverse. Distracted by this problem, it took Mrs. Donnelly a little longer to realize that the menu was not as planned. A check of the kitchen disclosed that the regular cook, who suffered from high blood pressure, had become sick and gone to bed. A cateress, hired to assist in the Mansion for the first time, had been left alone in a completely unfamiliar kitchen. "I will never know what my guests thought because I did not mention the troubles to anyone," Mrs. Donnelly recalled.

Another cook employed very early in Mrs. Donnelly's term presented a far different problem. It soon became apparent that her "sick spells" were self-inflicted. Mrs. Donnelly remembered the climaxing event:

> "One evening my husband came home from the office, I was out of town, and when he entered the house from the back basement door he did not see anyone. No one seemed to be on duty. He sat down in the nook by the stairway to read his paper. Hearing a peculiar noise, he got up to investigate but didn't find the cause.
>
> "In a little while he again heard the noise and this time he found the origin. In the dining room on the floor before one of the fireplaces lay the fat cook sound asleep and snoring."

It seemed the cook had spent the afternoon in a Jefferson City tavern. After several such escapades, the county sheriff called the Mansion and informed Governor Donnelly that the cook was in jail. "The Governor told him to keep her there," Mrs. Donnelly said. The search for a new cook was prolonged since most available employees were involved in war work. As a temporary solution, Barbara Pohlman took over in the kitchen until a cook from Springfield, Missouri, Catherine Dean, was hired and stayed through the remainder of Governor Donnelly's term. Of course, even an experienced caterer was hampered by the wartime rationing. The first family had no more food stamps than any other family and a good deal of skimping on personal meals was necessary before enough meat could be purchased for a state dinner.

Despite the shortage of preferred refreshments, the final months of World War II did include one memorable occasion at the Mansion. In February, 1945, Democratic women attending a meeting in the capital were invited to the Mansion for an afternoon reception. On hand to greet the guests was the Vice-President of the United States, Harry S. Truman. Several of the women consulted with Mrs. Donnelly about the proper way to address their fellow-Missourian. It was agreed to ask him. His reply was typical of the state's famous son. He laughed and said, "Just call me Harry."

As peace started to return in the spring of 1945, Missouri's first family was involved in ceremonies to honor military heroes of the United States and Europe. In June, the Donnellys went to Moberly to attend that city's celebration honoring its native son, General Omar Bradley who earlier had received Missouri's meritorious service medal. On June 21, 1945, the Donnellys were in Kansas City to greet General Dwight D. Eisenhower on his return from Europe. Mrs. Donnelly later recalled the occasion with pleasure mixed with chagrin. On the way to Kansas City, the Governor and Mrs. Donnelly had scheduled an appearance at the state college in Warrensburg. That stop combined with rain made them late and as they came to the outskirts of Kansas City a patrol car was waiting. The officers told the Governor it would be necessary for them to escort the state limousine with their siren sounding if the Donnellys were to make it to the airport on time. The Governor had never permitted a siren to be used in escorting him, but he consented this time. Mrs. Donnelly said their route was along the exact path marked for the General's motorcade and crowds already had gathered. "So, here we came, dashing through the streets in a mud-splashed car, escorted by the patrol with sirens wide open." Mrs. Donnelly said she was extremely embarrassed by the attention they attracted. However, they arrived just as the Eisenhower plane was landing.

A year later, on March 5, 1946, Missouri was the scene of a speech by Sir Winston Churchill that was to be long-remembered for its historical reference to the Iron Curtain which had descended between the free people and Communist

Courtesy Mrs. Phil M. Donnelly

Winston Churchill at a reception in Fulton following his speech at Westminster College. Others in picture, left to right, Governor Phil M. Donnelly, President Harry S. Truman and Dr. Franc L. McCluer, president of Westminster

countries. Mr. Churchill's route took him in a motorcade through the streets of Jefferson City, but he was unable to visit the Mansion. Mrs. Donnelly met the famous English statesman at a reception in Fulton following his speech at Westminster College.

Peacetime activities generally had been resumed by the time of Mr. Churchill's visit. Mrs. Donnelly was able to reopen a normal social calendar including informal open house on Tuesday and more formal dinners for state officials, legislators and newspaper reporters. The traditional Mansion open house on New Year's Day was rescheduled. In April, 1946, the Sophomore Pilgrimage sponsored by the state Federation of Women's Clubs was resumed. This annual event, started before the war, included a visit to the Mansion of outstanding students chosen from high schools throughout the state. Another school-associated event was the Sketch Day held in May for capital city students. The students involved would start an original sketch or painting early in the morning and submit their work for judging a few hours later. At the conclusion of the day, the sketches were hung on the iron fence surrounding the Mansion grounds with the winning citations attached for public viewing.

A first lady's concern extends to all events that touch her state home and her husband's administration, but each hostess of the Mansion has more intimate plans and projects that she undertakes. A perpetual concern through the years was the necessary repairs and maintenance work on the Mansion and grounds. Building materials still were in short supply as the nation's industries regeared to peacetime projects, but Mrs. Donnelly was able to do some work. The outside of the Mansion was repainted and kitchen appliances, including a new food freezer, were purchased. A window was enlarged into a doorway from the pantry and a stairway built to the driveway to provide an outside exit, other than passage through the basement. The center north bedroom on the second floor was rearranged to provide, for the first time, an upstairs sitting room for the first family.

A mystery which had plagued first ladies for years was solved when Mrs. Donnelly decided to renovate the dining room. The tapestry placed on the walls by Mrs. Folk following the fire in October, 1905 was removed. It was found that the paste attaching it to the walls was a breeding place for moths. The tapestry, which Mrs. Folk thought would last forever, was replaced with scenic wallpaper and new paneling was added to the lower half of the walls.

Another very personal project which had become traditional was the portrait painting sponsored by the honorary colonels of each governor. John B. Bohrer of California, a native of St. Louis, was engaged and painted Mrs. Donnelly in her satin inaugural gown. The portrait was unveiled at the Mansion on December 15, 1946 at a reception and tour for the colonels and their wives.

As her portrait was added, Mrs. Donnelly became aware that the Mansion walls were without pictures of many of the early governors' wives. She corresponded with Mrs. Park, co-author of *Women of the Mansion,* and it was decided to reproduce photographs from pictures cut from a copy of the book. Frames were made at the penitentiary and the likenesses of fifteen of the state's earliest hostesses were hung in the nook under the grand stairway.

A project very much in keeping with Mrs. Donnelly's interest in gardening was the renewing and completion of the park area between the Mansion and the capitol. The Starks had had plans drawn for the sunken garden and shelter house, but the site work had never been finished. Newer residents and visitors, puzzling over the site, referred to the area as the "What's It?" A veteran newspaperman, Boyd Carroll, referred to the area as a "formal entrance to a wall." Original blueprints were found and new plans were drawn with the help of

J. B. Jeans, an engineer with the state highway department. An appropriation of $15,000.00 was passed by the legislature after some personal lobbying by members of the Hawthorn Garden Club of the capital city. Efforts to keep ornamental fish in the small pool failed and Mrs. Donnelly settled on the addition of water lilies.

As the work neared completion, a movement was started to name the park for Mrs. Donnelly but she rejected the idea. A newspaper reporter commented: "Whether or not the small restful spot in the center of the city is ever given a name, Juanita Donnelly has left there the quiet reflection of a serene and gentle personality." During the final year of the Donnellys' term, "Freedom Week" was celebrated and more than one thousand persons from twenty states and Germany attended open houses at the Mansion. Mrs. Donnelly planted a "Liberty Tree," donated by War Mothers, in the Mansion park. She placed a flag

Grand stairway in Mansion showing nook and pictures of early First Ladies added by Mrs. Donnelly *Gerald Massie*

beside the tree with "a prayer in my heart that the bells of freedom that ring today will echo on throughout the ages."

But the prayer for peace was not to last through the administration of a new first family of Missouri elected in November, 1948 – Forrest and Mildred Williams Smith. It was the final occurrence of sequential name similarities in the executive office with the Governor-elect having the same first name as Governor Donnell.

It was an occasion for a dual celebration in January, 1949. Native daughters of Missouri were to take office as first ladies of the state and of the nation – Mrs. Smith in Jefferson City and Mrs. Harry S. Truman in Washington. The Missouri ceremony was set for Monday, January 10. The traditional "change" dinner was held in the Mansion Sunday night as the outgoing executive family, Governor and Mrs. Donnelly and their son, David, entertained the incoming family. Also present were the Smiths' two daughters, Forrestine and Mary Joe, and their husbands, Arthur Lynn Jr. and Frank Teterus.

An ice storm hit the state inaugural day disrupting communication and transportation. Many areas were without electricity for several days. The Donnellys were driven to their home in Lebanon immediately after the formal administration of the oath to the new Governor at noon and, thus, were able to complete the trip before highways became impassable. Governor and Mrs. Donnelly were to remain in Lebanon where the Governor reopened his law practice during the four years of the Smith administration.

Most of the inaugural crowds already were in the capital city ahead of the ice storm and most managed to negotiate the slippery hills and streets to witness the parade honoring Governor and Mrs. Smith. The honorary colonels, for the first time since 1941, were in full uniform which included not only the suit and hat but a cape lined in red. Mrs. Smith appeared at the grand march to open the inaugural ball in a floor-length white crepe gown designed by Howard Greer, a New York couturier. The straight lines of the dress were accented by horizontal bands of silver bugle beads in a braided design which circled the dress at three-inch intervals from the shoulders to the hem. Two executive grandchildren, eighteen-month-old Jody Lynn and fifteen-month-old Frankie Teterus, also had worn all-white when they held a white Bible for the new Governor earlier in the day.

Highways still were blocked with ice the next day and some fifteen close relatives remained an extra twenty-four hours as the Smiths' first house guests. The prolonged entertainment of guests shortened the time available for Mrs. Smith to start plans for traditional state dinners before she left for Washington. A few days after the state inaugural she and the Governor joined some five hundred fellow-Missourians for a trip to the presidential inaugural. The state delegation traveled in a special train of thirty-five cars.

Underwood & Underwood, Washington. Courtesy Mrs. Forrest Smith

Mildred Smith in her inaugural gown

It was the first time a native of the state had reached the White House and the Missourians made the most of the occasion. On inaugural eve, Governor and Mrs. Smith were hosts to President and Mrs. Truman and their daughter, Margaret, at a buffet dinner in the Shoreham Hotel. As a Washington newspaper columnist described the affair, "It was a bang-up party those Missourians gave for their favorite son." Some seventeen hundred guests attended, including the President's buddies from World War I – members of Battery D, 129th Field Artillery, 35th Division. Food was served from twenty-two tables and included glazed chickens, hams, fish, a stuffed pig, whole turkeys, curried shrimp and gelatin molds and cold vegetables of every variety. The dinner was held on January 19, preceding the presidential inaugural on January 20.

Most of the Missouri party returned on January 22 but the Smiths remained two extra days in Washington to rest for a busy state schedule which they faced at home. Because of this delay, a story was circulated that Mrs. Smith was sick. The wording in one newspaper headline made it appear that her illness was serious. As a result, the new Governor and First Lady were greeted by a very startled staff when they returned to the Missouri Mansion, both well-rested and in good spirits.

Within a week after the Washington trip, Mrs. Smith launched her social schedule with a formal dinner for elected state officials and their wives. It was not the first such state dinner for Mrs. Smith; she had been a guest at many official functions in the Mansion during the sixteen years while Governor Smith served four consecutive terms as state auditor. The Smiths actually had lived more years of their married life in Jefferson City than they had in their home town, Richmond, Missouri. They had met in Richmond while Forrest Smith was principal and the then Mildred Williams, daughter of Mr. and Mrs. Edwin Ridgeway Williams, was teaching at an elementary school following graduation from the state college at Warrensburg, Missouri. "It was a case of the principal carrying the teacher's books home," she recalled.They were married in Richmond on October 12, 1915. Both their daughters were born in Richmond before the Smiths moved to the state capital.

Governor Smith was quite gregarious and his petite wife, who had dark hair and sparkling eyes, was equally enamored with the guests who shared their life in the executive residence – either briefly to attend a tea or open house or for a dinner or overnight stay. Dignitaries from within the state invited to the Mansion included the British consul in St. Louis and the Belgian consul in Kansas City. Out-of-state notables who visited the Smiths were Vice-President Alben Barkley and governors of several states. Mrs. Smith recalled that there were few meals that "we didn't have company at our table." As many as one thousand visitors attended one of the New Year's open houses held by the Smiths.

A major part of their new life in the Mansion was shared by the Smiths with their daughters and five grandchildren, three of whom were born during the Smiths' administration. The daughters visited for all major holidays and took key roles in all major state functions, starting with the grandchildren's participation in the swearing-in ceremony. Antics of the grandchildren provided the Governor with many items for his newspaper column which he sent out weekly to rural newspapers in the state.

A granddaughter played an unexpectedly important part in the unveiling of Mrs. Smith's official portrait. The picture had been completed by the artist,

Charles F. Galt, in mid-December of the Smiths' first year in office. The painting showed Mrs. Smith in a melon-colored crepe formal, selected instead of her inaugural dress to provide a contrast to the pastel shades worn for portraits by many other first ladies. A group of some 125 honorary colonels and their wives had gathered at the Mansion for the unveiling on December 11, 1949. Forrestine, the Smiths' older daughter, was selected to remove the tapestry covering the painting. When the cord was pulled for the unveiling, the heavy cloth fell across two-year-old Jody, completely covering her. There was a hushed silence as the guests waited for the anticipated childish wail. Instead, Jody emerged from the covering with a broad smile, completely captivated by the unexpected game of "Hide and Seek" which she played so often with her grandfather.

All the grandchildren and their parents joined the Smiths for their first Christmas in the Mansion. Stockings were hung from the fireplace in the Gold Room for the two-year-olds, Jody Lynn and Frank Teterus, and the newest grandchild, nine-month-old Forrest Smith Teterus, nicknamed "Little Guv." As they rushed down the grand stairway Christmas morning, the older children were urged to "run and get what you want most." They both grabbed simultaneously a black and white plush panda that had been placed under the tree for Little Guv. The next hours proved distressing until two more pandas could be purchased when stores opened the next day.

Disaster was narrowly averted during another visit by two grandsons. The boys' mother, Mary Joe Teterus, was helping the First Lady with an afternoon reception on the first floor while the youngsters supposedly napped upstairs. As the last guest departed, Mary Joe found Frankie standing in the wash basin of the main bathroom on the second floor holding a near-empty bottle of orange-flavored aspirin. Fortunately, he had not consumed a harmful overdose because he had saved most of the "candy" for his little brother. Two other granddaughters, Elizabeth Louise Lynn and Mildred Anna Teterus, were born while the Smiths were in office and three of the grandchildren were baptized at a special ceremony in the Gold Room.

In June, 1950, during Governor Smith's second year in office, the United States became involved in another war. This conflict was in Korea. It did not result in such a total national effort as previous world wars and the first family was not limited by rationing or other wartime restrictions imposed on their predecessors in the Mansion – the Donnells and Donnellys. The only related project was a campaign by Mrs. Smith to raise funds for a memorial fountain at the New York headquarters of the United Nations, the international organization whose member nations had joined in the Korean conflict. The fountain, costing $75,000.00, was to be financed entirely by pennies, nickels and dimes donated by schoolchildren in the United States and its territories. Mrs. Smith was the state chairman and her campaign exceeded the goal of $3,000.00 set for Missouri.

Interwoven with the official demands made on her as the state's hostess, Mrs. Smith found time to pursue personal interests, such as music, needlework and flowers. Her musical talents had been advanced during her studies at Illinois Women's College, later McMurray College, and at a Kansas City conservatory. This training made her an especially appreciative guest when in March, 1950, she and the Governor made a trip to Kansas City to hear Margaret Truman sing. The President's daughter was touring the nation at the time and, as expected, an overflow crowd turned out for her Kansas City concert.

Needlework for the First Lady included a full range of projects, sewing, quilting and knitting. She planned her dresses and colors of her quilts "as carefully as any painter plans the colors of his canvases." One knitting project resulted in a memorable occasion at the Mansion when Mrs. Smith received a visit from a Fort Leonard Wood soldier. He had lost his eyesight and one leg during a training accident at Fort Wood. The young corporal, whose home was in Tuscon, Arizona, called on Mrs. Smith to thank her for the afghan she had knitted. It had been presented to him at the post hospital by Mrs. John A. Harris, wife of the Missouri adjutant general.

One of Mrs. Smith's major efforts in flower gardening was decidedly less successful than her knitting project. Governor Smith shared his wife's enthusiasm for flowers and made frequent public mention of the progress of flowers and trees that bloomed in the Mansion yard through the changing seasons, including redbud, jonquils, tulips and, finally, Mrs. Smith's favorites, the rose-colored zinnias. The Governor was particularly pleased when Mrs. Smith planned a new flower area for the south lawn facing a major hotel across the street. In the fall of 1950, Mrs. Smith bought one thousand crocus bulbs and had them planted in an M shape. The next spring only a handful bloomed. Mrs. Smith found that most of the bulbs had been planted too deeply by members of the detail of prison inmates assigned to yardwork. The Governor had to make a full explanation in his newspaper column to satisfy the many disappointed visitors who came to view the M-shaped garden the next spring.

On Sunday, August 18, 1951, a wedding was held in the Mansion. The bride, Alicia Sue Williams of Richmond, was the niece of Mrs. Smith. The ceremony in the state residence was proposed since the girl's parents had died in recent months. The wedding was at high noon with Governor Smith escorting the bride down the grand stairway. She wore a waltz-length gown of pale blue satin with overskirts of tulle. Assisting were the bride's little cousins, Frankie Teterus as ringbearer and Jody Lynn as flower girl. After a reception and dinner, the couple left for Ottumwa, Iowa, where the groom, Joseph Dennis Hayes, was a high-school teacher.

Many of Missouri's governors through the years have helped shape life in the Mansion as a reflection of their own interests and personalities. Governor Smith was the instigator of several social affairs at the Mansion, such as parties for special Ray County friends. On one occasion, he played special host to three unexpected dinner guests. Some seventy legislators had been invited to the Mansion and were served a turkey dinner. Just as the legislators were leaving three salesmen arrived at the front door. They had been "overserved" at a capital city bar and they mistook the Mansion for their hotel. The doorman thought they were legislators arriving late and admitted them to the front hall where Governor Smith took over. He served them some turkey and sent them on their way after a goodnatured visit lasting about forty-five minutes.

Governor Smith also made personal contributions to holiday menus at the Mansion. Each winter he took time for a goose-hunting trip. After one particularly successful hunt, his contribution helped round out an "all states" Christmas dinner which made use of gifts from governors of several other states. The menu included soup from Maine, a salad of oranges and grapefruit from Texas, white potatoes from Idaho, sweet potatoes from Louisiana, celery from Colorado and geese donated by the Missouri Governor. That same year the Mansion had a special Christmas tree sent by the governor of Virginia. It was cut from Jamestown Island, the site credited as the first permanent English settlement in the United States.

Very much by accident Governor Smith played a part in stepping up the tempo of repair work at the Mansion. Early in her administration, Mrs. Smith had rearranged the room designed as a library on the first floor. By adding some antique furniture, Mrs. Smith converted the area into a small living room, much less formal than the Gold Room across the hall. The front porch received a new tile floor, a copper roof and wrought-iron balustrades to replace the older railing. Further work was being planned when the schedule was disrupted by an accident in the dining room. Governor Smith was drinking milk at the exact moment his chair broke. Picking himself up from the floor, the Governor commented that he thought his "diet was going well until this happened." Thus, funds to repair dining room chairs had to be worked into the maintenance budget.

Additions made to the Mansion by Mrs. Smith included the first automatic dishwasher available to help with the tremendous cleanup chores in the kitchen. Steam lines were built to carry heat to the Mansion from the new fourteen-floor state office building constructed across the street from the executive residence. A painting contract was awarded for the outside of the Mansion and records show one hundred gallons of paint were required to cover the huge building. An attempt was made to remove the old paint layers by sandblasting as had been done to clean the capitol. That part of the work was stopped when it was found the blasting was harmful to the soft bricks which were by then eighty years old.

A final project was the redecorating of the third floor – an area which had lost its popularity as the scene of dancing and lavish entertainments.

With the completion of the third floor work, Governor Smith and the First Lady turned their concern toward a home for the future. On December 3, 1952, the Governor announced he had purchased a house in the southeastern section of the capital city, in the neighborhood where he and Mrs. Smith had lived so many years while he was state auditor. The Governor said their new home fulfilled Mrs. Smith's requirements – a bedroom and bath on the first floor and located on a side street away from traffic hazardous to grandchildren.

Very early in that final year, 1952, Governor Smith had effectively squelched reports that he might be a candidate for the United States Senate. The First Lady played a major part in that decision, continuing the role of her predecessors who injected their desires to guard the health of their husbands and the welfare of their children. In his official news release, Governor Smith said, "Mrs. Smith and our two daughters have strongly opposed any thought of my becoming a candidate for any office . . . My family believes that after a quarter of a century . . . as a public official . . . I am entitled to a little vacation." Ten years after he issued that statement, Governor Smith died following a heart attack. He had been active in civic causes and in planning for a new commercial television station in the capital city. Mrs. Smith continued to live in Jefferson City following the Governor's death.

An unprecedented inaugural-eve dinner was held in January, 1953. The same principals were involved as had gathered prior to the inaugural four years earlier. The only difference was the changed places of hosts and guests. As the Smiths retired from the Mansion, Governor and Mrs. Phil M. Donnelly returned. It was the first time in the history of Missouri that a governor had been elected to a second four-year term. Governor John Miller had served seven consecutive years very early in the state's history and was the first executive to occupy the first capitol in Jefferson City. But he was a bachelor and thus to Juanita Donnelly went the distinction of being the first state hostess to fulfill the position of first lady during more than one four-year term.

The crowds turned out in great numbers for the historic inaugural, but the First Lady observed the festivities with reservations. Governor Donnelly had resumed a successful law practice in Lebanon after his first term and Mrs. Donnelly had opposed a second campaign. She felt the demands of the state office were too taxing on the health of an executive. Mrs. Donnelly said her doubts had to give way before the many appeals for her husband's return. Thus, it was with conflicting emotions that she again took part in the traditional inaugural receptions and grand inaugural ball. For her second grand march, Mrs. Donnelly selected a gown from Neiman-Marcus, a renowned fashion store in Dallas, Texas. The sleeveless dress was a soft shade of blue silk faille with a low neckline. Two loose panels floated from the waist in the back while a panel on the front of the skirt was overlaid with matching blue lace.

For Mrs. Donnelly there were no reservations about her ability to fulfill her obligations as official hostess in the Mansion. She knew the social traditions; she was familiar with every nook of the state residence. It was a refreshing renewal of enjoyment of the Mansion gardens and her favorite bower, the little park in the corner. She planned with ease the required entertainments of legislators, elected officials, supreme court judges and news reporters.

A tremendous void in the Mansion, both personal and professional, was created with the resignation of Barbara Pohlman, the veteran housekeeper who had served first families for nearly forty years. Barbara first came to the executive residence with Mrs. Herbert S. Hadley in 1909 to help with the housework and the three small Hadley children. She had served as the mainstay of Mansion staffs, as the confidante of Mansion hostesses and as a friend to first families during ten administrations. However, during recent years the disabilities of advanced age made it obvious that her continued service was limited. Her retirement during the early part of Mrs. Donnelly's second term was an occasion accompanied with deep regret not only by the current First Lady but the many who had known Barbara through the years.

An outstanding entertainment during Mrs. Donnelly's second term was a Sunday afternoon reception honoring foreign students at the nearby University of Missouri. The University president, Elmer Ellis, and Mrs. Ellis, helped the Donnellys greet the guests who represented twenty-four countries. The Donnellys also entertained for lunch at the Mansion the Italian Ambassador to the United States, Manlio Brosio, and his wife and sister, along with the Italian consul and Mrs. Francisco Campanella of St. Louis. The First Lady recalled the extreme interest shown by the Ambassador in the Mansion constructed in a style so reminiscent of his homeland.

On April 16, 1955, the Donnellys' only son was married in Lebanon. It was the choice of David and his bride that the ceremony be held in a home-town church rather than the state Mansion, the setting for so many previous executive weddings.

As the Donnellys' second four-year administration progressed, Mrs. Donnelly had an opportunity to reflect on needs of her state home. She supervised a few essential projects, including painting the entrance hall and work on the iron fencing around the Mansion. The idea occurred to her that the building required "so much thought and work" that the planning should be directed by a permanent custodian. This suggestion was to be presented to the legislature in a few years.

Early in 1957, the Donnellys ended eight years as chief executive and first lady and returned to their home in Lebanon. As Mrs. Donnelly had feared, the second administration had taken its toll on her husband's health. Four years after the end of his administration, Governor Donnelly suffered a stroke. He died on September 12, 1961. Mrs. Donnelly still was living in her home in Lebanon in 1969.

Neither the Governor nor Mrs. Donnelly had favored a major item passed by the legislature early in their second term. The General Assembly had approved an appropriation of $250,000.00 sponsored by state Senator William H. Robinett, a Mountain Grove Republican, for construction of a new mansion. The amendment was supported by other legislators who were irritated by the continual high cost of upkeep of the existing state residence. The appropriation was passed only a few months after state building officials had issued an estimate placing the value of the Mansion at $242,000.00. That included $179,000.00 for the land and building and $63,000.00 for the furnishings. The movement for a new mansion was cut short on July 15, 1953 when Governor Donnelly vetoed the appropriation. The Governor stated the funding measure did not carry sufficient directive power to authorize the construction.

Thus, the Missouri Mansion, beloved by many and berated by a few, was permitted to continue its service to the state and its first families.

Chapter XIV

Missouri's Mansion with the mansard roof, after eighty-five years of dignified service to the state, was thrust suddenly into the national spotlight in January, 1957. The building had stirred comment previously as guests from other states spoke of its unique architecture and praised its splendid grand stairway. Attention this time was focused on the building's unpleasant features – the marks left by age – and on its uninvited rodent "guests" in the basement.

The controversy started rather unobtrusively when the new governor, James T. Blair Jr., remarked to friends at a social gathering two days after his inaugural that he didn't plan to live in the Mansion. There were reporters present and they later sought confirmation of this unprecedented statement. Governor Blair elaborated in vivid detail. He said the Mansion was rat-infested, the woodwork was worm-eaten, the wallpaper peeling. Plumbing on the first and second floors was of the chain-pull type watercloset of yesteryear. The Governor referred to the grand stairway as "Cardiac Hill" and noted the walk from the basement garage where state cars were parked to the second-floor bedrooms required a climb of more than one hundred steps. Governor Blair said he and the new First Lady had spent inaugural night in the Mansion only for the sake of convenience.

Inaugural festivities had been conducted in the traditional manner with no foreshadow of the announcement to follow. Turkey was served at the inaugural-eve dinner with the outgoing first family and their son and daughter-in-law, Mr. and Mrs. David Donnelly of Lebanon, entertaining the first family-elect, including Governor and Mrs. Blair and their two children, Mary Margaret and Jim Tom Blair III. The popularity of the members of the Blair family who had been prominent in state political circles for nearly half a century was attested by the enormous crowds present for the inaugural. Eleven railroad cars from St. Louis and six from Kansas City, including Pullmans and diners, pulled into the sidings at the capital city to serve as rolling hotels for visitors. The weather put on its normal bad show as temperatures stood at a jarring five degrees for the inaugural parade. Many of the some six hundred colonels donned long underwear beneath their colorful military uniforms for the parade but suffered later in the overheated capitol.

To accommodate the crowds, twin inaugural balls were held for the first time since the Hydes had two dances. The earlier dual affair was necessary to relieve the crush at the Mansion when it still was used for inaugural dancing. The Blair inaugural dances were held at the capitol and at the Governor Hotel located across the street from the Mansion. The new First Lady wore a white gown of *peau de soie* designed according to her specifications by Pauline Trigere, a top New York couturiere. The dress had a fitted bodice. Folds of material were draped over the left shoulder and the skirt flowed into a short train. The only ornamentation was a narrow belt of rhinestones. Mrs. Blair had suffered a painful injury to her right arm which failed to respond to treatment and at the inaugural reception she held flowers and smiled instead of shaking hands. Any extended handshaking left her in extreme pain for days.

With the Governor's son and daughter holding the Bible, the inaugural oath was administered by the new executive's younger brother, Circuit Judge Sam C. Blair. The ceremony marked the end of a career of more than thirty years for Governor Donnelly and the climax of a career of equal length for the new executive. Governor Blair had first served as city attorney in the capital city in 1925 – one year before he was married to Emilie Garnett Chorn, a native of Kansas City and the daughter of Mr. and Mrs. Samuel Kossoth Chorn. The two met when the Governor visited his sister who was a member of the same sorority as the First-Lady-to-be at the University of Missouri. Governor and Mrs. Blair were married in a private ceremony held at the home of friends in Kansas City. They immediately took up residence in Jefferson City where they were to remain throughout the years ahead as the Governor advanced through positions as mayor of Jefferson City, member of the legislature, lieutenant-governor and, finally, chief executive of Missouri.

After spending inaugural night in the Mansion, the Blairs had their suitcases returned to their private home in the capital city, some sixteen blocks from the capital area. In his revolutionary announcement rejecting further residence in the Mansion, the Governor noted that he and Mrs. Blair were fortunate to have their own home which had housed them for twenty-five years and would, he said, continue to serve them very comfortably for the remainder of his term as governor.

Such a statement issued by a less forceful executive would have attracted attention, but couched in Governor Blair's colorful language the quotations were clearly destined for wide circulation. The story was printed in newspapers from coast to coast, carried over nationwide radio and television networks and picked up by major weekly news magazines. Reaction ranged from outraged indignation to sympathetic understanding. One woman wrote offering to live in the Mansion because she was afraid the old house would be lonesome without a family "after all these years." A legislator suggested that rooms be rented out to state employees. A resident of Iowa sent a mousetrap. A voter wrote to remind the Governor of his campaign statement that he had "dreamed since childhood" of living in the Mansion. "Everyone learns that anticipation is greater than realization," the writer concluded. Blair's opponent in the recent gubernatorial campaign, Lon Hocker of St. Louis, reminded Blair that he had failed, in his list of objections, to mention "what is undoubtedly the Missouri champion in size

Private home in Jefferson City where Governor and Mrs. James T. Blair Jr. lived during Mansion renovations. Occupied in 1969 by Sam C. Blair

and luxuriousness of all poison ivy vines," hanging on the river garden wall beside the Mansion.

Mrs. Caroline Hyde Swift who lived in the Mansion as the daughter of Governor and Mrs. Arthur M. Hyde wrote a lengthy and cleverly worded answer to Governor Blair from her home in Massachusetts. Her story was published in major Missouri newspapers. She recalled an incident during her father's administration when Governor Blair as a very young attorney arrived at the Mansion to escort a visiting relative to a party. The Governor was dressed all in white and Mrs. Swift said she and a friend, who were watering flowers, couldn't resist the temptation to "turn the hose on the elegant gentleman. One wonders," she concluded, "whether his aversion to the mansion has any roots in his youth."

Governor Blair's statements about the Mansion immediately strengthened the conviction of a few legislators that the building should be razed. An undercurrent movement to do away with the executive residence existed at most sessions of the General Assembly, but backers seldom received majority support. No sooner had the Governor called attention to the inadequacies of the Mansion than the clamor for removal of the building gained momentum. One state senator suggested the Mansion site could better be used to ease the shortage of parking spaces in the capitol area. This proposal brought an immediate editorial reply from a newspaper in Columbia, home of the state university. The movement to raze the Mansion, the editor wrote, "reminds us of the ill-advised proposal of a university administrator some years ago that we slice the dome off Jesse Hall," the administration building at the university.

Buried beneath the public furor caused by the Governor's remarks were compelling personal reasons for the decision by the Governor and Mrs. Blair. It was not generally known at the time but Governor Blair had a heart condition. He had suffered two heart attacks prior to his election and had been advised by his physician to avoid stairs. Thus, his labeling of the grand stairway "Cardiac Hill" had a very real meaning to him and was one condition that made the Mansion almost prohibitive for the Governor's daily use.

Although attention was focused almost exclusively on the Governor's statements, another person was involved – the new First Lady. Emilie Blair, quite understandably, had a voice in the decision concerning the Mansion. Mrs. Blair was in complete agreement for personal reasons of her own. Throughout Governor Blair's career in public office, Mrs. Blair had by inclination stayed on the sidelines. She was a vivid and outgoing person but she firmly confined her social contacts to a small coterie of friends. She chose to avoid large public crowds and made campaign appearances only where her presence was a necessity. To the new First Lady, residence in the Mansion represented an unwanted commitment to public life with its contingent entertainment of large impersonal groups. This reluctance to move more actively into state and political functions, combined with the rundown condition of the executive residence, prompted Mrs. Blair to cast her vote to remain at home – a residence that the first family only recently had completely redecorated.

As the public reaction and debate reached a fervor which seemed to surprise even Governor Blair, a truce was requested. At a news conference several days after his inaugural, Governor Blair told reporters that he and Mrs. Blair would "like to respectfully request no further speculation" about the role of the Mansion as the state's executive residence. The Governor said all public functions required by custom would be held in the Mansion and a resident staff would be on duty to show visitors through the building. He concluded the conference with the observation that the future of the Mansion "is a legislative problem." A St. Joseph, Missouri newspaperman noted in an editorial that it was another "blunt-speaking Missourian" who pointed out that a piano was about to fall through the floor in one room of the White House. As a result of that statement by President Truman, extensive repairs were authorized by Congress and the national executive residence was restored completely.

Missouri's legislative assembly was not quite so generous as Congress but action was started. A special committee was charged with investigating costs of rehabilitating the building and the possible construction of a separate residence for the governor. With the help of a volunteer group of architects headed by John D. Sweeney of St. Louis the legislators considered several possibilities. The architects and construction experts surveyed the Mansion and all agreed that it was structurally very sound and would last indefinitely even if no repairs were undertaken. Mr. Sweeney reported, however, that every window needed to be replaced and interior wood, which "showed signs of fatigue," needed to be replaced or reinforced.

A Jefferson City contractor who did extensive probing of the building reported that thirty-eight rats' nests were found in the basement along with a tangle of dangerous electric wire. He found holes in the floor of one first-floor room. Red barn paint had been used years earlier on interior doors over the solid wood of the original construction. The contractor said the only really dangerous condition on the much maligned third floor was the narrow stairway which was the sole means of exit.

Most highly recommended by the architects in their final report was the complete restoration of the Mansion, returning it to its original appearance. Such a project would have involved about seventy-five per cent of the structure. The architects also recommended removal of additions which had altered the exterior appearance of the building, such as the kitchen wing and the second-floor porch. Fire escapes, the architects observed, might have to remain, although unsightly. "Here immediately, the old is in conflict with new," the architects said in their report. "People 'lived dangerously' eighty years ago in unprotected dwellings. Today, they do it in automobiles instead. The trick will be to maintain the spirit of antiquity, and to satisfy the demands of safety codes of the present day." The complete restoration, similar to the work done on the White House, was estimated to cost about $500,000.00.

As for a place for the executive family to live, the architects estimated new living quarters would cost between $150,000.00 and $250,000.00, depending on whether a separate site was purchased. The architects noted that the only possible place for construction of a separate residence adjoining the Mansion would be to the north, hanging on the river bluff, "a nice trick if it can be done." A modernized, air-conditioned living area for the first family within the existing Mansion was estimated at $100,000.00.

After three months of study, the legislative committee failed to reach a decision and recommended that the problem be turned over to a special interim committee which would meet while the regular session was in adjournment. No such interim committee was created and the problem was left for a special session of the General Assembly the next year. The special session voted a modest $40,000.00 to start general repairs and modernizing of three second floor rooms. Plans were dropped for a complete roof-to-basement renovation and for a separate executive residence either adjoining the existing Mansion or, as one person suggested, across the river on the Callaway County bluffs. Financing for a massive restoration project as outlined by the architects would have met oppostion in the legislature and Governor Blair had more pressing problems as he tried to advance his own state program which barely had been introduced when the Mansion controversy started.

While remaining in their private home, the Blairs carred out a limited calendar of social events in the Mansion. One of the first large entertainments planned by Mrs. Blair was a luncheon held at the Mansion for wives of state legislators on May 8, 1957. Among the guests was Clarissa Start, a noted columnist for the St. Louis *Post-Dispatch* whose husband was a member of the state senate. The columnist wrote that interest in the traditional event was "keener than ever" because of the controversy over the Mansion. The ladies were able to view the conditions since the repair proposals still were under study by the General Assembly at the time. Mrs. Blair, in pointing out the needs of the building, recalled how rotted tape on a Venetian blind had broken two days before the party sending the slats clattering to the floor. The First Lady was quoted as reassuring her guests that she personally was opposed to any effort to replace the Mansion. Mrs. Blair said she primarily was interested in repairs to the building and thought that "now, while a Jefferson City resident is in office and doesn't have to live in the mansion is the logical time."

Presiding over service in the dining room at the luncheon was Mrs. James T. Blair Sr., or "Mother" Blair as she was fondly called. The menu included, according to the columnist-guest, "creamed chicken on Swedish rosettes (those fancy fried thingamajigs that look like snowflakes), rolls and coffee and the most heavenly fruit salad." All the food had been prepared under the First Lady's close supervision. Mrs. Blair planned the menus and cooked the food herself or tasted for final approval all dishes served either her family or her guests.

Entertainment of legislators and state officials at stag dinners at the Mansion was scheduled by the Governor. For those affairs, he imported an entire crew of cooks and waiters from Stan & Biggie's, a St. Louis restaurant partly owned by Stan Musial, the Cardinal baseball star.

A final, large reception – the last such event before remodeling work

Emilie Blair, a copy of her portrait in Mansion

started – was held in the Mansion in January, 1958 as the First Lady's portrait was unveiled. Special guests were members of the Governor's staff of colonels and their wives and one female colonel, Miss Judy Murback of Sikeston, a former state beauty queen and a student at the University of Missouri. Mrs. Blair's portrait was painted by Daniel MacMorris of Kansas City and showed her wearing a pale pink formal gown of silk and lace. On Mrs. Blair's finger in the painting was a deep red star sapphire ring which the artist had added at the last minute to offset the general pastel tone of the picture. The make-believe ring became a reality a few months later when the Governor had a jeweler make an identical ring as a gift for Mrs. Blair.

A smaller Mansion party, more personal than the portrait ceremony, was held on April 29, 1958. The Governor presented his mother with the award of Mother of the Year in Missouri. The date also was the seventy-sixth birthday of Mother Blair whose spry and sparkling nature and forceful personality belied her years.

In mid-June, 1958, seventeen months after the Blairs took office, announcement was made that they were going to move into the Mansion. The Governor said the decision resulted from continued public criticism of their remaining in their private home. Some of the criticism had been goodnatured, such as the panning given the Governor at a Griddle Dinner sponsored by the Kansas City, Missouri Press Club at the height of the controversy. A song was sung to the tune of "This Old House" with the following verses:

"This old house is full of spiders,
"This old house is full of rats.
"This old house ain't fit for entertaining
"Good old Democrats.

"This old mansion is in tatters,
"This old place needs lots of work.
"If I'd known it last November,
"I'd have run for County Clerk.

"Ain't a'gonna need this house no longer.
"Ain't a'gonna need this house no more.
"Didn't get myself elected
"Just to fall right through the floor.
"Didn't get myself elected
"To a job of filling cracks.
"Ain't a'gonna need this house no longer,
"I'm a'gettin' ready to raise the tax."

Most of the cracks were filled and the tatters repaired as the Blairs packed for their move. An elevator had been installed from the basement garage to the second floor, eliminating daily use of the grand stairway. Two bedrooms and a sitting room on the second floor had been completely redecorated and air-conditioned. A small kitchen was built into a storage closet off the sitting room which served as a private living area for the first family. This family living room was redecorated with beige rugs and walls, chairs upholstered in gray satin and draperies of green damask. A decorating firm had to put an extension on its cutting table to manage the draperies which were fifteen feet long plus a nine-inch hem. The bedroom used by the Governor in the northwest corner of the second floor was decorated with gray walls and flowered draperies and contained the massive walnut furniture used during the Crittenden administration.

Beige carpeting, some 904 square yards of it, was added throughout the first and second floors combined with beige walls to emphasize the height and grandeur of the Mansion. Mrs. D.L. Chick of Kansas City, the First Lady's sister, advised on the redecorating. She also helped in selecting mauve and lime green fabrics used in draperies and upholstering for an effect which relieved past somberness of the executive residence.

Layers of paint, including that described as the "red barn" variety, were burned from woodwork and the huge doors inside the building, restoring the beauty of the natural wood. Plumbing and electric wiring were repaired. Outside the Mansion, a foot of dirt was removed from the lower walls and the entire foundation tuckpointed and waterproofed. After thermometers, placed by the Governor in nearly every room, recorded extreme variations in heat, it was discovered that one of the three pipes carrying heat from the Jefferson State Office Building was broken and it had to be repaired. Final estimates placed the cost of the repair projects at $129,078.00, including $80,000.00 specifically appropriated at two legislative sessions and the remainder taken from other funds available for use at the Mansion and the executive office in the capitol.

In mid-October, 1958 the Blairs moved into the Mansion and spent the first night in the building since their inaugural twenty-one months earlier. Governor Blair's first effort at adjusting to his new quarters was an attempt to cook a Sunday-night snack. He reported that he could find only one small skillet and a few knives. The next day he was in a nearby hardware store buying the utensils he perferred. The Blairs replaced the two home-sized stoves in the Mansion kitchen with a large restaurant-type range. With the correction of many of the building's inadequacies, the Blairs found life very comfortable under the mansard roof. Policing of "visitors" in the basement was turned over to a new cat, "Sylvester," who dominated not only the rats but also Mrs. Blair's German Shepherd, "Tiger Lily."

One of the Mansion renovation projects proved to be a continued source of dispute between the Governor and Mrs. Blair. The two never had been able to agree on the most comfortable room temperature and constantly were changing the air-conditioning thermostat until it would fail to work correctly. After repeated weekend emergency calls from the Mansion, Richard Schell, a contractor who was also a close personal friend decided to intervene. Acting in secret, the contractor sent an electrician to the Mansion with orders to set the thermostat at a reasonable level and then strip it of working parts. The cover and control lever were reinserted, but only as a sham. The Blairs could change the controls as often as they pleased without any effect on the mechanism.

Governor and Mrs. Blair were not informed of this goodnatured hoax until after their term was over.

The Blairs both had a background of long residence in the capital city and thus viewed the Mansion with greater familiarity than most incoming first families. The Governor first visited the Missouri executive residence as a guest of the children of Governor and Mrs. Hadley who served from 1909 to 1913. In later years, the Blairs' daughter, Mary Margaret, had attended a birthday party in the Mansion for the daughters of Governor and Mrs. Stark. The First Lady had been invited to the Mansion frequently during her many years as a legislative wife and then during her husband's two terms as lieutenant-governor.

An event of great sentimental importance to the Blairs occurred only a few months after their return to the Mansion to live. On February 6, 1959, their son, Jim Tom, married Mrs. Myrna Rothchild of St. Louis in a ceremony held at noon. The front hall fireplace which had been rebuilt after the fire during the Folk administration served as a background for an improvised altar. The service was performed by the Governor's brother, Judge Blair. The bride descended the grand stairway to music provided by a harp and violin. She wore a sky-blue wool dress with a portrait neckline and a small veil partly covering her face. The First Lady wore a white silk dress imprinted with black roses. A wedding luncheon was held in the state dining room decorated with pink and white carnations, sweet peas and snapdragons. It was the first wedding of a governor's son known to have occurred in any of the executive residences built by the state in Jefferson City. Several months after the ceremony, Mrs. Blair gave a large reception at the Mansion for her new daughter-in-law to meet friends from St. Louis, Kansas City and Jefferson City.

Mrs. Blair's specialty continued to be small parties for close personal friends, often with one honored guest such as notables in the arts. One such affair was given for William Rose, a Jefferson City native who later moved to England to start a career as an outstanding playwright. She also took a special interest in the preparation of a turkey dinner at Thanksgiving and Christmas for prisoners who worked on house or yard details at the Mansion. These holiday meals were served on long tables set up in the Mansion kitchen.

The Blairs both were interested in sports events and entertained regularly with a buffet luncheon at the Mansion prior to the traditional football contest between teams of the University of Missouri and the University of Kansas. Country ham and quail usually were on the menu. On another occasion a dinner party unrelated to a sports event was scheduled and just as the meal was served an important football game was in progress on television. To keep the food from getting cold, Mrs. Blair had a television set moved into the state dining room where guests ate in silence or talked only between plays. This same note of informality prevailed at other affairs such as a barbecue set up on the Mansion lawn for a houseguest from California. As serving started, a sudden torrential rain hit the city. Guests, barbecue, paper napkins and paper plates were moved into the Gold Room – normally the most formal area in the Mansion.

Special interests for Mrs. Blair included golf, cards, books and music; she moved her own high-fidelity record player into the Mansion. She, thus, was particularly enthusiastic about one official trip made with the Governor to hear Maria Callas, the noted soprano of Greek descent, scheduled for an appearance in Kansas City. The affair contained more excitement than was anticipated when the temperamental singer refused to appear the first night and the audience had to reassemble the following evening. On the second night, the start of the performance was delayed when building officials received a bomb threat. Governor Blair made an emergency appearance on stage to ask that the building be cleared. Police checked but the threat proved a hoax and the audience returned; the singer appeared and performed.

Another special trip on which the First Lady accompanied her husband included a dinner in Chicago for Queen Elizabeth II of England and her consort, Prince Phillip, who were on a goodwill tour. The affair was delayed when the Queen developed a toothache and a dentist had to be summoned to the royal suite. Governor Blair observed that the misfortune only proved the Queen was human and "could have a toothache like the rest of us common folks." Mrs. Blair recalled that both royal visitors were "very unassuming and easy to talk to." The Prince, she noted, could have been a "twin" to Stan Musial, the baseball star.

Because of the limited number of large state affairs, Mrs. Blair did not hire a personal secretary. She told friends she preferred only the special services of her maid and confidante through the years, Mrs. Lena Green, who moved to the Mansion with the Blairs. It was Mrs. Green who did most of the family cooking; special cooks or caterers were brought in only for major dinners. Mrs. Green acted frequently as tour guide for visitors. On one occasion, she was busy on the second floor of the Mansion while a group of young schoolchildren toured the grounds and gardens. Mrs. Green suddenly was aware of a commotion in the front hall and looked over the stairway just in time to see several young boys start a delightful slide down the rail of the grand stairway. Mrs. Green said later she secretly wished she could have helped them with their rides, but she knew they were not supposed to be in the building. She called a guard and, after several attempts, they escorted the amused youngsters out the door.

A final major party given at the Mansion in the fall of 1960 was an installation luncheon for the first class appointed to the Missouri Academy of Squires. This organization, unique among the states, was founded by Governor Blair to honor Missourians for outstanding service to their community, state or nation. Among the original class of ten squires was former President Harry

Truman and Mr. Musial of baseball fame. Again, a sports event played a part in this Mansion function as a World Series baseball game threatened for a time to disrupt the start of the ceremony.

Both Blairs left the Mansion admitting to a personal fondness for the old building. A newspaper editor noted that "if Missourians remember Jim Blair's term as governor for nothing else, they will long recall that he was the one who stimulated the state to do something about the ancient, run-down executive mansion which heads of Missouri had endured so long." Governor Blair rightly contended, the editor wrote, "that his job involves enough work without having to climb the stairs in the old dwelling or put up with its multiple inconveniences." Succeeding executives were to agree wholeheartedly to that assessment of the Blairs' contribution to the preservation of Missouri's Mansion.

As the traditional change of administrations was scheduled for January, 1961, the Blairs moved into a luxurious ten-room home on the edge of Jefferson City. A year and one-half later, on July 12, 1962, they both died in that home in a tragic accident which overwhelmed the capital community and the state. Both the Governor and Mrs. Blair had succumbed to carbon-monoxide fumes drawn into the house through part of the air-conditioning mechanism located in the garage. The fatal gas had formed when the Governor failed to turn off the motor of his car parked in the garage. Flags were lowered to half-staff through the period of the funeral. Burial was in a magnificent mausoleum in a Jefferson City cemetery.

There was no foreshadow of the tragedy to come as the inaugural festivities were celebrated in 1961, marking an end to the Blairs' active connection with politics. The "change" dinner on inaugural eve was a very formal black-tie affair and included both outgoing and incoming first families and their children. Early on inaugural day, which was accompanied by crisp and clear weather rare for these occasions, the Governor-elect, John Montgomery Dalton, and the new First Lady, Geraldine Hall Dalton, attended a pre-inaugural religious service. This was the first such scheduled church service to be held on inaugural morning. Arrangements were made after Governor Dalton told his wife shortly after his election that he wanted to start his term with a prayer. A small family service, similar to that held by the Starks, took place at the Daltons' private home in Jefferson City and then all state officials and their wives attended the formal worship at the Presbyterian church at 9 a.m. The service was sponsored by the Ministerial Alliance of Jefferson City and included Methodist, Baptist and Lutheran ministers as well as the Daltons' own Presbyterian pastor, the Reverend Frank Penick. A similar occasion was initiated by Governor Dalton a few weeks later when he attended the first governor's prayer breakfast to be held in Missouri.

It was a family affair when the oath was administered to the new

Governor. A personal Bible was held by the first family's daughter, Mrs. Julia Hall Hyland, and their son, John Hall Dalton. The administering official was the Governor's brother, state Supreme Court Judge S. P. Dalton. The First Lady was seated nearby between Mrs. Blair and former President Truman who greatly enjoyed political affairs at all levels of government. Simultaneous inaugural balls were held in the capitol rotunda and in the ballroom of a nearby hotel. Mrs. Dalton's ball gown, expecially designed for her by Philip Hulitar, was made from ice-blue *peau de soie* combined with re-embroidered silver metallic lace. A full

Geraldine Dalton and her portrait in Mansion

Gerald Massie

overskirt of the same fabric formed a deep train. The dress was a striking complement to Mrs. Dalton's prematurely white hair and deep blue eyes. It was the same dress worn for her official portrait painted only a few months later by Charles F. Galt.

At the end of the long day of festivities, the new first family got a sudden insight into the loneliness that could accompany their elevated station. Their children and families were staying in the Daltons' private residence so the weary couple was alone when they rode the new elevator to their second-floor living quarters in the Mansion. They discovered they both had failed to eat a meal and both were hungry. The refrigerators in the Mansion kitchen were secured with padlocks. It didn't seem quite proper that they should reappear in the still celebrating downtown area in their inaugural finery. They settled on sending out for sandwiches which they accompanied with warm tap water since no ice could be found. It was a rather forlorn contrast to the crowded festivities of the preceding hours. Less than two weeks later, the Daltons again wore their inaugural ensembles for the installation of President John F. Kennedy in the national capitol.

Mrs. Dalton's assumption of the role of first lady in her native state was an extremely natural transition. She loved people and entertained graciously. She had accompanied her husband on many of his campaign trips and found her travels provided an invaluable foundation for her years in the Mansion. She had gained a knowledge of the state and its problems and had added a host of friends. "There was an interesting person at every crossroad," she observed. Mrs. Dalton was introduced by the speaker of the House of Representatives soon after the inaugural as the "Governor's secret weapon." She obviously was a social and political asset to the Dalton administration but her talents for the position were hardly a "secret" from any observer with alertness to her abilities.

Concern with family events, both present and past, was vital to Mrs. Dalton who traced her ancestry to a Presbyterian minister of the Revolutionary War days. She was born in Cardwell, Dunklin County, Missouri, daughter of Mr. and Mrs. O.D. Hall. After a childhood in the "Bootheel" area of Missouri with its southern traditions, "Jerry" Dalton enrolled at Stephens College in Columbia. Her college days were interrupted by her marriage in 1925 to John M. Dalton, a young attorney whose parents lived in Columbia although he had a practice in Mrs. Dalton's part of the state.

Reflective of this concern with family were the first personal items moved into the Mansion by Mrs. Dalton. They included her grandmother's candelabra, a silver biscuit box which also was a family antique, her own silver tea service and the item she classed as "most important" – an antique crib for three-week-old Marian Frances Dalton, the daughter of the Daltons' son. "Fran" was their first grandchild but four more were born, one each year, during the Daltons' residence in the Mansion – probably a record for executive families of the state. The other grandchildren were Julia Elizabeth and Leslie Catherine Hyland born in 1961 and 1963 to the Daltons' daughter and John Hall Dalton Jr. and David Montgomery Dalton, born in 1962 and 1964 to the first family's son and daughter-in-law. Although the grandchildren made good use of the Dalton crib they were too young for the greatest of childhood joys of Mansion children – a slide down the grand stairway.

Mrs. Dalton approached her social calendar with the enthusiasm that comes from enjoyment. The traditional teas and receptions were scheduled and an added event, an Easter Eggroll for handicapped children on the Mansion lawn, was planned for the first time. Assisting the First Lady as a personal secretary was Mrs. Mary Margaret Mayfield who lived in an apartment on the third floor of the Mansion. Later, Mrs. Mayfield accepted a position with the federal government and was succeeded by Mrs. Lillian Gordon, wife of a capital city businessman. Other members of the staff included Mrs. Mary Etta Dexter, a cateress who had worked part time for three previous administrations; Arthur Hardiman, the official chauffeur who had driven state car No. 1 for some thirty years; and a housekeeper and a maid.

Basic and vital structural repairs as well as extensive redecoration on the second floor had been completed by the Blairs. But to Mrs. Dalton remained the challenging task of adding the finishing touches, particularly in the first-floor rooms. Requests for $50,000.00 for additions, repairs, and operations at the Mansion were approved at each of two legislative sessions during the Dalton administration and the funds were used from the front door to the third floor. Layers of varnish were removed from the heavily carved walnut doors at the front entrance which weighed several hundred pounds each and they were restored to their original luster. Hinges on the massive doors were polished, disclosing the date of July 18, 1869.

Repair work on dining room furniture was scheduled after a luncheon guest swung at a wasp and the sudden movement caused all four legs of his chair to break. As the legs were repaired, spindles in the chair backs, brittle with age, started coming to pieces. A craftsman at the School of the Ozarks in southwest Missouri was found who whittled new spiral spindles for the broken chairs and extras for future replacements. The original twenty-four chairs matching the expandable oval dining table had been reduced to twenty-three by the use of years. Plumbing repairs also became an emergency project when a leaky pipe on the third floor drenched the Governor's clothes in a second-floor closet.

Reupholstering was completed on the French gold-leaf furniture and other pieces used throughout the first floor. In the executive bedroom on the second floor, an old sleigh bed was brought from storage and refinished. A second sleigh bed which had been the property of the late Supreme Court Judge George Robb

Ellison was loaned to the Mansion temporarily by the Cole County Historical Society. Colors used in the executive living area were muted tones blending with the beige background selected by the Blairs. The soft blues which predominated were very reflective of the new First Lady's tastes in accessories and in her own personal wardrobe.

One improvement project carried out on the second floor was the complete renovation of a major guest bedroom for the use of Secretary of State Dean Rusk who was to visit the Mansion in connection with a scheduled speech at Westminster College in nearby Fulton. The walls of the bedroom, where Mrs. Dalton noted "the largest dimension was up," required forty-three rolls of paper. The main attraction in the room was the Prince of Wales bed with its large posts and canopy. According to tradition, this bed was in the hotel room occupied by the Prince of Wales, later King Edward VII, when he visited St. Louis in September, 1860. Facts of the bed's use by the Prince and the story of its removal to the state executive mansion never have been confirmed but the title seemed to suit the bed, regardless of its origin and occupants through the years. The old cords used to hold the mattress were replaced with springs by Mrs. Folk during her term, 1905-1909, making the bed much more comfortable for the distinguished guest expected by the Daltons.

Secretary Rusk was scheduled to arrive in May, 1961 but his visit was postponed when a Summit Conference was called. His presence was mandatory at such an important international meeting. The trip was rescheduled and Mr. Rusk arrived at the Missouri Mansion in June, 1962 for a stay of two nights. Mrs. Dalton discovered the Secretary was a man of great personal warmth which he did not project in major public appearances or over television.

For Mr. Rusk's first breakfast in the Mansion, Mrs. Dalton served hominy grits and country ham. The Secretary immediately suspected Mrs. Dalton had selected the menu in deference to his own background as a native of Georgia but was assured that his hostess also had a southern heritage. The discussion of grits brought to mind a childhood incident. Mr. Rusk said his father would make periodic trips to the mill to have the corn ground. He would return with two cans of Vienna sausages in his pocket which he would carefully dole out to his children. Because of this pleasurable memory, the Secretary said he relished the food at Washington receptions where he could eat all the little sausages he wanted.

As a result of Mrs. Dalton's meticulous research in advance of his visit, Mr. Rusk was pleasantly able to confirm the fact that he once was his wife's professor at Mills College in California. The next morning after this conversation, Clarence Cannon, Missouri's veteran congressman and noted parliamentarian, also was a guest at breakfast and acknowledged that he too taught his wife in college. Both Mr. Rusk and Mr. Cannon agreed that it helped to grade their

Prince of Wales bed. Photographed in Mansion in 1969

wives' papers before they proposed marriage.

Another national figure entertained at the Mansion by Mrs. Dalton was United States Senator Edward "Ted" Kennedy, younger brother of the assassinated president, who stopped enroute to a meeting in Kansas City. A total of nine governors from other states visited the Daltons overnight and dignitaries from throughout Missouri were frequent guests. At one evening reception for members of the Governor's staff of honorary colonels and their wives, Mrs. Dalton was assisted by all but one of the living former First Ladies. Mrs. Dalton recalled how Mrs. Park, seated at the table to serve coffee, was observed tracing her finger on a small patch on the tablecloth. Mrs. Park recalled with obvious amusement that she had paid thirty-five dollars for the cloth some thirty years earlier. "Now it seems it was a good investment, although I thought at the time it was terribly extravagant," she told Mrs. Dalton.

Luncheons and receptions for legislative and executive wives and tours by convention visitors were scheduled frequently. Contributing to a crowded social calendar was Mrs. Dalton's desire to share the Mansion with the many residents of the state. Other factors contributing to the crowds were conditions of the time, such as improved travel facilities and removal of the restrictions of wartimes as experienced in several previous administrations.

Tour groups were escorted through the Mansion either by Mrs. Dalton or by her secretary or both. The First Lady said many unique difficulties were experienced during tours, such as the time she found four strangers leisurely examining her bedroom. They explained that the door was unlocked so they just walked in to look around. Another problem was the overwhelming curiosity of guests who wanted to visit the Mansion kitchen. The First Lady had to draw the line since visitors frequently disrupted meal preparations.

A favorite time for the Daltons to invite guests was at breakfast. The First Lady and the Governor were early risers by habit and found that the quiet period at the beginning of a day "while thoughts are still fresh," lent itself to the dealing with serious state problems. The guests would be invited at 7:15 and the breakfast would last until 8 o'clock when the Governor left for the capitol.

Mrs. Dalton said she, on more than one occasion, would have guests for meals being served on all three floors of the Mansion at the same time. The Governor would be entertaining political or business leaders on the first floor; Mrs. Dalton would entertain on the second floor for women guests invited before the Governor's plans were known, and on the third floor, Mrs. Mayfield would open her apartment to last-minute visitors such as close personal friends or relatives who arrived from out of town.

As Mrs. Dalton entertained dinner guests she would, whenever possible, show them through the Mansion and share accounts of the history of the building and its furnishings. Her informed enthusiasm for the heritage of the Mansion was contagious. On at least two occasions, this enthusiasm resulted in pictorial and electronic productions which turned the public spotlight on the beauties of the state building as never before during its ninety-year existence.

Early in 1963, at the start of Mrs. Dalton's third year as hostess, a St. Louis television station, KMOX-TV, moved an entire C.B.S. film and sound crew into the Mansion for a televised tour of the executive residence. It took three days to film and during most of the nearly sixty minutes of the resulting program Mrs. Dalton was on camera, directing attention to a fireplace or a light fixture or an historic piece of furniture as she moved with the cameras from room to room. The prize-winning program was shown on February 27, 1963 and carried simultaneously on stations in St. Louis and Jefferson City. A year later, Southwestern Bell Telephone Company published a twenty-two-page booklet featuring magnificent color photographs of the Mansion. The idea for each of these ventures was conceived by executives of the firms who had been dinner guests of the Daltons.

In recognition for her work in the television production, Mrs. Dalton was selected as one of six outstanding women who made news during 1963. The citation, awarded by the St. Louis alumnae chapter of Theta Sigma Phi, a women's journalism society, noted that her television commentary "made Missouri history a very personal experience." In January, 1964, announcement was made of her selection by the *St. Louis Globe-Democrat* as one of the ten Women of Achievement for 1963. It was the first time this coveted award was presented to a woman residing outside the St. Louis metropolitan area. Mrs. Dalton was honored by the newspaper for her redecoration of the Mansion which she termed a "labor of love." In a special interview with the *Globe* publisher, the First Lady said her efforts were an attempt to "emphasize the positive and show people what they really have in the Mansion." Other honors extended Mrs. Dalton included selection as an outstanding Woman Who Works, and an award for her efforts to help crippled children.

Since two award luncheons at which she was to be honored were scheduled at noon, January 20, 1964, she was unable to be present to receive a citation from the Jefferson City Chapter of the American Association of University Women. This honor recognized Mrs. Dalton's efforts in the television program and also her good-will tour of Japan. Mrs. Dalton and the Governor made the nineteen-day trip to Japan during October and November, 1963 along with governors from eight other states. The tour was sponsored and planned by the United States State Department but was financed by the individuals involved.

Shortly after her return from Japan, Mrs. Dalton went to St. Louis where, on November 30, 1963, she christened a replica of Charles Lindbergh's famous plane, the Spirit of St. Louis. The copy was built for a movie about the pilot and his historic trans-Atlantic flight from New York to Paris. After the christening ceremony, the replica was flown on a tour of several states before it was put on display at the New York World's Fair.

On August 6, 1964, Governor and Mrs. Dalton made a return visit to the White House where they were overnight guests of President and Mrs. Lyndon Johnson. They had been with President Johnson earlier that year when he flew to St. Louis to take part in the St. Louis bicentennial observance. Their invitation to the White House was to take part in a dinner honoring Secretary General U Thant of the United Nations.

The trip to Washington was one of the final events of Mrs. Dalton's four active years as official hostess of Missouri. Two days before the trip, the state primary election resulted in the nomination of a candidate who would succeed as governor in the capitol while his wife assumed the role as first lady.

In a review of her four years, Mrs. Dalton observed that entrance into Missouri's stately Mansion "is a handclasp with history. You can't live there long and not grow to love the building," she said. "I always feel I grow a little taller every time I walk through those massive front doors." Among her greatest pleasures as First Lady, she listed the opportunity to meet challenging and interesting people and to share with them the pleasures of the Mansion. She also delighted in the variety of her experiences as First Lady of the state. "You have to be ready for the day -- every day and each is different from the preceding."

Mrs. Dalton's biggest problems were attempts by well-meaning people to "demand more than you can give." One day's mail contained four separate special requests -- one for an old hat, another for a button from one of the Governor's coats, a third for a jar of soil from the Mansion grounds. She couldn't remember the fourth but probably it was for a favorite recipe which she most frequently answered with one for chess pie or a grits casserole.

Mrs. Dalton kept detailed accounts of her entertaining and at the end of four years found that a total of 13,876 persons actually sat down to meals during her term. That's an average of nine people a day, every day -- a record she found overwhelming in retrospect. Every person who had ever lived in the Mansion was invited to make a return visit.

Jerry Dalton entered the Mansion at a time when unfavorable publicity about the state's executive residence had subsided but not disappeared. Four years earlier, the Blairs had resisted residence in the building and comments on its rundown condition had mushroomed into a nationally publicized controversy. One of the reasons the Blairs' complaints were so widely printed was that many other states had similar problems. New mansions were under consideration in nine other states at about the same time the storm broke concerning the Missouri Mansion. Governor Blair's protests later were recognized as the impetus that saved the Mansion for future generations of first families. Mrs. Blair lived in the renovated building for only half her term as First Lady but admitted to a friend that she grew to "love that old building."

In summing up four years as the state's chief executive, Governor Dalton told a newspaper interviewer that "no governor can operate successfully without support from his wife. Her work on the Mansion," he said, "will stand for many years." This was a fitting tribute to the first Missouri governor's wife who was suggested by a major newspaper editor as a successor to her husband. Although the editorial suggestion was regarded at that time more as an accolade than a serious political proposal, Mrs. Dalton's successor did, in later years, file as a candidate and become the Democratic Party's nominee for governor -- another first for a Missouri First Lady.

A traditional "change" dinner was held on inaugural eve as the Daltons entertained the governor-elect, Warren Hearnes; the first lady-elect, Betty Cooper Hearnes; and members of the incoming first family. Another of the guests was the Reverend A. B. Cooper of Charleston, Missouri, a Baptist minister and father of the new First Lady. Mr. Cooper should, perhaps, be credited as a major influence on the character of the next years in the Mansion. By nature of his profession, a minister is dedicated to the service of his parishioners and Mrs. Hearnes very early

Hearnes family as photographed for Christmas card in December, 1966. Girls, left to right, Lynne, Julie B., Leigh

Smith Studio

Smith Studio

Betty Hearnes

in her residency in the Mansion adopted the theme of unstinting service to the people of Missouri. The years ahead were witness to the success of her efforts.

Also present for the dinner were the three children of the new first family: Julia Britten, a mischievous six-year old; Leigh Eastman, a quiet, studious twelve-year old; and Lynne Cooper, at fifteen a teenager on the threshold of sophistication. These three were to contribute to an atmosphere of reduced formality inside the Mansion. It was the youngest, known as "Julie B.," who later helped select the brilliant red flocked wallpaper used in the dining room. This paper repeated the red from the background of the new needlepoint seat covers which featured dogwood blossoms. The covers for the two arm chairs and the several side chairs in the dining room were made by a group of women in St. Louis

County who volunteered for the project during Mrs. Dalton's term. It was also Julie B. who caused a speedup of work on the exterior of the Mansion after the First Lady spent most of one weekend ordering her lively daughter off the scaffolding which towered three stories high along the river bluff.

Touches of informality were introduced as the older Hearnes daughters added pennants and other mementos to walls of bedrooms dominated by antique furniture. The third floor bounced once again. The vibrations were caused, not by dancers as in earlier times, but by the use of a trampoline by the three girls. On one occasion the Governor conducted his affairs at the capitol with a stiff shoulder as a result of his introduction to the gymnastic equipment. Dinner guests were at first puzzled and then amused when a temporary absence by the First Lady brought an end to the rhythmic thudding from the third floor. Other new additions to the executive household were two dogs, a cat, a bird and a tank of guppies which seemed to increase their population daily.

These changes were yet to come on inaugural day. Preparations for the festivities started before dawn at the Hearnes' private home on the Missouri River bluff a short distance upstream from the Mansion. The executive residence itself had been temporarily vacated allowing time for a thorough housecleaning. The Daltons had moved back to their private home in Jefferson City where they were to continue to live in the years to come after the Governor started a law practice in the capital city.

Tension mounted in the Hearnes' household as the time neared for the inaugural events to start. The limousine and police escort arrived to take the new officials to a 9:45 a.m. worship service at the First Baptist Church. Formality and anxieties were eased on this occasion, as on many occasions to come, when Julie B. watched her father leave the house dressed for the first time in her memory in formal morning attire. "Daddy, come back here," she called frantically. He dutifully returned to the living room to listen to Julie's shocked revelation that his coat was "split up the back."

An unprecedented number of honorary colonels appointed by the new Governor contributed to record inaugural crowds. Eighteen hundred guests were invited for the military reception at the Mansion. Three inaugural balls were held for the first time in history and dance orchestras played in the capitol rotunda, in the ballroom of the Governor Hotel in downtown Jefferson City and in the banquet room of the Ramada Inn, a new motel complex on the southern edge of the city.

A counterpoint theme reflected the religious background of the large Cooper family which included eight brothers and sisters; all but one were present. An original hymn written by Mrs. Hearnes' sister, Rose Marie Cooper Jordan, was sung by the Baptist Church choir at the pre-inaugural worship. Perhaps the most attentive observer at all the ceremonies was the Rev. Mr. Cooper. In keeping with his personal conviction that no goal was too high -- nothing impossible, Mr.

Cooper had encouraged his son-in-law to make the race for the state's highest office. "He was the driving force while Mother was the steadying force in our family," Mrs. Hearnes recalled. Mr. Cooper also imbued his family with the idea that one should "live every day to its fullest -- as though it were his last." The new First Lady observed later that inaugural day 1965 was to be her father's last day lived to the fullest. He became quite ill and died thirty-nine days later following a prolonged hospital confinement in Houston, Texas. Thus, there was a delay before Mrs. Hearnes found the hours to rearrange her private home so that it could be advertised for sale and to start plans for an active administration. A formal mourning period, observed following deaths in previous executive families, was not part of the Cooper heritage nor was it expected generally in the 1960s.

A new secretary was added to the Mansion staff as Mrs. Hearnes called on the help of Margie F. Estes, a friend with whom she had been closely associated in musical activities. Another member of the Mansion staff was Mary Etta Dexter who was re-employed from the Dalton administration as cook. Arthur Hardiman, the veteran chauffeur who had driven the car bearing state license No. 1 for nine administrations, retired; driving duties were divided among family members and highway patrolmen.

Working with Mrs. Estes, Mrs. Hearnes inaugurated an accelerated schedule of public tours. Guests at Mansion parties, members of organizations in Jefferson City for conventions and friends of the first families had been conducted through the Mansion in previous administrations, but the new scheduling accepted members of small groups who made the trip to the capital city just for a tour of the executive residence. On one peak day, the First Lady, her secretary and close friends called in to help, conducted a total of twelve tours averaging thirty minutes each. A busy month saw fifteen hundred persons visit the Mansion for conducted tours.

Planning was started by Mrs. Hearnes for traditional social events such as dinners for legislators, state officials and visiting dignitaries. Regular weekly or biweekly "at homes," once expected of a first lady, had not been held in the Mansion for several years. The last such affairs, referred to as informal calling hours, had been held during legislative sessions by Mrs. Phil M. Donnelly during her first term from 1945 to 1949. However, Mrs. Hearnes started what she hoped would become a new tradition -- an annual dinner at the Mansion for members of the University of Missouri football and basketball teams and their coaches.

At separate teas on February 22 and 24, 1968, nine hundred honorary colonels and their wives were invited to view the new portrait of Mrs.Hearnes. The picture was painted by Fred Conway, a renowned St. Louis artist, who portrayed the First Lady in her inaugural gown of bright blue poie d'ange. The bodice of the gown, cut along sheath lines with a scoop neckline, was decorated with thousands of bugle beads in a heraldic design. The intense shade of the ball gown served to accent the vivid coloring of the First Lady -- deep reddish-brown hair, brown eyes and flawless fair skin.

Despite an increasingly busy social schedule, Mrs. Hearnes firmly reserved time to continue service to her church. She responded to appeals to substitute in the Sunday School and to play the organ for church services or special events. Thursday night still was set aside for choir practice. And as the first major holiday period approached following nearly two years of strenuous campaigning and adjusting to new duties, the Governor planned a trip to Hawaii for part of the vacation period. Mrs. Hearnes "begged off," saying she was too tired to face the necessary packing. Her primary reason for staying at home was that she had agreed to sing a solo for a church Christmas program. Her fatigue did prevail and she subsequently spent the holidays in bed with a severe case of influenza. There was no trip to Hawaii and no solo at church.

Church and music were complementary interests for Mrs. Hearnes and that fact was fortunate for the First Lady since her time free from state duties was so limited. She continued activities in a city music club which had been started more than half a century earlier by another first lady, Mrs. Folk. Later, Mrs. Hearnes returned to the University of Missouri at Columbia for special instruction in voice. These renewed studies were climaxed a year later when she appeared before the Democratic national convention in Chicago to sing the Star-Spangled Banner at the opening of the final convention session on August 30, 1968. Missouri's First Lady sang the national anthem in the traditional style, contrasted to previous soloists at the convention who adopted very personal interpretations.

Mrs. Hearnes' flawless performance was remarkable owing to a deep emotional upset. The day before she was to sing she received word that her brother-in-law, Audley Brown of Charleston, Missouri, had died suddenly in the Mansion following a heart attack. He and Velna Cooper Brown, Mrs. Hearnes' sister, were staying with two of the Hearnes' daughters while the Governor and First Lady were involved in convention activities. Mr. Brown was fifty-three years old. Mrs. Hearnes declined suggestions that she might prefer to cancel her appearance before the convention. "The easy thing to do would be to go home," she told convention reporters. "But Velna has asked that I stay and fulfill my obligation; we think Audley would have wanted it this way."

Betty Hearnes' association with church and music both were lifetime involvements. Although born in Arkansas, she moved with her family to Charleston when her minister-father expanded his evangelistic activities through southeast Missouri. Betty made her first appearance in a church choir at Charleston when she was five-years old. The Hearnes and Cooper families were acquainted, as are all residents of the same small town, but Betty didn't formally meet her husband, who was four years her senior, until college days. She was home from Baylor University in Texas, the third college she had attended on scholarships, when she had a date with the future governor. He was on leave after graduation from West Point. They were married on July 2, 1948, in the new Bethel Baptist Church of Charleston -- one of the fourteen churches constructed under her father's sponsorship. The church ceremony, at which Reverend Cooper officiated, marked a two-way exchange of more than wedding vows. Betty changed politics and her husband changed churches. "When we first started dating," Mrs. Hearnes observed, "the people at home said the only thing we had in common was residence in the same town in the 'Bootheel,'" an area of Missouri which juts down into Arkansas like the heel of a boot.

Betty Hearnes was introduced to politics during her husband's campaigns for the legislature and then for secretary of state, but her contributions to those efforts were limited by the demands of small children. However, it was an all-out family affair in the gubernatorial campaign with Mrs. Hearnes joining her husband on daily trips throughout the state. She shook many hands and made multiple speeches. Thousands of persons contacted during the campaign soon became aware that the candidate's young wife was a refreshingly forthright person. She had an ability to quickly identify with those she met and strangers soon became friends. There were many who admitted their vote was cast as much for Betty as for her husband.

Mrs. Hearnes' public appearances continued after she moved into the Mansion and organizations found her extremely willing to appear before audiences of all types. In one typical month, she accepted twenty-seven engagements before such groups as the wives of servicemen at Whiteman Air Force base, award-winning journalism students at Columbia, an organization of high school teachers and a state mental-health association. She appeared at the dedication of a new zither display at the state capitol, the opening to the public of a Boone County cave and the ribbon-cutting ceremony at a new department store building in St. Louis. These appearances, her secretary observed, were limited only by the First Lady's time and physical strength.

Although she made no personal appearances before the General Assembly, Betty Hearnes did do some serious talking to the legislators early in the administration. She successfully lobbied for passage of a bill to provide state financing for a Missouri Council on the Arts. Members of such a council had been appointed by Governor Dalton but their work was hampered by lack of funds. A request for appropriations for the program were included by Governor Hearnes in one of his messages to the 73rd General Assembly. "I didn't exactly ask him to support the bill but I guess he knew I would break his plate at home if he didn't do it," Mrs. Hearnes recalled with a laugh. The use of this colloquial expression was typical of Mrs. Hearnes' unassuming commentary on her own activities.

Mrs. Hearnes said her work for passage of the legislation was confined to explaining to the lawmakers the practical benefits that could result from a statewide arts program. "And the word just seemed to spread." One senator admitted he changed his vote after a colleague informed him that the issue under consideration was "Betty's Bill." The legislation passed and Missouri became the second state in the nation to provide public funds to support a state arts council. A few weeks later, Mrs. Hearnes was invited to Washington, D. C. where she appeared before the National Council on the Arts to explain the "fine art of politicking."

All these efforts by the First Lady were given formal recognition in December, 1968, when the *St. Louis Globe-Democrat* announced the selection of Mrs. Hearnes as one of the newspaper's ten Women of Achievement for 1968. She was cited for her work in public affairs.

An outstanding example of the activities that led to the St. Louis award was an event that occurred midway in the Hearnes' first term. It was the 1967 meeting of the Midwestern Governors' Conference. Chief executives of thirteen states and eight first ladies were guests of Missouri's First Family for five days of meetings and entertainment at the Lake of the Ozarks. This is a major resort area south of Jefferson City. It was still in its primitive stages when the National Governors' Conference came to Missouri in 1936 and Governor Park had provided planes for tours of the Lake region.

A year of planning preceded the Midwest Conference scheduled for August 26-30, 1967. A luxurious resort hotel complex, Tan-Tar-A, was selected for conference headquarters. Limousines and drivers were assigned to the visiting officials. A fleet of cruisers was donated by a yacht association to transport guests to events at other lake areas and to be available for pleasure cruises. Contingents of national guardsmen and highway patrolmen were assigned to security details. Thirty women and young girls acted as pages and guides and wore identical dresses of dark blue and white with a replica of the state seal on one shoulder.

"The governors chose to come to Missouri and we wanted to show them the best we had," Mrs. Hearnes said. This included the best not only in resort facilities, but in native scenery and food. Informal conference events were centered around the serving of fried channel catfish from the Missouri River and country ham cured in central Missouri. "And the weather cooperated with a perfect display of unbroken days of sunshine," Mrs. Hearnes recalled.

On her occasional days at home between meetings and speeches, Mrs. Hearnes attended to renovation projects at the Mansion -- a responsibility which must be met by each first lady. Many of Mrs. Hearnes' projects were necessary to arrange areas suitable for her family which included the first young children to reside in the Mansion since the Stark administration in the 1930s. Bedrooms and a lounge-study area were renovated on the third floor for the two oldest daughters. On the opposite side of the large ballroom, a new guest bedroom and dressing room were arranged after the floor of an unused area was reinforced to correct the sag of age. Family living quarters were redecorated on the second floor using the bright reds favored by the First Lady. In three second-floor bedrooms, new plank flooring reminiscent of the original was installed and layers of paint were burned away to restore woodwork to its natural warm tones. The elevator put in by Governor Blair to avoid "Cardiac Hill," was replaced with one which extended from the basement to the third floor.

Throughout the building, Mrs. Hearnes revitalized eight fireplaces. They were cleaned, new brass fenders were added to some and gas logs were installed so they could be enjoyed on cold days. A collection of antique table lamps was started, many purchased by the First Lady at auctions in rural areas of Missouri.

Mrs. Hearnes listed as a great source of pride the new Mansion library collection. An antique bookcase with glass doors was moved from the Governor's office in the capitol to house the books which included works of many Missouri authors. Other volumes were histories and biographical works needed to prepare speeches or papers. The books were a gift of the Missouri Library Association and the Missouri Academy of Squires. Special plates were designed to designate each book as part of the permanent Mansion collection.

Other changes in the Mansion resulted from the unsettled conditions of the 1960s -- a decade in which the nation had witnessed the assassinations of a president and his brother and of a prominent civil rights figure, as well as threatened attacks on other important figures in government. The problem was brought into sharp focus one day early in the Hearnes' administration when the Governor had come to the Mansion to rest during the noon hour. The only staff member present was Mrs. Estes, the First Lady's secretary, who was working in her office on the second floor near the family living quarters. Suddenly the quiet was disturbed by loud talking from the second-floor foyer at the top of the grand stairway. Three tourists had walked unchallenged into the basement, all through the first-floor rooms and up the stairs to the second floor before they were stopped by Mrs. Estes.

State highway patrolmen were assigned to the Mansion on twenty-four-hour duty. The patrolmen were in addition to the regular watchmen employed to check the Mansion grounds and to the state prison personnel who were assigned to guard inmates on yard and cleaning details. The Mansion front doors were locked from the inside except when staff members were on duty at the doors to greet expected guests. These changes reflected not only the concern for the safety of elected officials but also recognized the fact that young children were occupying the Mansion.

Instilling household responsibilities into three daughters is a challenge of major proportions in the state executive residence and a problem that particularly concerned Mrs. Hearnes. The older girls received a good introduction to obligations of a normal home before they moved to the Mansion. They continued to go to the Mansion kitchen to try new recipes or merely to help with family meals. But it was different for Julie B. who was too young for many household assignments before her father became governor. The only semblance of normalcy would occur on occasional weekends when guests were not expected. The cook was given time off and the First Lady and daughters prepared family meals. Other days of opportunity came during weekends and brief summer vacations at the private home built by the Hearneses in Charleston.

But there were many pluses to offset the minuses for the daughters of the First Family. They traveled with their parents to conventions and meetings in other states. They frequently met state and national notables, many of whom visited in their executive home. Appearances made as a substitute for their mother obviously contributed to the public poise of the young girls. The Mansion daughters, in turn, tried to limit the intrusion of their family's official life into their personal lives. Leigh once asked that the state car stop before it got to the school building so she could walk "like the rest of the kids." Julie B. reflected this need for conformity on the occasion when her fellow second graders were invited to the Mansion for a tour and refreshments. Notes for permission to take the trip were sent home with all children, but Mrs. Hearnes felt it was unnecessary for her to sign and return the slip. An hour before the group was scheduled to leave for the Mansion, Julie B. put in a frantic phone call and insisted her mother bring the signed slip to the principal's office. Mrs. Hearnes obliged, much to the amusement of the principal and teachers.

It was the youngest of the Hearnes family who brought attention to the temporary nature of residence in the state Mansion. During a discussion of campaign plans and election predictions, Julie B. interrupted with this wistful observation: "If Daddy doesn't get re-elected, I guess somebody else will get my bedroom."

But there were no changes in the Mansion in January, 1969. In an historic "first," Governor Hearnes was re-elected to a second consecutive term as the state's chief executive. The constitutional provisions which had prevented previous governors from seeking or serving consecutive terms had been changed early in the Hearnes' administration and he was the first Missouri governor in history permitted to succeed to a second four-year term.

As soon as her continued occupancy in the Mansion was assured, Mrs. Hearnes announced to friends that she was going to limit and redirect the pace of her life. But these changes didn't materialize as Mrs. Hearnes undertook the major project of her life as First Lady -- a massive restoration of the Mansion, both outside and inside. Plans for the restoration did not take shape all at once but developed from a series of ideas and from one startling discovery. This major "gold strike" came when Mrs. Hearnes found interior window shutters in the old Mansion library on the first floor. "I really wasn't surprised -- you might say more smugly hysterical," Mrs. Hearnes commented. During visits to restored nineteenth-century homes, particularly the country home of Henry Shaw in St. Louis which also was designed by the Mansion architect, Mrs. Hearnes had observed shutters in the windows. She had wondered why the architect, Mr. Barnett, had not designed similar window treatments for the state residence.

The discovery of shutters was made in the early part of 1969 and before that year ended shutters had been reopened and refinished in all the first-floor rooms. Only one half of one shutter was missing and had to be duplicated for the dining room. To add emphasis to the shutters, all the curtains and draperies were removed from the windows. The carpet installed during the Blair administration was removed and new plank flooring installed throughout the first floor except in the huge foyer or Great Hall and in the nook under the stairway. Removal of the carpet in these two areas displayed again the magnificent walnut parquet floor installed by the Starks and still in excellent condition. Area rugs were placed in the first-floor rooms, including one removed from the former executive reception room at the capitol. This reception area had been changed into an office for the governor.

To add to the comfort of executive families and to provide additional space for dinner guests, the first-floor porch was glass enclosed and heating was added. The porch columns had to be replaced but were faithfully reproduced to duplicate the originals. Similar work was planned for the second-floor porch where the flooring had been condemned as unsafe. Another project underway in early spring of 1970 was opening and refinishing of interior shutters which also were hidden beneath fifty layers of paint in the windows of the second floor. One set of shutters opened in an east bedroom was floor length, similar to a set in the dining room. This indicated to Mrs. Hearnes that extremely long windows in this area might have been designed originally to provide access to the roof of the front porch and to the first-floor back porch of the Mansion.

These interior projects actually came after work on the outside of the Mansion had started. The work on the outside bricks provided as much excitement for the viewing public as had the interior shutters for Mrs. Hearnes. An appropriation totaling $116,000 was approved in two sessions of the 74th General Assembly, enabling Mrs. Hearnes, working closely with state building officials, to complete plans for replacement of the slate exterior of the mansard roof. Leaks in the roof literally had washed one of the Hearnes' daughters out of her bed on the third floor during a nighttime rainstorm. The iron grillwork on the top of the building was repaired and cleaned.

But the roof was a token project compared to what took place on the exterior walls beneath it. A new chemical wash was found which could be daubed on the exterior brick walls. Water from high pressure hoses was used to wash off the acid along with layers of white paint. This process was not harmful to the old bricks

Gerald Massie

Missouri Mansion, 1968

as sandblasting would have been. It took nearly seven months to remove the layers of paint, including at least one layer of deep red added to the walls in 1889 by Mrs. Francis. The walls also were tuck-pointed. During that process, townspeople speculated over the outcome but Mrs. Hearnes kept silent and the observers politely watched and waited. Then, in November, 1969, newspapers informed the public -- the Mansion was to remain red.

Mrs. Hearnes said there was no great outcry of protest as had been expected. Most observers agreed that the color of the original bricks which had a definite pink tone, rather than deep red, provided a pleasing background for the pink granite pillars on the front portico. For the first time in years, the natural brick set off the contrasting white limestone lintels and the quoins. These were hand

Gerald Massie

Missouri Mansion, late 1969

dressed and installed when the Mansion was constructed to trim the windows and corners of the building. As for the appearance of the interior of the Mansion, the changes in the first-floor rooms brought the greatest praise from those among the Mansion guests who appreciated this type of atmosphere. It was a complete transformation. The elegance that results from plush carpets and fine fabrics was replaced by the simplicity of warm wood tones in the doors, in the windows and on the floor.

As the most extensive of the exterior and interior work was completed early in 1970, workers were united in their praise for Mrs. Hearnes' dedication to the restoration. "You might say she even gave her right arm," her secretary observed. She was referring to the accident in October, 1969, when Mrs. Hearnes broke her right elbow. She had fallen over workmen's tools as she hurried through a darkened dining room to show part of the work to the Governor who was equally enthusiastic about the restoration.

But there still was no obvious time in the remaining months of the Hearnes' administration for the realization of the First Lady's hopes for a less hectic schedule. Two major events over which she had no direct control were unexpectedly added to her calendar for August, 1970. The first was a meeting in Missouri of the National Governors' Conference, August 9 through August 13. Guests were to include governors or official representatives from fifty states and four territories and their accompanying parties. The guests were expected to number about five hundred. Planning also included accommodations for several hundred newspaper, television, radio and magazine reporters whose coverage was accelerated by the fact that thirty of the governors were to face election late in 1970. This was the first visit of the national conference to Missouri since Governor and Mrs. Park entertained the conference in 1936. Tan-Tar-A, the Lake of the Ozarks resort, again was designated as convention headquarters as it had been for the Midwest Governors' Conference. Actually, resorts throughout the lake area were cleared for the expected crowd of more than one thousand persons. Mrs. Hearnes said preparations were eased by using guidelines established for the Midwest Conference held in August, 1967. She also had attended fifteen other regional and national governors' conferences during the years her husband had been in office.

Later in August, 1970, the Hearnes' eldest daughter, Lynne, was married to Carl J. Sommerer II of Jefferson City. The groom was a student attending the University of Missouri law school. Both Lynne and her husband had to finish course work for degrees at the University in nearby Columbia after their wedding. It was the first marriage of a governor's daughter in the Mansion with the mansard roof in more than thirty years and the third such wedding in the state executive residence in Jefferson City.

Soon after the election in November 1972 determined the incoming First Family, Betty called Carolyn Bond and set a time for a tour of the Mansion. A few days later, she and Carolyn spent about three hours walking through the executive building while Betty explained special details and special problems. Betty said she decided against the traditional inaugural night dinner between the two families because she had found the evening "very awkward" eight years earlier. "The families are not necessarily good friends and the conversation often becomes strained." Mrs. Hearnes said she felt the traditional state dinner in December served as a suitable substitute. "Kit" and Carolyn Bond were automatically invited since he was then state auditor. Guests include all elected state officials and members of the state Supreme Court.

Extension of their time in the Mansion beyond the more usual four years intensified the sentiments of the Hearnes family when the day came in 1973 for a change of occupants. The end of Governor Hearnes' term in the executive office also ended the Hearnes' residency in Jefferson City which started with the years he was secretary of state. The family already had sold their private home in the capital city and built a new home in Charleston, the town which was part of the early lives of both Governor and Mrs. Hearnes.

Chapter XV

Carolyn Reid Bond, a young woman of striking stature, crisscrossed Missouri in 1972, appealing to the electorate in behalf of her husband. Less than a year later, Carolyn at 31 became one of the youngest First Ladies of the state and Christopher S. Bond at 33 was inaugurated as the youngest governor in history. Friends frequently compared the Bonds to the Kennedys -- President John F. Kennedy and his wife Jacqueline Bouvier Kennedy who was the nation's First Lady during the previous decade. Both First Ladies were noted for their fashionable wardrobes and for their work to carry out extensive renovations in their respective executive residences.

The eight years that Carolyn was to serve as Missouri's First Lady are historic for changes to the interior of the century-old state Mansion. Equally historic are the legal controls established during the Bond administration to supervise changes -- additions and/or deletions -- to the Governor's Mansion.

Carolyn and Christopher "Kit" Bond met in the spring of 1964 when they literally were thrown together -- playing touch football with mutual friends in Atlanta, Georgia. Kit left for employment in Washington, D. C., one month after their introduction and the courtship continued on a commuter basis. After three years, they agreed they were spending too much time and money with the airlines. They were married May 13, 1967 in Lexington, Kentucky, where Carolyn had lived as a student at the University of Kentucky. Carolyn was born in Louisville at a time when her father was employed at Fort Knox. Her family includes one younger sister, Charlotte Reid Blackwell, who lived in Atlanta in the 1990s. After her father's service in the Navy during World War II, the family moved to Owensboro, Kentucky, where Carolyn grew up and attended elementary and secondary schools.

Mrs. Bond's first exposure to politics came during high school days in Owensboro, when a social studies teacher challenged accepted standards in government and politics and "made us re-examine our ideas. He would stimulate us to question and make our own decisions." Carolyn pursued this independence when she broke with her family's loyalty to the Democratic Party to become a Republican precinct worker in Lexington, Kentucky, in 1960. These experiences served her well as she campaigned with Kit during his first unsuccessful campaign for Congress and later his successful campaigns for auditor and governor of Missouri.

Carolyn had the attributes of a fashion model. She was five feet, ten inches tall -- a height reached at such a young age that her distasteful nickname in the sixth grade was "Spider Legs." To add to her physical attractiveness, Carolyn's outgoing personality won her the title of "Miss Congeniality" in the 1961 Miss Kentucky contest.

As First Lady, Mrs. Bond's day in the Governor's Mansion started when she joined her husband for a jog on the sidewalks of downtown Jefferson City. Then, while the Governor fed the Bonds' two Basset hounds, Carolyn fixed breakfast which was limited to coffee, juice and rolls served in their private living quarters on the second floor. "We felt breakfast was a good place to cut calories and that is important when we would end many of our days dining on rich banquet foods." These personal meals occasionally gave way to the governor's breakfast meetings with legislators. Carolyn was involved in one of those events after a Jewish legislator lodged a good-natured complaint about the serving of ham and bacon as the only breakfast meats. At his suggestion, the legislator arranged with a St. Louis delicatessen to supply special foods for a kosher meal. Carolyn and her executive assistant, Sally Sprague, were in the Mansion kitchen at 7:30 that morning warming the bagels, sauteing the blintzes and arranging the lox for the breakfast.

Classifying herself as a slow starter, Mrs. Bond preferred to breakfast in a robe and leave grooming until after the Governor left for the capitol. She prefers the uncluttered lines of tailored clothes and finds bright colors best accent her olive skin and dark brown hair. One wardrobe adjustment dictated by her state position was the emphasis on more clothes for "dressy" occasions, particularly long dresses for special dinners and receptions. Each morning, Carolyn checked schedules with Mrs. Sprague who often accompanied the First Lady on trips throughout Missouri. The two were so similar in appearance that they occasionally were mistaken for sisters. Sally frequently helped the First Lady with tour groups but Carolyn made it a point to be on hand personally to greet the visitors at the front door. This was a formidable undertaking since the tours were held each Tuesday and Thursday, except for special times such as some summer months and Christmas. Also part of Carolyn's daily schedule was answering mail with the Mansion secretary and working with another helper who assisted with flower arrangements. Others on the Mansion staff included a housekeeper, a cook and a kitchen assistant.

Carolyn observed that management of duties for the staff was loosely knit. She usually met with them at noon in the Mansion kitchen for a quick sandwich, sometimes with soup. On many occasions, a similar lunch would be packed in a basket and sent to the capitol for the Governor and however many of his assistants he involved in a noon conference. Calls from the governor's office would be made at mid-morning with information about the number of the luncheon participants -- usually four to six. "Once he wanted service for 11 but we drew the line at that number." One housekeeping problem which was discussed but never resolved at the lunches with the Mansion staff was how to boost a vacuum attachment high enough to clean the tops of drapes when walls are so tall. Everything in the Mansion is so oversized, Carolyn commented, that housekeeping problems expand on a comparative scale.

During her first term as First Lady, Carolyn took time once a week to bowl with a team she organized while the Governor was state auditor. The team was named "Pachydames" in tribute to the political loyalties of its members. Carolyn's

T. Mike Fletcher

Carolyn Bond in front yard of Mansion on cover of *Missouri Life*, winter 1975 edition

team competed with another team, likewise mostly government wives, sponsored by Sally Danforth, wife of Missouri's attorney general and one of the First Lady's closest friends. Carolyn was given special recognition during that time for a bowling score of 226. Also in 1973, she netted a top tennis trophy at the Jefferson City Country Club. Almost any warm evening free of commitments would find the Bonds on one of the capital city's public or private tennis courts.

Tennis would postpone dinner even later than their usual hour of 7 or 8 p.m. That meal, unless they were entertaining guests, would often be a quick casserole fixed by Carolyn in the second-floor kitchen, a frozen dinner or occasional boxes of chicken from fast-food restaurants, served in front of the television set. Convenience foods were a necessity even for guests during the Bonds' first year in the Mansion since they had three different cooks. Carolyn explained that "our first cook, remaining from the Hearnes administration, retired; her assistant got sick and a replacement for both proved inadequate. It is hard to find a person who can cook for large crowds and then the next day turn out dainty tea cakes."

Inadequate staffing in the kitchen resulted in a change of arrangements for dinner guests. Visitors were mostly served buffet style rather than the more formal "sit-down" meals. Casseroles and salads would be prepared by caterers and brought to the Mansion while Carolyn would watch over the pots and pans needed for sauces and desserts. Visitors from foreign countries frequently meant other menu adjustments. For example, German industrialists considering Missouri as a site for a Volkswagen factory were served German wine and German chocolate cake. Carolyn stressed that all wines and champagne for guests were purchased by the Bonds with personal funds. That was in deference to critics who might object to the use of alcoholic beverages for Mansion guests.

At the start of her service as First Lady, Carolyn had considered enrollment at the University of Missouri to pursue another degree. She already held a bachelor's degree in speech and hearing therapy. After graduation with top honors from the University of Kentucky, she taught as a speech therapist in the Atlanta public schools before she completed a master's degree in guidance and counseling in 1966. She then worked for the IBM corporation, setting up tests for users of office products. She was one of the few female professionals in a world of engineers. This experience with problems associated with women in the work place was recalled later when she, while First Lady, advocated passage of the Equal Rights Amendment -- a position that was to prove politically controversial.

These early college studies helped shape her role as First Lady in other ways. Courses in speech, which earned her a top award in a statewide oratorical contest, provided Carolyn the skills for successful campaign appearances and later for appearances before the many state groups who invited her to be their speaker. She attributes the absence of a Southern drawl in her speech to the location of her childhood homes in Louisville, where she was born, and Owensboro, where she attended high school. These Kentucky towns are close to the Indiana border and not much farther south than central Missouri. Her work as a therapist for school children also prompted special activities at the Mansion such as an Easter egg roll on the lawn for mentally retarded children -- an event first held by Mrs. Geraldine Dalton. Mrs. Bond planned a special Day for the Handicapped at the 1973 State Fair. Some 1,800 persons, young and old, toured the Fairgrounds using a mapped area equipped with ramps for the physically handicapped. Members of Jaycee chapters throughout the state helped with this special event which resulted in an award to the First Lady by the National Association for the Physically Handicapped -- only the fifth such award made by the national group. Mrs. Bond also was a member of the Board of Directors of the Farmington Children's Home and of the advisory board for the Missouri Association of Retarded Children.

Carolyn observed that she was continually amazed at the effectiveness of the First Lady in serving as a catalyst for worthy causes. This function served her well when she identified with the wish of many governors' wives to preserve the Mansion as an important part of Missouri's history. A significant and permanent adjustment to supervision of the Mansion and its furnishings -- creation in 1974 of Missouri Mansion Preservation, Inc., (MMPI) -- resulted from Mrs. Bond's concern for the future of the state's executive building. MMPI is a nonpartisan, citizens' group directed by a board of some 20 to 30 members which raises funds for restoration work, coordinates public tours of the Mansion and has title to the furnishings bought by the group with private funding or items donated to the Mansion by interested citizens.

When Mrs. Bond approached the idea of a nonprofit organization to oversee the Mansion, she found only two or three other states had such groups. She used as models the oversight committees established for the White House in Washington D. C. and the one in Virginia for that state's executive mansion. Within the next 10 years, Carolyn found that almost every state had created some kind of oversight group for its mansion. Tied closely to the restoration projects and the MMPI was the publication of a book, *Past & Repast,* which recounts the history of the Mansion, includes before and after pictures of interior rooms and provides recipes, many of which were served at state dinners in the Mansion. The book was first published in 1983 and funds from the sales were earmarked through the years for restoration projects at the Mansion.

Early in the Bonds' first term, Carolyn enlisted a group of friends to serve as Mansion Docents. These volunteers conducted tours on Tuesdays and Thursdays and other special occasions. The Docents soon started the practice of wearing dresses cut from patterns ordered from the London Museum. The patterns were representative of the styles of the 1800s. Micca Ruffin, one of the first chairpersons of the Docents, noted that an adjustment had to be made to accommodate modern women. The original patterns had a confining seam under the arms which made it impossible to raise the arm. "I guess women in those days were only expected to use their arms in a limited way -- such as to lift teacups." The Docents later became a part of the MMPI.

The Mansion library, at the left of the front entry hall, was the first room restored under the auspices of the Mansion preservation group. The room features an overmantel mirror donated by the Bonds as their gift to the Mansion. Dedication of the newly restored library took place in August, 1976, as Missouri celebrated 155 years of statehood and the United States celebrated 200 years as a nation. This dual anniversary presented Carolyn with another opportunity to provide leadership for renewal and preservation of historic buildings. She was instrumental in the adoption of the Jefferson Landing area as Missouri's bicentennial project. That area is located between the Mansion and the capitol on the river bank where early residents and visitors to Jefferson City arrived by steamboat. The site which includes three restored structures -- the Lohman Building, the Union Hotel and the Christopher Maus House -- was dedicated by Governor and Mrs. Bond on July 4, 1976. As soon as the ceremony concluded, they boarded the state plane to attend that year's governors' conference in Philadelphia. Carolyn recalls that because of the late hour of the flight the view from the sky was "spectacular and certainly appropriate. It was dark and every place we flew over was having fireworks displays -- this is an outstanding memory." As part of the program for their conference, the governors and wives were invited to tea with Queen Elizabeth of England who was in this country for the bicentennial celebration. Mrs. Bond recalled the menu aboard the queen's yacht featured cucumber sandwiches and Pimm's Cup.

The year 1976 was a busy time for historical celebrations. In the executive Mansion in Jefferson City, a unique needlepoint rug commemorating the Bicentennial Year was dedicated, representing the work of 81 volunteers from all parts of the state. Individual canvases in the rug measured 14 by 16 inches and the completed rug measured 10 by 11 feet. Each piece featured the official flower of one of the 49 other states with Missouri's official flower, the hawthorn blossom, used in the border. Original plans were to place the rug in the nook beneath the grand stairway, but the steady flow of visitors led to a decision to display the rug on the brick wall of the first-floor back porch.

In October 1976 -- the last full year of the Bonds' first term -- Carolyn's portrait showing her in a formal gown of bright blue with green flowers was dedicated in a special ceremony. The portrait by St. Louis artist Gilbert Early of St. Louis represented contributions from 190 women and 35 Federated Republican Women's Clubs. The campaign for contributions was directed by co-chairwomen Cher Curtis of St. Louis and Anne Exon of Jefferson City. The fund drive was launched when two Brownie Girl Scouts touring the Mansion gave Mrs.

Bond seven pennies. They had noticed her portrait was not among those of earlier First Ladies. Carolyn said she was pleased with the portrait but found that seeing herself on canvas "is a little frightening."

In recognition of her work, particularly the restoration of the Mansion, Mrs. Bond received a special silver plate from C. Duncan Bauman, publisher of the *Globe-Democrat*, one of the two St. Louis newspapers at that time. Bauman announced that Carolyn was chosen as one of Missouri's Women of Achievement for 1975, joining two other First Ladies who received the honor -- Geraldine Dalton and Betty Hearnes. The publisher noted that Carolyn was selected for the "preservation of our heritage which is represented by the Governor's Mansion." The building, Bauman said, "houses the memories, the agonies, the successes and happiness of the governors and their ladies who have served Missouri for so many years."

Plans were to continue the Mansion restoration, room by room, during an anticipated second, four-year term as the state's First Family. However, like many events in politics, that second term was postponed for four years. There was an upset at the general election in November, 1976 when Kit was defeated by his Democratic opponent. Some critics, in retrospect, placed blame on Mrs. Bond. There were suggestions that she was too outspoken on political issues, such as the Equal Rights Amendment. Later analyses of the 1976 race by more professional critics show that there were many more harmful happenings which impacted the election -- events over which the Governor and Carolyn had little involvement nor control. These events were to serve as guides for a more successful election four years later.

Mrs. Bond concedes that her position on ERA probably cost votes. "This is going to happen anytime a political wife takes a visible role." However, she noted that criticism didn't curb Eleanor Roosevelt's campaigns for social issues. Nor did Mrs. Roosevelt's activities curtail the people's continued reelection of her husband to the nation's top executive post.

"The electorate has mixed expectations about what a First Lady ought to be. The voters want a First Lady to do meaningful things... but don't want her to meddle so much in policy. It is not always easy to carve out just the right role." Mrs. Bond philosophized that each First Lady has to decide what her role will be. "Each First Lady is a helpmate, traditionally, to the governor. Also, a First Lady has a wonderful opportunity to make things happen with her easy access to people and media. I feel it would be a wasted opportunity not to make meaningful things happen."

Kit Bond was the first Missouri governor in several years to have his eight-year tenure in the state's executive office split in the middle. The previous such occurrence came during the administrations of Governor Phil M. Donnelly, who served two terms which were not consecutive. Former Governor Warren Hearnes was the first state chief executive in history to serve two consecutive four-year terms. It previously had been prohibited for the governor of Missouri to succeed in office. However, Governor Hearnes proposed and the voters approved a constitutional amendment to remove that prohibition.

In November, 1976, Democrat Joseph P. Teasdale won the gubernatorial contest. Teasdale had tried for the top state executive post four years earlier but lost in the Democratic primary. Breaking of inaugural precedents continued during the change of administrations between the Bonds and the Teasdales. Again, as in 1973, no inaugural-eve dinner was held at the Mansion involving the outgoing Governor and First Lady and the incoming First Family. Lois May, Mrs. Bond's secretary, escorted the newly elected First Lady, Mary Theresa Ferkenhoff Teasdale, and her sister-in-law, Maureen Teasdale Galey, through the Mansion a few days before the change of administrations. Carolyn visited with TheresaTeasdale during that tour.

Another break with tradition occurred during planning for the inaugural parade. Governor and Mrs. Bond were to ride together in a car followed by a car with the incoming Governor and Mrs. Teasdale and their two-year-old son, William. Previously, the two governors had ridden together followed by a car with their wives. When inaugural day arrived, the rearrangement became unnecessary when the parade was canceled because of extremely bad weather. There was none of the usual waving to crowds by the First Families riding in open convertibles. They and other dignitaries got to the capitol as best they could over dangerously slick roads.

These changes in traditional events before and during inaugural ceremonies were not particularly noticeable to the public. However, a great deal more comment was engendered through the news media concerning the new First Lady's reluctance -- even refusal -- to be interviewed. Theresa Teasdale's avoidance of publicity was reminiscent of the years when Juanita Donnelly was First Lady. Mrs. Donnelly directed her energies toward her family and gardening. She chose to avoid public attention -- insisting that interviews and such should concern only her husband, the Governor. Mrs. Teasdale shared her predecessor's concentration on family matters. But her hobbies were different, involving horses and dogs. Prior to her marriage, she had trained dogs for shows and two of her most recent pets moved with the Teasdales to Jefferson City. The First Dogs were shelties, Heidi and Duffy, mother and son. They would frequently ride the Mansion elevator by themselves when Theresa was too busy to take the dogs for necessary outings. She would call the guards to alert them that the dogs were on their way to the basement. The First Lady's horse, Holly, was stabled at Lohman, a small community a few miles southwest of Jefferson City. Mrs. Teasdale rode Holly as often as she could but not as often as she would have liked.

Theresa's introduction to state political life followed closely her introduction to married life. She and Governor Teasdale were married October 13, 1973 -- one year after he lost his first gubernatorial race. He had been known during the 1972 campaign as "Walkin' Joe" because of his campaign excursions on foot through many areas of the state. He had served six years as prosecuting attorney of Jackson County but after his loss in the race for governor, he indicated to his bride that he was not interested in seeking further political office. That changed when his first son was born on election day, November 5, 1974. He told his wife he felt that was an omen, directing his decision to re-enter the campaign two years later.

Theresa Teasdale

So, it was an entirely new life style when Theresa came to Jefferson City in December, 1976 to tour the Mansion and become better acquainted with the city which would be her home for the next four years. She had been born in a hospital in Missouri but lived with her family across the state line in Kansas. Her father was a monument retailer in Kansas City, Kansas. Theresa's early education was entirely in Catholic schools in the Kansas City area -- St. Agnes elementary school and Bishop Miege High School. She attended business classes for two years at Fontbonne College in suburban St. Louis before she returned to Kansas City to work as a secretary for a lumber company and then for Braniff Airlines. She was introduced to her husband-to-be by a priest who was a friend of both the Ferkenhoff and Teasdale families. The bride and groom were older than most newlyweds -- she was 29 and he was 37. They spent the first years of their marriage in an apartment in south Kansas City while the former prosecutor practiced law.

When inaugural ceremonies were held January 10, 1977, Governor Teasdale became the first Roman Catholic to serve as the chief executive in the history of Missouri. However, Theresa was not the first Catholic in her position since Mrs. McNair, the wife of the state's first governor, also was a Catholic although Governor McNair was a Protestant. Ceremonies started early for the Teasdales with a pre-inaugural service at St. Peters Church located across the street from the capitol. The Mass of Thanksgiving was officiated by a priest, a rabbi and two Protestant ministers.

An overnight storm had dumped 10 inches of snow on the capital city, forcing cancellation of units scheduled to take part in the inaugural parade. Bands and other marching teams could not negotiate the slick roads. Mrs. Teasdale's first participation in inaugural ceremonies was to hold the Bible when her husband was administered the oath of office. She and their son also accompanied the Governor as he walked down the center isle of the House of Representatives to deliver his inaugural address. Theresa's initial social appearance was to greet the 20,000 guests -- or at least as many as could negotiate the slippery roads and sidewalks -- invited to a formal reception at the Mansion inaugural afternoon. The climaxing event was the inaugural ball at the capitol. The First Lady wore a designer gown of printed metallic brocade in a shell-pink shade which complemented her creamy complexion and dark brown hair. This was the same dress she wore for her portrait presented to the Mansion in 1995, some 18 years later. The delay, she said, resulted from the fact that two more babies were added to the First Family during the Teasdales' term.

Because of her avoidance of media interviews, Theresa was said to be "shy." Those who knew her better, such as her secretary, Gloria Overfelt, said a better description would be that she was just "a very private person." In a less formal conversation, she was quite open and warm. After she had been in the

Mansion for seven months, she told friends she could still walk around Jefferson City without being recognized. And that, according to friends, was the way she wanted it. She felt strongly that any media stories should be about her husband, the Governor. She saw her role as a wife and mother -- not a person of concern to the public.

Capital city news reporters were miffed because of their inability to interview Theresa. They were accustomed to First Ladies of recent years who were comfortable with and even welcomed media attention in order to publicize their projects and programs. The reporters took their complaints to the Governor who explained that his wife "doesn't want the public limelight." Theresa, he added, "is going to maintain a very low profile by her own choosing."

Soon after the inaugural festivities came to an end, Theresa became abruptly aware of the loneliness of a large house in a strange town. She recalls that the Governor was out of town. Billy was asleep when she decided to walk through the first floor rooms of the darkened Mansion. It was in the Great Hall that she encountered an equally startled security guard who had been told that all members of the executive family were out of town.

During another trip out of town, Governor Teasdale introduced the First Lady to top-level executive humor. The Governor was in Washington, D. C. Theresa received a call from him one night and he said a friend wanted to say "Hello." A strange voice introduced himself as Jimmy Carter. After several minutes of dubious reaction on Theresa's part, the Governor finally convinced her that he was attending a function at the White House and it really was the president on the phone. The White House was the site of another occasion that Theresa remembers as the highlight of her years as First Lady. She was one of 16 persons invited for an audience with Pope John Paul II when he visited the United States and Washington D. C.

Theresa Teasdale's first major household activity as First Lady was to find furnishings for the family living quarters on the second floor of the Mansion. In previous administrations, the family rooms had been furnished primarily by the state. However, when Kit Bond was elected governor, he and Carolyn sold the home they had in Jefferson City while he was attorney general and moved their personal furniture to the Mansion. The decision logically was to store many of the state furnishings from the second floor or use the pieces elsewhere in the Mansion. Some pieces were declared surplus and sold. So, when the Teasdales moved in they were startled to find vacant rooms for their personal use since the Bonds had taken their things with them.

The Teasdales' immediate solution was to move to the third floor where there were three furnished bedrooms. Their bedroom had twin beds, both of which were too short for the Governor who was six feet, two inches. Their son Billy had a bedroom by himself across the ballroom from his parents. Commenting on their accommodations, the Governor said: "It's been an inconvenience since we've lived there over two months and we've lived in one room and that's just a bedroom with twin beds. The bed is short, our son sleeps clear across the old ballroom in the other room by himself. We don't like that. We don't have a dining room set; we don't have a divan, we don't have porch furniture, we don't have a regular size tv set, we don't have anything that normal families have. I think for a Governor and First Lady to have to live under those circumstances, it's fair to say that's somewhat of a hassle."

By early the next year, 1978, the living quarters were fairly well furnished. A $35,000 appropriation had been provided by the General Assembly. Theresa brought together various pieces of traditional and Queen Anne furniture -- some new, some antique and some reclaimed from state storage. Blue wall-to-wall carpeting was installed and sheer panels ordered for the long windows. Some of the furniture such as a curio cabinet in the family's living quarters belonged to the Teasdales. All the pieces except a few personal items were intended to remain as furnishings for the private quarters of succeeding first families.

Another concern of the new First Lady was the scheduling of Mansion tours conducted by the Docents. Traditional entertainments also were continued, such as breakfasts and dinners for the legislators and for the media. Mrs. Teasdale normally attended and guests found her a gracious hostess. One such dinner was disrupted when the lights in the dining room were mysteriously dimmed and then brightened. Mansion maintenance staff members were summoned but the mystery remained until the controls were located in a corner. There unseen and unnoticed was Billy having a good time with dimmer switches.

Shortly after his father became governor, Billy made his own impression. The younger Teasdale loved to imitate his father giving speeches. He would slip into groups touring the executive mansion to invite visitors to "a big party at my house." On occasion, Billy would interrupt his father's news conferences by trotting up to the Governor for a "big hug." Billy delighted in staying for lunch with his father in the capitol. His mother said she was unsure of the menu for the Governor, but she was quite certain that Billy had either peanut butter sandwiches or hot dogs or both.

In later years, Billy remembered his life in Jefferson City and his enjoyment of the state's executive residence. When he returned with his parents for the dedication of Theresa's portrait, he termed the Mansion "awesome." The First Lady said she tried to shield her family and keep their life style as normal as possible, but there still were intrusions. An example was the highway patrolman who accompanied Billy to pre-school classes and later to kindergarten. Although the trooper was not in uniform, he carried a gun which certainly impressed young Billy. One reaction to executive life displayed by Billy, according to his mother, was to talk louder in the Mansion. "He seemed to feel he had to raise his voice to be heard in those tall rooms."

State building officials worked at "childproofing" the Mansion to accommodate the youngest child in residence since the Stark administration in the late 1930s. The work included special locks on windows and doors. Also, play equipment including a fort, swing set and sandbox, all constructed of heavy wood, was designed for the side yard of the Mansion. Part of that structure remained for amusement of young visitors some 20 years later. The First Lady recalls that Billy particularly enjoyed the third-floor ballroom which was nearly vacant at that time, except for a billiard table. He could ride his Big Wheels without damaging the walls or floors. Another favorite toy was the electric train set which was a gift from an organization of train enthusiasts from St. Louis.

Later in the Teasdales' administration Billy had playmates added to his family. On September 24, 1978, Governor and Mrs. Teasdale announced adoption of their second son, John Patrick Teasdale. Billy was to be four-years old in November of that year. On July 22, 1979, their third son was born in a Kansas City hospital and named Kevin Joseph Teasdale. It was the impending birth of Kevin that touched off a major media event that the Governor called "The Great Noodle Scandal" and the newspapers labeled "Meals on Wheels." The Teasdales rented a home and moved to Kansas City for two months to be near the First Lady's obstetrician and also close to the hospital where the baby was to be born. A second and equally compelling reason for the move was to make way for more extensive restoration work at the Mansion. The repairs included strengthening of the back stairway, rewiring, refinishing of floors and construction of a steam tunnel to connect the Mansion with a nearby state office building.

The furor over food was touched off when published reports stated that meals were being prepared in Jefferson City by the Mansion cook and transported to Kansas City daily by security guards. Staff of the Governor's office countered with arguments that only a few casseroles had been prepared using food already in the refrigerator. "It certainly was better than letting it spoil," the Mansion secretary noted.

The guards who provided the wheels for the meals were part of the security detail assigned normally to a governor and his family. Most of them were state Highway Patrol officers in plain clothes. During previous administrations, some of the guards were employees of the Department of Corrections who were needed to supervise inmates assigned to duties inside and outside the Mansion. However, Governor Teasdale had decided against using inmates. He felt there would be an increased risk since some of them might have been sent to prison by the Governor when he was prosecuting attorney in Kansas City. Young men were hired on a temporary basis to serve at special events in the Mansion; they were most often students at Lincoln University, a state facility located in Jefferson City. In addition to the refusal to use inmate labor around his family, Governor Teasdale

Teasdale family at Christmas, 1979. Pictured, left to right, are Billy, the Governor holding John, Theresa holding Kevin, and First Dogs Heidi and Duffy

also had extra security equipment installed at the Mansion. By spring 1980, a $43,000 system of remote television cameras, a remote control at the traffic gate into the Mansion grounds and an intercom system had been installed.

Governor Teasdale shared the concern expressed by Governor Lloyd Stark about the safety of young children in the Mansion and this concern prompted Teasdale to request funding for the extra security equipment. There were other parallels between the Teasdales' life in the Mansion and the Starks' administration from 1937 to 1941. When the Starks entered the Mansion, they had two daughters -- the youngest at two the same age as the Teasdales' first son. When

Kevin Teasdale was born in 1979, he was the first baby born to a first family since a third daughter was born to Mrs. Stark in 1938. This daughter, Susan Spotswood Stark, lived only 11 days. The final parallel, and a sad one, occurred when Mrs. Teasdale suffered a miscarriage in July 1980 while the Governor was campaigning for re-election. Theresa was in Kansas City at the time.

A few First Ladies through the years have expressed some concern over the Mansion cooks' intrusion on a wife's responsibility for meals. It should be recalled that Mrs. Hearnes frequently would give the cooks days off so her daughters could gain experience in homemaking and mealmaking in the Mansion. However, Theresa enjoyed spending time in the main kitchen, visiting with the cooks, Georgia Herron, who had worked for two previous administrations, and Vera Sanders, who had worked for the Hearnes and briefly for the Bonds. The First Lady said they helped expand her culinary skills which were still rather elementary since she was a recent bride.

In retrospect, Theresa remembers her favorite times in the Mansion as events connected with the major holiday periods of Thanksgiving and Christmas. Thanksgiving was the time for gatherings in the Mansion of the immediate families of both the Governor and First Lady. If all attended, there would be 14 adults and 18 children, after John and Kevin were born. And that didn't count aunts and cousins. Only once were the family dinners held at Christmas and that was the Teasdales' final Christmas in Jefferson City. The holiday schedules in the Mansion were filled every year with other traditional events such as the candlelight tours when the electric train would be brought down from the third-floor ballroom and used under the Christmas tree, traditionally placed either in the entry hall or in the double parlors of the first floor.

On December 19, 1979, a special Christmas party was held for some 175 handicapped children from homes in St. Louis, Kansas City and Fulton. They ranged in ages from five to ten years. Characters from Six Flags over Mid-America, a major amusement park in the St. Louis area,entertained the children and the choir from the Missouri School for the Deaf in Fulton performed. The Teasdales commented that the event was planned because many of the children would not otherwise be able to see the Executive Mansion.

Soon after the Teasdales' Christmas dinner for their families in December, 1980, the events of four years earlier were replayed in reverse. Governor Teasdale had lost his re-election bid to his previous opponent -- Governor Bond. So, the Teasdales moved out of the Mansion and the Bonds moved back. Inaugural traditions again were broken. This time, the outgoing governor and family didn't take part at all in the inaugural parade. There again was no "change" dinner involving the two families on inaugural eve. After the election in November, the Teasdales vacationed in Florida and didn't return to public view in Jefferson City until time for the deliverance of the oath of office to Governor Bond on Monday,

January 12, 1981. Immediately after that noon ceremony, the Teasdales walked to the capitol basement garage and drove off to Kansas City where they had purchased a home and the Governor established a private law practice.

Carolyn Bond's return to the Mansion signaled the restart of the major Mansion renovations under the direction of the Mansion preservation group, MMPI. That restoration program had been basically on hold during the Teasdale administration, except for some necessary repairs and installation of security devices. There also was a major alteration concerning Carolyn's schedule, as far as days in Jefferson City versus days in the Bonds' private residence in Kansas City. During the Bonds' second term, she spent a lot of her time in Kansas City, except for major events in the Mansion. That change from being a very visibly proactive First Lady created considerable speculation among capital city folks. The conviction by some that Carolyn was responsible for her husband's defeat in 1976 was identified by those few as the reason she was not seen as often in the Mansion during the Bonds' second term. In reality, she was equally active in pushing restoration of the Mansion, but that work was not as apparent to the general public.

Carolyn identifies another factor as the main reason for spending more time in Kansas City -- the birth of the Bonds' son, Samuel, less than one month after they re-entered the Mansion for a second term in January, 1981. The Bonds' childless state had been a very minor campaign issue during his bid for re-election in 1976. Shortly after they announced that Carolyn was pregnant in the fall during the 1980 gubernatorial campaign,the Bonds were in St. Louis for a debate with Governor Teasdale. Carolyn recalls that Mr. Teasdale walked up to the Bonds, congratulated them and joked that they must really be serious about re-election this time. Another amusing high point was the headline in a leading newspaper on inaugural day that stated the Governor was "Figuratively Eclipsed" by his pregnant wife when he took the oath of office.

After the electorate voted the Bonds into the Mansion for a second term, Carolyn began dealing with the problem of finding a maternity dress that would be suitable as an inaugural gown. She solved the dilemma when she found a dress in her favorite bright red and bought it two sizes larger than the size 10 she regularly wore. She also had the sides merely basted rather than stitched and the skirt unhemmed. That was in November. Two months later, she had the dress finished to suit her size at the time. The Bonds' baby was due in February but he was born January 26 -- three weeks early.

With her son as the main reason she limited her time in the Mansion during her second term, Mrs. Bond's second reason was her goal to complete the Mansion restoration. "To proceed at that pace would require constant construction during all four years, making the Mansion a very difficult house to live in. I knew I could not give Sam the upbringing I wanted in that house." A third factor had to do with the interior design business she had started in Kansas City during the time between the governor's terms. "My business was doing very well and I wanted to keep that going." Also, she supervised the publication of the book *Past & Repast* in a record time of ten months.

Taking advantage of the freedom from daily duties in the Mansion, Carolyn traveled the state to help raise support for the Mansion restoration. She visited executives of foundations and top officials of Missouri's major industries to seek donations and grants. She also organized bus tours during which women from various areas of the state would be driven to the capital city for lunch. Carolyn would be present at the Mansion to point out details of rooms already finished and explain plans for further restorations. "These ladies formed a statewide network of support. They provided funding and, equally important, spread the word to their friends about our work in the Mansion." Carolyn's efforts paid off handsomely, with some $1.3 million raised to underwrite the restoration efforts.

Between these frequent special events and major entertainments,Carolyn and Sam stayed in the Bonds' home in Kansas City. She had strong feelings about retaining their private home. When Governor Bond was elected to his first term, the Bonds sold their home in Jefferson City. "The last place you probably ever want to be when you lose an election is in Jefferson City. The day after the November election in 1976, we realized we had no home to go to in January -- it was very traumatic. We literally camped out for a year." After the final round of events in the capital city, the Bonds moved into Kit's parents' home in Mexico, Mo., and stored their furniture in the basement. The next move was to the farm house of a friend in Jackson County nearer to Governor Bond's office with the Great Plains Legal Foundation. After two or three months, they purchased a home in Kansas City but then had to move into its carriage house until remodeling was complete. Carolyn said that this nomadic experience prompted her resolve to "never again to be without a home of my own."

To free Carolyn from day-to-day responsibilities in the Mansion during the Bonds' second term, they recalled a family friend and former Mansion staff person to help with hostess duties. The Bonds had met Frank and Lois May when the Mays held campaign parties for the Bonds at the Mays' home in Bonne Terre. Later, the Mays moved to Jefferson City and bought an older house west of the capitol with plans to spend their spare hours restoring their home. Lois observed with good humor that she "immediately got involved, instead, in restoring the Governor's Mansion.

"Carolyn called and said she had such a big house that she needed a little help -- just a few hours with menu suggestions, entertainment tips and that type of thing." Lois' primary responsibility during the Bonds' first term narrowed into daily flower arranging for the state Mansion. "The only reason I started doing flower arrangements was because the governor's Mansion has a finite budget; it might be the smallest budget in the state, but it can be the most visible." Carolyn recalls that Lois skillfully used wild flowers gathered through the central Missouri countryside. On one occasion she created patriotic bouquets by putting bunches of Queen Anne's lace in blue-food dye and others in red dye and leaving others natural white to arrange them for Fourth of July parties.

During the Bonds' first term, Carolyn worked closely with Lois to develop menus for parties. Carolyn recalls that any recipe that said "Serve Immediately" was automatically eliminated. In planning meals at the Mansion, the logistics of the food had to be considered as well as the taste, texture and appearance. Casseroles were used frequently because they could be prepared in advance and heated. Carolyn says that she and Lois did lots of crepes, wrapping them around chicken, crab meat, ham, beef and lamb, and then preparing unique sauces which also were made ahead of time, heated later and poured over the crepes. The largest number of people invited on one occasion during Carolyn's first four years in the Mansion was during the 1976 bicentennial celebration. There were from 350 to 400 persons served outside on the Mansion lawn. Round tables for ten were covered with white full-size cloths and overlaid with smaller green and white plaid ones. All the cloths were made in the Mansion with Lois supervising prison inmates assigned to work in the executive residence. "If you can teach a young man to serve a formal dinner, you can teach him to run a sewing machine and make a tablecloth," Lois commented.

Due to the ongoing restoration of the Mansion, meals were served all over the house. Lois recalls that lunch was planned for the second-floor porch. At 11 o'clock the scaffolding was still up and the painter was at work. By 12 o'clock, the scaffolding and drop cloths were gone; the tables were set ready for the meal. Lois compared her schedule to the activities of gerbils, those little animals who run around and around the same wheel.

A continuing concern of many First Ladies has resulted from the prison inmates who are assigned to house cleaning and food serving duties in the Mansion. The only major problem recalled by Carolyn occurred the day the refurbished double parlors were being dedicated. The guests were invited, but the furniture hadn't arrived. The furniture came the day before the ceremony and inmates were assigned to help Carolyn with arranging it. One inmate referred to as "Bob" kept looking outside and drifting back to the kitchen until he was sent back to the parlors. There usually were six inmates assigned daily to the Mansion. Because of the extra activity, there were seven that day.

Carolyn was directing traffic in the parlor and Lois was typing instructions for the inmates concerning table assignments and serving courses. A highway patrolman came in and asked Lois how many inmates were assigned that day. Annoyed at being interrupted, she reminded the patrolman that there always were six. As Lois added their names to the assignment cards, she remembered that there was one extra. The patrolman had checked because a neighbor had called, saying that someone in a white jacket was seen jumping over the Mansion fence and speeding away on a motorcycle. Sure enough, it was Bob -- the one who kept looking out the kitchen window to see if a friend had left his motorcycle.

Carolyn recalls that the most hair-raising experiences occurred in connection with dedication of restored rooms in the Mansion. "Murphy's Law was in full force -- things seemed destined to go wrong." As restoration of the library was nearing completion, a date was set and invitations mailed. A beautiful table with a marble top which had been ordered for the library arrived but wasn't opened immediately. When the table was uncrated, it was found that the marble top was in 100 or so pieces. On the advice of Mary Pat Able, the director of MMPI, the pieces were sent to St. Louis where they were glued together and the top polished. An insurance reappraisal showed the value had not changed. It was learned that marble-table tops are often broken and if the repairs are done correctly, the accident doesn't change the value.

Another untimely near disaster occurred when preparations were nearing completion for dedication of the restored dining room. The men hired to install the rug had arrived and were staying on the third floor of the Mansion. The rug was manufactured in long strips which had to be sewn together and the border sewed on before it was installed. Finally, on Sunday afternoon only a few days before the dedication was scheduled, the truck arrived with the rug strips and it was found that one was soaking wet. The workmen threw up their hands, but something had to be done. It obviously had to be dried and it had to be stretched during the drying or it wouldn't fit. There were frantic moments. Rug stretchers were brought in and dehumidifiers and fans installed. "It took 24 hours to dry, but we made it on time -- just barely."

Christmas and the candlelight tours are occasions that bring special delight to all who have been involved in the Mansion since the tours were first held by the Bonds. Preparations start in July and continue until December. Lois May recalls those occasions vividly. "The Mansion would look so beautiful. People would be lined up around the block. Kit and Carolyn would be at the front door to greet the guests. A stringed ensemble would play. And when I would hear the members of the Cantorum add their voices with Christmas carols, I would always break down in tears." Lois expressed the reactions of Carolyn and later First Ladies concerning life in the Mansion and particularly the candlelight tours. "The greatest joy I found from the Mansion was sharing it."

The candlelight tours are held in the early evening for two nights in December with the general public invited. Seasonal flowers and greenery are placed through the first-floor rooms and a tree, tall enough to complement the walls of the Mansion, is artfully decorated and antique toys displayed around the base. Candlelight tours using the same Christmas theme were continued through

Bond family at Christmas, 1984. Pictured, left to right, are three-year-old Sam, the Governor and Carolyn. Family pets, left to right, are Lincoln, Meriwether Lewis and Ozark

administrations that followed the Bonds. However, other special events planned by Carolyn were not continued, such as the special ceremony in May 1974 honoring the oldest Missouri-born grandmother with the largest number of descendants.

Asked about highlights of her eight years, Carolyn remembers "how much fun Kit and I had." She identified as one of the best social affairs the party on inaugural night in 1973. "We had promised the people who helped us in the campaign, most of them young people, that if we won we would have a rock band play in the Mansion to celebrate." She recalled that after the rock band was invited from nearby Columbia, home of the University of Missouri, "we got nervous about how the band members would dress. So, we called and asked them to wear formal jackets and black ties in order to be properly dressed for the occasion. They arrived with dinner jackets and black ties -- plus blue jeans and tennis shoes."

Two weddings of friends were celebrated at the Mansion. One for a Jewish friend was held outside in the rose garden. It was close to the Fourth of July. Just as the groom broke the glass -- a traditional part of a Jewish ceremony -- someone in the neighborhood exploded a fire cracker. Carolyn noted that the coincidence never could be duplicated -- "it was just one of those moments that happen." Dignitaries entertained at the Mansion by the Bonds included former Prime Minister Edward Heath of Great Britain and the Japanese Ambassador to the United States Yoshio Okawara. During the Bonds' first term, Secretary of State Henry Kissinger and his wife were among notable guests.

A major event during the second term was the third birthday party for Sam. "We invited nine of his little friends and a photographer. We made the trip from Kansas City on Amtrak. Entertainment included clowns, an electric train around the table in the dining room and lunches from McDonalds. The littlest ones took naps on the floor of the third-floor ballroom. At one point, we toured the historic buildings at Jefferson Landing and then visited Kit in the capitol. We didn't get back to Kansas City until 10 at night; the mothers still talk about it." When the children napped in the ballroom on the top floor, the area was undergoing complete renovation. The restored ballroom was dedicated in December1984 -- a ceremony which also marked the completion of 10 years of restoration of the Mansion. The ballroom is the width of the Mansion, terminating in rounded bays at each end. Three chandeliers of brass and crystal provide light for the room and are reflected in pier mirrors donated by a friend from Springfield, Mo. Placed throughout the room were the gold-leaf chairs and benches acquired by the state at the close of the 1904 Louisiana Exposition held in St. Louis. That gold furniture previously was used in the double parlors on the first floor of the Mansion. Also in the ballroom is an ornate billiard table which has been a major attraction on the third floor since the term of Governor John S. Marmaduke, who died while in office in December 1887.

Six bedrooms which once surrounded the ballroom had been reduced to three through the years to accommodate bathrooms and an elevator. Furnishings in those bedrooms include a walnut suite donated to the Mansion by former Governor and Mrs. Thomas T. Crittenden in memory of their daughter, who died in the Mansion of diphtheria in 1882. Another third-floor bedroom features the Van Dyke suite donated to the Mansion by the Missouri State Society, Daughters of the American Revolution and by the Old Tavern Board of Managers and Advisory Board of Arrow Rock. During the dedication of the ballroom, Mrs. Bond recognized the work of Theodore J. Wofford of St. Louis who had served as architect for the restoration work throughout the Mansion. The Bonds had only a few weeks to enjoy the executive building in its restored state when their second term ended in early 1985.

A unique feature of the change of administrations in January 1985 was the first time in 56 years that one Republican governor turned over the state to another Republican governor. Therefore, as might be expected, the transition between First Ladies was much more congenial than it had been in recent years. Kit and Carolyn Bond had developed a personal and political friendship with the incoming governor and his wife, John and Janet Ashcroft, during the years that the couples had lived in Jefferson City while the husbands served in state offices. Governor Bond had appointed Ashcroft as state auditor in January 1973 to fill the two years remaining when Bond resigned to accept election as governor of Missouri. Two years later, Ashcroft was appointed an assistant attorney general and, in 1976, he was elected to the first of two terms as attorney general of Missouri.

As a result, Jefferson City had been home to Janet Ashcroft and her family for the 12 years previous to his election as governor. They moved from their farm near Springfield when he was appointed auditor and built a two-story brick home in Jefferson City. They sold that house after he was elected governor, but maintained the farm through the years as an "emotional backstop" from the stresses of political life. The farm was their first home after John and Janet were married the same month she graduated from the University of Chicago Law School in December, 1967. "This was all new to me," Janet said, referring to life in a rural area of southwest Missouri. "I had grown up around concrete."

She was born Janet Roede in Albany, N. Y., in 1944. Her father was a career military officer. While she was quite young, the family moved to La Grange, a suburb of Chicago. She told interviewers that the women in her background were "extremely strong, outgoing people." It also was obvious that advanced education for all in the family was high in the Roedes' priorities. Her mother returned to finish college while Janet was in high school. Janet and her twin sister both had graduate degrees.

"There was never any question whether I would grow up and have a career. At first, I wanted to follow in my mother's footsteps and be a teacher. But somewhere between my sophomore and junior years in high school I decided I was going to be a lawyer." After completing an undergraduate degree at a private school, Mount Holyoke College in Massachusetts, she was accepted into law school at the University of Chicago.

Like the later switch to farm life in Missouri, enrollment in the University of Chicago required a role adjustment -- from an all-female college to a law school where she was one of only 10 women. "No girl could walk into the library without every man looking up." It was at U. of C. that she met John Ashcroft who also was a law student. They made an informal, prenuptial agreement never to argue on opposing sides of a case.

So, as newlyweds, they shared cases in their law firm and chores on their farm, such as tending the garden and feeding newborn calves with large baby bottles. They also taught business law at Southwest Missouri State University in Springfield and wrote law books. The preparation for legal cases, however, was divided -- she did most of the research and John interviewed the clients, particularly those in the Greene County jail.

The Ashcrofts' first child, Martha, was born in 1969 while they still were living near Springfield. Their first son, Jay, was born shortly after they moved to Jefferson City in 1973. The third child, Andrew, was born four years later. In 1975, Janet accepted appointment as general counsel for the Missouri Department of Revenue where she prepared opinions interpreting the tax and licensing laws of the state. She resigned that post in 1977 after Democrat Joe Teasdale upset Bond in the race for governor. Janet said she didn't want "to be fired for political reasons as the wife of a Republican office holder."

During her remaining years in the Missouri capital city, Janet divided her time among various volunteer positions, such as her principal concern with the Assembly of God Western Hills Church. She also was active with the YMCA, Missouri Citizens for Life and the Wonderland Camp Foundation for special children. As First Lady, one major activity was a Bible study group which met in the Mansion once a week. She also worked with various organizations to support research into Alzheimer's, a disease which afflicted her father in his later life. Her hobbies were swimming, biking, jogging and skiing, both water and snow. It was the latter activity that resulted in a broken leg while she was First Lady. She had being snow skiing in Montana. A staff member in the Governor's office described both the Ashcrofts as sprinters -- "you'd better be prepared to race walk if you're going with either of them."

Janet stepped onto the fast track well before she entered the Governor's Mansion. As soon as the general election was over in early November, 1984, the Ashcroft family took a ski trip. They returned in mid-November to prepare for their first change of homes since coming to Jefferson City. During the Christmas holidays that year, one newspaper reporter wrote that Janet "has figures not sugarplums, dancing in her head." As the organizer of inaugural ceremonies for her husband, she helped arrange details of two major food events -- a special luncheon immediately after the oath-taking at high noon followed by a post-inaugural reception at the Mansion. The occasions called for such items as 600 pounds of roast beef, 1,500 buns, 1,400 cookies, including chocolate chip made from the First Lady's own recipe for the Governor's favorite cookies. Other offerings at the reception were 24 pounds each of Bavarian and creamy butter mints, 300 gallons each of punch and coffee.

Janet coordinated with officials at the state Adjutant General's office who obtained 40 military police and 26 National Guardsmen, and supervised the use of 50 gallons of white paint and 250 sheets of plywood for the inaugural platform, and 2,500 chairs for inaugural guests. These items were needed for the ceremony held on the south side of the capitol with the platform built over the steps and the chairs arranged on the driveway.

Festivities ended with state officials in formal attire marching from the governor's office on the second floor of the capitol, down the circular stairways to the rotunda floor. Traditionally, the march was climaxed with the Governor and First Lady dancing the first number to open the inaugural ball. However, Governor and Mrs. Ashcroft, as members of the Assembly of God Church, decline to participate in such activities as dancing. Instead, the Governor combined his musical talents on the piano with the nationally known jazz trumpeter Al Hirt who was a guest soloist at the ball. The two delighted the audience with special renditions of "The Missouri Waltz."

As guests applauded from the crowded rotunda and the second floor balconies, the Ashcrofts departed the capitol to start their residence in the state's Governor's Mansion. Janet had been given tours and special advice about her life as First Lady by Carolyn Bond shortly after the election. She observed that "it's so nice to be going into the Mansion with a very cooperative first family residing there." Janet also met in advance with the five state employees on the mansion staff -- a manager, housekeeper, cook, baby sitter and secretary.

But touring a building and living there are obviously differing experiences. Several months after the move to the Mansion, Janet told friends that on some days she wouldn't mind moving back to their own home. "This house (the Mansion) is a lot harder to live in than I thought it would be." She noted that the formal state executive residence somewhat cramped the customary casual style of the First Family. She added that the Ashcroft children were cautioned against wandering from the family's private quarters on the second floor to the first floor where they might interrupt public tours or private luncheons.

The First Lady also noted that family communication was complicated. When the teenager in the family, Marti, received a phone call, she could not easily be located. The search extended through three stories of a building where each floor was nearly equivalent to two floors in other homes. Just as the previous first ladies had made adjustments to accommodate family needs, such as moving to or remaining in private homes in Kansas City, so did Janet rearrange schedules better to suit the requirements of the three Ashcroft children.

One change imposed by Mrs. Ashcroft brought public objections from the

Jefferson City Chamber of Commerce and political protests in the form of a legislative resolution introduced by a Democratic member of the House of Representatives. The cause of the protests was Mrs. Ashcroft's decision to reduce the days the Mansion was open for public tours. Previously, since Carolyn Bond had established the Docents as specially trained guides, the Mansion was open regularly for individuals or groups on Tuesdays and Thursdays. Janet chose to schedule the tours only on Tuesdays, with special arrangements on Wednesday. The First Lady observed that the tour schedule was "not in the statutes." Other changes to conform to family needs included more unobtrusive adjustments such as the relocating of light switches.

When Mrs. Ashcroft was described as "strong willed," the First Lady agreed with the characterization. "Yes," she said, "if it comes to protecting my family and preserving our integrity." This concern with family members and family values prompted an exchange between the Ashcrofts and administrators of the Jefferson City School District. The Ashcrofts questioned a play presented during "An Evening of Drama." It was one of the five plays directed and performed by students of the Jefferson City Senior High School. The Ashcrofts were present to watch their daughter in another of the plays. The performance questioned by the Governor and First Lady dealt with the plight of a young pregnant woman who contemplated suicide after her boyfriend suggested an abortion and then deserted her.

The president of the school board, when asked for comment, said he felt Mrs. Ashcroft had a legitimate point in that "for the very young, the play might have been inappropriate. But I think that the other parents also had a legitimate point of view that the play did depict a real-life situation for young people in today's society." He noted that the theme of the play was that there was hope and that suicide was not the answer. Mrs. Ashcroft stressed that she should "be able to act like any other parent."

The First Lady's standards also impacted the personnel who performed various functions in the Mansion. Several adjustments were made in the organization and membership of the Docents or Mansion tour guides to conform with Mrs. Ashcroft's requirements. A Mansion cook was fired because she extended a social invitation during working hours to a security guard. The executive assistant at the Mansion commented that "we all have high standards. It's better for the whole operation of the Mansion that those standards be observed."

Prison inmates had returned to duties in the Mansion when Governor Bond was re-elected. When the Ashcrofts moved to the Mansion, some 13 specially selected trusties were assigned to help serve meals, clean and do laundry. It was during the administration of former Governor Teasdale that the inmates were replaced by temporary help because of the security requirements for the Teasdales.

At the first of every week, Janet would send menus to the kitchen for family meals with restrictions on cholesterol and fat content. The cook also was provided a list of each family member's likes and dislikes. Mrs. Ashcroft kept notes on food served guests to avoid duplication in case of repeat visits. Most frequent luncheon guests were senior citizens, of whom many were active in Alzheimer's support groups. Apparently overwhelmed by the majestic surroundings of the Mansion, one visitor bowed elaborately to the First Lady, as if she were meeting royalty. Mrs. Ashcroft eased the tension by sharing with her guests her own dilemma: "It's your house, but it's our home."

One particularly elegant part of the entertaining at the Governor's Mansion was use of the silver table service and other silver serving pieces originally bought by the state in 1944 when the battleship USS Missouri was commissioned for duty in World War II. When the battleship was taken out of service at the end of the War, the silver was returned to the state. In the spring of 1985, it became the center of a minor nonmilitary skirmish between the Navy and the state. The battleship was being recommissioned for duty and the captain came to Missouri for a ceremony in which the ship's bell was being reclaimed. The officer informed state officials that he would be pleased if the silverware also was returned to the ship.

However, Governor and Mrs. Ashcroft declined the return, stating that Missouri taxpayers had paid for the silver service, which included an extremely large and elaborate punch bowl, teapots and candelabra. One central Missouri newspaper editorialized that the Governor should return the silver. The newspaper noted that state guests at the Mansion "will not suffer if they have to eat from Sears, Roebuck and Co., dinnerware like the rest of us." A compromise was reached and the Navy received all the silver, but agreed to lend the punch bowl for special occasions at the Mansion. The exchange was brief, since the battleship later was permanently decommissioned and the silver service, as one newspaper noted,was "sentimentally welcomed home after bearing silent witness to nearly a half-century of ceremonies and sea war." It was on the deck of the USS Missouri that Japanese officers formally surrendered ending World War II.

In March of the Ashcrofts' first year in the Mansion, Janet planned and successfully carried out a "surprise" for the Governor. While he was busy at the capitol, she had his concert grand piano moved to the second floor of the executive residence.

Six movers used brute force and a two-wheeled cart to push the 880-pound instrument up the 36 steps of the sweeping stairway while members of the Mansion staff and news reporters and photographers watched apprehensively. At times, the piano teetered precariously close to the hand-carved walnut railing.

Janet admitted to covering her face at one point, but assured observers that she had checked with the Division of Design and Construction to make certain the stairway would support the load. When the Governor discovered the surprise during lunch at the Mansion, he rewarded those remaining from the move with special music. The piano had been a gift from Janet when the Governor won re-election as attorney general in 1980. The concert grand on the second floor brought to four the number of pianos in the Mansion at that time. An 1889 Chickering grand piano was located beneath the grand stairway in the nook on the first floor. Also on the first floor in the double parlors was a Steinway grand piano and an 1880-era Renaissance Revival upright piano was in the ballroom on the third floor. A piano tuner worked most of one day to prepare all four instruments for a special event for volunteers who had helped in Ashcroft's campaign for governor. In addition to his skill on the piano, Governor Ashcroft also was known as an accomplished gospel singer.

At Christmas time in 1985, the Ashcrofts celebrated their first year in the Mansion by observing many of the events which had become traditional -- formal dinners for state officials and two nights early in the month when the general public was invited for candlelight tours. Christmas day started with a holiday breakfast featuring some family traditions -- freshly squeezed orange juice and Janet's homemade coffee cake. Christmas dinner for the Ashcrofts, whether in their private home or in the state's executive residence, included roast turkey,

Ashcroft family at Christmas 1990. Left to right, Andrew, Janet, Jay, the Governor and Martha

sweet potato casserole, green beans, a variety of salads, rolls, and pie for dessert -- the Governor's choice always was pecan.

On January 9, 1989, Janet and her family renewed their residence at the Executive Mansion. For the second time in history, a First Family extended its term for a second, consecutive four years. The first time a governor was elected for a consecutive term was 20 years earlier when Warren and Betty Hearnes continued their stay in the Mansion. There was another tie to the Hearneses connected with Governor Ashcroft's re-election. That tie was in the person of Ashcroft's Democratic opponent in the 1988 gubernatorial election -- Betty Hearnes, the first woman ever to be nominated by a major political party to run for the state's top executive post. And it was an outgrowth of that contest that occasioned the removal of Betty's portrait from the first floor of the Mansion. Janet Ashcroft told friends that she noticed that Betty's image was looking from the portrait over the Governor's shoulder as photographers were taking pictures in the Mansion after Ashcroft's re-election. The First Lady said she only meant that Betty's portrait should be moved temporarily, but the painting was to remain in the basement for the remainder of the Ashcrofts final four years.

Inaugural festivities in 1989 basically were a repeat of 1985. On inaugural eve, the Governor and Mrs. Ashcroft and their three children joined with other worshippers at a special prayer service at the Assembly of God Church in Jefferson City. The Prayer of Dedication and Consecration for the governor-elect was delivered by his father, Dr. J. Robert Ashcroft, president emeritus of an Assembly of God college in Springfield, Mo.

A change for the swearing-in ceremony at high noon was the opening of 7,200-pound bronze doors situated atop the south steps of the capitol. The doors, which are more than 18 feet high and 12 feet wide, had recently undergone restoration. The First Family rode to the capitol for the inaugural ceremony in the family's yellow 1973 convertible. Mrs. Ashcroft said 19-year-old Marti quickly claimed the front passenger seat so she could be closest to the heater. The Governor again provided a climax to the Grand March and signaled the start of the Inaugural Ball by playing a medley on the piano in the capitol rotunda.

Mrs. Ashcroft told interviewers that she thought her husband would face less pressure in his second term. "I think it's a little bit more relaxing when you're not going to be running for office.... There's no question that you don't have to think about raising the money to run a big campaign." She added that she hoped the family would get to see the Governor more during the second term. "What really bothers me is that our children too often go to bed without seeing their father, and he's off to the office before they're up in the morning."

The second term for the First Lady basically was an extension of her activities started in her first four years. She already was serving as chairman of the Alzheimer's Disease and Related Disorders Task Force in the state and was

Missouri's liaison for the national ADRD association. Janet also had helped establish local chapters of the ADRD in Missouri communities. In 1988, she initiated a new program concerned with Alzheimer's disease which was described as the first of its kind in the nation. It was a program to train police officers, fire fighters and emergency medical workers to recognize people who suffer from Alzheimer's. She explained that her father, who had Alzheimer's, had a "wandering problem." On a number of occasions, he was found by police officers a significant distance from his home.

Another very personal but little publicized activity which continued was Janet's association with the group of Jefferson City women who met weekly to study the Bible. The study group started when Governor Ashcroft was attorney general and was extended by Mrs. Ashcroft throughout her remaining years in Jefferson City. At first, the group met in homes of members or in various churches. After Janet became First Lady, she suggested the group meet in the Mansion since it was centrally located. She noted it also would be easier for her since security personnel had to travel with her whenever she left home. Women in the group represented all ages and all religious denominations, Protestants as well as Catholics. They met regularly every week, except on holidays and during summer months.

In early January, 1993 the happenings of eight years earlier were reversed. A moving truck pulled up to the state Executive Mansion as a symbol of the impending transition of power. State law sets a limit of two, four-year terms for a governor and the Ashcrofts had reached that limit. The truck was to take the Ashcrofts personal belongings back to the family farm near Springfield and some also to a rented house in Jefferson City. As a concession to 15-year-old Andy, the only one of the Ashcroft children still in high school, Janet agreed to remain in Jefferson City until the school year ended. As her service as First Lady also was ending, Janet reflected on eight years of living in what she termed as a museum-type structure with round-the-clock security. "It's not that I dislike politics," she told interviewers. "I just really relish being an ordinary person. People see me in local stores all the time and they understand that's the kind of person I am." She identified as a major drawback to public life the difficulty in maintaining her personal friends. "My friends thought they were bothering me to call me up. I felt like I was kind of isolated and away from things."

This penchant for personal privacy was strongly evident in her second four years in the Mansion. Shortly after she first moved to the Mansion she observed that she had been in political life for several years, but "I'm finding that the wife of the governor is a totally different ball game. There's no normalcy in our lives anymore." She told reporters that as First Lady, she expected to carry on her own separate life just as she always had, along with the second life of representing the state as the governor's wife. She said she planned to volunteer for whatever programs she chooses, including an anti-abortion group. "I think I'm a human being and a voter and a citizen, so I have a right to promote what I believe in."

But things changed. Janet soon became less vocal. Early in her role as First Lady, she had spoken publicly against the Equal Rights Amendment as unnecessary. But that statement apparently ended her involvement with that controversial issue. Perhaps she recalled the political repercussions that had followed Carolyn Bond's campaign for passage of the Amendment. During the final years of her service to the state, Janet's activities received minimal publicity. The few items that continued to appear in the media concerned her role as a highly involved parent, such as her complaint about the high school play. She also had filed a protest concerning a high school teacher who downgraded a theme that her daughter had turned in beyond the deadline. Probably the most public happening was the time she asked an employee of the state library to open the facility on Sunday so her son could complete his research for a school report.

In her comments on her activities as First Lady, Janet observed that she was, on most occasions, not speaking for the state -- she was speaking for herself as a mother. But as her predecessors learned, the comments of a First Lady are more often interpreted differently by the interested public of the state.

Chapter XVI

Time is approaching in 1996 for First Ladies of Missouri and their latest executive residence to enter the third century of service to the state. In 1821, Marguerite de Reilhe McNair became the first First Lady. She used as an executive residence a house in the St. Louis area along the Mississippi River on the eastern border of the state. The First Lady in 1996, Jean Carpenter Carnahan, occupies a Victorian Mansion built in 1871 on the banks of the Missouri River in the center of the state.

This latest First Lady brings a blend of creative energy to Missouri's executive residence which she delights in sharing with all who enter the massive walnut front doors. Even before her term began, Jean Carnahan noted that each First Lady could be most effective if she focuses her contributions. She reflected on her experiences as the mother of three sons and one daughter -- all lawyers. "It just seemed natural," she said, to direct her activities primarily to the children of the state. These services are successfully underway as Missouri approaches the year 2000 and the 21st Century.

A unique feature of the Carnahans' administration is the emphasis of the Governor and First Lady on duality. They both were featured in the official photograph printed in the state manual for 1993-1994. They also were pictured together on the state highway map for 1994. These features are historical firsts since governors were pictured alone in previous years. Mrs. Carnahan further participated as a major planner in the inaugural ceremonies scheduled for the Governor's assuming office in January, 1993. Having noticed that there were sizeable gaps in activities available for visitors, Jean directed the scheduling of the Missouri Heritage Festival on the day of the inaugural. Ethnic artists and craftsmen from all parts of Missouri demonstrated skills at eight sites near the capitol. The festival events were available to all who attended various inaugural activities. Later that day, political and personal guests were invited to the Mansion for receptions -- first for inaugural leaders and volunteers and later for state officials and special friends of the Carnahans. Refreshments included apple cider, brownies, muffins, sandwiches and chocolates. The festivities were capped with the traditional grand march and inaugural ball in the capitol.

This sharing of recognition and responsibilities by the Carnahans extended to sharing of disappointments. During the summer of 1993, their first year in office, they planned a trip to Italy. It was to be a major vacation after the many months of campaigning. The Missouri River was rising when they left the state, but most residents regarded it at that time as little more than the usual summer freshet.

The Governor and Mrs. Carnahan were in Rome when officials recognized that conditions were building toward the most devastating flood in recent history. After a 19-hour vacation, the Carnahans returned. They were back in the Mansion by the time the river surrounded most of the capitol area, cutting off highway traffic from Jefferson City to the northern half of the state. The First Lady joined in sandbagging efforts and other emergency activities, such as packing and serving food and reading to children in shelters. "I felt like my being there and pitching in encouraged the volunteers," she said. "One elderly widow told me she had lost everything, including her cat. It was so sad; all we could do was hug each other."

The trip to Italy was not rescheduled so Mrs. Carnahan turned her attention to her role as First Lady. Being the wife of a political leader was not a new experience for her; the Governor was elected municipal judge in Rolla six years after they were married. Jean, an only child, was born in Washington, D. C., where her father worked for the government. She and Mel Carnahan met in a Baptist Church youth group. The next morning they found they were in the same class in high school and were seated near each other since both last names started with the letter "C." They started dating when they were 15 and continued dating for five years, in high school and college. They both attended George Washington University. On their second date, he told her he was going to marry her and run for political office -- predictions which were to prove accurate.

Jean noted that Mel had promised his father that he wouldn't marry until he finished college, so he completed four years in three. "I hadn't made any such promise, so I still had one more year in college after we were married." They were 20 years old. The Carnahans' first son was born a year and a half after they were married -- a few months following her college graduation with a degree in business administration. "After we started our family I never did work outside our home -- only with our children and on Mel's campaigns." Since her husband joined the ROTC program in college, he served two years as a second lieutenant in the Air Force following graduation. The young family's next move was to Mel's home state of Missouri so he could attend law school at the University of Missouri in Columbia. He graduated in 1959 and they decided to make their permanent home in Rolla.

"My mother thought we were moving to the end of the earth. So, to remind me of home, she would send me apples from Winchester, Virginia, an area in the

Blue Ridge Mountains where our family would often make a fall pilgrimage. Then she came out here and saw that Missouri had wonderful apples of its own so she quit sending them." Jean found Missouri quite a contrast, but her residencies in Columbia and Rolla were not too different. Even though her family had lived in the area of the nation's capital city, they had made their home in nearby communities. "I had known nothing but small towns."

The Carnahans' second child was born during the time the Governor was attending law school and the third and fourth were born in Rolla. "We chose to make our home in Rolla because Mel's brother lived there and because Mel thought at that time he wanted to run for Congress from the Eighth District." The Governor's father, A. S. J. Carnahan, had served that district in the U. S. House of Representatives for 14 years. Mel, however, didn't follow his father, directing his attention instead at local and state offices. He was elected sequentially as municipal judge, state representative, state treasurer, lieutenant governor and, in 1992, as governor.

During her husband's campaigns, Jean cleared the dining room table and set up headquarters in their home. Mrs. Carnahan said her work resulted from financial necessity and personal interests. "I did whatever needed to be done because we often had no money for staff persons. I always liked to write so I wrote the campaign brochures. I also enjoy meeting people so I did some handshaking." Through the years she developed an intense interest in computers and when her husband started his statewide campaigns, she worked with experts to develop a data base for fund raising.

"When the phone rang at Mel's political headquarters, I was, at first, the only one around to answer. But things changed. When he won the Democratic nomination for governor, we had this big campaign office in Clayton. One day I called that office and said 'Hello, this is Jean.' The receptionist asked: 'Jean who?' And I knew that we had come a long way from the dining-room table."

One of Mrs. Carnahan's first initiatives as First Lady was to start a special program for grade-school children living in central Missouri. "I felt we needed to create some activity that would give children a special time at their state governor's Mansion and it has proved most rewarding -- they are so awed by what they see and experience." The Children's Hour was started during the Carnahans first year in the Mansion. Jean conceived the project with her special insightful enthusiasm and found two Jefferson City women to plan and supervise the activities. Both women had been deeply involved in Mansion activities in previous administrations. Micca Ruffin had directed the Docents for some 12 years, starting in the first Bond administration, and Gloria Overfelt was personal secretary to Mrs. Teasdale.

Some 200 children are issued special invitations to each monthly event which is scheduled from 10 to 11 on Saturday mornings during the school year.

When they arrive, the children are divided, those in kindergarten through grade two in one group and those in grades three, four and five in the other. One group watches a special activity on the first floor while the other group is directed to the third floor to see the restored ballroom. At the end of 30 minutes, the groups are switched. "There are 36 steps on the Grand Stairway to the second floor," Micca said. "We have the children count the steps silently to reduce the noise level as they walk to the third floor."

Rules concerning the Children's Hour stipulate that parents must stay

Dennis Garrels

Jean Carnahan

outside the gate and the children walk by themselves to the front door. "Sometimes the children are very intimidated," Micca observed. "One little girl kept waving back to her daddy at the gate. He cautioned her to hurry 'or you might be late to the ball.' With that, she gave her party skirt a switch, blew her daddy a kiss, and ran up the stairs to the porch." Programs are planned to connect an activity to the history of the state or the Mansion. In January, a skit commemorates the birthday of the Mansion. Flamenco dancers are related to the Spanish heritage of many Missourians. Mrs. Carnahan tries to be present for most of the programs. She took part in one that featured country line dancers in the ballroom. "We really rattled the chandeliers," she recalled.

Two other major children's activities were started by Mrs. Carnahan during her first two years as First Lady. In the fall of 1993, in addition to the Children's Hour, Jean started a Halloween SPOOKtacular. Six Flags over Mid-America, a St. Louis theme park, helped stage the SPOOKtacular during two evenings in October. The Mansion was transformed into an eerie haunted house. Featured attractions on the grounds between the Mansion and the capitol were Looney Tunes characters, a headless horseman, a walk-around graveyard, games and a costume parade. Inside the Mansion, Six Flags' performers thrilled youngsters with a musical comedy, "Love at First Fright" and a Halloween marionette show. Governor and Mrs. Carnahan dressed for the occasion, wearing costumes resembling the television Munster family.

During the second year, 1994, the SPOOKtacular was held only one evening and an afternoon performance was added. New attractions were a thirty-foot inflated gorilla which hovered over the front porch, a Phantom of the Opera organ player on the front lawn, and larger-than-life inflated dinosaurs. That year Mrs. Carnahan wore a green and purple outfit with gold bells and a black spiked-hair wig. "It started out as a jester and turned out looking like an eggplant," she laughed in describing her costume. Some 10,000 adults and children attended the SPOOKtaculars during each of the first two years.

In the spring of 1994, the first Walt Disney Children's Arts Festival was held involving activities on the grounds throughout the capitol-Mansion complex. Funding for the Festival is shared by Missouri Mansion Preservation, Inc., the Missouri Arts Council and the Lillian B. Disney Foundation, named in honor of Walt Disney's widow. To help with the financing, country-western star Jim Stafford of Branson, Mo., presented a benefit performance at the Mansion during the preceding Christmas season. Mrs. Carnahan laid the groundwork for Disney Foundation backing when the late Walt Disney's daughter, Diane Disney Miller, visited the capital city for dedication of a bronze bust of her father. A native of Missouri, Disney was famous as the creator of Mickey Mouse. The Disney Foundation obligated funding for three years; this seed money decreases each year.

The First Lady noted that while the festival is named for the famous cartoonist, the activities bear little resemblance to the renowned Disney theme parks in California and Florida. Disney characters are busy elsewhere and, secondly, the admission to the Missouri Arts Festival is free for the 12,000 to 15,000 children who attend from more than 90 elementary and secondary schools.

Jean comments that the "festivals allow kids to express their artistic ingenuity. I'm hoping this will give them a chance to nurture their creativity and recognize it in others." Attractions and activities include producing a play or

Lady on the Newel Post as installed in 1995. Photograph by Lisa Hefferman Weil, courtesy of Missouri Mansion Preservation, Inc.

designing large inflatable art in a tent on the Mansion grounds, performances of marionettes, African-American story telling, juggling, Spanish dancing, and singing of Ozark ballads. One workshop shows how an animated cartoon is produced. A petting zoo lets children "pet and sketch." The festival continues for three days. "It's a fitting tribute to a man who was dedicated to incorporating art into the lives of children," Mrs.Carnahan said in reference to Disney. Each year, the First Lady also continues the traditional event staged for children -- the Easter Egg Roll on the Mansion grounds for youngsters with handicaps. Once, when the weather was bad, the event was moved indoors and a pet lamb was imported for the occasion.

Even additions to the furnishings inside the Mansion and attractions on the grounds are reminiscent of children. They include the reinstating of the Lady on the Newel Post and a new fountain in the front yard. The newel post figure is remembered by children of previous administrations who were grateful to the Lady as a stopping place for a slide down the balustrade of the Grand Stairway. Others recall trying to hide behind her to observe grown-up events to which they weren't invited. Research shows the bronze figure of a lady holding a lighted globe was removed during remodeling during the administration of Gov. and Mrs. Lloyd Stark in the late 1930s. The original statue was located but it was too damaged to reuse so a similar one, made by the same manufacturer, was found and returned to the post at the base of the stairway in the Great Hall of the Mansion.

The front-yard fountain has ties with children of the past and present. It is set on the same site of the original fountain installed during the administration of Gov. Lon V. Stephens, 1897-1901. One photograph showed three children playing in the fountain -- presumably the youngsters of Gov. and Mrs. Herbert Hadley who served from 1909 to 1913. Through the years the fountain deteriorated and parts were removed. When Mrs. Carnahan got the idea for restoration, the only reminder was a metal ring which marked the spot in the yard.

"Undoubtedly, children who lived here in previous years played in that fountain all the time. It must have been a great attraction to them." To represent those children, the First Lady worked with an artist to include four-foot statues of two boys and one girl as part of the design of the fountain. The girl is trying to stick a toe in a spray of water. A boy is extending a hand as he reaches for water cascading off the upper dish of the fountain and another boy is pointing to a catfish in the water. Jamie Anderson, the artist selected to create the fountain, is a resident of the Carnahans' home town, Rolla.

The fountain repeats motifs found in ornamental metal planters on the Mansion grounds: the angular grace of a blue heron, replications of oak leaves, wild-grape vines and the elegant lines of cattails. The artist, who is the mother of three children, commented that the statues represent the wonder and excitement of children... "the whole thing is just a joyful expression." The fountain is ten-and one-half-feet tall. In the spring of 1996, large machines lifted and placed it on a plaza of Missouri red granite.

Financing for the fountain was provided by private donations from three women: Carol Crawford Philipson of Jefferson City, whose contribution was in memory of her husband, Robert Crawford, a state legislator, an administrative assistant to former Gov. James T. Blair Jr., and secretary of state for a brief time; Kathy J. Weinman-Steve of St. Louis, philanthropist and advocate for child-abuse victims, and Willie Podesta Young of Omaha, Neb., whose donation was in memory of her husband, George D. Young, also a Missouri legislator and former

Fountain in front yard of Mansion in 1996. Photograph by Lisa Hefferman Weil, courtesy of Missouri Mansion Preservation, Inc.

superintendent of the state insurance department. The three benefactors were recognized at a black-tie dinner in the fall of 1993 hosted by the Carnahans to benefit the MMPI.

An unexpected attraction at the dinner was the official portrait of Mrs. Carnahan. "I didn't want any special unveiling fanfare," she said about the portrait which was hanging in the Great Hall for viewing by visitors to the formal party, including the portrait artist, Gilbert Early of St. Louis. The portrait shows Jean in a short-sleeved pink linen suit, standing in the library of the Mansion. She is holding a slender branch covered with blossoms of the dogwood which is the state tree of Missouri. The pose is in contrast to other portraits in which the First Ladies chose more formal dresses. "I think the suit is in keeping with the times and with my lifestyle," Jean explained. One other portrait was returned to the first floor of the Mansion as one of the first official acts of Jean Carnahan. The portrait of Betty Hearnes had been stored in the basement. The "rehanging" of the former First Lady resulted in some interesting headlines in Missouri newspapers.

The black-tie dinner was just one event on the long list of entertainments hosted by the Carnahans. "My concept of living in the governor's Mansion is that I am here to be of service to people," Jean commented. "Living here gives you an opportunity to do something worthwhile... providing you with a brief window of time. I always feel like I am in a hurry to get everything done." And that feeling of urgency becomes quite evident when her calendar for her first three years as First Lady is reviewed. The Mansion is opened on the average of at least once a week for teas and ceremonies honoring special events and special persons, such as a blind man living in Jefferson City who celebrated his 100th birthday. In addition to the activities for children and social events, Mrs. Carnahan serves as honorary chair of the Missouri Center for the Book established at the state library to honor authors who live in the state and to encourage the study of books and print culture. She is a board member for William Woods University in Fulton. Jean and the Governor have taken part in television spot announcements concerning various health issues and encouraging the use of seat belts for children. Jean again was on television as part of a program in which the capital city was featured on the "Good Morning America" show.

To recognize these contributions, Mrs. Carnahan was selected as the first woman to receive the Robert C. Goshorn Award for public service. This award was created by directors of the Goshorn Foundation in memory of the long-time publisher of the Jefferson City *News Tribune*. Previous recipients were U. S. Senator and former Gov. John Ashcroft and U. S. Rep. Ike Skelton of Missouri.

Also added to her calendar of public events, the First Lady carries out renovations and additions needed in the 125-year-old Mansion. Special activities such as the formal gala held each year help underwrite the programs of the Missouri Mansion Preservation group started by former First Lady Carolyn Bond.

"I feel like the directors of MMPI and I effectively work together -- I come up with ideas and they choose the ones that make sense and help carry them out." The executive director of MMPI, Mary Pat Abele, exchanged compliments with the First Lady. "Jean has a wonderful ability with words and such a wit about her. She's extremely creative. She has great ideas, but she also has a very realistic outlook on what it takes to implement those ideas."

Other construction activities early in the Carnahan administration included replacing the ceiling in the third floor bedroom known as the Crittenden room. The ceiling began to sag so that project was put on fast forward before visitors were showered with plaster. Also on the third floor of the Mansion were new additions to the ballroom area. An ornate mirror complements a wooden mantle which was constructed and painted to look like marble.

Renovations in the planning are new carpet and wallpaper for the back stairway, recovering the billiard table on the third floor, new furnishings and wallpaper for the second floor room used by Mrs. Carnahan as her study and redecorating a guest bath on the first floor.

A third-floor room which was used as a study in previous administrations was being redecorated by the Academy of Squires, an honorary group of outstanding Missourians started by former Governor Blair and continued through the years. Mrs. Carnahan said it would become a Victorian-style drawing room -- a place for guests staying in the third-floor bedrooms to assemble. An entertainment center would be installed, containing a television set and a tape/disc player.

In addition to items considered remodeling and/or maintenance, Jean extended her efforts to modernize the Mansion by installing computers. She uses the system to build an inventory of Mansion furnishings, showing where each item was bought, by whom, and how much it cost. She also created a computerized catalogue of all the art in the Mansion. That collection has been expanded, at least temporarily, with the addition of paintings by the famous Missouri artists George Caleb Bingham and Thomas Hart Benton. The paintings were either given to the Mansion or are on loan. The First Lady has installed a data base used for fund raising by MMPI. The computers help in scheduling of Mansion events, in producing a newsletter and in printing invitations and menu cards.

The computers are used by the cook to multiply ingredients of recipes when needed and to keep track of menus for special guests and groups so items are not repeated on return visits. The Mansion cook during Mrs. Carnahan's tenure was Sheri Wolf who worked for Governor and Mrs. Bond and briefly for the Ashcrofts. She resigned when her husband became ill and was replaced as chef by Jerry Walsh. Other Mansion staff are Joyce Bunch, manager; Paula Earls, administrative assistant, and Jean Davidson, the housekeeper who also bakes rolls and arranges flowers. Trusties from the prison system carry out housekeeping duties, work in the kitchen and help serve at special events. Mrs. Carnahan noted with particular interest the penchant of prisoners to hide bits of food, "just like a youngster who had been hungry at some time. We have found cokes hidden behind stereo equipment."

Commenting on life in the Missouri governor's Mansion compared to private homes, Jean observed that youngsters seem to adjust the fastest. "Our grandchildren found their way around very quickly. It took me six weeks to find the light switches. The first night I was in the Mansion, inaugural night, I remember the feeling that I had been left behind in a museum and at any moment someone was going to come around the corner and ask me to leave... that the place was closing. This building is just so much bigger than life. You have to live up to the house."

As for future structural changes, Mrs. Carnahan said a large tent owned by the state would be a most usable addition. She noted that tents had been rented for special events, such as the MMPI fund-raising gala and for the arts festivals. "A tent in the front yard is great as a gathering point -- as an extension of the house." She had asked an architect to design such a tent, but it became too fancy. It would have cost as much as a house.

Asked about special adjustments as hostess in the Mansion, Jean recalls how visitors tend to arrive early. "I set a start time and then find people come as much as 30 to 45 minutes ahead of that time. This caught me off guard at first, but now when I schedule an event, especially a large dinner, I plan for music and appetizers for the early arrivals."

Jean says she has been most surprised by the latitude afforded the position of First Lady. "I could live here and that would be fine, or make as much of the opportunity as possible. Mel and I came to the Mansion at a very good time in our lives. Since we do not have small children we have to see after, we can have the house open a lot more. I have more time to entertain -- and I love that."

When she leaves the Mansion at the end of her husband's administration, Mrs. Carnahan says she will tell her successor to "keep the traditions and start some new ones. I've worked to discover what those traditions are and I'm trying to reinstate the ones that haven't been followed recently. I think that's very important to the house and to the history of Missouri."

The First Lady hopes to contribute to the history of the state in a special way. She is writing a book about the families that have lived in the current governors' Mansion, "particularly stories about the children who lived in this wonderful home."

If she has one regret about her current position, Jean Carnahan says it is the nagging feeling that there isn't enough time. "I feel I'm rushing all the time and working against a deadline. That adds to the excitement of living here. You don't know what you're going to be doing next."

Epilogue

Missouri's First Ladies have served their state and their families for 175 years. Each has struggled to balance the duties of her unofficial position and the demands of her family. Each has arrived at decisions in some ways similar and in other cases very individualistic. Each faces the common struggle of providing support for her husband as governor while preserving privacy for her family.

Each First Lady has contributed to the history of Missouri. The accounts of some are diminished with the passage of years and the absence of records. Early in the story of the state's First Ladies accounts of the life of the Missouri Indian princess or of the role of the wife of a territorial governor were accorded only brief mention in records of the times. Later ladies often were more distinctive. They joined their husbands on stage and created their own records through their individual activities.

One recent First Lady attempted to turn the political tables and assume the top executive office of the state. Betty Cooper Hearnes, after her family's eight years in the Mansion, chose to take a personal part in state government. The Hearnes family had returned to their home in Charleston, Mo., in January, 1973. Six years later, Betty entered a special election and won a seat in the state House of Representatives. She won re-election four times until 1988 when she answered the call of the Democratic Party to seek the office of governor. Betty won the primary but lost in the November election to John Ashcroft, a popular governor who was seeking his second term.

Mrs. Hearnes made one additional unsuccessful effort in 1990 to regain her seat in the legislature. In 1996, she is living in Charleston and serving as chair of the state Mental Health Commission. Warren Hearnes has a private law practice and also is executive director of Southeast Missouri Legal Services, an appointive position with the federal government.

After the Bonds left Jefferson City in 1985, Carolyn Bond remained briefly in Kansas City. She and Kit moved to Washington when he was elected to the U. S. Senate in 1986. She continues her successful business as an interior decorator and in 1995 accepted a position as director with the American Architectural Foundation. In June, 1994, announcement was made from the senator's office that he and Carolyn were separating after 27 years of marriage. Their divorce was finalized in June, 1995. Carolyn in 1996 continues to live in Washington with the Bonds' son, Sam, who attends a private school on the grounds of the National Cathedral.

Theresa Teasdale's life style has not changed appreciably since she left Jefferson City in January, 1981. The family lives in Kansas City where Joseph Teasdale continues the private law practice he started when he completed his four-year term as governor. In 1996, their three sons attend a Catholic high school-college in Kansas City. Theresa's First Dogs from the Mansion have been replaced with Ellie, a golden retriever who walks with her on most days. Her struggles with culinary skills, previously enhanced by Mansion cooks, currently are being further enriched by classes at a cooking school in Kansas City.

The Ashcrofts' place of residence keeps changing since they left the Mansion in January, 1993. Janet immediately rented a home and remained in Jefferson City while their younger son completed the school year. In the spring, she moved to St. Louis County where John Ashcroft had joined a law firm. In August, 1994, he won nomination to the U. S. Senate and was elected in November. They maintain two residences in 1996 -- a house on the Hill in Washington and their farm on Little Sac River near Springfield, Mo. Daughter, Marti, is married and the Ashcrofts' two sons are in college.

Missouri's executive residence -- the one-time home of all these ladies -- stands on the river bluff in Jefferson City with its exterior largely unchanged since it was built in 1871. The major changes to the outside occurred during the 1937-1941 administration of Gov. and Mrs. Lloyd C. Stark. A kitchen wing was added to the south side of the Mansion and the outside of the building was painted white. Thirty years later, the exterior brick was restored to its original rosy red under the direction of Betty Hearnes.

The interior of the Mansion in 1996 astonishes those seeing it for the first time or those remembering it from earlier years. The residence no longer is subject to the preferences of each successive hostess. A few persons who were frequent visitors as friends of previous first families express nostalgic regrets that they no longer can identify couches, chairs or styles of furnishings reflective of earlier First Ladies.

Most visitors are awed by the elegance of this official building in the center of Missouri. The metamorphosis of the interior started under the direction of Mrs. Hearnes who discovered the shutters hidden in window casings under layers of paint. She restored the shutters and bared the wooden floors. Carolyn Bond, using her decorating skills and insatiable energy, devoted her eight years as First Lady to transforming the interior of the Mansion to reflect the styles of the 1870s. Carolyn was able to bring about creation of Missouri Mansion Preservation Inc., a private, not-for-profit, and nonpartisan group which has legal ownership of many of the Mansion furnishings and supervises all changes and/or additions. MMPI raises funds from private sources to restore the Mansion. Since its creation in 1974, the group has contributed substantial financial support for Mansion projects.

The Mansion today is a showplace for the Renaissance Revival style of furnishings and wall and window treatments -- a style which flourished from the early 1860s to about 1885. Decorators describe the furnishings of that period as massive in scale yet restrained in character. Details include sculptural figures and symmetrical patterns. The first room completed by MMPI was the Library to the left of the entryway. Special touches include stencil patterns and gold leaf on the ceiling and cornices at the windows. Carolyn and the supervising architect, Ted Wofford of St. Louis, emphasize that the underlying philosophy of the project is a "living restoration" -- a restoration authentic to the period when the Mansion was built, yet adaptable to functions held by first families of the present and future.

Throughout the now opulent rooms, there are on every wall reminders of the First Ladies who lived in the Mansion with the mansard roof as well as earlier wives who lived in less splendid houses, including the first governor's wife who lived in a rather plain home in St. Louis. These reminders of years past are the portraits of executive wives, most of them created while they lived in the capital city or added to the Mansion later in efforts to complete the visual history of Missouri's First Ladies.

Similarly, this revised book is dedicated to bringing to current the written history of Missouri's First Ladies: Their Homes and Their Families.

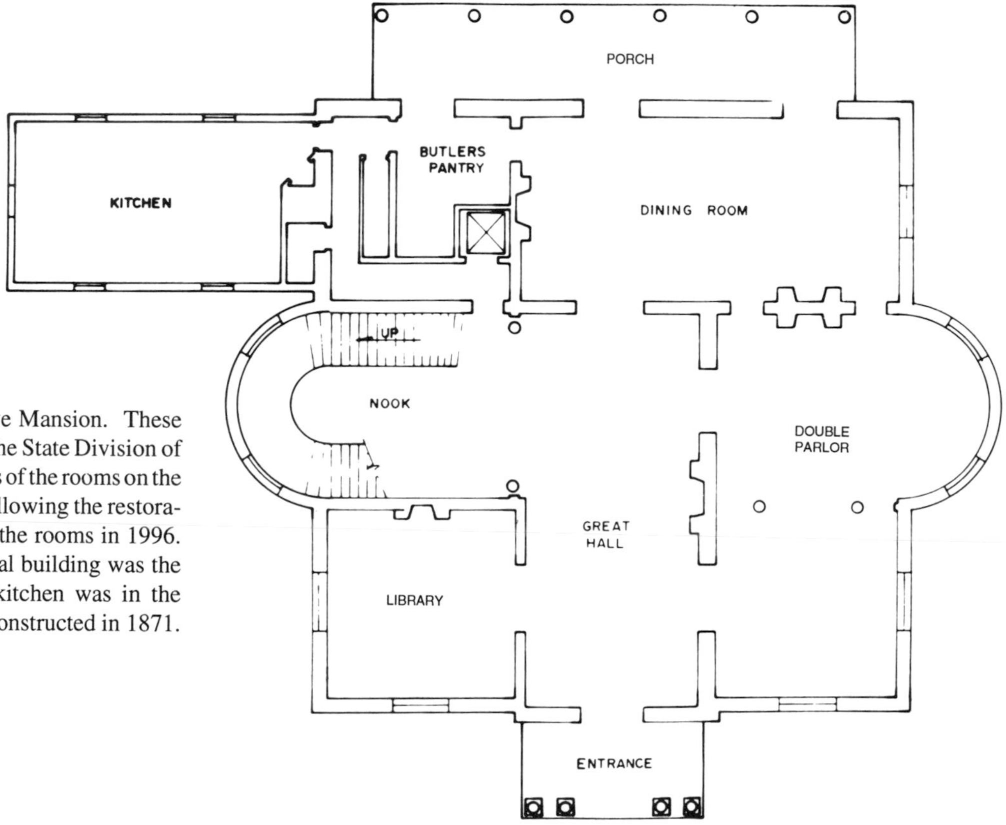

FIRST FLOOR

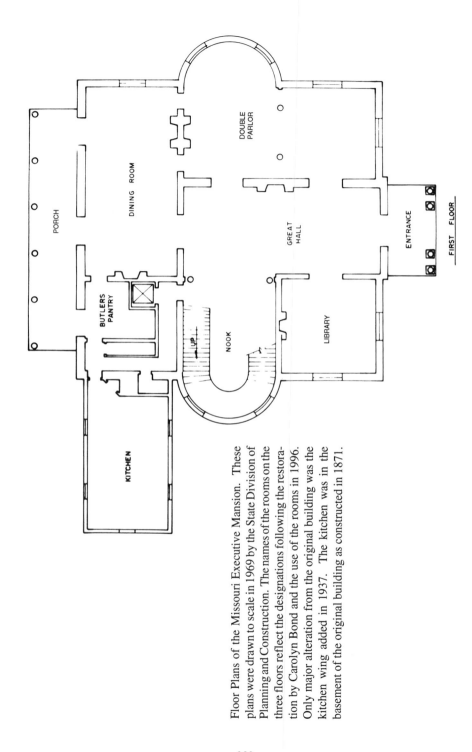

Floor Plans of the Missouri Executive Mansion. These plans were drawn to scale in 1969 by the State Division of Planning and Construction. The names of the rooms on the three floors reflect the designations following the restoration by Carolyn Bond and the use of the rooms in 1996. Only major alteration from the original building was the kitchen wing added in 1937. The kitchen was in the basement of the original building as constructed in 1871.

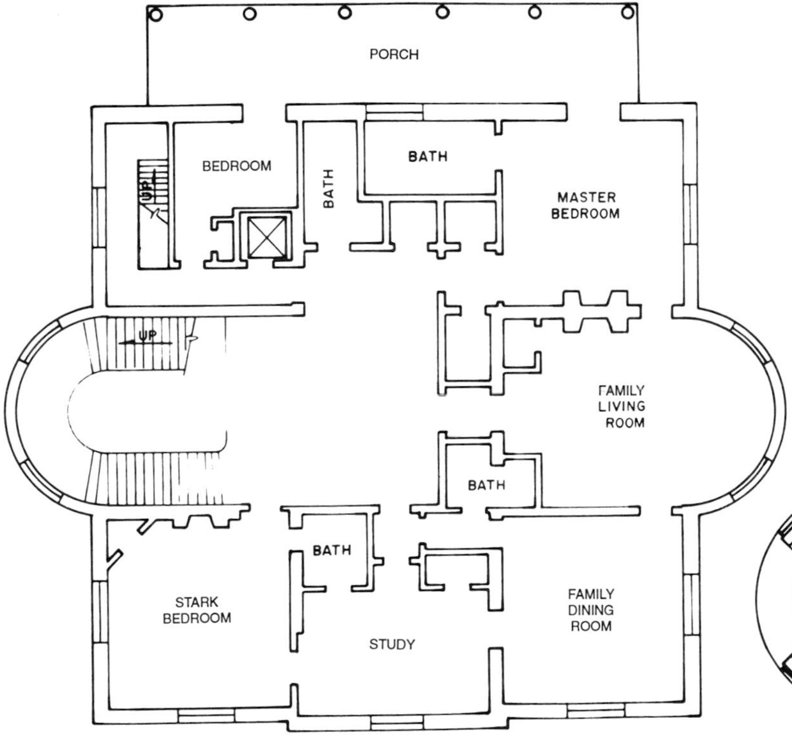

SECOND FLOOR

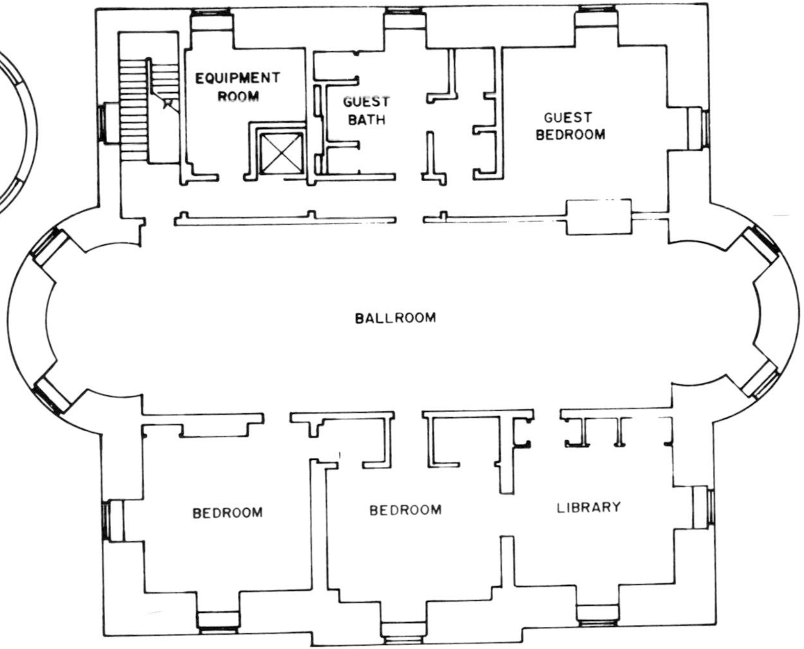

THIRD FLOOR

First Ladies of Missouri, 1805-1996

Name	Husband (Governor)	Birth Date	Married	Inaugural	Death	Children
TERRITORIAL						
	(Amos Stoddard)					
Anne Biddle Wilkinson	James Wilkinson	Not Available	Nov. 12, 1778	1805	Feb. 23, 1807	3
	(Meriwether Lewis)					
Mary Mason Howard	Benjamin Howard	Not Available	Feb. 14, 1811	Not available	March 21, 1813	None
Julia Hancock Clark	William Clark	Nov. 21, 1791	Jan. 5, 1808	June 2, 1813	June 27, 1820	5
STATE OF MISSOURI						
Marguerite de Reilhe McNair	Alexander McNair	Jan. 29, 1787	March, 1805	Sept., 1820	June 17, 1863	10
Nancy Opie Ball Bates	Frederick Bates	April 19, 1802	March 4, 1819	1824	March 16, 1877	4
	(Abraham J. Williams)					
	(John Miller)					
Emily Haley Dunklin	Daniel Dunklin	Feb. 2, 1797	April 28, 1815	Nov. 22, 1832	Nov. 17, 1851	7
Panthea Boone Boggs	Lilburn W. Boggs	Sept. 20, 1801	July 29, 1823	Nov. 23, 1836	Sept. 23, 1880	10
Eliza Ann Young Reynolds	Thomas Reynolds	Not Available	Sept. 2, 1823	Nov. 18, 1840	Jan., 1869	1
Lavinia Sappington Marmaduke	M. M. Marmaduke	Sept. 22, 1807	Jan. 4, 1826	Feb. 9, 1844	Feb. 14, 1885	10
Emma Richard Edwards	John C. Edwards	Jan. 8, 1834	May 4, 1854	Married later	Nov. 29, 1925	11
Nancy Roberts King	Austin A. King	1806	1827	Dec. 27, 1848	Oct. 2, 1857	8
Martha Head Price	Sterling Price	May 2, 1810	May 14, 1833	Jan. 3, 1853	March 5, 1870	7
Elizabeth Skinner Polk	Trusten Polk	Feb. 7, 1819	Dec. 26, 1837	Jan. 5, 1857	Nov. 22, 1896	5
Ursley Oldham Jackson	Hancock Jackson	July 15, 1805	March 8,1821	Feb. 27, 1857	March 4, 1880	11
	(Robert M. Stewart)					
Eliza Sappington Jackson	Claiborne Jackson	March 4, 1806	Nov. 27, 1838	Jan. 3, 1861	July 5, 1864	3

Name	Husband (Governor)	Birth Date	Married	Inaugural	Death	Children
* Heloise Sprague Reynolds	T. C. Reynolds	About 1828	Nov. 28, 1848 or 1849	Dec. 6, 1862	Jan. 25, 1872	None
Caroline Coalter Gamble	Hamilton Gamble	1800	Nov. 8, 1827	July 31, 1861	June 12, 1864	3
Olivia Oliver Hall	Willard P. Hall	About 1845	June 22, 1864	Jan. 31, 1864	June 9, 1926	3
Mary Clarissa Honey Fletcher	Thomas Fletcher	Feb. 3, 1827	April 16, 1851	Jan. 2, 1865	Dec. 19, 1907	2
Mary Johnson McClurg	Joseph McClurg	Not Available	Oct. 18, 1841	Deceased	About 1861	8
Mary Gunn Brown	Benjamin Brown	About 1842	Aug. 17, 1858	Jan. 9, 1871	Feb. 17, 1888	8
Virginia Lard Woodson	Silas Woodson	May 23, 1846	Dec. 27, 1866	Jan. 8, 1873	Jan. 25, 1907	3
Mary Jenkins Hardin	Charles Hardin	Oct. 6, 1824	May 16, 1844	Jan. 12, 1875	Sept. 27, 1904	None
Mary Whitney Phelps	John S. Phelps	Jan. 8, 1812	April 30, 1837	Jan. 8, 1877	Jan. 25, 1878	5
Caroline Jackson Crittenden	Thomas Crittenden	Aug. 1, 1839	Nov. 13, 1856	Jan. 10, 1881	Jan. 27, 1917	4
	(John Marmaduke)					
Martha McFadden Morehouse	Albert Morehouse	May 16, 1838	Jan. 10, 1865	Dec. 28, 1887	Jan. 10, 1900	3
Jane Perry Francis	David R. Francis	Jan., 1855	Jan. 20, 1876	Jan. 14, 1889	March 20, 1924	6
Sarah Winston Stone	William Stone	Nov. 8, 1852	April 2, 1874	Jan. 9, 1893	March 16, 1933	3
Margaret Nelson Stephens	Lon Stephens	Aug. 1, 1859	Oct. 5, 1880	Jan. 11, 1897	April 17, 1929	None
Mary Bird Dockery	Alexander Dockery	March 15, 1849	April 14, 1869	Jan. 14, 1901	Jan. 1, 1903	8
Gertrude Glass Folk	Joseph W. Folk	Feb. 12, 1872	Nov. 10, 1896	Jan. 9, 1905	March 18, 1952	None
Agnes Lee Hadley	Herbert Hadley	March 27, 1876	Oct. 8, 1901	Jan. 11, 1909	Feb. 4, 1946	3
Elizabeth Myers Major	Elliott Major	April 28, 1869	June 14, 1887	Jan. 13, 1913	Nov. 8, 1941	3
Jeannette Vosburgh Gardner	Frederick Gardner	April 30, 1872	Oct. 10, 1896	Jan. 8, 1917	June 4, 1943	3
Hortense Cullers Hyde	Arthur M. Hyde	Sept. 17, 1881	Oct. 19, 1904	Jan. 10, 1921	Sept. 4, 1962	1
Nelle Tuckley Baker	Samuel A. Baker	July 7, 1880	June 1, 1904	Jan. 12, 1925	Nov. 19, 1966	1
Frances Delano Caulfield	Henry Caulfield	Feb. 28, 1875	Oct. 22, 1902	Jan. 14, 1929	Feb. 10, 1961	4

* *Wife of Confederate Governor*

Name	Husband (Governor)	Birth Date	Married	Inaugural	Death	Children
Eleanora Gabbert Park	Guy B. Park	July 28, 1888	Nov. 16, 1909	Jan. 9, 1933	Feb. 25. 1984	1
Katherine Perkins Stark	Lloyd C. Stark	March 23, 1901	Nov. 23, 1931	Jan. 11, 1937	April 19, 1993	3
Hilda Hays Donnell	Forrest Donnell	Aug. 18, 1885	Jan. 29, 1913	Feb. 26, 1941	Oct. 16, 1976	2
Juanita McFadden Donnelly	Phil Donnelly	April 28, 1891	May 22, 1915	Jan. 8, 1945	Dec. 14, 1980	1
Mildred Williams Smith	Forrest Smith	April 6, 1890	Oct. 12, 1915	Jan. 10, 1949	March 16, 1973	2
Juanita Donnelly	(second term)			Jan. 12, 1953		
Emilie Chorn Blair	James Blair Jr.	July 28, 1903	July 17, 1926	Jan. 14, 1957	July 12, 1962	2
Geraldine Hall Dalton	John M. Dalton	July 1, 1909	Nov. 22, 1925	Jan. 9, 1961	July 19, 1989	2
Betty Cooper Hearnes	Warren Hearnes	July 24, 1927	July 2, 1948	Jan. 11, 1965	___	3
Betty Hearnes	(second term)			Jan. 13, 1969	___	
Caroline Reid Bond	Christopher Bond	Oct. 20, 1941	May 13, 1967	Jan. 8, 1973	___	1
Theresa Ferkenhoff Teasdale	Joseph Teasdale	March 7, 1944	Oct. 13, 1973	Jan. 10, 1977	___	3
Caroline Bond	(second term)			Jan. 12, 1981		
Janet Roede Ashcroft	John Ashcroft	Aug. 11, 1944	Dec. 23, 1967	Jan. 14, 1985	___	3
Janet Ashcroft	(second term)			Jan. 9, 1989	___	
Jean Carpenter Carnahan	Mel Carnahan	Dec. 20, 1933	June 12, 1954	Jan. 11, 1993	___	4

Selected Bibliography

PUBLIC DOCUMENTS OF THE UNITED STATES OF AMERICA

The Territorial Papers of the United States, Clarence Edwin Carter, ed. Vol. V, Territory of Mississippi 1798-1817; Vol. XIII, Louisiana-Missouri Territory, 1803-1806; Vol. XIX, The Territory of Arkansas, 1819-1825. United States Government Printing Office, Washington, 1948.

PUBLIC DOCUMENTS OF THE STATE OF MISSOURI

Board of Public Buildings, Jefferson City, Record Book 1, 1953-1965;Record Book 2, 1966-, and accompanying folders. These records contain listings of biddings and work progress on public contracts.

Journal of the House of Representatives of the State of Missouri. Adjourned session, Jefferson City, 1871-1872. Legislation to furnish new mansion, 77; Report of committee on program to receive Grand Duke Alexis, 300-301.

Laws of the State of Missouri. First session, Sixth General Assembly, Jefferson City, 1831, Divorce bill for Eliza Sappington and Alonzo Pearson, 111-113.

________. First session, Seventh General Assembly, Jefferson City, 1832. An act requiring construction of new executive residence, 76.

________. Adjourned session, Twenty-Sixth General Assembly, Jefferson City, 1871-1872. Appropriation to buy lot on Mansion grounds and furnish mansion, 6.

________. Twenty-Seventh General Assembly through Seventy-Second General Assembly, Jefferson City, 1873-1963, all volumes. Sections dealing with mansion appropriations.

Missouri Division of Vital Statistics, Jefferson City, Certificate of Birth, Geraldine Hall Dalton, July 1, 1909, File No. 44240.

________, Certificate of Death, Fannie D. Caulfield, February 10, 1961, File No. 61-006377.

________, Certificate of Death, Jeannette Vosburgh Gardner, June 4, 1943, File No. 16112.

________, Certificate of Death, Ollie L. Batt, June 9, 1926, File No. 19551.

________, Certificate of Death, Mildred Williams Smith, March 16, 1973, File No. 73-006327.

________, Certificate of Death, Hilda Hays Donnell, Oct. 16, 1976, File No. 76-207483.

Official Manual of the State of Missouri, Secretary of State, ed., Jefferson City, 1891-1996, all volumes.

The Messages and Proclamations of the Governors of the State of Missouri, Floyd C. Shoemaker, et al. The State Historical Society of Missouri, Columbia; all volumes I-XX.

PUBLIC DOCUMENTS OF OTHER STATES

Florida State Board of Health, Bureau of Vital Statistics, Jacksonville. Certificate of Death, Margaret Nelson Stephens Johnson, April 17, 1929, File No. 6829.

Department of Public Health, State of Tennessee, Nashville. Certificate of Death, Gertrude Glass Folk, March 18, 1952, File No. 52-05864.

COUNTY RECORDS

Cole County, Office of County Recorder, Deed Record Book A, pg. 74, state buys lots from Angus Langham et al., 138, 148-149, sale of lots on Mansion grounds; Deed Record Book B, 86, 302-303, sales of lots on Mansion grounds; Deed Record Book C, 15, Deed Record Book M, 73, 159-160, change of ownership of Mansion lots; Deed Record Book No. 73, 32 and Deed Record Book No. 79, 80, 83, 85, 86, 89, 90, 91, state repurchases lots on Mansion grounds, Jefferson City, Missouri.

Cole County, Office of County Recorder, Marriage Record Book B, 184, wedding of B. Gratz Brown-Mary Gunn; Marriage Record Book C, 352, marriage of Gottlieb Martin-Fanny Elsner, Jefferson City, Missouri.

Cole County, Probate Court Records, Estate No. 316A., will of Governor Thomas Reynolds, 1844, Jefferson City, Missouri.

MANUSCRIPTS

Blair, James Thomas Jr., Papers, 1957-1961, 5152 folders, 25 volumes; Joint Collection, Western Historical Manuscripts Collection, State Historical Society of Missouri Manuscripts, Columbia, Missouri.

Brown, B. Gratz, one folder of letters regarding building and furnishing of governor's Mansion, 1871-1872; State Archives, State Historical Society of Missouri, Columbia, Missouri.

Brown, B. Gratz, letter, 1850; Joint Collection, Western Historical Manuscripts Collections, State Historical Society of Missouri Manuscripts, Columbia, Missouri.

Brown, B. Gratz, letter, 1872; Joint Collection, Western Historical Manuscripts Collection, State Historical Society of Missouri Manuscripts, Columbia, Missouri.

Carson Family Papers; Missouri Historical Society, St. Louis, Missouri. Collection includes correspondence concerning B. Gratz Brown family.

Caulfield, Fannie Delano, My Life in the Mansion, 10 page booklet; copies in possessionof Mrs. Jane Caulfield Cordonnier, 6306 Washington Ave., St. Louis, Missouri.

Caulfield, Henry S., Papers, 1904-1966, 117 folders, 10 scrapbooks, includes diary or day book of Mrs. Caulfield, and Mansion Guest Register; Joint Collection, Western Historical Manuscripts Collection, State Historical Society of Missouri Manuscripts, Columbia, Missouri.

Collet's Index to St. Louis Church Registers, Baptisms; Missouri Historical Society, St. Louis, Missouri.

Connelly, Mrs. Clyde D., Early Women in Missouri, Daughters of the American Revolution, 1921-1923; typescript in files of Missouri Historical Society, St. Louis, Missouri.

Donnelly, Juanita, Typescripts I, II, first person accounts of her years as First Lady; in 1970 in possession of Mrs. Phil M. Donnelly, 252 South Adams, Lebanon, Missouri.

Donnelly, Phil M. Papers, 1944-1957, 8178 folders, 14 boxes, 62 volumes; Joint Collection, Western Historical Manuscripts Collection, State Historical Society of Missouri Manuscripts, Columbia, Missouri.

Duncan, Jenkins, Hardin Family Papers, 1821-1860, two folders; Joint Collection, Western Historical Manuscripts Collection, State Historical Society of Missouri Manuscripts, Columbia, Missouri.

Dunklin, Daniel, Papers, 1815-1877, 42 folders; Joint Collection, Western Historical Manuscripts Collection, State Historical Society of Missouri Manuscripts, Columbia, Missouri.

Folk, Joseph Wingate, Papers, 1902-1952, 43 folders; Joint Collection, Western Historical Manuscripts Collection, State Historical Society of Missouri Manuscripts, Columbia, Missouri.

Hadley, Agnes L., Daybook of Mrs. Agnes L. Hadley, 1909-1913; Cole County Historical Society Museum, Jefferson City, Missouri.

Hadley, Herbert Spencer, Papers, 1876-1943, 1065 folders, 50 volumes; Joint Collection, Western Historical Manuscripts Collection, State Historical Society of Missouri Manuscripts, Columbia, Missouri.

Hardin, Charles Henry, Papers, 1842-1892, 10 folders; Joint Collection, Western Historical Manuscripts Collection, State Historical Society of Missouri Manuscripts, Columbia, Missouri.

Hardin, Mary B., Diary, 1854-1860, 86 pp.; Joint Collection, Western Historical Manuscripts Collection, State Historical Society of Missouri Manuscripts, Columbia, Missouri.

Hardin, Mary B., Diary, 1867, 183 pp.; in 1970 in possession of Mrs. John H. Hendren, 1628 West Main Street, Jefferson City, Missouri.

Hyde, Arthur Mastick, Papers, 1919-1925, 1828 folders; Joint Collection, Western Historical Manuscripts Collection, State Historical Society of Missouri Manuscripts, Columbia, Missouri.

Inaugural Dresses, ball gowns and other items of apparel of 15 First Ladies or state hostesses of Missouri, descriptions on cards and dresses on display; Cole County Historical Society Museum, Jefferson City, Missouri.

Index to St. Louis Register, Baptisms, Marriages and Burials, 1766-1781, from the Archives of the St. Louis Cathedral, 1912-1913; Missouri Historical Society, St. Louis, Missouri.

James, Mary Burton, undated typescript of speech on inaugural gowns of Missouri; Cole County Historical Society Museum, Jefferson City, Missouri.

McNair, Alexander, Papers; Missouri Historical Society, St. Louis, Missouri.

Marmaduke, Lavinia Sappington, Bible record, copied by Daughters of the American Revolution, Marshall Chapter; mimeographed copy on file at the State Historical Society, Columbia, Missouri.

Marmaduke, Meredith Miles, Papers, 1823-1886, 3 boxes; Joint Collection, Western Historical Manuscripts Collection, State Historical Society of Missouri Manuscripts, Columbia, Missouri.

Mitchell, Ewing Young, Jr., Papers, 1841-1949, 4018 folders, 2 boxes, 7 volumes; Joint Collection, Western Historical Manuscripts Collection, State Historical Society of Missouri Manuscripts, Columbia, Missouri.

Park, Guy B., Papers, 1932-1936, 2255 folders; Joint Collection, Western Historical Manuscripts Collection, State Historical Society of Missouri Manuscripts, Columbia, Missouri.

Paxton's St. Louis Directory and Register, 1821; copy on file at the Missouri Historical Society, St. Louis, Missouri.

Pennington, Steve; typescript, May 9, 1968, 21 page architectural study of the Missouri executive mansion; in possession of Steve Pennington, 1822 Taylor Drive, Jefferson City, Missouri.

Price Family Papers; Missouri Historical Society, St. Louis, Missouri.

Salmon, Harvey Wallis, Papers; Missouri Historical Society, St. Louis, Missouri. This collection includes letters regarding the death of Gov. C.F. Jackson.

Simmons, Lucy, The Life of Sterling Price; Master's dissertation, 1922, University of Chicago, Chicago, Illinois.

Smith, Forrest, Papers, 1940-1953, 6642 folders, 13 volumes, 8 card file boxes, including original copies of weekly newspaper columns; Joint Collection, Western Historical Manuscripts Collection, State Historical Society of Missouri Manuscripts, Columbia, Missouri.

Smith, Mildred Williams, handwritten papers concerning a first person account of her life as First Lady, 1949-1953; in 1970 in possession of Mrs. Forrest Smith, 1006 Fairmount Court, Jefferson City, Missouri.

Snyder, Dr. John F., Collection; Missouri Historical Society, St. Louis, Missouri. Collection includes correspondence concerning Gov. and Mrs. John Phelps and Fort Orleans.

Spanish Governors of Louisiana, Dispatches of., 1766-1796, 11 books with English translations; Manuscripts and Rare Book Section, Howard-Tilton Memorial Library, Tulane University, New Orleans, Louisiana.

Spencer, George D., Papers, 1948-1960, 653 folders, 9 boxes, 1 scrapbook, including report of Special Mansion Investigating Committee; Joint Collection, Western Historical Manuscripts Collection, State Historical Society of Missouri Manuscripts, Columbia, Missouri.

Stark, Katherine Lemoine, typescript, personal account of her years as First Lady, 1937-1941, and separate typescript of biographical material; in 1970 in possession of Mrs. Lloyd C. Stark, Aberdeen Farms, Eolia, Missouri.

Stark, Lloyd C., Papers, 1931-1941; 12, 401 folders, Joint Collection, Western Historical Manuscripts Collection, State Historical Society of Missouri Manuscripts, Columbia, Missouri.

Stephens, Margaret Nelson, Diary, No. 1, Sept., 1894 - August 26, 1896, No. 2, Executive Mansion, July 1, 1897 - April 20, 1903; in possession of Charles Leonard, Ravenswood Farm, Belair, Cooper County, Missouri.

Stone, William Jack, Papers, 1878-1935, 113 folders, 1 scrapbook; Joint Collection, Western Historical Manuscripts Collection, State Historical Society of Missouri Manuscripts, Columbia, Missouri.

Tally, Stephenie Hillegeist, Genealogy of the Boggs Family, 1965, typescript; Reference Library, State Historical Society, Columbia, Missouri.

Works Progress Administration, Historical Records Survey, 1935-1942, 14,696 folders; Joint Collection, Western Historical Manuscripts Collections, State Historical Society of Missouri Manuscripts, Columbia, Missouri.

CLIPPING COLLECTIONS

Cole County Historical Society Museum, Jefferson City, Missouri, six scrapbooks containing newspaper clippings, legal documents, letters, concerning history of central Missouri and state history in general.

Dalton, Jerry, two large scrapbooks containing newspaper clippings, personal items, invitations, photographs; in 1970 in possession of Mrs. John M. Dalton of Jefferson City, Missouri.

Missouri State Library, folders of newspaper items concerning Carolyn Bond, Missouri Mansion, Governor Teasdale, Governor Ashcroft, Governor Carnahan; Secretary of State's Office Building, Jefferson City, Missouri.

Park, Eleanora, six scrapbooks containing newspaper clippings and personal items concerning Mrs. Park's early life, the early life of Guy B. Park, the political life of Gov. and Mrs. Park, and the life of Thomas W. Park, father of Gov. Park; in 1970 in possession of Mrs. Henrietta Park Krause, Columbia, Missouri.

St. Charles County Historical Society, newspaper clippings concerning St. Charles history; in 1967 in possession of Mrs. Edna McElhiney Olson, archivist for society, at her home, 125 North Fifth Street, St. Charles, Missouri.

Smith, Mildred Williams, two scrapbooks containing newspaper clippings and other mementoes of her years as First Lady, in 1970 in possession of Mrs. Smith, 1006 Fairmount Court, Jefferson City, Missouri.

Stephens, Margaret Nelson, one scrapbook of newspaper clippings and personal mementoes including period 1897-1898, one album of some 200 snapshots; in 1970 in possession of Charles Leonard, Ravenswood Farm, Belair, Cooper County, Missouri.

NEWSPAPERS

(All issues in the files of the State Historical Society, Columbia, Missouri, except as noted)

Chillicothe Constitution, Chillicothe, Missouri, Jan. 2, 1903; Jan. 9, 1903, pg. 7 Cols. 1-5, death of Mrs. Mary Dockey.

Free Press, St. Louis, Missouri, Feb. 28, 1833, pg. 3 col. 6, notice of bidding for construction of new governor's residence.

Jefferson Enquirer, Jefferson City, Missouri, Sept., 1840 - March, 1841.

Jefferson Inquirer, Jefferson City, Missouri, April, 1841 - Dec., 1849; Feb. 23, 1850 - Oct. 14, 1854; 1855; 1856 - Sept. 29, 1859; June 10, 1860 - Jan. 26, 1861.

Jeffersonian Republican, Jefferson City, Missouri, April 30, 1831- Dec. 17, 1831; Jan. 12, 1833 - Dec. 28, 1835; Jan. 2-Dec. 31, 1839; Jan. - Dec. 28, 1839; Jan. - Dec., 1840; Jan.-Dec., 1841.

Jefferson City Post-Tribune, Sunday News and Tribune, Jefferson City, Missouri, Jan., 1941 - Jan., 1945.

Jefferson City Sunday News and Tribune, Jefferson City, Missouri, Nov. 20, 1966; pg. 1 col. 8, death of Mrs. Nelle Baker.

Jefferson City Tribune, Jefferson City, Missouri, July, 1882 -Jan., 1901, all issues.

Kansas City Post, Kansas City, Missouri, Jan. 26, 1907, pg. 2 col. 2., death of Mrs. Virginia Woodson.

Kansas City Star, Kansas City, Missouri, June 10, 1926, "Grief Kills A Mother," death of Mrs. Ollie L. Batt.

Louisiana Courier, New Orleans, Louisiana, June 7, 1822, pg. 3 col. 3, burial of Manuel Perez; May 1, 1843, pg. 2 col. 5, death of Col. Charles De Lassus. (New Orleans Public Library)

Marion County, Palmyra Spectator, Palmyra, Missouri, Nov. 23, ,1921, pg. 9 cols. 3-4, "Eccentric Governor Freed All Women in State Prison."

Missouri Gazette, St. Louis, Missouri, April 17, 1813, pg. 3 col. 4., death of Mary Howard, wife of Gov. Howard; July 3, 1813, pg. 3 col. 4, Gen. William Clark accepts as governor of territory; Oct. 1, 1814, pg. 3 col. 3, death of Brig Gen. Benjamin Howard.

Missouri Intelligencer, Franklin, Missouri, June 11, 1821, pg. 3 col. 1, special commission on site of permanent seat of government recommends two possible locations; June 25, 1821, pg. 1 cols. 2-4 and pg. 2 col. 1, complete report of special commission on site of permanent seat of government and lists of advantages and disadvantages; Aug. 5, 1822-June 16, 1826, all issues.

Missouri Intelligencer, Fayette, Missouri, June-Dec., 1826, all issues.

Missouri State Times, Jefferson City, Missouri, Jan. 3, 1863-July, 1868; Jan. 8, 1869-Dec. 30, 1870, all issues.

Mount Vernon Chieftain, Mount Vernon, Missouri, Feb. 6, 1936, pg. 2 col. 1, reprint of item concerning death of Mrs. John Phelps.

New-Orleans Bee, New Orleans, Louisiana, May 2, 1843, pg. 1 col. 5, death of Col. DeLassus. (New Orleans Public Library).

St. Joseph Daily Gazette, St. Joseph, Missouri, Nov. 4, 1882, pg. 2 col. 2, death of Gov. Willard P. Hall, pg. 4 cols. 1-2, biography of Gov. Hall.

St. Louis Home Journal, St. Louis, Missouri, May 2, 1868, pg. 2 col. 6-7, "From Central Missouri." (St. Louis Public Library).

St. Louis Missouri Democrat, St. Louis, Missouri, March 17, 1871, House passes Senate Bill appropriating $50,000.00 for new Mansion; March 18, 1871, pg. 3 col. 2, reaction to passage of mansion bill.

St. Louis Post-Dispatch, St. Louis, Missouri, Nov. 10, 1940, feature story by Clarrisa Start about Mrs. Forrest C. Donnell; March 4, 1941, feature about Gov.

and Mrs. Donnell by Curtis Betts; April 4-6, 1943, stories of visit of Grand Duchess Charlotte of Luxembourg; May 2, 1943, plans for unveiling portrait of Mrs. Donnell.

St. Louis Republican, St. Louis, Missouri, Aug. 19, 1878, pg. 8 col. 2, exposure of grave of Gov. Howard in grading of street. (Missouri Historical Society).

Springfield Daily News, Springfield, Missouri, Sept. 21, 1936, "The Waste Basket"; Oct. 8, 10, 1936, "The Old Timer."

Springfield Weekly Leader, Springfield, Missouri, Jan. 31, 1878, pg. 3 col. 2 death of Mrs. Mary Phelps.

The Maryville Republican, Maryville, Missouri, Jan. 11, 1900, pg. 1, death of Mrs. A. P. Morehouse.

The Peoples' Tribune, Jefferson City, Missouri, Oct. 4, 1865-Dec. 26, 1883, all issues.

The Princeton Post, Princeton, Missouri, Oct. 21, 1904, pg. 1, story of wedding of Arthur M. Hyde.

ARTICLES

Anderson, Frank, "Missouri's Confederate State Capitol at Marshall, Texas." Missouri Historical Review, XXVII (April, 1933), 240-243.

"Are Inaugurations For the Officers or Their Wives?" Missouri Historical Review, XLIII, (April 1949), 312-313.

Bek, William G., "The Followers of Duden–The Approaching Storm." Missouri Historical Review, XVII (April, 1923), 334-339.

Boggs, William M., "A Short Biographical Sketch of Lilburn W. Boggs." Missouri Historical Review, IV (January, 1910), 106-110.

Boggs, William M., "Reminiscences of William M. Boggs, son of Governor Lilburn W. Boggs," Missouri Historical Review, VI (January, 1912), 86-90.

Broadhead, G.C., "The Location of the Capital of Missouri." Missouri Historical Review, II (January, 1908), 158-163.

Brown, Edward, "Alexander McNair, First Governor of Missouri." St. Louis Catholic Historical Review, Catholic Historical Society of St. Louis, I (July-October, 1919), 231-242.

Carondelet to Howard, "Letter of Instructions." Missouri Historical Society Collections, III (January, 1908), 71-91.

Cary, Mrs. Lalla Marmaduke, Obituary. Missouri Historical Review, XXX (July, 1936), 459.

Chouteau, Col. Auguste, "Journal of the Founding of St. Louis." Missouri Historical Society Collections, III (1911), 335-366.

Collot, George H. Victor, "Descriptions of St. Louis, Report of French Staff Officer." Glimpses of the Past, Missouri Historical Society, I-III (March, 1934), 20-30.

Crittenden, Thomas F., "Selections from the Autobiography of Governor T. T. Crittenden." Missouri Historical Review, XXVI (October, 1931), 3-11; (January, 1932), 142-152; (April, 1932), 241-255.

De Wyl, Dr. N.E., "Archaeological Explorations in Cole County, Mo." Missouri Historical Society Publications, I (1880-1899), 19-20.

"Earliest Picture of St. Louis." Glimpses of the Past, Missouri Historical Society, VIII (July-September, 1941), 71-98.

Faye, Stanley, "The Arkansas Post of Louisiana: Spanish Domination." The Louisiana Historical Quarterly, XXVII (July, 1944), 629-716.

Finkelnburg, Gustavus A., "Under Three Flags, or The Story of St. Louis Briefly Told." Missouri Historical Society Collections, III (1911), 201-232.

Folmer, Henri, "Etienne Veniard de Bourgmond in the Missouri Country." Missouri Historical Review, XXXVI (April, 1942), 279-298.

Garraghan, Gilbert J., "Fort Orleans of the Missoury." Missouri Historical Review, XXXV (April, 1941), 373-384.

Geise, William R. "Missouri's Confederate Capital in Marshall, Texas." Missouri Historical Review, LVIII (October, 1963), 37-54.

Gordon, Robert, "Listening in on 'Governor's Night'." Missouri Historical Review, XLV (October, 1950), 106-107.

Gregg, Kate L., "The History of Fort Osage." Missouri Historical Review, XXXIV (July, 1940), 439-488.

________, "The Missouri Reader-Explorers in the Valley." Missouri Historical Review, XXXIX (April, 1945), 354-388; "De Bourgmont", (July, 1945), 512-528.

Haskell, Agnes Lee, Obituary. Missouri Historical Review, XL (April, 1946), 455.

Hill, Ed C., "Has The Site of Fort Orleans Been Discovered?" Missouri Historical Society Collections, IV (1914), 367-370.

Jackson, Claiborne F., "Letter of Governor Claiborne F. Jackson." Missouri Historical Society Collections, II (April, 1903), 21-23.

Judson, Frederick N., "The Administration of Governor B. Gratz Brown." Missouri Historical Society Collections, II (April, 1903), 24-44.

Karst, Emile, "Convict Fiddled Out of Missouri Prison." Missouri Historical Review, XXXV (July, 1941), 666-667.

Kirkpatrick, Arthur Roy, "Missouri's Secessionist Government." Missouri Historical Review, XLV (July, 1951), 124-137.

Lee, John F., "John Sappington Marmaduke." Missouri Historical Society Collections, II (July, 1906), 26-40.

"Letters of Thomas Caute Reynolds, 1847-1885." Glimpses of the Past, Missouri Historical Society, X (January-June, 1943), 3-54.

"Letters of William Carr Lane, 1819-1831." Glimpses of the Past, Missouri Historical Society, VII (July-September, 1940), 47-114.

Major, Mrs. Elliott W., Obituary. Missouri Historical Review, XXXVI (January, 1942), 255.

McDermott, John Francis, "Museums In Early Saint Louis." Bulletin, Missouri Historical Society, IV (April, 1948), 129-138.

"Missouriana-Service Organizations For Civil War Soldiers." Missouri Historical Review, XXXVII (April, 1943), 321-325.

Nelson, Arthur W., Obituary. Missouri Historical Review, XXVI (July, 1932), 416.

"Not Even The Outward and Visible Signs." Missouri Historical Review, XXXVI (April, 1942), 393-394.

Papin, Edward Villere, "The Village Under The Hill, A Sketch of Early St. Louis." Missouri Historical Society Collections, V (October, 1927), 18-37.

Peterson, Charles E., "Colonial St. Louis." Bulletin, The Missouri Historical Society, III (April, 1947), 94-111; (July, 1947), 133-149; IV (October, 1947), 11-30.

Philips, Judge John F., "Hamilton Rowan Gamble and The Provisional Government of Missouri." Missouri Historical Review, V (October, 1910), 1-14.

Primm, Wilson, "New Year's Day In The Olden Time of St. Louis."Missouri Historical Society Collections, II (January, 1900), 12-22.

Quaife, M.M., "Detroit Biographies-The Sieur de Bourgmont." Burton Historical Collection Leaflet, Detroit Public Library, VI (March, 1928), 49-63.

Scott, Mary Semple, et al., "History of Woman Suffrage in Missouri." Missouri Historical Review, XIV (April-July, 1920), 281-384.

Shackleford, Thomas, "Early Recollections of Missouri." Missouri Historical Society Collections, II (April, 1903), 1-20.

Sharp, Grace Marmaduke, "The Marmaduke and Some Allied Families." William and Mary College Quarterly, Second Series, No. 15 (1935), 151-172.

Shoemaker, Floyd C., "Fort Orleans: The Heritage of Carroll County." Missouri Historical Review, LI (January, 1957), 105-112.

Smit, William M., "Old Broadway, A Forgotten Street and Its Park of Mounds." The Bulletin, Missouri Historical Society, IV (April, 1948), 153-163.

Stadler, Frances Hurd, "A Letter From Lizzie Price." The Bulletin, Missouri Historical Society, XIX (July, 1963), 340-344.

Stipes, M.F., "Fort Orleans, The First French Post on the Missouri." Missouri Historical Review, VIII (April, 1914), 121-135.

"The Butt End of the Joke." Missouri Historical Review, XXXVI (April, 1942), 390.

Thompson, Cyrus, "Reminiscences of Official Life In Jefferson City, 1865-1875." Missouri Historical Review, XXIII (July, 1929), 550-567.

Temps, Vieux, "Old French Times." Glimpses of the Past, Missouri Historical Society, IV (January-March, 1937), 35-38.

Thwaites, Reuben Gold, "William Clark: Soldier, Explorer, Statesman." Missouri Historical Society Collections, II (October, 1906), 1-24.

Van Ravenswaay, Charles, "Missouri Cookery." Bulletin, The Missouri Historical Society, III (January, 1947), 53-59.

"Vest's Reminiscences of Governor Thomas C. Reynolds." Missouri Historical Review, XXXIII (July, 1939), 594-595.

Viles, Jonas, "Missouri Capitals and Capitols." Missouri Historical Review, XIII (January, 1919), 135-156; (April, 1919), 232-250.

PAMPHLETS

New England Historical and Genealogical Register, published quarterly by New England Historical Genealogical Society, Boston, III (April, 1849), 195; LXIII (April, 1909), 158. Both issues list notice of marriage of Thomas C. Reynolds and Heloise Sprague.

Olson, Edna McElhiney, "Historical Saint Charles, Mo.", 1967. Published privately in St. Charles by author.

Peterson, Charles E., "Colonial St. Louis, Building a Creole Capital," Missouri Historical Society, St. Louis, 1949.

Quigley, Martin, "St. Louis, The First 200 Years," First National Bank, St. Louis, 1954.

St. Vrain, Paul Augustus, "Genealogy of the Family of De Lassus and Saint Vrain," Kirksville, Mo., March 16, 1943.

Smith, Melbourne, "Life Sketch of Joseph Wingate Folk," Privately published reprints of articles originally published in The Farmington Times, Feb. 5, 12, 19, 1904.

BOOKS

A Biographical History of Nodaway and Atchison Counties, Missouri. The Lewis Publishing Company, Chicago, 1901.

Adamson, Hans Christian, Rebellion in Missouri: 1861, Nathaniel Lyon and His Army of the West. Chilton Co., Philadelphia and New York, 1961.

Alvord, Idress Head, Descent of Henry Head 1695-1949, In America. Mid-State Printing Co., Jefferson City, Mo., 1949.

Arthur, Stanley Clisby and Kernion, George, Old Families of Louisiana. Harmanson, New Orleans, 1931.

Barns, C.R., Switzler's History of Missouri. Published by the author, St. Louis, 1879.

Bates, Onward, Bates, et al. of Virginia and Missouri. P.F. Pettibone & Company, Chicago, 1914.

Beck, Lewis C., A Gazeteer of the State of Illinois and Missouri. Charles R. and George Webster, Albany and New York, 1823.

Billon, Frederic L., Annals of St. Louis In Its Territorial Days From 1804 to 1821. Printed by the author, St. Louis, 1888.

________, Annals of St. Louis, In Its Early Days, 1764-1804. Printed for the author, St. Louis, 1886.

Bossu, Mr. Captain in the French Marines, Travels Through That Part Of North America formerly called Louisiana. Translated by John Reinhold Forster. Printed for T. Davies in Ruffel-Street, Covent-Garden, London, 1771. 2 vols.

Boyer, Mary Joan, Jefferson County Missouri in Story and Pictures. Tri-City Independent, 1956.

Bryan, John Albury, Missouri's Contribution To American Architecture. St. Louis Architectural Club, March, 1928.

Bryan, William S., and Rose, Robert, A History of the Pioneer Families of Missouri. Bryan, Brand & Co., St. Louis, Mo., 1876.

Burson, Caroline Maude, The Stewardship of Don Esteban Miro, 1782-1792. American Printing Co., Ltd., New Orleans, 1940.

Caldwell, Dorothy J., Missouri Historic Sites Catalogue. The State Historical Society of Missouri, Columbia, Mo., 1963.

Collins, Lewis, revised by Collins, Richard H., History of Kentucky. Collins & Co., Covington, Ky., 1882, Vol. II.

Conard, Howard L., Encyclopedia of the History of Missouri. The Southern History Co., Haldeman, Conard & Co., proprietors, New York, Louisville, St. Louis, 1901. 6 vols.

Crittenden, H.H., The Crittenden Memoirs. G.P. Putnam's Sons, New York, 1936.

Darby, John F., Personal Recollections. G.I. Jones and Co., St. Louis, 1880.

Davis, W.B. and Durrie, D.S., An Illustrated History of Missouri. A.J. Hall and Company, St. Louis; Robert Clarke & Co., Cincinnati, 1876.

Devoy, John, A History of the City of St. Louis and Vicinity. Compiled and published by the author, St. Louis, 1898.

Dillon, Richard, Meriwether Lewis, A Biography. Coward-McCann, Inc., New York, 1965.

Edwards, Richard and Hopewell, M., Edwards's Great West. Published by Richard

Edwards, St. Louis, 1860.

Egle, William Henry, Pennsylvania Genealogies. Land S. Hart, printer and binder, Harrisburg, 1886.

Federal Writers' Project, California, A Guide to the Golden State. Hastings House, New York, 1967.

________, Missouri, A Guide to The "Show-Me" State. Duell, Sloan and Pearce, New York, 1941.

Ford, James E., A History of Jefferson City. The New Day Press, Jefferson City, Mo., 1938.

Fortier, Alcee, A History of Louisiana. Goupil & Co., Paris; Manzi, Joyant and Co., successors, New York, 1904. 4 vols.

Geiger, Louis G., Joseph W. Folk of Missouri. The Curators of the University of Missouri, Columbia, Mo., 1953.

General History of Macon County. Henry Taylor and Company, Chicago, 1910.

Gill, McCune, The St. Louis Story. Historical Record Association, Hopkinsville, Kan., and St. Louis, Mo., 1952. 3 vols.

Hardin, Mary Barr, Life and Writings of Governor Charles H. Hardin. Buschart Bros., St. Louis, 1896.

Hay, Thomas Robson and Werner, M. R., The Admirable Trumpeter, A Biography of General James Wilkinson. Doubleday, Doran and Co., Inc., Garden City, New York, 1941.

Head, Idress, Historical and Interesting Places of St. Louis. Missouri Historical Society, St. Louis, 1909.

Historical, Pictorial and Biographical Record of Chariton County, Missouri. Pictorial and Biographical Publishing Co., Salisbury, 1896.

History of Boone County, Missouri. Western Historical Company, St. Louis, 1882.

History of Buchanan County and St. Joseph, Mo. The History Publishing Company, Midland Printing Company, St. Joseph, Missouri, 1915.

History of Cole, Moniteau, Morgan, Benton, Miller, Maries and Osage Counties, Missouri. The Goodspeed Publishing Co., Chicago, 1889.

History of Greene County, Missouri. Western Historical Company, St. Louis, 1883.

History of Howard and Chariton Counties, Missouri. National Historical Company,

St. Louis, 1883.

History of Howard and Cooper Counties, Missouri. National Historical Company, St. Louis, 1883.

History of Randolph and Macon Counties, Missouri. National Historical Company, St. Louis, 1884.

History of Saline County, Missouri. Missouri Historical Company, St. Louis, 1881.

Houck, Louis, A History of Missouri. R.R. Donnelly and Sons Company, Chicago, 1908. 2 vols.

________, The Spanish Regime in Missouri. R.R. Donnelly and Sons Company, Chicago, 1909. 2 vols.

Hyde, William and Conard, Howard L., Encyclopedia of the History of St. Louis. Southern History Co., New York, Louisville and St. Louis, 1899. 3 vols.

Jackson, William Rufus, Missouri Democracy . . . A History of the Party and its Representative Members-Past and Present. S.J. Clarke Publishing Co., Inc., Chicago, St. Louis, Indianapolis, 1935. 3 vols.

Jacobs, James Ripley, Tarnished Warrior, Major-General James Wilkinson. The MacMillan Co., New York, 1938.

Johnson, Allen and/or Malone, Dumas, Dictionary of American Biography. Charles Scribner's Sons, New York, 1928-1933. 12 vols.

Johnson, W.F., History of Cooper County, Missouri. Historical Publishing Company, Topeka and Cleveland, 1919.

Kennerly, William Clark with Russell, Elizabeth, Persimmon Hill. University of Oklahoma Press, Norman, Oklahoma, 1948.

King, Grace, Creole Families of New Orleans. The MacMillan Co., New York, 1921.

Kirschten, Ernest, Catfish and Crystal. Doubleday and Company, Inc.,Garden City, New York, 1960.

LePage du Pratz, Antoine Simon, History of Louisiana. Vol. III, translated by Beatrice Paddock, Wichita City Library, 1936.

Lionberger, I.H., The Annals of St. Louis and A Brief Account of Its Foundation and Progress, *1764-1927*. Mound City Press, St. Louis, 1928.

March, David D., The History of Missouri. Lewis Historical Publishing Co., Inc., New York and West Palm Beach, 1967. 4 vols.

Marshall, Thomas Maitland, The Life and Papers of Frederick Bates. Missouri Historical Society, St. Louis, 1926. 2 vols.

Meyers, Duane, The Heritage of Missouri, A History. State Publishing Co., Inc., St. Louis, Mo., 1963.

McClung, Quantrille D., Genealogy of Carson-Bent-Boggs. Published by the Denver Public Library, 1962.

McDermott, John Francis, The French in the Mississippi Valley. University of Illinois Press, Urbana, 1965.

Monette, John Wesley, History of the Discovery and Settlement of the Valley of the Mississippi. Harper and Brothers, New York, 1846. 2 vols.

Musick, James B., St. Louis As A Fortified Town. Press of R. F. Miller, St. Louis, 1941.

Park, Eleanora G. and Morrow, Kate S., Women of the Mansion, 1821-1936. Midland Printing Company, Jefferson City, Mo., 1936.

Parker, Lester, Missouri's New State Capitol, Official Guide Book. Stephens Printing Co., Jefferson City, 1924.

Parrish, William E., Missouri Under Radical Rule 1865-1870. University of Missouri Press, Columbia, Mo., 1965.

________, Turbulent Partnership, Missouri and the Union, 1861-65. University of Missouri Press, Columbia, Mo., 1963.

Peterson, Norma L., Freedom and Franchise, The Political Career of B. Gratz Brown. University of Missouri Press, Columbia, Mo., 1965.

Pickard, John, The Missouri State Capitol, Report of the Capitol Decoration Commission. 1917-1928. No publisher listed.

Pictorial and Genealogical Record of Greene County, Missouri. Goodspeed Bros., Chicago, 1893.

Rea, Ralph R., Sterling Price, The Lee of The West. Pioneer Press, Little Rock, Ark., 1959.

Reaves, L.U., St. Louis, The Future Great City of the World. 1875. No printer listed.

Rutt, Chris. L., History of Buchanan County and the City of St. Joseph and Representative Citizens. Biographical Publishing Company, Chicago, Ill., 1904.

Scharf, J.T., History of Saint Louis City and County. Louis H. Everts and Co.,

Philadelphia, 1883. 2 vols.

Seebold, Herman, Old Louisiana Plantation Homes and Family Trees. Pelican Press, Inc., New Orleans, 1941. 2 vols.

Settle, William A. Jr., Jesse James Was His Name. University of Missouri Press, Columbia, Mo., 1966.

Shepard, Elihu H., The Autobiography of Elihu H. Shepard. George Knapp & Co., St. Louis, 1869.

________, The Early History of St. Louis and Missouri, 1673-1843. Southwestern Book and Publishing Co., St. Louis, 1870.

Shoemaker, Floyd C., Missouri, Day by Day. State Historical Society of Missouri, Columbia, Mo., 1942-43. 2 vols.

________, Missouri's Struggle For Statehood. The Hugh Stephens Printing Co., Jefferson City, Mo., 1916.

Shreve, Royal Ornan, The Finished Scoundrel. The Bobbs-Merrill Company, Indianapolis, 1933.

Spencer, Thomas Edwin, The Story of Old St. Louis. Con P. Curran Printing Co., St. Louis, 1914.

Stevens, Walter B., Centennial History of Missouri. The S.J. Clarke Publishing Company, St. Louis-Chicago, 1921. 6 vols.

________, St. Louis, The Fourth City. The S.J. Clarke Publishing Company, St. Louis-Chicago, 1909. 3 vols.

The Battle of New Orleans-Plantation Houses on the Battlefield of New Orleans. Published by the Battlefield of New Orleans, 150th Anniversary Committee of Louisiana, 1965.

Stewart, A.J.D., The History of the Bench and Bar of Missouri. The Legal Publishing Company, St. Louis, Mo., 1898.

The United States Biographical Dictionary, Missouri Volume. United States Biographical Publishing Company, New York, Chicago, St. Louis and Kansas City, 1878.

Thomas, William L., History of St. Louis County. S.J. Clarke Publishing Co., St. Louis, Chicago, Philadelphia. 1911. Vol. 1.

Turner, Beatrice Clark, The Chouteau Family. 1934. No publisher listed.

Wetmore, Alphonso, Gazeteer of the State of Missouri. C. Keemle, St. Louis, publisher; Harper and Bros., New York, printers, 1837.

Wilkinson, James, Wilkinson, Soldier and Pioneer. Published by the author, 1835 Canal Bank Bldg., New Orleans, 1935.

Williams, Walter, History of Northwest Missouri. The Lewis Publishing Company, Chicago, New York, 1915. 3 vols.

Williams, Walter and Shoemaker, Floyd C., Missouri, Mother of the West. The American Historical Society, Inc., Chicago, New York, 1930. 3 vols.

The Index